Teaching Skills in Further and Adult Education

Teaching Skills in Further and Adult Education

Third edition

David Minton

Australia • Canada • Mexico • Singapore • Spain • United Kingdom • United States

THOMSON

Teaching Skills in Further and Adult Education: Third Edition

Copyright © David Minton and Thomson Learning 2005

The Thomson logo is a registered trademark used herein under licence.

For more information, contact Thomson Learning, High Holborn House, 50-51 Bedford Row, London WC1R 4LR or visit us on the World Wide Web at: http://www.thomsonlearning.co.uk

British Library Cataloguing-in-Publication Data
A catalogue record for this book is available from the British Library

ISBN-13: 978-1-84480-140-4
ISBN-10: 1-84480-140-3

First edition published in 1991 by Macmillan Press Ltd
Reprinted five times
Revised edition 1997
Reprinted 2000, 2001, 2002 and 2003 by Thomson Learning
This edition published by Thomson Learning 2005
Reprinted 2005 by Thomson Learning

Typeset by Gray Publishing, Tunbridge Wells, Kent
Printed in China by C & C Offset Printing Co, Ltd

Contents

PART 2	Developing the learning programme 117

PART 4	Growing responsibilities 331

List of figures

Preface

Most people who come into teaching in adult and further education will be entering an unfamiliar world; not only is being a teacher very different from being a student but the context in which teaching occurs has been subject to great change and development in recent years. This new edition takes account of developments in the twenty-first century, so that the new teacher may feel more at home in this new world. The emphasis remains the same: it sets out to provide effective guidance and support to enable new teachers, whatever the context they may be working in, to be effective in their role.

Teachers are responsible for learning programmes for their students and they should also be concerned for their personal development. I set out what I believe to be good practice in defining effectiveness in the design and implementation of learning programmes. To implement this good practice need not be difficult, but it does require commitment and willingness to learn from the experience of teaching.

It is government policy that all new teachers receive support and guidance of a *mentor* when they join a team in an institution. They will be required to undertake professional initial training. Colleges offer supportive programmes of teacher training and tutoring like the City & Guilds Further and Adult Education Teachers' Certificate where peer-groups learn as colleagues.

This book is intended to supplement programmes of training for the new teachers who benefit from shared learning and group activities. It can be used as a valuable resource by teachers working independently, but with mentor and tutor support to share their perceptions and offer feedback and advice.

Whatever the content of the teaching programme and wherever the context of the teaching, the book will prove a reliable companion and guide as you explore your new role as a teacher.

David Minton

Acknowledgements

I was privileged to work with a remarkably able group of moderators during the rapid changes that occurred in further education during my years with City & Guilds and had the support of colleagues there. It was the experience of working with tutors in most of the FE colleges, visiting their classes and observing teachers in hundreds of workshops and classrooms, running training sessions and listening to their views of effectiveness in teaching which shaped the convictions expressed in these pages. I have set out a tiny number of all possible case studies that seem to me to throw up important questions. I am deeply grateful to those teachers who have given me permission to cite them.

John Temple, Geoff Jones and Hugh Jones were a tutoring team for the City & Guilds Further and Adult Education Teachers' Certificate with me. Their creativity and critical judgements focused my thinking while I was writing the first edition. I gratefully acknowledge the help, insights and guidance I had from Anne Castling during preparation of the second edition, particularly dealing with Assessment and Testing where so much has changed. Nor would the book have been possible without the expertise and good humoured persistence of my editor, Anne Webster.

What is contained in this book I learned from students and colleagues with whom I have worked for more than thirty years in the UK, also teaching in Africa, America and Asia for a dozen years more. Some of them appear fleetingly in case studies. Their willingness to share their experiences with the new teachers through the pages of this book will undoubtedly encourage those teachers greatly.

In revising the book for a third edition in the new century I acknowledge with gratitude the help, advice and insights into the new concept and practice of FE provided generously of time and friendship by tutors and students in FE and HE colleges and officers at CGLI and at Thomson Learning, particularly Stella Wilson, Lin Wilson, Rosemary Cooney, Sue Marshall-Clarke, Cathy Hairsine, Elizabeth Halford, Peter Hadfield, Patricia Barylski, and John Winckler, and Lib Wright without whose encouragement and patient persistence the revision could not have happened.

The author and publishers wish to thank the following for permission to use copyright material: Geoff Croxon, for the cartoon on page 2. Fran Chard, for her description of the 'Sculpting' activity. Clare Minton for her drawing of the new cartoons. Gaynor Dunlop, Julie Schmidt, Vivienne Thorneycroft-Smith, Evelyn Wendleken and Sarah Nishi for their Case Studies.

Figure 19.2 is derived from a paper presented in 1989 to the Industrial Society by ECA of London. Tony Buzan for material from *Use Your Head*, W.C. Hooks, 4th edn, 1995. Federal Publications (S) Pte Ltd for two cartoons from *Fun With Chinese Characters* by T.H. Peng, 1980. DfES for the reproduction of material.

Every effort has been made to trace all the copyright holders, but if any have been inadvertently overlooked the publishers will be pleased to make the necessary arrangements at the first opportunity.

PART 1	**Effective class teaching**

Introduction: the teacher's role

| I TAUGHT SPOT HOW TO WHISTLE | I CAN'T HEAR HIM WHISTLING | I SAID I TAUGHT HIM I DIDN'T SAY HE LEARNED IT. |

EJ and Spot.

We can almost feel EJ's frustration.

Few come to teaching without any experience, although they may not consciously be aware of having had a go at it. People enjoy teaching others: children, friends, parents, adults, subordinates, dogs, cats, lions. They 'get a kick out of it'.

They feel they have knowledge or skills, something to share. Often they have an enthusiasm for something, or experience to communicate. Usually, it is in an ordinary social context, such as wishing to make others feel jealous, perhaps, about the great place they've been to on holiday: 'If you go, you must see ...' Or in role-modelling: children copying their parents' household tasks or leisure pursuits.

EJ's attitude is typical. 'I can whistle, you can too. You simply do this!'

How many teachers are satisfied with just having got through what they set out to teach without finding out if the students learned anything at all? What's wrong here? Spot didn't learn to whistle; why? Was it the way EJ set about teaching him? Would EJ have been more successful if he had used a different technique? Does the dog have a problem EJ does not understand, or does not want to understand?

Who says Spot should whistle anyway? Is it for EJ or for Spot? Is EJ concerned with Spot's achievement or only with his own? Is Spot motivated to learn? How could EJ motivate him? Would it help if he whipped the dog, or fed him chocolate? Is EJ expecting Spot to do something he is incapable of doing, or sees no point in doing?

We could ask so many similar questions. Teaching can be the most fulfilling and the most frustrating of human activities. But we should always ask: who is it for?

REMEMBER! ... A teacher's prime task is to engage the student in the learning process. What the student does to learn is more important than what the teacher does to teach.

Observing

Have you watched parents with a small child? Perhaps you have brought up children of your own. Parents watch and guide their child constantly. They shape its growth. They inhibit antisocial and dangerous behaviour. They encourage the child to achieve skills and understanding, and to develop certain attitudes. They surround the child with actions, words and objects that stimulate responses from the child. And they learn themselves by experience how to get the 'right' response. In fact, they are creating, usually quite unknowingly, a learning environment for themselves and their child. They are learning the job, and growing with it both as people and as parents.

Watch a very young child explore its environment. Then observe older children and adults, and make some comparisons.

REMEMBER! ... The first important skill a teacher needs to develop is the ability to observe behaviour in a learning environment.

Exploring

What do you do when you go into a new place? meet new people? arrive in a new town or country or shop in a new store?

You explore.

Watch the people who come into your class for the first time. What do they do?

They explore the environment.

They will probably look for clues as to how to behave there, who the other people are, where to sit, what to wear, and so on. A classroom environment is full of information: the way the furniture is arranged, what it is like, the equipment in the room, the dress of the teacher and the other students, information on the walls and in books – or lack of it.

Why do they look for such clues? Perhaps, so that they can modify their own behaviour to fit, avoid being 'out of place'. They want to feel comfortable there.

You can watch them explore their learning environment and gradually adjust to it. And you can take control of what happens if you want to.

REMEMBER! ... The basic learning activity is exploring: wanting to find out.

Teaching and learning

As the teacher, what is your part in the learning activity of your students? This book is primarily concerned with exploring the role of teacher. Teaching is as much a learning experience for the teacher as it is for the students. You need to use every teaching session as an opportunity to learn: to watch student behaviour and assess the learning that occurred so that you can improve the learning experiences for them. We call this process 'evaluating'. The book is intended to act as your guide: to provide signposts and suggested itineraries, things to do and things to look out for, to help you to establish good practice.

In undertaking the teaching of adults you are embarking on a most exciting journey of discovery, of yourself and others, that will last as long as you continue teaching. There will be no point at which you can say confidently, 'That's it! I've got it! I'm now a fully competent teacher.' But if you learn from the experience of teaching you will achieve confidence and skill. You will understand more about how people learn.

The more you understand people, dealing with them, involving them in the excitement of their own self-discovery and learning, the more they will surprise and fascinate you. There is no limit to the fascination of people. That is the great joy of teaching.

Questions

The book is about questions.

Questions alert the brain: Look out! new information is coming. A child is full of questions. In order to learn our brains must be alert, searching, looking for answers to questions.

Many textbooks are only about answers – and frequently the reader is not told the questions to which these are the supposed answers. They set out to provide short cuts, to eliminate the necessity of thinking.

Teaching is a journey of discovery – discovery about yourself and other people. You have come for the journey, for the challenge of thinking things through and of problem-solving – for the satisfaction of being effective as a teacher, and doing a good job.

If the book closes down your curiosity and your eagerness to go on learning more and more, it will have failed in its purpose.

Cycles

The establishment of good practice means a repeated cycle of preparation, teaching and review. The questions become more searching and more interesting as you come back to them.

When you have observed what people do, you will want to know why they do it. If you set about asking them, you will receive quite complicated answers. You will want to get behind these answers to underlying motivation, to 'real' reasons, and so to value systems, fears, anxieties and social pressures.

CASE STUDY 1

Carol had a Saturday morning class of people who wanted to learn word processing, databases and spreadsheets. The group included both men and women, aged between their middle twenties and late forties. A few were experienced typists; some were parents with children in local schools; some worked in offices or in retailing; two were self-employed. They were all motivated by the need to get to grips with the introduction of computer technology into their home or working lives. Some were afraid that they would not be able to cope at work or help their children.

They showed a great deal of anxiety.

Discussion

Think about these questions:

1 What do you think they were anxious about?

2 How would that affect what they did and their learning?

3 What would you do to help them if you found yourself in the same position as Carol?

Comment

It is important to know what it feels like to be in the situation of the students in a class. If you know how they feel, the barriers and anxieties they bring with them, you will be able to help them overcome the barriers and learn successfully.

We each have a perception of ourselves, our status, our potential or lack of it: our self-image. American education, for instance, values a good self-image highly; and a great deal of effort goes into improving it.

For many, not only has formal education failed to stimulate their creativity, it has damaged their self-confidence. It has convinced them that, compared with others, they are stupid or at least not clever, and so engendered mental blockages. Many adults have a fear of formal education, of teachers and exams. They have developed complexes and barriers to learning. One of the great delights of adult education is to see students make quite startling discoveries about themselves.

If you cut down a mature tree, you can count growth rings year by year. You can distinguish the good years for growing from the bad years. Although the tree is largely what was determined by its genes at conception, it was shaped by accident and weather, by where its roots have sought their nourishment, by the nutrients or poisons that it found, by disease or by competition with other trees.

People are far more complex than trees, but each is the result of how far environment and experience have promoted or inhibited growth, realised or stunted potential, and shaped his or her self-image. You will probably learn as much about yourself as about anything else as you reflect on the experiences of teaching that you will undertake and work through the activities and tasks in this book.

Models

Learning is unstoppable. You learn all the time – otherwise you could not cope with new situations as they arise. If you did not learn, you could not deal with the world. You would constantly stub your toe on the same step or burn your fingers, miss the chair when you go to sit down, press the wrong button on the television set. Learning is also cumulative. Once you have dealt successfully with an experience you find it easier the next time you encounter a similar situation. When we walk into a room or encounter, say, a new machine for the first time, we look for clues to help us to categorise it. We have 'models in the head' about most things. They enable us to learn quickly how to deal effectively with the new place or machine or people.

Where do our models come from, including our models of ourselves? We are constantly creating them and modifying those that we already have from our experiences.

We hardly have to think about it usually. We instantly recognise a room as, for instance, a sitting room or a kitchen. Equipment and layout tell us how we are to behave there. We do this by transferring learning from one experience and context to another.

It is not true, however, that when we consciously set out to learn something, we can always do it easily. Why the difference? Why is it often apparently hard to learn things? There must be special factors at work preventing learning from happening.

One reason is the way, already mentioned, that the past experience of many people has unfortunately convinced them that they will not be able to deal with it very easily, if at all. They have formed a poor self-image; and created barriers that stop them from learning. As teachers we can improve learning by bringing the process to the surface so that we can look at it. We can try to understand what is going on for the students and for us. We must try to see it, and feel it, from the students' point of view.

Reflecting on our own learning experiences will help us to do that – for example, how we felt on our first day at work: what happened for us, and how we changed as we learned.

Growth through experience

We talk about growing with the job. Learning is growth through experience. We need to grow as teachers and stimulate growth in our students. There is no short cut. Some grow and flourish more quickly than others do. This is not simply a matter of luck. It is more a readiness to learn – to reflect on experience and to explore alternative methods and approaches. It may depend on ability to adapt and willingness to take risks, to engage in creative problem-solving. It depends crucially on our belief in ourselves.

REMEMBER! … Maturation is an important part of
learning processes that cannot be hurried.

SECTION A A guide to the book

CHAPTER 1	How to use the book: learning through activity

REMEMBER! … You have to do it to learn it, if you don't do it you don't learn it. And it is important to do it right.

Learning requires activity on the part of the learner. You have to do something in order to learn. Reading is one such activity. But when we read, our concentration span is quite short and so we soon stop taking things in. We need to pause frequently and review what we have read – to try to process it for ourselves in some way. There has to be time for it to become part of our own perception.

You will find learning activity in every section of the book. Some learning activities require simply a change of approach, variety in what you are doing; some ask you to do something – to get up and do it, such as rearranging furniture to improve the environment where you or students are attempting to learn. It is important to do these things. It is the way to learn, and the way to develop competence.

There is a pattern in the learning programme in the book. The learning activities are integrated into that programme. Undertake them as soon as you can after you have read the appropriate section. They relate to three aspects of learning.

1 The first, described as **Activities**, concerns your own needs and self-discovery. They will enable you to explore your strengths and build up confidence, skill and understanding, and will help you to get yourself properly organised and working in methodical and efficient ways. Activity 1, below is an example.

2 The **Tasks** focus on your preparation for teaching: these will help you to develop the good practice to be effective.

3 **In addition, Case studies** are set out with questions to draw out the lessons that may be learned. Merely reading the case studies will not extract the benefit that may be had from using the experience of others. You must think about what happened and why, and compare that experience with your own. It is even better if you can share your thinking in a peer group discussion.

REMEMBER! … Learning is most effective at a point of need.

YOUR MODEL OF TEACHING

You come to teaching with your own 'model in the head' of what teachers do and why, and of how learning happens for the students.

You will also have feelings about what you want to learn from any book on teaching or from training sessions you may attend.

Learning is change of many things: including knowledge and ideas, beliefs and attitudes, skills, habits, insights, approaches that we make to our work and to other people, our self-image. We need to monitor these changes in ourselves and our students.

To observe change we have to know what the initial state is that is to grow and change. We also need to bring to the surface what we think and how we behave in order to have a view of it.

So it is important to work through the following questions now before you read on.

1 What do you consider to be the role of the teacher of adults?

2 Analyse and explain your 'model in the head' of teaching and learning and how they relate to each other. (It may help if you describe students in a context that is familiar to you: how the class works, and what are the expectations of both students and teacher.)

3 Write down what you feel you need to learn in order to be an effective teacher of adults. Decide what your priorities will be, and try to explain to yourself why you believe that.

4 Try to explain your model to a group of others and respond to questions. You may also have the chance to listen to accounts by others of their 'models of teaching'. You may be surprised at what different ideas there are; and different expectations from a book or a course of training.

BUILDING UP TEACHING MATERIALS

You will need to keep materials in order and develop a system to file your work. It is a good idea to have a file for your own learning materials such as completed Activities/Tasks in this book and other materials you will want to gather. These should be filed in date order so that you can later reflect on your own learning by reviewing your work. If you use a computer for your work it helps to facilitate what you need to do because folders/files can be named to make retrieval and sorting into date-order easy.

You will need files for lesson plans and teaching/learning materials.

The use of computers and computer software (ICT) has greatly improved the ability to store and retrieve all manner of 'data'. Teaching/learning materials can be accumulated in large quantities and stored in a computer. Usually, I find it is helpful to keep both data files in the computer and printed materials from other sources in a folder or a box file. It is not easy to 'input' materials which are not your own into a computer even using a scanner.

'Hard copy', printed out materials of your own, can be stored using ring binders or boxes or other filing systems; you must be able to 'retrieve' it without too much searching. The big advantage of hard copy is that you can easily compare and put together all sorts of materials. It is more complicated to do this in a computer. It is also quicker to 'scan through' papers and to make comparisons.

Visual materials are much easier in this form too. You should have a box-file for the audio-visual aids (AVA) and other resource materials you use or gather together for your classes. I find that the printed out material is easier to look at and to evaluate in terms of appearance, usability, content and language than when it is on a screen in a computer. It has to do with seeing the whole of a thing rather than the bits. In any case, the real thing is always rather different from 'virtual reality': what things look like on a computer screen. You can also, of course, print in different colours and on different coloured paper, which is very useful for colour-coding to facilitate filing.

One enormous advantage of computer filing is that it is relatively simple to modify materials, to redo sections, move pieces of work around or insert them into other documents and so on. All teachers should be reasonably adept in keyboard skills and the use of text-processing, graphics, spreadsheets and other straightforward computer software. They often come 'bundled', as in Microsoft Office.

Learning paths and maps

You must tackle learning a bit at a time, in digestible amounts. But these will only make sense if they link in successfully to what you have already learned and to your perception of things – your world as a 'whole'. Your perceptions will change with time. Compare how you see things now with even a few years ago.

You will find in any case that you and your students select, quite unconsciously, from whatever learning experiences you provide. You and they select those bits you can make sense of and can link with present knowledge and understanding. The rest will probably be ignored, at least for the present.

For example, you can easily overwhelm your brain with information about the assessment of student learning. You will find that when you actually need to assess what your students have learned in a particular context, you will search for an appropriate method. By using that method, even if you do it rather badly, you will come to an understanding of how it works; you are then ready to try to explore assessment processes in more detail.

This book has been designed to plot a learning path and to guide you through it. But every learner has specific needs, and each will modify the design and use it in a way that suits them. That is inevitable.

Consider again exploring an unfamiliar town or building or store. You may start by looking at a map. The map is an abstraction. It made perfect sense to the person who drew it. But it may only really make sense to you after the experience of visiting the place. We can use a map to help us explore physically and so come to understand both the town and the map. A design-plan is understood thoroughly only if you make something following instructions in the plan, whether it is a dress pattern, a recipe for a pudding or a drawing of a machine part.

The same is true of a book of this kind. To undertake any task in teaching – or in anything else – you must define the task. This involves asking appropriate questions and seeking information. If we ask the wrong questions, or the wrong kind of questions, our perceptions of what we are about are likely to be distorted.

The book is intended to enable you to identify questions in relation to tasks in your teaching role. These questions become more searching as experience increases and you encounter new contexts and different groups of students.

Growth cycles

Learning and growth are cyclical. We constantly revisit areas of experience, redo the same tasks, and practise the same skills. We grow to be a whole person through this experience. The learning programme in the book reflects cyclical reality. Your learning will be more successful if you undertake the Activities and Tasks in the order set out in the book. There is an order of precedence in which we need to accomplish things. But nothing is once for all. Every group and every class you teach should be approached through repetition of the Tasks: it is by repetition that we embed good practice.

To learn, we need to know what it is we are setting out to learn. Afterwards we need to revisit the learning to fix clearly in our minds what has been learned, and so link it to other learning.

REMEMBER! … A teacher's prime task is to engage the student in the learning process. The student must take an active role in order for learning to occur.

The structure of the book

The book is in four parts, related to increasing responsibility.

Part 1 assumes that you will be responsible for ensuring effective learning for a learning group, whether it be a class, a workshop or a ward. It is concerned to establish the way of setting about the job, the good practice. To do that you have to understand certain principles and you must develop confidence and other positive attitudes. You need to take control of your own learning and of the conditions under which your students will learn.

To help you, there is advice on 'peer-teaching' with a group of your peers, as part of a course programme, to gain insights and confidence.

You are then guided through the various aspects of what is involved in dealing with your own students: preparation, classroom management, creating a learning environment, running the class, controlling what happens, communication and the use of feedback and assessment. Good practice is defined through performance criteria, to provide a model in the head of what you are trying to achieve. There is a great deal of emphasis on evaluating, what happens for you and your students, your teaching and their learning.

Part 2 builds on the learning in Part 1, but requires greater depth and breadth. It develops as a case study or a reflective diary of your own learning, as you design and plan a learning programme for your students. The programme will develop over a defined time span, with a series of teaching sessions. By reflecting on what happens, you build up your insight into your role. The purpose is constantly to refine and improve what happens.

The expected performance will be to more demanding standards than in Part 1, because there is growth and increasing maturity. There is much more advice in Part 2 on methods and approaches to help you. Much of this takes the form of 'do this or that', but please understand that in making these suggestions I am not trying to close down your own creative thinking. This advice is not intended to be 'right answers' for you in your context and role. You need to evaluate it against your own experience and needs you perceive in your context. What is important is the questions you ask, the decisions you make, what you observe happening and your evaluation of what happens.

Part 3 provides a survey of educational psychology and theories of learning as developed in the last century. The model of practice set out in the book is based on an understanding of these theories. I have chosen to present the theory after you have had enough experience, so that you will be able to read it critically by comparing it with what happens for you and your students. This is a book, so you can choose to read it first or now if you want to, or again and again!

The last philosopher's work I discuss is Sir Karl Popper, who changed the way that scientists thought about what they were doing. They used to look for evidence to confirm their theories, but he showed that it was much better to look for things that the theory failed to explain or predict. It is only in that way that you get better theories. The same is true of any advice or theory in teaching.

For this reason, emphasis is placed also on developing your study skills. You need to help your students to develop their study skills, because the emphasis in teaching in FE/AE today is on learning programmes which are negotiated and agreed with individual learners.

In this regard, this book is intended as a model. It is to be used by individuals as a programme of tasks and activities designed as a learning path but the experience will be much richer when shared with other learners. The learning will be greatly improved and accelerated by having a mentor/tutor to be for you a mirror and guide.

But the book is yours. You may explore various parts in an order that meets your perception of what your needs are. However, the book is not really designed to be 'dipped into'. No one can make real sense of 'unconnected bits'.

Part 4 provides a guide to your future learning and development. FE is intended to be lifelong education for all, opportunities for anyone to return to study and learning, to 'go back to school' as the Americans say. Initial training is what it says it is. All teachers need to be continuing their own education if only because the world of FE is constantly evolving to keep pace with the society that it serves.

The **Appendix** provides a snapshot of the road DfES intends FE to travel in this decade.

ASSUMPTIONS

The following assumptions are made about you as student and teacher.

1 You will be functioning in a teaching context where you can undertake tasks in relation to a real teaching situation.

2 You will have some responsibility for a learning group and for designing a learning programme or a number of sessions for them.

3 You will have the opportunity to undertake teaching assignments, to develop competences in the various aspects of the teaching process, to match your ability against 'performance criteria'.

4 You will be able to find a mentor who will support you in your teaching context, and preferably someone who has expertise in your own subject specialism.

5 You will also be able to join a teacher training course so that you will have tutors to provide structure and feedback within a learning programme.

6 You will have some opportunity to share with others in team and/or group work, so that you will get critical but supportive feedback on what you are doing.

7 You will be able to reflect on the learning and gradually build up a model of good practice.

Tasks in progression

The TASKS for Part I are set out below as an overview of progression:

CHAPTER 2	# Learning to learn: developing study skills

REMEMBER! ... Developing study skills are essential.

To study successfully, you need to decide

- what you need to know
- what it would help you to find out
- where you can best and most easily find the information
- how to make the best use of it.

Teachers need to establish rules and a work-orientated environment for their students to create positive working behaviour. What is true of students is true of your own behaviour. No two people are the same, nor are the contexts where they have to work. Every learner must take responsibility for creating the conditions under which he or she will work and study.

Major factors are:

- space-management
- time-management
- self-management.

Space-management

You need personal territory for study, just as you need a kitchen for cooking. Make it easy. Like a carpenter, work with the grain of the wood. Get to know yourself and how you work best. Set out a territory, adopt a system that suits you and establish rules and a pattern to follow. No carpenter will work without a bench and a tool rack. No cook without kitchen utensils and a practical kitchen.

Not everyone is tidy. Some work better with clutter around them, but still seem to know where everything is. That is really what matters. Don't waste energy and time looking for things when the need arises. A good idea or good thinking may disappear while you look.

Many do find it easier to have a 'proper system' of shelves and files.

PREPARATION FOR STUDY

Write down the things you will need to do where you study. How easy will it be to do them? You could be systematic about it and make a table:

Things to happen here	How easy is it? (ring your score)	What I need to do
Reading	a b c d e	Have a reading lamp
Making notes	a b c d e	
Writing	a b c d e	
Computing (IT)	a b c d e	

Make your own list

Is there enough light to read by? What kind of light do you need? Poor light leads to eye-strain and tiredness. Will the chair be an upright hard chair? and if so, will it give back support if you use a computer? Or will it be an easy chair? Is there space to establish your territory, to spread out what you need? Will you need extra space on shelves, or room for machines? Are things to hand when you need them?

Distraction

You need to pay attention to what you are doing. Some people find 'wallpaper' music helps. Some work better in silence. Some prefer to look out on to a busy road, others choose a blank wall. Some find that looking at a wall makes them feel shut in; they will work better sitting on the other side of the desk with space in front of them. Colour has a strong effect on some people, pictures on others.

Time-management

Try things out; experiment to find what improves your sense of well-being. Things distract us, maybe irritating little things. Set aside time for yourself, so that you can say 'this is my study time'.

Brain behaviour works by pattern-making. How goal-orientated are you? Can you shut out distraction and get things done? Or are you easily diverted? Are you more person-centred or more goal-centred in the way you think and behave? If person-centred, you may place greater value on human transactions than on tasks you need to do, and you will find it hard to concentrate on what needs doing. How will you handle that? If you are goal-centred, how do you react to people and they to you? Are you really interested? Some people appear to be sequential in their behaviour, dealing with one thing at a time. Others are happier to have many things on the go at once. Table 2.1 compares the two kinds.

Sequential people tend to plan by hours, set priorities and list actions: things to do and when. They do not find it hard to set targets and goals, and to concentrate on the job. In social affairs they tend to be punctual; they regard keeping to time as

Table 2.1 People-centred or goal-centred.

Sequential people	Multi-task people
Try/do one thing at a time: time is tangible and divisible	Try/do many things at once: time is intangible and elastic
Concentrate on the job	Easily distracted; like interruptions
Take time commitment seriously, emphasise keeping to schedule	Think time commitment good, but put much more emphasis on human transactions
Emphasise promptness/timing: but only make casual short-term relationships	Timing is flexible, related to assessment of who it is: prefer long-term relationships
Strong preference for keeping to plans and getting the job done	Change plans/details easily and often: commitment is to people not to job

important, and they establish a schedule and stick to it. They have a strong preference for order and promptness, and are strongly goal-orientated. In social affairs, they make judgements about individuals in regard to time-keeping, promptness and punctuality. They may also find long-term relationships hard and suffer fools badly.

Multi-task people have an elastic view of time. Their goals are imprecise and confused by all the different tasks they have in hand. They tend to be distracted easily and invite interruptions – they may even create them themselves. They acknowledge system, schedules, agendas and dead-lines as desirable but not pressingly important. They constantly change their decisions, arrangements, plans. They are interested in people, not the job, and in maintaining relationships: that is, they are strongly people-orientated.

You will no doubt recognise people you know of both these types. They tend to be intolerant each of the other. People, however, are tall or short – or any size in between. Honestly assess your own characteristics to help you get yourself organised.

Teachers need to be strongly people-orientated. They need to be able to establish relationships and commitment – to inspire trust and liking in their students. But to be a good manager you must get things done. Find a rhythm that will suit your personality.

Self-management

Time-management and stress-management are related

Imposing schedules on yourself that are impossible for you, maybe because they do not fit with your personality or your style of working, can lead to stress. Equally, disorganisation is very stressful for the person who likes order. In the end it is much better to set targets and keep to schedules if you can, because stress increases with failing to do things that need doing.

You must somehow develop goal-seeking behaviour

Time is precious. Set yourself short-term goals. Plan ahead, but not more than three weeks ahead. Plan regularly, and revise your plan every day. Check where you are and what you need to do now.

REFLECTIVE DIARY

You cannot reflect on learning experiences you cannot remember.

Teachers need to be keenly aware of how learning happens for them if they are to help their students learn. As you explore the role of teacher, you need to monitor change as it occurs for you.

I once read in an examination script: The village school consisted of one teacher and seven other children. There is real truth here! As a teacher you will be learning all the time from decisions you make:

- what goes well and what goes badly
- what takes you by surprise
- what you find you can do easily or what proves hard
- what students do, what they find difficult or master easily
- what you observe and what you learn about yourself
- how people behave as individuals and groups
- sudden insights when your perception of something changes.

1 At the time these things happen, you need to make a note for yourself with the salient facts. Note too what you feel.

2 Keep a diary in which you record later reflections on your notes, while they are still fresh in your memory.

3 Later still, look back and see if your view has changed. See if it now forms part of a pattern that begins to make sense.

4 Later again, try to organise your learning experiences into some structures or patterns such as:
   - student behaviour
   - learning activities
   - teaching techniques
   - important insights.

The purpose of the diary

The principal purpose of the diary is to encourage you to reflect on learning experiences: what you observed, what it felt like, how it might have looked to others, what you intend to do after you have thought about it.

REMEMBER! … What the diary is for is much more important than what it looks like.

It must make sense to you when you come back to any entry. It can be in any form as long as it makes sense to you. You can write it or record it – on a pocket cassette recorder perhaps. It may be in a book or in a card index file or using a computer; this last has the advantages noted earlier.

Date each entry so that you can monitor changes in the way you perceive things, so that you can see how your ideas develop with experience. Files in a computer will do that for you. To see what this means, try to recall a few occasions when you were acutely aware of having learned something – when your learning was accelerated. You might have said: "Oh! I see it now!" as something that was puzzling you fell suddenly into place, giving you a new way of perceiving it. This often happens. It is like the moment when you see the picture as you assemble a jigsaw puzzle.

Perhaps, you suddenly realised why someone you knew was behaving oddly, or you found out the purpose of the unlabelled button on the television set. Or you might have discovered something about yourself, some ability you did not know you had. You might have surprised yourself by tackling a problem: "I didn't know I had it in me!"

CASE STUDY 2

Once I was looking for a residential adult centre in an unfamiliar town. I had a map, which I had misinterpreted. I was sure the place was a large house approached up a drive behind a gate on to the road. That was my 'model in the head' of what I was looking for, what I expected to see. Two people I asked gave me directions, and I still walked straight past the place. Why? In fact it was part of a terrace of houses along the main road. I did not see what I expected to see, so I walked past it.

Consider occasions when you failed to see something you were looking for. Why was that? What were you expecting to see? What did you actually discover?

SECTION B Gaining confidence

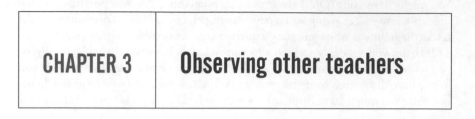

CHAPTER 3	Observing other teachers

ACTIVITY 4

CLASS VISIT

1 Find a colleague or a teacher in a context you are familiar with: the more experienced the teacher the better.

2 Negotiate with the teacher an opportunity to visit one class s/he is teaching. Students and teacher will need to know why you want to come and what you will be doing. Even experienced teachers may be a little reluctant to have an observer in the class. This is because any intruder into a class may be disruptive, even someone who just sits at the back and does nothing. Once groups form and gel, any visitor remains an outsider and affects group behaviour.

3 Find out as much as you can from the teacher, so that you have a view of the class before you visit.

Make a record along the following lines:

Date of visit:	...
Class and teacher:	...
The students:	Male/female, numbers, ages, employment status, married/unmarried, and so on
	Any specific groupings (for example, motor vehicle trainees, playgroup leaders)
	Any other factors the teacher thinks important to tell you about
The purpose:	Relationship to any course, intended outcomes, qualifications aimed at, job prospects, who pays
The place:	What the environment is, what it is like, special features/equipment

The time:	Time of day, frequency of meeting, and so on
Learning goals for this class:	…

The visit: building a picture

Armed with the above information, you can prepare for the visit. When you visit someone's class, you need to make it clear to both the teacher and students what you are going for. Your purpose is to share an experience with teacher and students: **to observe as accurately as you can what actually happens – what is going on in the class – to avoid making value judgements**.

Inevitably you, the teacher and the students will all have your own feelings about the experience. Quite often these strongly influence what happens. **You are extending your experience by sharing that of others**.

In order to do that, you have to be receptive and alert; you must arrive at the experience with questions. You cannot simply be passive and 'let things happen'.

Go armed with questions

The information above will help you to make sense of what you observe. It will help you to recognise what is happening in the class if you have a preliminary picture of it to take with you. Without it, you can miss important aspects of what is happening or be puzzled by what you observe. But be particularly careful to 'observe' things which are familiar, too. If the context is too 'normal' for you, it is harder to see it than it is for someone who doesn't know it well.

Set out below is a structure to enable you to get the most out of the experience. Discuss this beforehand with the teacher, who may point out things in relation to a particular context that may have been omitted from this set of questions, designed as they are for general application.

BUILDING UP A PICTURE

Make notes for yourself along these lines, but invent the questions YOU think are important.

Environment: *room*: size, condition, age, lighting, heating, etc.
furniture/equipment: what is present, layout, desks or tables
purpose: what is it designed for? what style of teaching/ learning?
constraints: what may cause problems for the intended learning activity

Students: dress, groupings, age
any things that surprise you
relationships with the teacher or within and between the groups

---

Activity:	teacher activity
	student activity
	how they relate
	note timings and change of activity: movement, breaks
	and so on
Other:	

Sharing perceptions

What you should take away from the experience is a picture that you can reflect on in private. This will arise partly from what the teacher tells you beforehand and partly from what you see. It is important 'to keep an open mind'. This is much harder than it might appear; it is very hard not to respond with value judgements to any experience.

You need factual statements rather than judgements. Avoid making notes like: 'the students were bored' or 'they were excited', or 'the teacher explained the topic very well'. You cannot know how the students felt or how they saw what the teacher did.

How far the environment, equipment, learning/teaching material and behaviour help or inhibit the intended learning are judgements. Don't try to guess why the students or the teacher behaved as they did. Just note carefully what they did.

Factual statements concern such things as the environment, the dress of students and teacher, the equipment and resources used, and the behaviour of students and teacher – what they actually did, their level of activity, the sequence of events and so on: how learning was achieved, what the students did in order to learn.

You want to observe what actually happens, rather than what you may go expecting to see. I missed the adult centre because I was expecting to see a different kind of building; you may fail to see important things because you are looking for or expect to see something else. The problem is worse if the context is very familiar because you stop asking questions, so you don't really 'see it' at all.

But no two people will perceive the same experience in the same way. Each comes to it with an individual mind-set and questions. Clearly, we all select from what we hear, smell, touch and so on. It is just impossible to take it all in.

In discussion with the teacher after the experience, you can share and compare your perception of what took place. You can ask the questions that have occurred to you as you watched, about why certain things happened, maybe, and especially about the student learning activity.

Reflecting on the experience: consolidation

Avoid sharing your feelings with the teacher. You can explore your own feelings in your reflective diary, and later with a group of your peers if you have an opportunity. To discover what you have learned, you will probably have to wait a while, thinking over what happened and getting it into perspective. Then try to set down what you have discovered. This will help to consolidate the learning. What does this mean?

We have to revisit an experience, we have to rehearse it again, in order to embed it in our memory. But we cannot do that unless we shape it some way – in pictures and in words. We may take away visual memories and sounds, but usually we frame things in our thoughts as words.

Consolidation is this revisiting. One of the most effective ways of revisiting an experience is to share it with someone else, telling them about it and responding to their questions. Try to tell them what happened and how you felt about it. This is normal human behaviour.

Using the peer group

It is very helpful to share the experience of observing a class with a group of your peers, especially if they have had similar experiences to tell you about. The effort you make to explain what you saw, heard and felt will concentrate and focus the experience for you.

REMEMBER! ... You will probably discover that you do not know what you think until you hear what you say.

Later reflection

Your views of what happened when observing a class will change with time; and you should try to be aware of any changes in your perception. Telling the peer group and listening to their comments helps to bring these into focus. Look at your previous comments in your diary. What has changed?

<table>
<tr><td>**CHAPTER 4**</td><td>**Peer-group teaching**</td></tr>
</table>

First find the questions

What is peer-group teaching? What is it for? How should it work?

Once, in a restaurant in Villefranche in Beaujolais, I had a dish of the most delicious garlic mushrooms. Madame ran the restaurant, Monsieur did the cooking. Foolishly, I asked Madame for the recipe. '*Monsieur, it is not what, it is who,*' she said. The difference between one dish of garlic mushrooms and another depends on who has cooked it. I had asked the wrong question. Asking wrong questions is what people do a great deal of the time. They get unhelpful answers.

There are no foolproof recipes for a good lesson. There are only teachers. We must concentrate on 'who'. Teaching behaviour depends critically on teaching experience. Teacher educators have little control over real classes that teachers teach so they may choose to use simulations where they can control what happens, what teachers are asked to do, and the conditions and pressures that they face.

It has become standard practice to set up simulations in training for everything. Airline pilots are trained on a simulator, a highly sophisticated, very expensive piece of technological wizardry which puts the trainee through an experience that feels like the real thing. All the senses – sight, hearing, balance, movement – are used to create a grand illusion. The pilot is then put under stress. From normal take-off and landing, the pilot is made to deal with emergencies, engine failure and so on to ensure that he, or today she, will be able to cope with whatever happens. Whenever a pilot changes from a familiar aircraft to another, certainly from flying warplanes to civilian passenger planes, they use a simulator. A minimum number of 'flying hours' must be clocked up before a certificate to fly is awarded, and it is much cheaper and more effective to do many of them on a simulator. Trainees must, of course, fly a real aircraft under supervision. What matters is the transferability of the training to 'real' conditions, but you can hardly put the pilot into a 'real emergency' during training.

With the realisation that the present training and testing for car drivers do not prepare people at all adequately for real driving – indeed it avoids putting them into situations that require rapid response and ability to cope under stress – there is a move to using technological simulators in this field too. They may be a large-scale version of Virtual Reality, which today can be experienced in your home by computer. If you have ever been on rides in theme parks such as Disney World, you will be aware of what it feels like to be in one of these things. I use the words 'feels like' because these methods are *experiential*; the trainee/participant goes through a learning experience. The simulation experiences are intended not only to change people's behaviour, but their perception of the job and their self-knowledge.

Affective learning

This is educational jargon for changing how people approach things, emotional and attitudinal change. It is recognised that changing behaviour means changing not only what people do, but the way they think of it: their attitudes to themselves and the things they are asked to do. To take an extreme example, if I propose to walk across a wooden plank suspended far above the ground between two high buildings, I must know that I can do it. I must have a firm belief in my ability. How do I get the belief or the knowledge unless I actually do it? It is not unlike a pilot, perhaps, who is mentally prepared for any emergency that might happen, but which s/he has never faced before.

People learning to walk the tightrope start close to the ground and go on to using a safety net until they are confident enough to do without it. Someone who is frightened of water should not be taught to swim by being thrown into the deep end of a swimming pool. Even if the victim survives, the terror of water and of drowning is likely to become embedded and inhibit rather than enhance their ability to cope.

The astonishing thing is that most people do cope with such an experience. People do survive their first terrifying drive on the motorway, where they have to react much faster, and deal with so much more baffling information, and suffer so much more aggression, than their training prepared them for.

One effect can be that they learn bad behaviour, they become equally aggressive, say, or discover techniques to defend themselves from the dangers they perceive. These then inhibit good practice. We should think about that in relation to learning to teach. How many teachers are essentially in a defensive mood when they enter the classroom, having been thrown in the deep end and told to swim or drown? As a way of learning anything, immersion has certain advantages. We do not usually make tiny steps in learning, we make great leaps from one state of being to another. If we try step-by-step gradual approaches, the learner usually gets way ahead of us and is likely to become bored. You can watch it happening with people using programmed learning from manuals to learn computer operating systems or software applications. They get bored and jump ahead, eager to get on and do something interesting. In the end they come unstuck and then: *If all else fails read the instructions!* Just following the instructions usually fails, too!!

So long as my motivation to succeed is high enough, I can go through hell and high water. From the point of view of my self-image, succeeding against the odds, overcoming fear and solving problems is very effective. In the end, I must risk drowning in order to swim. All learning involves taking risks. Playing safe inhibits any possibility of change.

But there are bound to be casualties, since there is a level of risk. Who calculates the risk? What is an acceptable casualty rate? We reduce the risks as far as possible with training airline pilots because the costs of failure are very high. But we accept a scandalous rate of failure and casualties on our roads. And what about in our classrooms?

Air crashes are still put down to pilot error. However experienced pilots or brain surgeons are, they still have to take risks, and they make mistakes in their professional judgements. Arthur Cranmer, a famous professional singer in the UK, related a conversation he had with a surgeon. '*You and I are alike – neither of us can afford to make mistakes.*' The surgeon replied, '*Yes, but I bury mine.*' And what of teachers?

We rely on professional judgements in pilots, doctors and teachers. The judgements they make are based on their knowledge and experience; they depend critically on the depth of that experience and the learning that has occurred as a result of that experience.

Simulation in teaching

The simulations that teacher educators use vary widely. Their choice may depend on their 'model in the head' of what teachers do, on assumptions they make about how learning happens or how it is transferred from one context to another.

There was a fashion in teacher education to analyse teaching into an array of teacher skills that could be developed, perfected in isolation, then brought back together into a 'global performance'.

Micro-training is a better description. Sophisticated set-ups were built at great expense to allow this to happen. A commonly used method was modelling: having students watch a 'good' teacher in a micro-session demonstrating the skills, then their practising the same skills and video-recording their performance so that they could evaluate it against that of the model to improve it. But the problem of transfer to a real situation remained. Because the use of skills is only one part of what makes it possible for me to be effective in a given situation, I must integrate my skills with all the other things I need, such as confidence, intelligent decision-making and so on. In teaching, it is what the students do in order to learn that matters, at least as much as the skill of the teacher. A skilful performance by the teacher, impressive as it may be, will be of no value unless it also engages students actively in learning.

Early arguments for 'competency training programmes' were based on the assumptions which underlie this approach to training. Since it is impossible, they say, to practise all the skills a teacher needs at once, let us develop them individually. There is, I believe, a misconception here of how changes in behaviour occur. If I practised for ever the individual skills needed to walk my plank between my two buildings (whatever I analysed them to be), when it came to setting off across the plank the very terror of falling would drive my skills away. After all, I could walk across the plank easily without training if it were on the floor.

A problem with skills training of this kind is that it focuses on what tutors have decided about the methodology teachers will use. It inhibits creative thinking by the student teachers about methods of teaching/learning after observing their own classes: it fails to encourage their ownership of the decisions.

There is no doubt, however, that there are important skills teachers need to acquire and practise. I believe they are best practised at a point of need, that is, with your own students. What then should we do with our peer group?

Planning lessons with a peer group

The lessons described below occurred within a teacher peer group attempting to achieve agreed learning goals in a training programme.

Purpose

What are the lessons for? There are many answers:

- to provide enrichment of the learning through sharing ideas and feedback
- to learn experientially by being both a student and a teacher
- to face and overcome the fear of putting on a performance as a teacher
- to challenge assumptions about how learning can be promoted
- to develop confidence and insight
- to encourage a creative, student-centred approach
- to provide the opportunity to experiment and take risks
- to encourage risk-taking by removing the consequences of failure in a real context
- to broaden the range of methods a teacher has the confidence to use.

Each lesson should be approached as a simulation of real class teaching, but within tighter constraints of time. It would not be sensible to ask your peers to role-play 'your students' as they are in reality. Your peers have to be themselves. The 'teacher' must deal with the learning needs they really have, not those that some others might be supposed to have. Because the constraints of time and place are real, they provide the same challenges as in any teaching situation:

- the need to think through what is to happen
- thorough preparation in relation to achieving learning goals
- producing teaching/learning materials
- observing student reaction and attempting to meet their learning needs
- responding to feedback in the lesson
- being ready to adapt where it clearly is needed.

But there is also a chance for formal feedback and evaluation from your students to let you know *how it felt for them*, what worked, what didn't, what they learned, and what they failed to learn. They are very likely to be supportive and sympathetic because they know *how it feels to be you*, so the pressure of the fear or fact of failure is much less worrying. It should encourage you to be more adventurous. You must learn from the experience 'as a whole'.

The intention is to create an experience which is not dissimilar from the real thing. This is most important, because what matters is to be able to transfer learning from simulated experience to a real one. **One thing you might well learn is that learning can be fun.**

Where?

The environment where any teaching/learning occurs must be appropriate and support rather than hinder the learning activity. This has clear implications for where any lessons happen. If 'your students' need specialist equipment in order to learn, it is easier to take them to that specialist area than to try to recreate it in a room designed for some other activity. Some equipment is far too big to be moved around anyway. One thing you are learning is how important it is to ensure that the environment supports what students and teacher are trying to do. In some cases, you can move the students and/or the furniture in a classroom. In many other contexts, this is not helpful. No one can learn computing without sitting at a computer; you cannot turn on a lathe without a lathe, throw a pot on a wheel without a wheel.

Certainly, many things can be imported, but at considerable effort. Teachers do carry laptops around in the boot of a car, there are portable projectors and screens. I have seen fascinating craftwork done in peer-group lessons, even using water, after spreading plastic covers over tables. All this is easier to understand from examples. I am most grateful to those students who have allowed me to use their ideas and to report their lessons.

CASE STUDY 3

Sandra, a teacher of students with learning difficulties, thought about what she wanted her peer group to learn. The peer group was made up mostly of part-time teachers from a wide variety of backgrounds: nursing, hairdressing, motor vehicle work, catering, plumbing, engineering, computing and teachers of students with learning difficulties and disabilities. The greatest advantages of group work of this kind derive from the richness of experience and challenge in the group.

It was clear to her that most of them had little experience of working with students like hers for whom learning is a much slower process than for 'normal' students. Sandra decided that if they were ever to find themselves working with such students they needed to know *what it felt like to be unable to learn*; and that she would put them through the experience.

She produced work-cards for each 'student' which gave simple instructions as to what each had to do, but the cards were written in letters of the Greek alphabet. She provided paper, patterns, scissors and so on, because they had to try to make something.

The class had 15 minutes to complete the task on the work-cards: it was the time allowed for the lesson. Sandra had thought carefully about the time constraint. She said nothing to them except that they should read what was on the cards and get on. Of course, they could not read the cards. Here is an example:

$$\tau\eta\kappa\ \theta\epsilon\ \sigma\kappa\iota\sigma\sigma\rho\sigma\ \iota\nu\ \theta\epsilon\ \lambda\epsilon\varphi\tau\ \alpha\nu\delta.$$

The class asked her to explain it to them. *'Why? Can't you read it? It's in English.'* Sandra then read it. *'Take the scissors in the left hand.'* *'Oh! is that what it says?'*

The instructions deliberately made them clumsy by setting them to do things backwards or upside down, using the left hand if they were right-handed and so on. They made a mess of it. They laughed at their own clumsiness and what others were doing. It was fun. But it was serious learning too. At the end, Sandra asked them what they had learned. They said they knew now what it was like to have a learning difficulty, what it felt like to be clumsy and unable to cope, to be unable to read, to be or appear to be stupid. Then one engineer said, *'But you haven't taught us anything.'* You may imagine what a good discussion arose from that remark!

Discussion

What can we learn from a case study like this? Here are some questions to think about and/or discuss.

1 What would you have said to the engineer at the end?
2 What model of teaching did he have that made him say that?
3 What model of teaching was Sandra using?
4 Do you sympathise with the engineer's point of view? If so, why?
5 Why did this class of adults laugh so much when they could not do what they were trying to do?
6 What can we learn from this about adult learners?
7 Can you think of ways of exploiting an idea like Sandra's in your own classes?
8 Could you plan a peer-group lesson along these lines?
9 Make a note of ideas you could use: come back to them later.

Comment

Sandra was new to teaching, but she had had years of experience in helping Scouts and other people. She started with a simple question and a simple idea.

REMEMBER! … Try to be straightforward: avoid being complicated and 'clever'

Sandra thought through what she wanted the group to learn, how they should learn it and what they had to do in order to learn. She set up a learning experience for them to go through. This involved them in attempting to do something that they found difficult, so discover things about themselves that they did not know.

There were clear learning goals. Sandra knew what they were. She could have made it clear to the group what they were to learn, but she felt it would affect the process of discovery. They were able to say afterwards, and confirm, what they had learned. Usually it is better to share the learning goals at the beginning. Sandra was right in this case, of course.

The method she chose involved her in considerable effort to prepare cards and materials. During the session she had little to do; she could concentrate on watching the learners and giving a hand when asked. The students were very busy; the lesson was entirely a learning activity, mainly discovery learning on their part. There was a lot of variety in what happened in the class in 15 minutes. The students could say what they had learned at the end to consolidate.

REMEMBER! … Preparation pays off. Thinking through and preparing properly matter even more than enthusiasm and giving a performance.

Sandra came into her own mainly during the final session when she made them consolidate what they had learned by getting them to tell her about it.

Finally she was able to exploit the comment made by one of the group to stress principles on which she was working and to make them clear.

The students went away from the experience changed in important ways. Principally, it had made them think. They found out things about themselves and others that were important. It almost certainly affected the way they thought about learning difficulties students experience. All this stemmed from just 15 minutes of learning experience. This was learning by leaps: a great deal of important learning is of this kind.

CASE STUDY 4

Tony, who was in the same group, taught plumbing. He decided not to fol-low the easy option of giving a mini-introduction to pipe-work but to share an enthusiasm of his, a working hobby that he pursued with his wife on market days. He went round the markets dealing in antique pottery. He was very knowledgeable about pottery, and had a good collection.

The room was set out with comfortable chairs and some tables. Tony set a representative sample of plates on the tables. He had made photocopies from a catalogue of makers' marks, which are usually stamped or printed on to the bottoms of plates to show the manufacturer and the year of manufacture.

Armed with these, groups of two or three students were asked to identify and date sets of plates. They moved round the tables to do this, picking up the plates and examining them closely, looking for and com-paring the makers' marks.

At the end, Tony marked the groups' scores and helped them to under-stand where they had gone wrong. He revisited the learning with them and consolidated it. He communicated his own enthusiasm, and talked about the feel and look of the glazes, the patterns and so on.

In the evaluation of the class afterwards, there were expressions of genuine enthusiasm and excitement about what they had found out. It had opened their eyes to a whole new area of interest they had not known existed. Some brought their own plates the next week to be iden-tified and dated. And so did I; I was particularly fascinated by a Toby jug I had, which turned out to be French, not English as I had supposed. I have continued to learn. So have they.

Discussion

Consider the following questions.

1 What preparation did Tony have to do?

2 Tony's input of information came after the students had had the opportunity to discover about the marks for themselves. What do you think was the advantage of that?

3 Would they have learned better or worse if he had given a lecture first?

4 What was the advantage of doing it in small groups?

5 What was the point of marking the scores?

6 What lessons can you learn that you can apply in your class?

7 Make a note to yourself about these things. Review it later.

Comment

Most teachers rely heavily on only one of their students' senses: hearing. They do so without any idea how to develop the listening skills such reliance requires.

It is a great pity, because for most people hearing is a poorly developed and inaccurate faculty. We are even worse at listening: our concentration span is about 15 minutes. We are much better at seeing than we are at hearing, particularly since television has replaced radio as our principle leisure activity. Seventy per cent of what we learn we learn through seeing. It was probably because our ancestors relied so much on their eyes that they took to walking on their hind legs, to give themselves a better view of the world.

Furthermore, teachers ignore the importance of touch, of handling things. If you really want to know about something, you explore it with all your faculties. In order to look at it closely, you pick it up, feel it, weigh it in your hand, smell it, even taste it maybe. A baby does all these things when s/he explores the world. This is what the students did with these plates. Tony loved pottery, the feel of it, the look, the different glaze mixes that were used, and how the different makers produced the tell-tale characteristics. He communicated its sensuousness to us. His plates were the products of loving craftsmanship.

Most real-life learning is of this kind. People explore, walk through their environment, handle objects, smell, touch, feel. Most adult leisure classes are about hands-on activities, 'doing it' so as to learn. Teachers and textbooks tend to make things 'academic'. Why do we so often take the fun, the exploring, the doing out of learning?

There was a great deal of cognitive learning in the class. I now know a little about china marks and I can recognise differences in plates and glazes which I certainly did not know before. I wanted to know more. My interest had been aroused. I had been shown how to set about learning more. More learning by leaps.

Tony's class ran over its allotted time. When something so good was happening, it would have been stupid of me, as the tutor, to stop it too soon – and that is another lesson. The ability to adapt is essential. Often, teachers are trapped by their own rigidity and determination to get through what they planned, they stop student learning just as it is about to take off – to everybody's annoyance.

A small group of students wanted to try an experiment in learning with their peer group. They had learned about the difference made to learning by using structure. They used two low tables set in different parts of a large room. A collection of the same things was displayed on each of the tables. On one table, the many objects were set out in random order, deliberately jumbled up with no possible logic to connect them. But on the other, they were grouped so that a learner could easily recognise the category to which each object belonged. For example, ink, pen, paper, a book and paper-clips were placed together; a screwdriver, screws, a tape-measure and a hammer, and so on.

The students were selected randomly in groups. Each group was then allocated one area of the room and not allowed to see the other. Members of the two teams were to complete in memorising the contents of the table in front of them. The contents were covered with a cloth. The cloth was removed and they were asked to look at the table and its contents for 2 minutes. The cloth was put back and they were then individually to write down as many objects as they could remember.

The scores were then added up and people were invited to talk about the difficulty they had in memorising the objects. The team who tried to memorise objects randomly distributed on their table had had great difficulty, but the other group, with objects set out in categories, found it not too hard. Neither team, of course, knew that the thing had been rigged. They were amazed that one team had done so much better than the other.

Of course, the real learning came when each team was shown what the other had to learn. '*Oh well! If I'd had that …*'

Again, in this case the learning goals were known to the persons who devised the game, but were only divulged to the students at the end when they had perceived them for themselves.

Discussion

1 What do you think was the advantage of having a small group plan a lesson together?

2 This was a game set up as a competition between teams. What might be the advantage of that?

3 How do you think the losing team felt when they saw the arrangement of the objects on the table for the other team?

4 How effective do you think this kind of approach might be in getting students to learn an important principle?

Comment

Games are very powerful learning tools. The competitive element, if used well, properly controlled, can create a strong motivation towards achieving group or individual goals and improve the level of achievement overall. Used badly, games are disruptive and spoil cooperative, friendly relationships.

The peer group here had come together well by the time this game was devised, so that everyone in the group was able to relate well to the others. Even so, the losing team felt they had been cheated. This probably had something to do with self-image. What is important is that the learning was highly experiential. It was much more powerful for the losing team than for the students who found it quite easy. We often learn a great deal more from having to work hard to do something than from a task that is easily accomplished – if we have to come back from failure.

Fran taught personal relationships and coping skills with various groups, including adult students with moderate learning difficulties. She wanted to show her peer group how she set about getting people to understand how relationships develop; for instance, what might go wrong in a marriage and why. Here is her description of the activity as a handout, which was not given to the students until after they had had the experience.

SCULPTING

Begin with two willing volunteers. Choose any situation you like. You could choose the family, because it is a common experience. If you want to explore conflicts and relationships at work, you could choose that instead. In the descriptions that follow I assume you are looking at family relationships.

1 Place your volunteers In positions which you feel convey the relationship that would exist between a couple in a newly formed relationship. Ask the group to tell you what the postures suggest – affection, closeness, protective, absorption and so on.

2 Now move the time scale on – two years perhaps – and introduce the first child (another member of the group).
   You can do the rest of the exercise in one of two ways: *either* continue to position additions to the group and explore feelings, *or* allow additions to stand where they feel most natural. If you are working in a real situation with a group it is best to use the second method because you can explore why they have stood in that position – for example, closer to one person than to another.

3 Continue to add 'family members'. They need not all be children; some can be elderly relatives, for instance. Either use volunteers, or choose people if you know them well. You can also remove members – perhaps a sister who has married, a brother who has moved away to take a job, a partner who leaves home and then comes back, one member who has died.

4 At each new addition/subtraction, explore with the group their feelings about the changed situation and how they would prefer the relationship to develop. Let them adjust their postures and then talk with the other group members to see how they now feel.

5 At intervals, encourage the group members who are observers rather than participators to say what the groupings suggest to them. See if 'family members' agree with their impressions.

6 Finally, ask the first couple to stand exactly where they are while the others return to their seats. Explore with the whole group how the original body postures of the 'parents' have changed and what this might indicate about the changed nature of the relationship. Why has it changed? How could this be avoided.

Fran conducted the exercise above for about 15 minutes. The peer group found it entertaining. At the end, comment was hardly necessary, but it led to a fascinating discussion.

Discussion

1 What advantage do you think there might be in getting people to 'be' someone else and to try to express their feelings about it? (This was *not* role play, which would require the students to play out a scene of some kind, but wordless 'sculpting' of postures to express feelings and relationships.)

2 Fran was using examples of 'body language' here. What do you think is meant by that phrase?

3 Why is body language so important?

4 Was the teacher able to predict what would happen?

5 How far should she have tried to control and shape what people chose to do?

6 What effect would that have had on the learning?

7 What effect do you think the experience had on the learners?

8 Can you think of other ways to use an idea of this kind?

9 How well would you need to know your students to use this kind of technique successfully?

Make a note of any ideas/thoughts you could use.

Comment

Such complex ideas as the relationships between people, how they change with time, under different pressures, are very difficult to deal with. Usually, they become abstractions, or get bogged down in anecdotes and discussions of people's personal problems. This method was marvellously powerful in creating an abstraction at the same time allowing individuals to explore relationships in their own way. Sculpting produced striking visual images and made people walk through an experience. This was as fascinating for the observers as for the participants. People were encouraged to draw their own conclusions, there was no ready-made moral, no advice from Fran. My conclusion was that you have to work hard to hold a relationship together with so much going on to force people apart.

What we discover for ourselves may be much more creative learning than what other people tell us. This was another example of a simple but powerful idea well used.

John needed to explain a particular concept to his class of modern apprentice plumbers. He wanted his students to understand how to calculate the heat loss from a building and hence how much heat you needed to put into it, as well as be able to apply a formula. They had to visualise the problem, to have a mental model. The rooms were in three dimensions and heat loss in six directions: through the four walls, the ceiling and the floor. The students needed also to take into account the number of rooms inside a house.

John felt that it would be a good idea to try to explain the principle to people who knew very little about plumbing in a peer group, to experiment with them first before doing it with his students. He and I agreed it could be done by using a doll's house. So he managed to get hold of a large doll's house and brought it to the class.

The students were asked to examine the house in small groups and then to work out in their groups what factors had to be taken into consideration in designing heating input into the house, and in particular to discover the problems of heat loss. Each group was asked to come up with a solution to the problem.

It took them very little time to analyse that heat loss problem, and their solutions were quite fascinating. They saw that insulation was as important as heat input and why. The students told the teacher what the problem was, and jumped way ahead in understanding other principles as well.

Discussion

1 What was the advantage of using a physical, tangible object?

2 Why do people generally find it so hard to deal with abstract ideas and principles?

3 Would it have helped if the students had known the formula for calculating heat loss/heat input?

4 What was the advantage of setting them the task in teams?

5 What do you understand by a 'principle'?

6 Why are they so important to grasp? Why are they sometimes so hard to grasp?

7 Can you think of ways of using this idea?

8 What principles do you need to get across? Write them down and think of ways of achieving that.

Comment

It is usual to present principles to students as abstractions, but a principle is much better understood in a concrete/real situation. When you explore something physically in the round, you are using all your faculties rather than just that part of the brain that deals with language and concepts. Equally, you will create your own abstraction in words that makes sense to you. There are marked differences in the ability of groups of students to deal with abstractions. We need to observe carefully how hard it is for any particular group: their level of difficulty will depend critically on their experience as well as on the ability to visualise something as a mental model. Many people find that extremely hard: to be able to visualise something, especially to 'see' it 'in the round', rotate it in the head, imagine it from a number of different angles. It is the reason so many people find it hard to remember how to get somewhere, even if they have done it before – or to read maps.

Creative use of simulations

Simulations allow us to rehearse teaching techniques on a small scale and 'get the feel' of how they work, without the fear of the consequences of failure.

It is important to take risks – to try, and maybe to fail. We can learn a great deal from such experiences. For instance, if the students had become really angry when they found they had been tricked in the game with the objects on the tables (unlikely, but possible), the teacher could have explored with them why they felt like that, and think of ways of dealing with it. The only way you will find out what tremendously good things can happen in simulations such as peer-group teaching is by taking part in them. However many examples I might give, they lack the excitement and challenge of being there either as student or teacher, sharing the learning of others and matching your experiences with theirs.

Simulations do not have to be confined entirely in time or space. It is perfectly acceptable for example to set the group things to do before your lesson – perhaps as a game.

For instance, if you want to interest them in local history, it is good to get them to do some simple research first. You could ask them during the week, whenever they are about the district, to look out for things of interest, anything that catches their eye and that might have a history to it. At the lesson, get 'the class' to tell you what they spotted, then show them how and where they could find out about what they have observed. You will, no doubt, be able to explain many things that they will find, but if there are gaps in your knowledge, too, you can use those to advantage.

All this focuses their attention, they arrive with questions to alert the brain, where a lecture on the history of the town, or a catalogue of 'interests', might evoke nothing but yawns. They develop the ability to look and to observe, to research for information. The questions are theirs, not yours, or those of a history book. It is all much more fun.

Another approach is to give them a list of places to discover or questions that can be answered only by searching through the town. 'What is on the weather-vane on the Town Hall?' 'What colour is the lion on the White Lion?' It is possible to make it a competitive game too. You could even award prizes!

Take risks. Be inventive. And, whatever you do, prepare thoroughly.

Effectiveness

There are numerous examples of successfully inventive lessons. Peer-group work can bring about a startling release of creative energy once teachers stop worrying about their own performance and concentrate instead on student learning.

Many peer-group lessons involve demonstrating techniques. A lesson is about learning; it is not a challenge to the teacher to prove something. Most of the many demonstrations I have seen were adequately done, but a fair number were so 'clever' that all they did was convince the students that this was a kind of magic they could never learn. Others encouraged 'students' to believe just the opposite.

It is hard for teachers to remember what it was like when something they now do so easily was difficult for them to do at all. Their present skill has come 'naturally' without their having to think about it. All skill learning is like this. With sufficient practice it is a matter of habit, 'memory in the muscles', so that the concentration of the skilled person can be given to other things such as the design of the object that is being created, while the skill takes care of itself. Skills, after all, are not an end in themselves, their purpose is to enable us to create something, maybe a document or a table or a meal. It is also hard to slow down, to demonstrate a skill at a pace that the students can 'see'. At the same time you have to ensure that all the students can see what you are doing. This can be hard if you have to demonstrate on a flat surface to 20 people, or if you have to have your back to them when working at a lathe, say, or with a 'patient' on the floor or on a bed.

To be effective, demonstrations must provide opportunity for the students to have a go. So the students must be able to learn the skill/techniques quickly. For example, 'catering students' can learn to make quite reasonable 'roses' by peeling tomatoes thickly with a sharp knife, well within the 15 minutes allowed. Students can learn to do a fireman's lift, simple resuscitation, how to find someone's pulse and measure the heart rate or how to bandage an arm – or almost anything that is simple, easy to follow and achievable within time constraints. There are many things you cannot learn in 15 minutes: how to use a typewriter or a computer or how to write a poem. But I did once learn a children's song that taught me Cantonese numbers.

Obviously, you have to decide where your lesson is to happen, what equipment/ resources you will need. You cannot plaster a wall or lay bricks in classrooms designed for teaching other things, any more than you can reasonably ask students to dice a macedoine of vegetables on a desk. I have seen wet clay presented on large trays with desks protected by polythene so that students could experiment with it. But if you want to throw a pot on a wheel you have to go to the wheel, you cannot bring it to the class.

You do not have to be trapped in a normal classroom, but remember that if you are going to ask students to meet in a specialist environment, they need to know where it is, how to find it. It may be important they wear the 'right' clothes. They must know in advance and come prepared. **All this requires thinking through, planning and organising.**

Evaluating peer-group lessons

Ask before the event:

- What are the students setting out to learn?
- What am I going to get them to do in order to learn that?
- What preparation do I need to do, and by what time?
- How will they know what they have to learn and whether they have succeeded or not?
- How will I know whether they have learned what I intend?
- How will I consolidate the learning?

Ask after:

- Did it go as intended?
- What actually happened?
- Why?

Evaluation must be seen as entirely concerned with consolidating the learning. We are trying to learn about learning, and what the teacher's behaviour and thinking has to do with it. We also need to know where we are going if we want to know if we have arrived there, or somewhere else. Your evaluation of how effective the lesson you prepared and implemented was should be matched with perceptions of others, principally your mentor or tutor. In the case of peer-group lessons, you can also get the reactions of 'your students'. If you are starting from the learning needs of 'the students', as you should be, their views of how it was for them, what happened in terms of their learning, are the most revealing.

Let us be clear what simulations such as peer-group lessons are for. Any simulation is about learning, not the performance of the teacher. Evaluation is about how effective the learning has been, not with scoring various teacher skills. They are not a means of assessing competences of a teacher. If they are used for this purpose, most of the excitement and fun will disappear, and so will much of the potential for learning.

Evaluation is an opportunity to revisit a learning experience, so that the group as a whole can take a reasoned view of what actually happened and why, and draw some conclusions from it. To do that, first you must establish the facts; this is where sharing perceptions of the group is most valuable. Consider again the advice on observing a class on page 18. You can compare your view, the teacher's view of what happened, what s/he noticed and felt with those of the students. And if they differ, so much the better.

How did 'the students' *feel* in trying to learn through the method chosen by the 'teacher'? Did they feel threatened, confused, stimulated? Did they find it easy, hard, interesting, annoying, exciting, challenging, infuriating? Were they amazed at their ability, or depressed by their failure, or bored by the whole thing? If some succeeded and others did not, what was the difference? And why?

Perhaps, there was some gender stereotyping. In some exercises, women generally seem to do better than men, and in others not so well. If that does happen, it could lead to asking why that is so. Does it relate to self-image – that's what men/women do? Or to experience? Or to conditioning?

I am not going to suggest all the possible questions. But in the end that is what it is all for: *to find the questions*. It is no help to learn theories about how people learn if you have little practical experience against which to test them, or to make judgements about their validity.

Feedback: you need a mirror

The more experience of teacher–student interactions you have, the more fascinating the questions will become. You need to look at how you learn, how you feel about what is happening to you, if you are to have an insight into how it is for your own students. But it is hard to see things the way they do.

Your peers are able to provide feedback about how it was for them. Your tutors will provide a different perspective because they have greater experience and understanding. Their advice will be invaluable. They will 'chair' feedback evaluations with the peer group.

Some tutors prefer also to video-record each lesson and, usually after a suitable lapse of time, allow you, the teacher of the lesson, to watch it. There are advantages in doing this, but also dangers. It very much depends on how the camera is used, who is making the recording, what is recorded. It is easy to raise the wrong kind of self-awareness, the teacher is so concerned about what s/he is like and what s/he is doing that what is happening for the students, what they are doing to learn, can no longer be the focus of their attention. Many teachers find the prospect of being recorded daunting. I still do, I hate it. So do most tutors if they are honest.

What should the video-camera record? Cameras exclude most of any experience and narrow the attention on to specific things. The closer the image comes, the more that is excluded. That is in fact what a camera is designed to do! It is of benefit if you want to focus attention on that bit. What we need to do in evaluating a lesson, however, is to have a view of 'the whole' experience, both for the teacher and the students. This is extremely difficult to do with a camera, unless it is set up with a wide view of the room, but that is very hard to watch. Yet if all that is recorded is what the teacher is doing, student reaction and involvement will go unrecorded.

It might be more advantageous to record what the students are doing, as in the Case Studies above, but there is a danger of excluding the teacher. Whatever means is used of providing feedback, it should include as much as possible rather than exclude parts of it, to provide a picture of the whole experience and so avoid distortion. To use a camera creatively to help a viewer share an experience, to walk through it as it were, takes considerable expertise and skill. A tutor cannot be doing that at the same time as watching the lesson. If the camera is set up in a static position, that is tedious to see.

In the end, it is the verbal exchanges, question and answer that consolidate the learning. The evidence as a recording can be very helpful, tutor and student watching and discussing together. This is what happens when football coaches analyse matches with their players.

Tasks

Task 2 sets out some structured ideas for planning a lesson with a peer group. In Task 3 you evaluate one by reflecting on the experience.

PREPARING A PEER-GROUP LESSON (CHECKLIST)

Learning goals

1 Clarify for yourself what you want the students to learn.

2 Set these out as statements of learning goals. Make the statements simple. For example; The students will
- locate a fracture in a limb
- make a sling
- make the patient comfortable.

3 Try to ensure that what you describe can be done in the time, and can be observed happening.

Method

1 Think about how the students are going to learn.

2 Try to ensure they will learn, as far as possible, by being required *to do something actively*.

3 Think about what they might enjoy attempting to do.

4 Are they going to work individually or in groups?

5 Will there be any element of competition?

6 How practicable is it? Where can it be done?

7 What are the things they and you will need?

8 How much organisation time will you need for the room or the equipment?

9 Will you need a specialist room? How do you organise that?

10 What information will the students need beforehand? Will they need a map?

11 What clothes will they need to wear? Do they need to bring anything – ingredients?

12 Anything else that you can think of?

Input

1 What do you have to provide as input to get it going?

2 Will this be you talking, or will there be instructions on paper?

3 Will you need to demonstrate something?

4 How much time will you need to do your bit?

5 How much time do they need? What is to be the balance?

6 How much can be prepared beforehand?

7 Will you prepare handouts? overhead projector transparencies? a computer presentation?

8 Will you need to ensure that the proper equipment is available and in place?

9 Will they need anything beforehand? Must they do anything in advance?

10 How will you grab their attention? How will you make them want to learn?

Preparation

1 Make clear for yourself what you need to make or prepare

2 Give yourself deadlines – 'do this by' such and such a day. Have a checklist.

3 Have it all together and ready.

4 Make sure everything works!

5 Have a cue-sheet, showing teacher activity, student activity and timings.

Consolidation

Ensure that there is time to focus on what they have learned.

EVALUATING PEER-GROUP LESSONS (CHECKLIST)

TASK 3

Facts

1 What did you expect to happen? Did it happen that way?

2 What actually happened? Can you describe it?

3 Did the students understand what they had to do? and do it?

4 How well did they do it? Did anything surprise you?

5 What would you do differently next time?

Learning goals

1 Restate for yourself what you wanted them to learn.

2 Do you think your view of that has changed? Why?

3 Did they achieve the goals? Did they know? How did you know?

4 What else did they and you learn?

5 Did anything about the learning surprise you?

Method

1 Was the method you chose appropriate for the learning?

2 How active or passive were the students?

3 Did you get the balance right, do you think?

4 Did they enjoy what they did? Why, or why not?

5 Were there any problems? Could you have foreseen them?

6 How well did you cope with making it all happen?

7 Did they cooperate, or was there any tension?

8 Did you get the practicalities right?

9 Did they have the right things to learn with? Was the place right?

10 How could you have improved what happened?

Input

1 What about your preparation and what you actually did?

2 Did it take too long? Was it clear?

3 Was there too much information to absorb? Was it confusing?

4 Was everything ready? Did it work? What else did you need?

5 Did the environment support the learning or did it cause problems?

6 If you did it again, how would you change it?

Consolidation

1 What did they learn?

2 What did you learn?

Once you have your own evaluation you can compare it with what your students said.

CHAPTER 5 | Teams

REMEMBER! … The ability to work as part of a team is an essential skill in all walks of life.

Why is it so important to practise working as part of a team? Employers will always value good team members above those who want to do their own thing, or who find it hard to work with colleagues, or to make a commitment to team achievements. Businesses are run by management teams, colleges are no exception. The effectiveness of teams depends on the mix of personalities. If we want students to become adept at problem-solving, developing the insight, skills and confidence which are needed, we really have to encourage them to work in teams, to share and to support each other. What is true of students is true of teachers. A team is a group of people working together to achieve agreed goals, as in a football match! Apart from any other consideration, it is much more fun. It is very satisfying to achieve shared goals together with a group of colleagues. We learn so much from each other.

Full-time teachers share preparation rooms, which provide opportunities to discuss any issues with colleagues. In all institutions teams of teachers have identified team leaders who develop course programmes and resources together. The team provides a point of challenge testing their capabilities to the full.

Part-time teachers often feel isolated from other teachers, left to cope largely on their own without adequate support from the institution they work in. In the evenings they may feel they are there when everyone else has left. It is not a comfortable situation to find oneself in, particularly in the present climate of accountability with additional pressure on teachers to achieve results. It is in recognition of this that government policy is to establish a mentorship system in specialist areas for all teachers in training. We all need support, even if it amounts to no more than a listening ear. It is usual to specify roles within a team to exploit each member's strengths. But teams will only work well if the members develop the appropriate skills and attitudes.

Humans are social animals. It is normal human behaviour to work together in a social group. History records solitary geniuses who had a profound effect on their society. But human beings would have achieved little if each had worked in isolation. We should have no great cities, nor even village communities. We live in a technological age, the outcome of competitive cooperation, in which individuals with specialised skills and knowledge work together. Our students need to function well in this kind of society. To do so they need to develop not only specialised skills, which will give them employment in specific roles, but interpersonal skills and positive attitudes to others, especially in problem-solving situations. Unfortunately, the present accreditation system undervalues important learning of this kind by certificating only individual skills and achievements.

How do we develop these skills and attitudes? It is mainly through the experience of trying to solve problems together with others. It is a cumulative learning experience for us as individuals as we build up confidence to tackle problems in a creative way. For example, suppose you are driving a car at night down a completely dark road. You see lights coming towards you. From experience you can make a reasonable, we may say 'an educated guess', as to what those lights are. You predict how the 'oncoming car', not 'the lights', will behave: that it will keep to the side of the road away from you and safely pass by. On the basis of this prediction, you are able to decide what you should do. It is not always easy even then to discern the shape of a bend or to mentally calculate how to drive it.

Well, of course, you could be wrong! We need to be able to predict what is going to happen in most situations we meet. We learn to do this by our experience of similar things happening in the past. We cannot deal with people or things that happen without some hypotheses, guesses, to guide us. But it is necessary to test our hypotheses, and in the situation just described that could be rather frightening. If we have guessed wrong, we are in trouble.

When we are faced with new and challenging circumstances, with problems we may not have met before, or where our theories are not working very well, we are puzzled as to what to do. We are forced to try out new ideas, new tactics to cope with them. If the lights coming towards you present a totally unfamiliar pattern which makes no sense to you, you cannot make 'an educated guess' as to what they are, you cannot make any predictions or take any positive action. You are best advised to stop and wait to see what happens.

If there are other people in the car, you can consult with them. Perhaps if you put your heads together, you will come up with a workable hypothesis and an action plan.

This is normal human behaviour. Social animals work most effectively in groups rather than alone. The only way we can explain how a creature as physically weak as *Homo sapiens* has come to dominate much stronger animals is in terms of this combining of strength and intelligence. After all, the most terrifying 'animal' in the jungle is a column of soldier ants 'on the move', where the whole is much greater than the sum of the parts. The same is true of all good teams. Bad teams are likely to make a mess of things. Those are usually teams in which personalities clash and there is antagonism or a lack of common purpose. Individuals pull in different directions.

But individuals alone are less likely to solve problems than are cooperative groups. Managing is essentially the harnessing of the energies of groups of people who have agreed goals which they are committed to achieving together. Those countries as well as business enterprises that value the group above the individual have achieved technological dominance in the last 50 years.

Setting up a team exercise

First, there must be a context in which the team exercise will occur. It is much easier to practise the skills as an extension of peer-group teaching. But it needs a whole day to do it properly.

Identify teams of three or four teachers and invite them to plan a learning activity to last for about 30–45 minutes. Planning and preparation must take place well ahead of the day.

All the same considerations apply as for individual lessons (or indeed, for planning learning of any kind). What is special is the greater potential for creative thinking and design of the learning. Again, the model is:

- explore ideas
- choose one and shape it
- design a session
- implement the learning activity
- evaluate it with the group.

CASE STUDY 8

Karen, Christine and Frances formed one of several teams set up from among a class of teachers in training who were given the task of planning team teaching exercises for a day's programme of peer-group teaching.

They thought of a simple task like answering the telephone and how hard people find it. So, they set up a large room with telephone sets, arranging them into six different contexts in different parts of the room. They wrote instruction cards, each defining a different situation and a problem using the telephone. The situations included:

(a) asking a difficult bank manager for a loan

(b) answering the phone in a shop with an insistent customer on the phone, and another in the shop

(c) dealing with an answering machine

(d) having a one-sided conversation and taking down instructions by telephone.

The teachers started proceedings with a role play of a secretary who committed every possible error in dealing with the phone. It alerted the students to problems they might encounter and was fun to watch. It created a good atmosphere.

Students then went round in pairs to experience all the situations. The team had positioned an observer at each station to note what each pair of students did as they followed the instructions.

At the end the students reported what they had discovered and the observers what they had observed. The learning was then agreed in relation to certain principles.

Discussion

1 What do you think was the benefit of choosing an activity that was already familiar?

2 What was the point and the effect of having the 'demonstration' at the beginning?

3 What kind of 'errors' do you imagine the secretary committed?

4 What are the major problems of using the telephone in your experience?

5 Do you think the four above are typical of difficult situations?

6 Can you imagine others? Have you experienced others?

7 What was the point of having observers?

8 What do you think the peer group will have learned from the experience?

9 How would you handle the evaluation and feedback at the end?

Comment

The team exercise was fun. Students explored a range of different but perfectly realistic situations to discover important principles about communicating by telephone. Having observers meant that there was an opportunity to take different views of the same experience. The observers were able to compare different people doing the same tasks. The pairs of participants could explore their own feelings. And sharing the experience with a partner allowed the students to extract maximum benefit from the whole exercise. The teachers learned a great deal also about generating ideas and about making students work together as a team.

TASK 4

PLANNING A TEAM EXERCISE

Plan a team exercise as a lesson, or a class, with some of your colleagues working as far as possible as a team – to gain the experience.
　　Implement and evaluate the plan. What have you learned?

SECTION C Your own class

CHAPTER 6	Getting started

What are your students going to do in order to learn?
What are you going to do to help them to learn?

Teaching

First, look again at the checklist you used at the end of Peer-Group Teaching. All the same questions arise with any class you will take. But answers will be conditioned by many other factors you need to consider.

One of the factors that looms large for new teachers is having the confidence to control the class. There is a great deal more to running effective learning sessions than your ability to maintain control of a class, to deliver your material clearly or manage the learning activity you have devised. All these skills are required and no class is likely to be successful without them. But these are about what you are going to do. For a fuller discussion of classroom management read Chapters 9 and 10.

REMEMBER! ... Managing learning is managing the class. You are there principally to engage the students in a learning process.

In developing your skills and competence as a teacher, you must keep this constantly in mind. Whatever you do, however well you do it, their learning depends critically upon what they do in order to learn. This must be your starting-point for planning learning sessions. If you are over-anxious of your ability to manage, how well you are performing, what the students think of you, how critical the head of department or tutor is going to be of 'your performance'; it may be difficult for you to avoid concentrating largely on what you do, not even seeing what your students are doing. In observing other classes, therefore, concentrate your attention on the students: how they are responding to what the teacher is doing, on the balance of activity? Who is doing most of the work in the class?

Think about the role of a doctor with a patient. The doctor has to deal with perceived needs of individuals, listen carefully to what each patient says, ask appropriate questions to elicit relevant and helpful information and make a professional judgement about the patient's needs in order to prescribe a course of therapy. Often enough, what the patient tells the doctor may be distorted or even untrue. S/he has to interpret that in relation to other diagnostic information. Students behave in much the same way with teachers and they with them. The responsibility for getting well lies as much with the patient as with the doctor. The doctor may prescribe a regime, advise a change of life-style, or eating habits, or work patterns, but it is what the patient chooses to do that affects progress. If s/he goes on over-eating, refuses to take the pills or muddles and/or abuses their use, it is the patient who is mostly to blame, although the doctor must ensure that the patient understands what the instructions mean.

I remember a surgeon saying to me: 'A surgeon can only do damage. It is the body that must do the healing.' The body's capacity to heal and rebuild itself always amazed him. He set me thinking about teaching. It requires real effort on the part of students to learn, and a level of commitment to doing it. A teacher has to create the right conditions for learning and find ways to motivate the students. But s/he has to start by trying hard to understand the students' needs, and particularly their perception of what is going on.

You should be able to generate excitement for your subject and communicate enthusiasm. But often enough, you will feel the need to do much more. In the present climate of accountability, you will want to be certain the students 'get it right', achieve the results that matter to them and to you. In doing so, be careful you do not take away the excitement that comes from intellectual or physical challenge. There is a danger you may do all the thinking and all the work, only requiring students to sit quietly, listen and remember what you tell them. What will they learn? Think carefully about it.

Learning

What makes someone want to learn, to move on from where they are now, when it clearly requires a lot of effort? Who will want to change unless they are discontented with the way things are now? or unless they truly believe there is something important for them personally in what they achieve? Perhaps a teacher should be like the grit that gets into the shell of an oyster. How does it feel for the oyster? An itch? An irritation? A pain? Whatever effect, the result may be a pearl, beautiful or misshapen, but a precious object nevertheless.

REMEMBER! … The effort to achieve the learning goals
must come from the students.

A learner has to worry at the thing. Many teachers provide the pearls ready-made. Students are asked to value them highly for what they are, to store them in their bags. But they are borrowed, put into a bank. It is the pearls the students make themselves that they really value, that matter for them, and that will have a significant effect on their thinking, behaviour and self-esteem.

| CHAPTER 7 | **Lesson preparation** |

In the next few chapters we will consider separately each part of the process involved in preparing for and teaching a class, beginning here with the preparation of a lesson.

Any new experience is difficult to grasp as a whole because there is such an enormous amount of information, so many different and confusing things to try to take in all at once. Initially, we explore and deal with the bits of any experience as they arise. Only later can we try 'to make sense of it all', if we have the chance to look back over what happened and try to get it into perspective.

You will have had this happen to you many times. With anything new, whether trying to read a book, to make a new thing you have never tried before, visiting an unfamiliar town, a new department store or a supermarket, there has to be a learning period.

We can, however, adopt a strategy, a way of going about it, that will enable us to deal with the new experience more effectively. In a department store we can use the store guide. With a text book, we could decide first of all what information we want, then search the book for it, rather than plough through everything the author thought we should be told. That is what we do in a supermarket, though they are designed to ensure the customers walk past lots of tempting and distracting packaging to find what they want. We can watch a television programme with the same questioning attitude. People are usually passive with their brains switched off or in neutral when sitting in front of the television set, or even reading a book. Searching for information is not, however, the same as 'dipping into a book'; it is actively looking for something.

Think about starting a new job. What happens when you arrive? You can wait to be told by your new employers whatever it is they feel is necessary for you to know. Of course, this will be important information. But the trouble is they cannot start from what you already know and what you don't know, nor can they address their remarks to what you feel is of importance to you to find out, nor in a sequence that will suit you, unless you tell them. Most of what they tell you will only make sense when you need to know, at a point of need. They cannot know the difficulties you experience as you try to come to terms with your job. You must say what is worrying you. You must ask questions, ask for help. You should encourage your students to do the same.

From past experience, we can identify for ourselves what we feel it is important for us to find out. We can then set out to discover these things. This will enable us to make sense of the experience much more quickly.

Think about that from the point of view of your students as they join a new class. If you look at things not only from your point of view of the teacher taking on a new class but also as the students coming to the class may see it, you will recognise what needs to happen early in the proceedings.

You need to share with the students your perception and theirs of what the class is about, find out where they are starting and what they see as their learning needs, why they are in your class. I asked you to do this for yourself early in this book. We need to ask ourselves certain kinds of question when we start thinking about teaching a class; and to go on asking more and more questions as we gain experience by teaching the class.

What questions? They are of the kind: who? what? where? why? how? when? This book has been written around these questions and is intended to help you to explore them. The answers are yours.

TASK 5

FINDING THE QUESTIONS

REMEMBER! … Preparation pays off: thinking it through, having things ready.

In preparing to teach we need to ask questions such as these:

Who?

Who am I going to teach?
What age are they? What is their background?
Why are they in this class?
What do they want, or what do they need to learn?
Why do they need to learn it?
What are they expecting to learn?
What do they know already? What can they do already?
What experience do they bring with them?
What are they expecting from me?
Where are they starting from? Where should I start?

What?

What are they going to learn? How can I share that with them?
What do they have to do in order to learn that?
What do they need in order to do that?
What are they going to learn with?
What do I have to do in order to provide that?
What do I have to do to help them to learn?
What kind of problems are they likely to have in learning?
What can I do to make their task easier?
What can I do to anticipate these problems and make learning easier for them?

Where?

Where are they going to learn? Where am I going to teach?
What kind of support and help will they find there?
What kind of difficulties are they likely to find there?

What equipment can they and I use?
Where is that and how do I get hold of it, set it up, find out how to use it?
Where can I prepare?
What preparation and/or reorganisation must I do?
Where can I go for help and advice?

When?

When and how often does the class meet?
How much time have I/they got for each class?
How much time for the whole programme?
What time of day will it happen?
What effect is the time of day likely to have? How often we meet each week?

How?

How are they going to learn?
How am I going to teach?
How fast can I go? What pace of learning?
Can they all go at the same pace?
How will we agree our learning goals?
How will I get them working and committed to the learning?
Can I assume they will want to learn what I am teaching?
How do I engage them in the learning?
How far can I trust them to be responsible for learning?
How shall I know whether they are learning – and what?
How shall I get feedback, and how shall I use it?
How should I adapt what I do to what they need?
How flexible should my learning/teaching programme be?

How will you answer the questions?

Initially, by asking your employer. When you meet your class, in discussion with them. In peer-group teaching, I focused on 'how' and 'where' questions in planning learning for your student group. In planning your own class, you have to consider other factors, such as motivation and purpose, needs and expectations, effects of the teaching environment and of time of day. The context of the teaching has to be clearly understood. Most importantly, you have to find out all you can about your students which will help you.

Questions must be simple and direct. They must lead to useful, clear answers, and to action you can take. There is really no point in trying to discover information you cannot use when planning the teaching programme.

Who?

In very many contexts, students are not used to teachers showing interest in discovering their views, being concerned to draw them into discussion about the learning process. If you ask personal questions about them, many will resist, and may even be offended. They may well take the view that as you are the expert, they expect you to make the course interesting for them; how can they contribute if they don't know about the subject? On the other hand, many will come with considerable experience. It is most unlikely that all the students will be starting from the same base-line, unless, in FE terms, they are very young. It is even more unlikely that they can all learn and make progress at the same pace. In recognition of this, the emphasis in FE today is on learning programmes for individuals.

Students do know about themselves, which you do not. Most people will welcome the chance to talk about themselves, about what they feel they need. Teachers often report that their students were grateful and welcomed the opportunity to talk to a teacher who 'wanted to know about me'. It is the critical starting-point of a process of building up a spirit of trust between students and teacher. If it goes wrong or is handled badly, it may make things harder. Certainly, it is perfectly easy to find out most of what you need to know without asking the students at all. If your class is part of a larger programme, the other teachers, or the head of department, will know what you want to ask. In nearly all institutions there is now a counselling team who use sophisticated materials and expertise to ensure that all students are guided in their choice of options and their progress monitored to ensure success.

Nevertheless, your questions may be of a different kind, and their questions will be more pointed.

> **ACTION**
>
> Consider ways in which you might find out about your students. Write down the options and think about what you have to do.

What?

You and your students must share and agree the learning goals. Students need to know what they are setting out to learn. They must also know what you are going to teach. And these must be the same. Frequently and unfortunately, they do not seem to be the same. Many classes fail because the students did not know what it was the teacher was trying to teach them, or what they were supposed to learn. It is not unusual for students to come to class with a fixed expectation of how and what they will learn, and experience a mismatch with the teacher. This is why it is so important that all agree what they are about. Is everyone starting from the same place? Learning goals should be set out clearly. 'What are the students going to learn?' is the question you must ask first. 'What am I going to teach?' can only be answered after that.

This is not the same as arriving at the first session, or any lesson, with a blank page and asking them what they want to learn. Negotiated programmes must start by the teacher declaring the options available. Your students expect you as the person with knowledge and experience to have a clear idea of what they are supposed to be about, what they have to learn, and how. That is the starting-point.

It is a process of sharing. Telling them is not enough. You must ensure that they understand what is intended, and they agree it is what they are ready to do. In some of the Case Studies later in the book you will find examples of a serious mismatch of expectations between teacher and students.

Clarify for yourself what you want the students to learn. It is best to have a general statement of overall learning for a programme, called Aims, with more detailed statements of learning goals for each lesson plan within the programme. The students and you need to know where they are going and how they are going to get there, and what they need to learn along the way. It will help you to sequence learning activities in a helpful way, and provide essential links to make the learning easier to perceive and assess.

Once aims and learning goals are agreed, type them up. Ensure that each student has a copy. Learning goals for each lesson should be given to your students at the start so that they know what they are to learn, and you and they can assess the effectiveness of the learning at the end of the lesson. You will have to decide how you are going to do that. If the learning is through tasks, they are also the form of assessment.

They should be able to link learning in one lesson to learning in the next lesson, and so build up a structure. With no idea of the structure, students find it hard to make sense of things. Learning goals are always a compromise between what the students feel they want to learn, and the teacher's perception of their needs; for instance, what they have to do to pass the assessment. Of course, assessment should arise from the learning and not be imposed on it. If the form of assessment is externally determined, there ought to be a working match. In preparing a teaching programme, you have to make assumptions. Make clear to yourself what your assumptions are – as I did in writing this book. Examine them, review them carefully again once you have met the students and worked with them to check where the assumptions you have made might be wrong. It is easy to continue with a lesson style and structure based on wrong assumptions.

Be ready to admit when it is necessary to change. That depends on your readiness to observe what actually happens in your classes. The most valuable role your mentor can play for you is to be a mirror, so that you can see things clearly the way others see them.

Julie wrote the following: Overview of my teaching practice and a typical student group.

CASE STUDY 9

I have been teaching Word Processing and Excel Stage I and II for 18 months. I mainly teach by implementing demonstration, imitation and assess students by giving exercise worksheets. The students I teach range from 20 to 75 years old. Their aim is (generally) to acquire or enhance computer skills and knowledge, not to achieve a specific qualification.

When I first started to teach computer skills I always had problems with my lesson plans running to time. Each week I carefully mapped out how long each demonstration would take, designed and prepared information and exercise worksheets. I had thought carefully about how I was going to deliver the topics required by the scheme of work. However I found that after each session I still had problems with covering all the Aims and Objectives.

When assessing my students in the first session I identified that some of them had better typing skills than others. Some were touch typists and able to complete the worksheets much quicker than others. It was important that the slower students had time to complete the exercise sheets to enable me to assess the learning, before I demonstrated the next topic. The more able students found themselves wanting more after completing the tasks. Therefore I prepared extension worksheets for the 'more able students' to help to maintain their interest while waiting for everyone to finish. This was my main problem.

By the third session I concluded that I had wrongly addressed the problem of my students' needs. Instead of giving extension worksheets to the more able students, I should have supplied differential exercise worksheets by redesigning the original exercise sheets to suit the slower typists' needs. The sheets needed to contain the minimum amount of typing but include all the Aims and Objectives necessary to asses the learning and understanding. I then needed to give the more able students the original exercise papers. This would try to ensure that all students complete the exercises at the same time.

This helped my lesson plan run to time in two ways:

1   Time was not wasted waiting for slower students to finish their work

2   Slower students were not making lots of mistakes and becoming frustrated, trying to catch up with more 'able students'.

It also instilled motivation into the group because everyone was achieving together and learning at their own pace.

Discussion

1   What assumptions did Julie make about her students when she first did her lesson planning?

2   What did she discover and when did she discover it?

3   What was her main concern when she first started planning her teaching?

4   She identified problems at the end of each session; why did she have these problems?

5   When did she realise what the major problem was for her students?

6   What was her first strategy for dealing with that problem?

7   What did she discover then?

8   What did she feel was a better way of dealing with it?

9   Why was that more successful?

Comment

There is an overwhelming demand in colleges by students of all ages who want to learn computer skills. The reasons are obvious. It is almost impossible to 'get on' anywhere without them. It is clear from Julie's experience that it is very hard to predict who is going to turn up in such a class. Yet all the manuals and programmes for learning computer skills start from an assumption that all the learners will learn the skills as sequential, structured packages, because that is how a computer program is designed. It is easy to assume that all learners will progress at the same pace, because it fits neatly into planning the teaching programme.

It is very hard to break out of this mould – to design learning that goes at the pace of individual learners, or that addresses individual needs.

AIMS

Set out the **overall aims** or learning goals for your class. Make the statements simple. You might say: The students will

- understand the various methods and techniques for making *x*
- develop skills necessary for using the techniques
- use the techniques successfully to produce examples of *x*
- use the equipment and materials efficiently/effectively
- be able to evaluate the quality of the product.

1 How will you make sure these aims are reasonable and make sense?

2 Who needs to look at them or agree them? Your tutor? Your head of department? Your students?

3 When should that happen?

4 How will you ensure that you and the students are committed to achieving these learning goals?

How?

REMEMBER! … People learn what they do; if they don't do it they don't learn it. But they must do it right.

Are the students going to learn individually or in groups? Consider Julie's class above. Think about how your students are going to achieve the aims. What learning tasks are likely to be most successful? Why is that likely to be so? What should you the teacher do? What is your role in the process? There is little value in their seeing a demonstration, however excellent it might be, if they do not have the chance to 'do it themselves'. It is essential to watch someone turn metal on a lathe, or carve a piece of wood, or ice a cake, or implement a computer program; but if I want to learn how to do these things I have to do them. My eye–hand coordination, my clumsiness, the weight of an object in my hand, the speed at which things can happen, my lack of understanding of symbols, or the sheer impossibility of making something do what I want it to do, can only be known when they happen to me and through my own reactions.

Students themselves bring tremendous resources to a class in the richness of their experience. What is to be learned in your class must link into and arise out of their experience. How are you going to exploit that experience? How are they going to make sense of it, starting from where they are? Is it possible to find out where their base-line is?

> **ACTION**
>
> Make a list of the ways in which your students might learn.
> Make a list of the possible ways in which you might teach the class
> Choose one way. Try to say why that one.
> Sketch an outline of what is to happen in your class.
> Think about who is going to do what, and when.
> What will they need? what will you need?
> What preparation is necessary to have things ready?

Sharing

To understand the nature of the questions teachers need to ask I have incorporated a few examples of actual classes as Case Studies. They are drawn from different countries: contexts change but learning and teaching present similar questions everywhere, at least in my experience. We learn by sharing our experience and our discoveries. That is what this book is about. The Case Studies are not to be seen as 'models' of the 'right way' to deal with situations. It is just what happened then and there. You have to decide what might work for you and your students. Nor is it just humans who learn from others. The animal world presents hundreds of examples. In Yokohama, Japan, urban crows are a nuisance. People put their rubbish bins in designated locations every other day. A common type of plastic bin had a lid that fastened down by a screwing action. It seems that one crow discovered how to unscrew the lid, tear the plastic bag inside to strew the contents all over the road. Within days, all the crows in Yokohama knew how to do it. The local government banned the use of those bins in favour of others fastened with clips. The crows were highly motivated learners, of course!

> **CASE STUDY 10**
>
> Karen was to teach word-processing in the School of Business Administration in a college in the UK. She was new to teaching. Her class was a full-time business administration group of 16-year-olds. They had no experience of producing real documents in a working environment, although they had some basic keyboarding skills. She tried to discover from other teachers about these students, but she felt safe in assuming they were like she had been at that age. So she felt reasonably happy she could understand their needs.
>
> As a new teacher, Karen played safe using the model of teaching/learning that she knew best. She had been taught word-processing using a textbook.

The textbook had worked for her so why not for these students? What she had not thought about was how many students the method that worked for her had *not* helped. She had been highly motivated and able to learn her skills whatever method was used by the teacher. Many students learn from what appears to be very poor teaching.

The textbook provided a 'lock-step' approach. It assumed that every student needed to learn the same thing at the same time, in the same way and at the same pace. Clearly, this cannot possibly be true. Individuals have personal learning patterns and learn at a pace that suits them.

Rote-learning has a place. Skills like keyboarding need repetitive practice. Learning to be a secretary or a keyboard operator in the real world requires a different approach, however. The skills are a means to an end; what matters is the ability to create letters and other documents of a quality an employer needs. And that requires all sorts of other skills.

Karen quickly discovered that some of the students who chose to sit at the front of the class did the exercises in the book at a pace she felt happy with, and at the same pace. Most of the class got left behind, and some who chose to sit at the back did very little work. The room was clearly set up to encourage the approach Karen had adopted. The workstations stood in rows facing down a long room to the teacher's desk and a whiteboard at the front. Karen could not supervise the students who were misbehaving at the back, because they were a long way from her and hidden by the machines.

Karen observed that for most students her teaching strategy was unsuccessful. She decided to redefine her learning goals. What the students needed was not just to learn the orthodox methods of paragraphing and so on from the book as a kind of abstraction, but to have 'tasks' that simulated real world demands and which gave a point to what they tried to do. She decided on a new strategy.

She prepared packages for all the students to enable them to adopt the role of a keyboard operator in an estate agent's office. They had to use the word-processing program to complete tasks which an employee in this role would undertake in the selling of a house: advertisements, the house details, the design of a brochure with a photograph, a window display, letters to buyer, seller, solicitor and other agents, and so on. Each student had a worksheet identifying what they had to do, as well as other resources. The pressure and excitement of the simulation radically changed the students' behaviour.

Karen spent a great deal of time in the preparation of the sets of materials, then she found herself in the class with little to do except to encourage students and respond to requests for help from individuals. Which happened only occasionally. She was anxious because she didn't seem to be doing her job as teacher, but as tutor I encouraged her to do nothing and just watch. The 'naughty' students at the back got on as quickly as those at the front. One girl noticed a mistake in a letter as she took it from the printer, looked at her neighbour and said, 'I'll still beat you', and quickly edited the text. These two had done nothing in the previous classes.

Discussion

1 What were the assumptions Karen made about the class?

2 Why did she choose to use the model of teaching/learning she had experienced as a student?

3 Why was it unsuccessful in this case?

4 Try to explain the differences between her first strategy and her second.

5 Why was the second more successful in involving all the students?

6 What do you think she had to do to use this method well?

Comment

Most people play safe. 'If it worked for me, it should work for them', but are they like you? Maybe it will, but what if it doesn't? We all learn from role models, and the obvious model for new teachers is the teacher who taught them. After all, their present success is a fair assessment, isn't it? If this model of teaching is also implicit in the way rooms are set up and equipped, and in the textbook you have been told to use, naturally, you will accept that model and try to make it work. You may even come to believe there is something wrong with you when it fails. It is very hard for a new teacher – or a new anything – to question such things.

Your role

There has to be energy in a system for anything to happen. Where does it come from? How much of the energy in the class has to come from you? How can you get the students to work in order to learn? If you do all or most of the work, will they actually learn anything? What is the right balance between what you do and what they do?

Time spent preparing teaching and learning materials will be well rewarded by the energy and excitement that it will facilitate in the learning, as in Karen's class. In the preparation for your class, it is important to decide how much you will need to talk and for how long, how you will get the students working and how quickly. What do you need to prepare for them to do that?

How much do you need to do as your part of the class? Remember that students can only deal with a limited amount of information at any one time. Trying to cram a whole mass of facts or words or symbols or ideas or practical skills into them all at once is very ineffective.

People need to absorb and preferably master a few things at a time, to do something with the new learning so that they have ownership of it. A variety of learning activity with timed changes helps to overcome this problem.

Once you have decided what they are going to do, you can think about how much time will be needed to do it. Then you can work out how much time you will need to make the input that will get them going. The form of the input is critically important in terms of motivation and understanding. Even if you want to get through a large amount of information, you will need to present it in sections of no more than 15 minutes at a time, and then make them do something to learn and assimilate what you have presented. Often, a teacher will assume that students have understood what has been presented and hurry on. Even if they have understood, by the time they have attempted to grasp the next package the first one is gone. In any case, almost inevitably some will be way ahead and some still at the starting gate. Try to see it from their point of view. Ask: What is hard here? What is it that a student will find difficult to understand or to do? You can then approach it by tackling that difficulty.

Getting ready

How much can you prepare beforehand, and in what form? What would best help the students to learn, and get them active? Do they need to have something in their hands that they can use? So, would it be better to present your information – or instructions or whatever – on paper as a handout, or as a visual presentation, using an overhead projector (OHP) transparency, or a computer-generated presentation? It has become standard practice for students to use Microsoft Powerpoint in schools; but older students and teachers may not be so familiar with designing teaching materials by using it.

More questions:

- What do you have to get ready?
- What teaching aids do you need?
- Where are they?
- Are there ready-made materials somewhere?
- Will you have to make anything,
- Must you carry equipment to the room? If so, where?
- How can you find out what is available and have access to it?
- Is there technician support? How do you get help?
- Can you get the room set up before the students arrive? (This matters enormously!)
- How much time do you need beforehand to set things up and make sure that they work?

Be prepared. You will be on your own and in charge – but you can get help. There is nothing more frustrating than to wrestle in a class with something that won't work: an OHP with a dud lamp, say, or a video machine that doesn't function, or a projector. It is a good idea always to carry a small screwdriver to repair the plug that has a loose wire – of course, practise doing it beforehand! Your own supply of OHP and whiteboard pens, and indeed chalk. I have found that students appear to eat chalk, and classrooms in many places have chalkboards and little more. Nowadays, it seems that everything walks if it is not locked up. Do you know how/where to get the key:

- to your classroom?
- to the video/DVD/projection box?
- to AVA?
- to the cupboard where pens, chalk or other essentials are probably locked up?

Do you know

- where to find the register?
- how to complete it?
- where the students can get coffee, maybe?
- where the fire exits are?
- what to do in case of a medical or fire emergency?
- important telephone numbers?

Do you know the college/institution rules about student attendance? time-keeping? behaviour? smoking areas if any? resource centres? opening/closing hours? and so on.

Your class as a sharing group

Consider how to promote group sharing through group activities. They can learn much more together and from each other than on their own. To enable this to happen, you have first to establish a group identity that is supportive of each member of the group. You will need to think about how to get your students sharing. Whatever you decide, it must be practical and possible within the time available.

CASE STUDY 11

ICE BREAKING

Vivienne, who teaches a Counselling Skills Course to mature students, wrote:

On the first evening of the course I wanted to integrate the group as quickly as possible because during this year-long course they would be doing a lot of experiential work, which demands a high degree of mutual trust. Here is my description of an ice-breaker exercise I set my students to help them to learn each other's names.

The classroom is set out with the chairs in a circle in the middle of the room, as opposed to the traditional desk and chairs layout, giving us a circular space in the middle. I told my students to take time (say 5 minutes) to observe all their fellow students. Then I asked the students to take a sheet of paper and a pen, to stand and circulate, approaching each student, asking their name and writing it down on their sheet. Then they were to say in turn: 'The thing I noticed about you was …'; e.g. 'your warm smile', 'your wonderful pink shoes', 'your curly red hair'.

They then wrote down their comment on their sheet opposite the appropriate name.

This proved to be a real ice-breaker, causing much hilarity and almost a party atmosphere. Each student then had a list of everyone's name with a memory-jog (a mental picture), which they could memorise before the next week's session. I also took part in this exercise and found it a wonderful way to learn my students' names very quickly without the usual name badges or cards. When you can address students by their names they feel valued, and it certainly helps with the group dynamics, if the group can gel quickly by feeling at ease with each other.

Discussion

1 What was Vivienne's purpose in using this 'ice-breaking' exercise?

2 What was special about her class? Would this technique work with any class? Yours?

3 What is the advantage of everyone knowing each other's names?

4 Why is it important for the teacher to use the names of students?

5 How can you find out the names of your students? And remember their faces to use their names?

6 Why was it important for her to move the furniture and create a circle for students to face each other without desks in front of them?

7 Why did it turn into a 'party' atmosphere? Why did these adults laugh so much?

8 What was the effect of her joining in the exercise? Was it important for her to do this?

9 What could you do with your class?

Comment

There are many interesting things here. First is the removal of barriers between teacher and student and between the students themselves. Vivienne wanted to 'integrate the group'. The arrangement of chairs and desks 'tells' students how they are to behave, what is supposed to happen there. Think of any room you go into. You hardly have to wonder about it, you know at once what is to happen from the furniture and the way it is arranged. Rooms are full of messages. You are hardly likely to want to sleep in a kitchen or cook in a bedroom.

Chairs in a circle like this suggest a party game and that is what happened; rather like children at a party, these students felt they were playing. Which was very helpful, because there is something embarrassing about facing other people with no protection such as a desk between you, for bare knees. Part of the point is to overcome this by confronting it. There is a feeling of rudeness, too, in making a personal remark before you are introduced, even if it is a compliment.

Asking each other's names is only the beginning. No doubt, they asked what people preferred to be called. In English custom, we need to be invited to use Kate or Katy as against Catherine or Mrs Jones even! Levels of formality are also levels of social separation. Vivienne wanted to be part of this student group, not apart from it. Learning names by using 'mnemonics' is a clever idea, too.

These were mature adults, from the context apparently mostly women. What might happen if you tried to do this with a mixed group of teenagers? What does that tell us about adult learners? Or about teenagers?

Lesson plans

Your lesson plan is essentially a cue-sheet. The plan of the lesson should be clearly in your mind, and related to the use of teaching and learning materials that you have produced. But it is helpful to have a paper you can refer to from time to time to check where a lesson is going: whether it has got lost or is basically still on the intended programme. It is not unusual for teachers to lose their way in a class; nor for them to adhere too strictly to a plan and not respond to student needs as they arise. A lesson plan should state the learning goals for the lesson – with some indication of how you and your students will check whether each has achieved those goals. It really is important that they do this for themselves. It should identify teacher activity and student activity, with a clear relationship between these two and an indication of the use of time. Also what both teacher and students will need and use. Remember that student learning activity is itself an assessment of their ability to cope with the learning, identified as tasks to complete. A reasonable test of someone's ability to produce something, or of skill in using a technique or a piece of equipment, is doing it. You learn what you do. If you do it wrong, that is what you learn, unless someone helps you to realise it is wrong and you do it right. This last is terribly important because once learning is embedded it is very, very hard to unlearn it. The students can assess their own performance. It is highly desirable that students make their own assessments of their achievement and progress. It is obviously essential that their assessments are matched with – and modified by – your assessment of their achievement. It is possible to design a pro forma to help teachers in planning classes where these conform to a well-established pattern as on a college timetable. What is essential is that you do not allow use of a proforma to limit your own inventiveness. Here is an example of a proforma that I hope allows sufficient flexibility for planning a wide variety of learning activities. (It is in shortened format; to use it you will need wider spaces for your information.)

Lesson plan proforma

Overview

Class/group:
   Room:
   Equipment available:
   Constraints:
   Time available:
Important notes:
   Students – who are they?
     how many?
     ages?
     why are they in this class?
Learning strategy:
Learning method:
Learning goals:
Preparation:

Individual classes   (1, 2, 3, …)
Date and time:
Learning goals:

Activity
Who? How long? Doing what?

A
B
C
D
E

(or more)

Consolidation.   What to do before next class.

Notes.   Preparation and setting up.

A lesson plan for Karen's class

How might Karen's lesson plan fit into this proforma?

Lesson plan proforma

Class:	Business Administration Word-Processing 2C
Room:	Computer Room 3B
Equipment available:	Workstations with computers and printers, OHP, whiteboard filing cabinets, cupboards
Constraints:	Workstations in rows in a long room facing the whiteboard
Time available:	2 hours a week (could plan over several weeks or a term)
Important notes:	
Students – who are they?'	Full-time college students. Must have GCSE English, grades A–C
How many? Ages?	35, all 16+, all female
Why are they in this class?	Business course preparing for clerical jobs. Not very ambitious
Learning goals:	to take responsibility for a real piece of work to use their own initiative and take pride in presentation to set out letters and advertisements properly to use correct and appropriate language to use the right style in business letters to complete everything by a deadline
Preparation:	Make a folder for each student (could work in pairs?) Find the materials – get them from an estate agent Maybe better if different property for each student? Plan and photo of each property – outline information: name, address of owner, valuation and so on

Instruction sheet (Sheet A) what to do, order/sequence:
letters to clients, newspaper (solicitors later?)
advert for the paper – a display for the window
a brochure with details of the property

Class 1
Setting up the simulation

Date and time: Wednesday 12th January 3–5 pm

Learning goals for   to understand exactly what they have to do
the lesson: to clear up any misunderstandings: question/answer
to examine the folder of materials, find out what is what
to plan: what to do, when, what is needed and so on
to plan: who to see, what to look for, questions to ask
to decide: the right format and style of business letter;
a good style for display and newspaper adverts

Activity
Who? How long? Doing what?

A Myself (15–20 minutes)
Hand out folders. Explain what's in them and what we are going to do:
a project for 6 weeks to half-term.

B Students (10 minutes)
Examine contents of folder. Make sure they understand what is in it and what
they have to do. Read Sheet A. Any questions? Are they clear about everything?

C Myself (20 minutes)
Question and answer round the class. Tell them they have to go and visit an estate
agent:
what questions will they need to ask? what will they look for? bring back?
Get their ideas. Build up ideas on the board/OHP
Where? who? what to ask? what to look for? what to take away?
What models can they use?
Make sure they each have a copy of the ideas put on the board.

D Students (30 minutes)
Planning: sorting out, making notes about what to do.
Create a programme for themselves.

E Myself (10 minutes)
A business letter to an estate agent asking for help:
set up a visit, what they want and why?

F Students (20 minutes)
A letter to an estate agent asking for information with an explanation of what
they are trying to do.

G Myself (5 minutes) Consolidation.
What to do before next week.
Make sure they bring their folders with them each week!

Notes on preparation.   Prepare Sheet A and folders.

Examples of lesson plans

This section includes examples of lesson plans without a proforma style. Their style suits me, but you must develop your own; there are many different approaches to the kind of structure and presentation such plans take.

What matters is not the plan itself, but what it is about, what it enables to happen. The plan is a tool. It must be flexible and usable: it should alert you to what needs to be done, and when, and by whom. The learning process you set up depends on what you think the whole thing is about: what it is for, who it is for.

Many lesson plans state only what the teacher is going to do: what aids the teacher is going to use, the content the teacher is going to cover. They are rather like lessons in which a video camera is pointed only at the teacher and records what the teacher does. A video-recording should be of what the students do, together with what the teacher does to make that happen. What are students doing while the teacher is teaching? After all, what matters is that the teacher observes carefully what the students do and don't do. Many video-recordings made on that basis would be very dull to watch.

Class:	Evening class in local history, one evening a week for 10 weeks	**LESSON PLAN 1**
Duration:	Two and a half hours, Thursday 6.30–9 pm	
Location:	Adult Centre; classroom with tables and chairs	
Equipment:	Whiteboard, OHP, photocopying available	
Facilities:	Central coffee-break area with easy chairs	
Students:	Age range 35–55, four men, 12 women	
Main purpose:	Personal interest, no examination	

Session 1

First evening session: Getting Started.

Purposes

- To get to know each other
- To share interest and motivation: what do we bring?
- To agree learning goals and programme to achieve them
- To establish working procedure – set targets.

Learning goals for Session 1

The students will:

- share their reasons/expectations in joining class
- agree what we are all setting out to learn
- establish good working relationships as a group
- identify a learning programme and responsibilities.

Evening programme

A Teacher Activity A (10 minutes at most!)
   Welcome students and introduce myself: who, why I'm here

Set up and explain 'ice-breaking' activity
Divide students into pairs (mix up men and women if they have
separated themselves out);
  they may have to move
  Provide an interview brief (very short, some cues).

Paper A

B Student Activity B (10 minutes)
Each one of a pair to interview the other and change over (5 minutes)
Make brief notes – my cues as starting-point.

C Student Activity C (30 minutes)
Each student introduces his/her partner to the class.
(Note: must ensure it's light-hearted and fun. Spot a 'jolly' character to
start it off, set the tone.)

D Teacher Activity D (5 minutes at most)
Tell them what we are going to do after the break.

Coffee break   (Ask them to be back in 10 minutes)

E Teacher Activity E (20 minutes)
Set out my own interest and background in local history
Outline: How to find information
           What to look for: clues, evidence, gathering information and
           ideas.
(Note: make it interesting! photos, old newspapers, artefacts on a
table to handle/hand around.)

F Student Activity F (15 minutes)
Students, in pairs again, examine the articles and try to see what can
be learned from the ones they look at. They make notes.

G Student Activity G (30 minutes)
Each pair comes to the front to explain what they have discovered.

H Teacher Activity H (5 minutes)
Consolidation of the learning: what we have learned.
Use students' ideas as far as possible.
Learned about: how to go about local history
                 what interest can be found in ordinary things
                 each other, the group.

I Teacher Activity I (5 minutes)
Setting up the programme for the 10 weeks

Paper B

Tell them my learning goals
Learning approach to be used: individuals or groups to
agree the topics to tackle; they share the tasks – agree who
will research, what they will prepare and who will present a paper to
the class.

Paper C
> Present my own outline: what I think is important and why
> Get them to take Papers B and C away with them and think about them
> Make their own programme around mine: what to add
>   special interests
>   research each to do

J   Teacher Activity (5 minutes)
> Agree with them: what to do next week
>   what they will do before then.

Complete the register

Thank them for coming – what a pleasure and so on.

Note to myself: Preparation

1   Set out learning goals   Paper B
2   Design my own outline programme   Paper C
3   Design my interview cues paper   Paper A

Before the class

- Arrive early.
- Get the keys I need.
- Get the register and make sure I know how to complete it!
- Find the caretaker and make friends.
- Make sure the room is comfortable: check heating, windows.
- Check on fire drill and evacuation procedures.
- Set up tables and chairs as I want them – committee style.
- Set the 'articles' table – make it as interesting as I can!!
- Make sure there are copies of the lesson plan, Papers A, B, C.
- Ensure OHP, etc. is in place and working, in case I need it.
- Ensure there is chalk or whiteboard pens and other things I need.
- Find out the drill for coffee, paying, etc.: when, how, who.

Class:	Full-time course in catering
Subject:	communication skills
Duration:	one hour, twice a week
Location:	drama studio with some tables and chairs
Equipment:	lighting, whiteboard, OHP
Facilities:	central refectory and student areas
Students:	20 men and women, ages around 17+
Main purpose:	to improve interpersonal skills

Overall aims

To improve communication skills and confidence in dealing with clients
To integrate work in accounts with writing skills
To improve team-working
To stimulate good working practice.

Methodology

An extended simulation for a term
Class divided into teams: a management game
Each team to 'set up' a catering company for weddings.

Learning goals for course

The students will:

- improve their interpersonal and communication skills
- have increased confidence in dealing with clients
- establish good working relationships in teams
- use accounts to improve understanding of need
- understand, have insight into managing a small business.

Programme for sessions

Session 1:   Setting up teams and agreeing learning goals
                  Setting competitive goals and targets
                  Establishing working practice
                  Team behaviour
                  Roles and responsibilities
Sessions 2–8:   While teams are working, practise skills team by team
                  Use feedback opportunities: tackle problems
Sessions 9–10:   Presentation by each team of what they have done.

Lesson plan for Session 3

Face to face with the customer – how to handle it

Method: role play

Learning goals (enabling overall learning goals 1–2)
The students will:

- be able to establish a welcoming, helpful manner
- explore with the 'customer' what he/she wants
- guide the customer carefully: advise, be helpful
- clarify what is required and agree to cost it.

(Note: in a subsequent session the students will prepare a proposal/estimate to meet the customer's requirements and cost it. The customer will receive different estimates and choose one, taking into account the whole package. The 'bottom line' is whether they can make a profit on a sufficient scale to keep going.)

Programme

Teacher activity:

1 Make sure teams know what they have to do

2 Check on progress so far and understanding of activity and goals

3 Set up the role play of customer and caterer, explaining it

4 Provide a cue-sheet for the role play   *Paper 1*

5 **After role play**, evaluate what happened with the teams.

Student activity: Take roles and work them out
                    Observe carefully and note what happens
                    Reflect on what happens
                    Evaluate performance
Teacher activity: Explain what each team has to do now.   *Paper 2*

Time allowed for each team: 30 minutes.

Note to myself: Preparation

Design role play guidelines, cue sheet and guidance *Papers 1 and 2*.
Set out room to facilitate role play.

John was appointed as an education officer to Northern Nigeria. He found himself in an isolated town south of the Sahara desert. The people were Muslim with strong traditions. English was the language of education and government; the main language spoken there was Kanuri, many also spoke Hausa. John was teaching in a government secondary school preparing students to take examinations in English set overseas. All were young men who had passed local examinations in English and knew they were privileged to be at the school. They were keen to do well, because getting the examination passes would open up top jobs for them in the future. But there were strong cultural barriers affecting their learning and John's understanding of them.

He was to teach English, European History and Health Science. The History syllabus was all about the Expansion of Europe and the Industrial Revolution. But Europe was no more than a word for the students, and at that time no industrial revolution had happened in that part of Africa. How do you create a feeling for industrial towns or factory life for people who have only ever known an agricultural society, and for whom the possession of a bicycle represented considerable wealth? Health science was a more promising topic. This required some basic knowledge of the human body: where various organs were, how they worked, what their function was, and especially what part they played in the health of the person. Perhaps, more importantly, what could go wrong.

Africans tended at that time to be afflicted by most of the diseases that affected people in Europe, plus a profusion of illnesses that were specific to Africa, or which had largely been controlled elsewhere. Many were insect-borne and most were preventable. This last was the real point of these students' learning Health Science, although they also needed to pass the examination.

John thought about them. What were their needs? Why was it thought they needed to know about the Industrial Revolution? It was hard for him to convince himself of the necessity, let alone convince the students. It was pointless 'knowledge' to be mugged up for an examination. But they certainly needed to understand Health Science. John felt he could count on a high level of motivation. People are fascinated by themselves and their own bodies, more than by almost anything else, and these young men had a strong desire to be fit and well. They all had the experience of being ill; most had relatives who had suffered from a whole range of ailments. All had had malaria and knew what many of the diseases felt like when you contracted them. This was not an abstraction, but very real. They also had their own bodies to relate experience to. John decided to use it. The main obstacle to learning Health Science was the large amount of specialised vocabulary they had to learn, a 'naming of parts' with medical terms and conditions. And John had no access to organs in bottles or laboratory equipment.

What they needed, he felt, was some way of visualising what the body was like inside. They needed to be able to *see* how the body worked, how the various parts fitted together as a whole, how the separate organs and their functions related to the whole 'machine', what a malfunction could do and its likely effect.

His solution lay in a plastic construction kit of the human body he discovered advertised in a magazine. He sent for the kit. As a group, they had all the bits and a diagram to help them to assemble 'this male body', which he set up as a group project. They had to fit the bits together. This allowed them not only to see things in the round, but to handle them, trying to fit them together into the places they belonged. You have the diagram: you have to build it. They had a great time and they learned the parts very quickly. They were also able then to understand the diagrams in the textbook and to draw diagrams themselves to show how the parts worked. They learned technical terms quickly, and passed the examination.

Most importantly, however, they learned Health Science as 'real' and absolutely relevant to their needs: practical knowledge related to their own life and well-being. It was not simply something to swot up in order to pass an examination – and then forget.

Discussion

1 What do you remember of many of the 'subjects' you mugged up for examinations at school?

2 What was the essential difference between what John had to teach in History and Health Science?

3 Why should this make so big a difference in learning?

4 What factors did John feel he could exploit with them?

5 Why were these so helpful in relation to the learning goals?

6 What was it in the method he chose that made it successful?

7 Would it work with any students in any context?

Comment

One stubborn barrier to learning occurs when students (and sometimes the teacher) can see no point in what they are being asked to learn or do. As with Spot in the cartoon on page 2, students might well ask what it is for or who it is for. Learning has to seem relevant and important, otherwise it will become a rather pointless game of 'beat the examiner'.

Unfortunately, this is an all-too-common experience in schools everywhere in the world. In FE, it is a scandalous waste of learning time and opportunity. And it is a major cause of unruly, even hostile behaviour in classes of young people. *'I didn't choose to do this and I don't see why I have to do it. Interest me if you can!'* Adults can be just as hostile: see Case Study 16 on page 97 (Lincoln) and Case Study 17 on page 106 (Florida).

What a difference it makes when they can see relevance, when the learning is in a form they can relate to! When the learning becomes fun!

Using experience and prior learning

One clear advantage of using the energies and resources within a student group is that they will start from where they are and not attempt to start from where the teacher believes them to be; or, as is often the case, from where the teacher is. A teacher can only make assumptions about a group, it is even harder to be clear as to individual learning needs.

To integrate their *prior learning* (what students bring with them to class from experience and previous schooling, working and life) students must use their new information and skills to create new perceptions and this must change their behaviour. It is not possible to ignore prior learning, because it determines what students select from what you present to them. New ideas and new thinking must link, can only link, to what is already processed. Skills can only build on previous skill levels.

What teachers provide is information and opportunity: to acquire knowledge and skills and to gain insights. Information, misleadingly called knowledge, is presented neatly packaged as a 'drive-through take-away'. Unfortunately, that is all it remains unless the students process it in some way to make it part of their own knowledge structure. Packages remain as useless lumber in the memory if they are simply stored to be repeated as answers to tests. Information only becomes knowledge if you do something with it (Figure 7.1). Knowledge is a process, a constant

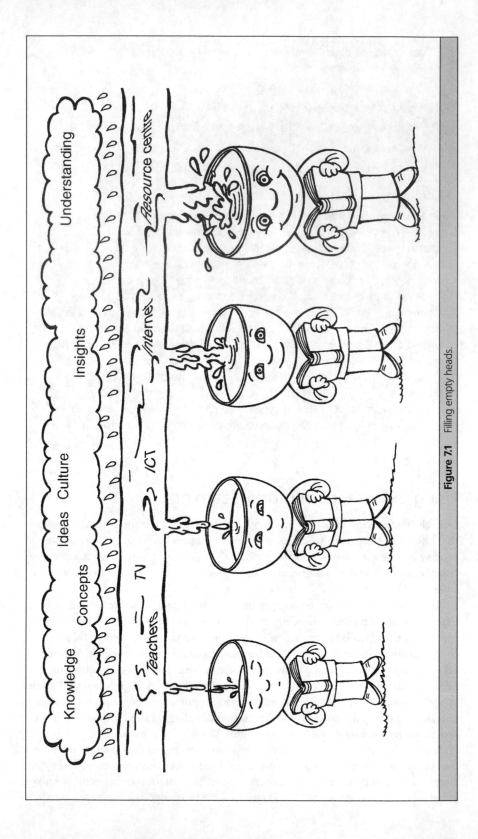

Figure 7.1 Filling empty heads.

change in perception, and not just an accumulation of packages. The same is true of skills. Learning, knowledge, change are all largely synonymous, the same thing.

Pace

Pace in learning is a major concern. How quickly can you expect an individual to learn something? In a class, how can you discover a way of dealing with different levels of readiness, or ability, that affect the pace at which each student can learn or cope with learning tasks?

Some methods will promote learning more quickly and cater for student differences. Many of the students in Karen's class in Case Study 10 would hardly have learned anything if she had not seen a need to change her teaching strategy. Nor will learning answers from a textbook for a test change our perception of ourselves or of our world, as John discovered in Case Study 12.

The methods both chose accelerated the learning dramatically. No doubt, Karen's students would eventually have learned how to work properly, perhaps when they were employed in an office somewhere. By using a simulation, Karen hastened the process. She ensured that each one progressed at her level of readiness and commitment to learning. It gave them something to do that they found interesting. They all progressed faster and gained insight into the *why* as well as the *what* they had to do. They saw the learning as relevant and important to them.

Readiness is mainly the result of past learning experience. People usually do not know what they know, where they have got to in their learning, nor where they are going. They often have no idea what they can do either, until they are asked to do it. They have to learn to use the experiences they have accumulated, to reflect on them and integrate what they know and can do by bringing it to the surface. Some courses are designed to do that. One obvious example is Drama. A technique that can be used – with considerable care – in other subject areas is 'role play', as in the Catering Class of Lesson Plan 2 on page 65.

We have to find some way for them to explore their stored resources and their accumulated experience, by matching it against new challenges. Equally, and often more urgently, we have to help them to remove the barriers to learning that previous learning has probably created for them. How fast can the process go?

Learning/teaching materials

Most new teachers, and many established teachers, rely heavily on textbooks. The trouble is that this allows the author to decide what students are going to learn and how they are going to learn it. Some institutions insist on all teachers using the same textbook. As in Karen's case, the assumptions made by the author were not helpful.

A book is a resource to be used wisely. It should not dictate what happens in a class. A crutch can eventually prove a handicap and should then be thrown away. One result of relying on a book is that it takes away the need to think things through.

New teachers frequently lack the courage to take charge, to take risks. They look for what is or appears to be safe. Some adopt a pattern of defensive behaviour, and this may become embedded. Similarly, new teachers can find it difficult to challenge what seem to be established patterns in the classroom or workshop. Often, a caretaker seems to dictate how a class will run. Some teachers lack the nous, or the courage, to move the furniture in a room to promote the activity they planned, however hard that actually makes it to do that activity. Students are made to attempt interchanges with other students by twisting uncomfortably in their chairs. It is one reason for making friends with the caretaker.

It is not necessary to try to produce 'professional' teaching/learning materials and aids. Just searching in resource areas in colleges and schools might produce useful stuff. What you need may be available, but you don't know about it or where it is to be found or accessed. Whatever you make or get, make sure it really is helpful to students. I have seen astonishing effort made by new teachers in producing teaching aids, which are far too elaborate for their purpose. It is a major problem with new computer programs for producing presentation materials. The test is: will it help them to learn? Anything can be a teaching aid used in the right context. Tony's plates were effective learning aids; so were Sandra's instructions written in letters of the Greek alphabet. If there is something available which is real, it is better than any simulation of it. The main criterion is: how useful is it?

Usually, you can follow the principle of 'the simpler, the better'. Instructions on a worksheet need to be clear and simple to understand. The less an OHP transparency has on it, the easier it will be to grasp, and the more effective it will be. Look at the cartoon on page 70. It could hardly be simpler, more effective.

Try not to upset people

Most things are done for a purpose.

- Put things back as they were when you leave.
- Clear the board of your work, it will only be a distraction to the next class.
- Lock up everything you are expected to lock up.
- Return the keys to the proper place.
- Put the register back in its slot.
- Don't take things home that others after you will need.
- Fill in any required information.
- Complete absence reports if required to do so.

CHAPTER 8	Tasks and performance criteria

REMEMBER! … What is important is that you are effective in your role.

A teacher is to be judged by what his/her students do and what they achieve. Concentrating on teaching performance in training has the danger of diverting attention from improving student learning. The *FENTO Standards for Teaching and Supporting Learning in FE in England and Wales*, published in 2003, stressed the interrelation of teacher performance and student performance and the role of the teacher in teaching teams.

Language used in education, as in other disciplines, changes with time. Education more than most other human activities is subject to change. Current emphases are *accountability* (the pressure to show results), *standards* (yardsticks against which to measure teacher performance), *competences* (identifying specific skills and knowledge), and *effectiveness* in the teacher's role. Teachers who lack competence in skills cannot do even an adequate job for students, let alone a good one. (Please read the Appendix.)

The achievement of *FENTO Standards* is the process of becoming effective as a teacher *in a context*. No teacher exists in a vacuum. Everyone has a role in a specific learning environment with identifiable students, where s/he must develop skills, insights and attitudes to an acceptable standard. Teacher training is to ensure that what is achieved in one context is relevant and transferable to any new context – which is the major purpose of stating such standards. You will certainly wish to become a competent teacher. It is one of the purposes of this book to define *standards* you should achieve and *competences* you ought to demonstrate in teaching. You will want to raise your level of understanding and skills well beyond competence, for teaching is about decision-making, creative interactions with students to promote learning, managing the learning and learning environments.

Many factors determine how effective people are in their roles, some definable as criteria for personal performance, but others relate to environment, contextual constraints, interpersonal skills, working in teams, relationships, confidence and adaptability. Much is determined by students who enrol for courses: by the society, employment fields and other similar factors that affect them. This is where growth in the job is most marked as a teacher gains experience.

Mentor and criteria

For teachers, teaching is the most important learning experience. You need to be eager to learn from that experience.

Overall, a person's learning and perception of learning is achieved by reflecting on experience. The first part of this book outlines a process, a journey along which a teacher in any context may gain insights and confidence in his/her role. No one can reflect on experiences of learning or teaching unless s/he can first observe what happens.

This is actually quite hard to do, since the closer we are to something, the less of it we can see. It is much easier to observe what others do than what we do ourselves. To see ourselves we must have a mirror. Some other person can act as that mirror for us (even our students if we are ready to listen to them). To be really helpful, the other person should be someone we can feel has experience of the problems and experiences we are dealing with and is sympathetic to our needs, but who is also prepared to be open and honest. An over-indulgent tutor or mentor is no help to anyone. But we must have something to share, some structure that will help our interchange. It cannot just be statements about what each of us 'feels'. We need to define the things we are looking for, what we are hoping to see, what *good practice* looks like.

We need to know, *before we do something*, what it is we have to do in order to do it well, how to set about it properly. We also need to know how what we do will be judged or assessed. Finding out afterwards that we have failed is demoralising, even worse if we are given no idea what we did wrong or failed to do. Stating performance criteria, standards of performance, will enable teachers and mentors to know clearly what patterns of behaviour they are both looking for. It will provide 'out there', non-subjective things to concentrate on and discuss rather than 'in here' feelings. Performance criteria relate to setting out to do Tasks, and observing what happens in order to reflect on it afterwards, to have common ground to share with your mentor and your tutor.

Set out in the rest of the book are Tasks. They define the learning path, the learning process of becoming a teacher. They are things to do in a logical sequence related to the job of teaching. The Tasks are *generic*: essential elements of teaching in any context, wherever it occurs. The Tasks may be tackled in a different way according to the context where you are teaching (what normally happens there, what others do), but there are patterns of behaviour that will make for more effective teaching in any context. FENTO is mainly about the generic knowledge, skills and personal attributes addressed in this book, but is also concerned that all new teachers receive help with developing skills and insights in teaching their specialist subjects from practitioners in those fields.

Since the context of teaching will be whatever it turns out to be, we cannot be over-precise in stating performance criteria, though achievement in any one context must be transferable to another. I have used the idea of *performance criteria* throughout to focus on the skills and attitudes which you need to develop. These match closely the FENTO Standards but are not intended to 'deliver' them in an instrumental sense. They explore the essential aspects of your role to become an effective teacher. The term '*performance*' is used here to mean '*behaviour as a teacher that can be observed and assessed*' in a real teaching situation: classroom, workshop, laboratory, ward, or where the teacher has responsibility for the learning of an identified group of students. It is not about '*putting on a show before an audience*', who might cheer or hiss and boo!

The *criteria* are judgements to be made. We have to rely on judgement in making assessments. Clearly, the quality of the judgements depends on the level of experience of whoever is making them. There has to be a sharing of perceptions, just as there is in observing a class and peer-group teaching. The teacher has the principle responsibility for assessing his/her own performance against agreed and stated criteria. But this will be more valid and constructive if an experienced mentor can be involved, not only in assessing by using the performance criteria, but in the whole learning process by providing positive feedback.

What is needed is that you, as teacher, should perceive clearly what is required to be effective in the role you fulfil at the level of responsibility you carry. That is partly defined by a statement of performance criteria, and partly by feedback from your mentor who shares the context in which the teaching occurs; who should also be a specialist in your own field and able to focus your learning so as to develop subject specific techniques and methodology. Naturally, you can expect to turn to your mentor for information and advice. It is not intended as a one-way street. Indeed, rather the opposite; your mentor is your guide, not usually your assessor. A tutor may fulfil both functions, but the former is by far the most important.

As you read on, you will encounter performance criteria for each way of looking at the role of teacher and what happens with your students. They are intended to help you understand the principles that are involved in what you do; they define *good practice*. They are intended as 'spectacles to wear' to view a particular aspect of your teaching experience. An 'aspect' means a point of view. There are many aspects that view the same experience from different angles. Hence, the criteria are cumulative not separate. Communication is not to be seen as about a different experience somehow isolated from Lesson Planning or Assessment.

Study these criteria, and match what you do against them. Where you meet with a clear lack of success in achieving any of them, ask yourself why that is so. Look carefully at what you are doing to evaluate what has happened and what needs to happen.

The criteria all start from the effect on the learning of your students of what you do as teacher and how it promotes their competence.

Good practice and maturation

Do not be over-anxious to achieve all the criteria that relate to performance in the first class you take. These criteria are not goalposts between which you can shoot the ball once and then feel '*I don't need to do that again*'. They are signposts: they point a direction of travel. Each time you prepare a class, you will understand more. It is a process of maturation and it cannot be hurried. Every time you try to meet them they will show you more of the road. You will find you can always do better; what we are about is the establishment of a pattern of good practice in your preparation for classes. This means a repetition of the pattern in preparing for *all* your classes because it is only by reflecting on experience that you will learn. You have come for the journey. Enjoy it.

LESSON PREPARATION

A lesson plan is a cue-sheet. What matters is the thinking that leads to the choices you make and the way you design your plan. Develop a style that suits you and where you are, the kind of students you deal with.

1 Find out what you can about your students to be useful in planning a learning programme for them.

2 Use that information in planning learning sessions.

3 Decide how you will go about agreeing aims, learning goals and their learning activities with them.

4 Design at least one lesson for your group. (Think about what you have learned from peer-group teaching and from your experience as 'student'.)

5 State your learning goals for the lesson(s) in ways your students will understand. How you will agree them with them. Are you prepared to be flexible at all?

6 Identify clearly Activity: what you will do, when, for how long – and what the students will do. How these relate.

7 Try to ensure you have thought it through. How the students will learn and how the activities you have designed will help.

8 Make sure you think clearly about feedback. How the students and you will find out what they have learned.

9 Identify clearly what learning and teaching materials you and they will use.

EVALUATING YOUR PREPARATION

Look critically at your lesson plan(s). Read through the criteria below.

1 How well do you feel you match up to these criteria?

2 Have you shared your evaluation with a mentor?

3 What do you think you should concentrate on improving?

Performance criteria

8.1 Information is obtained of your student group: their ages, educational background, past experience.

8.2 Questions were asked about motivation and personal learning goals.

8.3 This information has been used in planning learning sessions and learning activities.

8.4 What the students bring with them, their prior learning, is taken into account.

8.5 The teacher has a pretty good idea of where the students are starting from.

8.6 Students and teacher have shared their perceptions and have agreed learning goals for the lessons.

8.7 Lessons are planned to achieve the specified learning goals.

8.8 Where appropriate, the learning goals are consistent with the requirements of examining bodies.

8.9 Teaching methods and learning activities are designed appropriately.

8.10 The lesson(s) will engage students actively in learning.

8.11 Learning materials and teaching aids are chosen as likely to promote the intended learning.

8.12 Methods of obtaining feedback and assessing the learning are identified.

8.13 There is flexibility to allow for the different pace of learning of individuals.

8.14 There is flexibility to allow for changes in the programme if need be.

EVALUATING THE EXPERIENCE/REFLECTION

TASK 9

1 Use your lesson plan (or series of lesson plans) in a teaching context and evaluate its effectiveness by observing carefully and noting what actually happens.

2 Match perceptions of what happens in your classes to the performance criteria below, and use them to shape what you do.

3 If you have the chance, share your evaluation with your mentor and agree an evaluation statement.

Performance criteria

9.1 The lesson has specified (and/or negotiated) learning goals clearly stated and shared with students.

9.2 The structure and content of the lesson is known by students and takes account of the identified needs of individuals.

9.3 Teaching methods are appropriate to the specified goals.

9.4 Students are monitored and observed throughout the lesson.

9.5 Learning problems are identified during the lesson and the programme (or lesson plan) is adapted to take account of them.

9.6 Learning materials and teaching aids are used thoughtfully to promote the intended learning.

9.7 Individuals and groups are managed well. Control of the session is maintained. There is linking and structure.

9.8 Learning is assessed by the students and the teacher and is consolidated at the end, with clear links between lessons.

Evaluating a teaching session

You will need to think about the following in relation to your initial lesson plan.

Facts

Class: students, course, time, duration, place

1 What did you expect to happen? Did it?
2 What actually happened? Do you and your mentor agree?
3 If there are differences, make a note of these.
4 How well did your students carry out the activity?
5 Were there any surprises?
6 What was really important in what happened there?

Learning goals

1 Did your view of the learning goals change?
2 Did the students achieve the goals? How well? How do you know?
3 What else did they learn? Did anything surprise you?
4 Did they/you consolidate the learning? Take it away?
5 How do you expect them to use it?
6 How will they link to next session?
7 Was the method you chose able to provide assessment of the learning?

Method

1 Was the teaching method you chose appropriate?
2 Did the students *do* much to learn, or were they mainly passive?
3 Did they enjoy what they did? Why, or why not?
4 Did they understand what to do and why they were doing it?
5 Did they have the right things to learn with?
6 Could you have improved the organisation? the room? the equipment?

Input

1 Was your input right? Did it take too long? Was it effective?
2 Were the teaching aids and learning materials effective?

3 Were instructions clear? Was there enough or was there too much information?

4 Was everything ready? Did it work?

Communication

1 Did the students work as a group? Was that partly down to you?

2 Were there any problems for individuals or groups? What did you do about them?

3 Did you feel sufficiently skilful? Comment on that.

4 What about the students' attention, their enthusiasm, their concentration?

Consolidation

1 What did you learn? What would you change, or rethink?

2 What do you need to work on now? What do you need to improve?

REMEMBER! ... You can use the same list after every lesson for
the next 40 years as I have done, particularly the last two questions.
There will never be a time when they are unnecessary.

Although I use performance to mean 'observable behaviour', you need to be as sensitive to how 'a performance' went as any concert pianist, for whom every concert is a learning experience even if s/he is playing the same Beethoven Sonata for the 99th time.

CHAPTER 9	**Managing learning and your class**

Class management

Activity 1 asked you to set down what you felt you needed to learn to be a teacher of adults. Many new teachers will have replied, '*I need to know how to control the class.*' What did they mean and why did they feel it to be a need?

All planning works on assumptions. There is an assumed contract between a teacher and the learning group s/he is responsible for. In the majority of cases in FE/AE, there is an understanding and an easy relationship based on this contract, as long as the students feel that what they are doing is purposeful and that they are making progress. If there is an apparent mismatch between the needs and expectations of the class and what actually happens, this relationship may sour. Students must feel a respect for their teacher.

It is vital that all agree early what they are there for. Your job is managing the learning. Any manager wants to feel in control, but what is it that you as a teacher can control? We shall explore the answer to that question in this chapter.

REMEMBER! … Your first job as the teacher is to establish the class as a group working together.

How quickly that can be done is unpredictable. Some classes will settle down almost at once, while it may feel like weeks before others gel. This depends on the relationship a teacher makes with his/her students, but many factors may not be within the teacher's control. It is difficult in a book to anticipate the huge variety of circumstances, age range, environments, personalities, helpful or disruptive elements encountered in FE/AE. One way forward is to consider the experiences of others. That is the reason for reading and discussing case studies. They are not intended as 'models' to copy, so much as ways of thinking things through. What is possible with your class is a matter for your judgement.

Certainly, you need to control the environment and the learning materials. This book is full of advice about those. What about the people? You cannot manage people in the same way that you manage a machine or a room. I believe that the new teachers above were afraid of loss of control. A fear of students and what they might do pressed on them, and they had little confidence in their own ability to manage the people in the class.

Unfortunately, I can do no more than make some general statements and suggestions because I cannot predict your circumstances or who will come to your class. One thing is certain, you cannot manage others if you cannot manage yourself.

Self-organisation was mentioned in the discussion of study skills in Chapter 2. We have also discussed other factors in management, such as stating clearly what you and your students are about, and preparing competently, having things ready and properly structured.

REMEMBER! … Preparation is all-important.

You will find that your students respond well if you appear ready and well prepared, showing interest in them and involving them in 'ownership' of the learning goals; if they know clearly what they are to learn and what they have to do in order to learn. It is a combined effort: them and you together. They will usually want to cooperate with you.

Roles, rules and responsibilities

Teachers will adopt a defensive behaviour if they feel insecure. Being well organised addresses this first problem because you can then concentrate on your students. Confidence in managing your resources, your teaching/learning activities and the environment communicates positive messages to students.

Your students will look to you to lead. That means, at least, that you should know where you are intending to go and how you want to get there. It means establishing roles and responsibilities in the class. No groups can work successfully without rules that govern interactions and behaviour. You must win the respect of your students.

In establishing the group, you need to create the framework of understandings within which it is going to work. Usually, these are known to all from previous experience of learning groups. Most of the important rules governing behaviour of groups are unspoken, but are clearly understood. But it might be necessary to spell them out at the start if the behaviour of the students requires it. Rules must include their responsibilities, their side of the contract that they enter into to be in your class: attendance, handing in work by a dead-line, completing tasks to an acceptable standard, treating all equipment with care – and many others. Adults are actually often worse than youngsters in this!

There may be established patterns of behaviour that inhibit the kind of learning activity you wish to see in your class and between classes. Students in full-time education can be confused between what is expected in one class and what is not tolerated in another. This is worse if students commute between different institutions with different cultures. Students, particularly adults, look for clues to behaviour, dress, language registers and attitudes in each class – importantly, from you as the teacher.

You must make it clear *from the beginning* what is acceptable in your class, and what is not. This is a matter of observing behaviour and interfering to shape it. It is not unlike what parents do with their young children. If your class uses equipment, computers perhaps, they must know how to treat it properly, not to abuse or damage it. There are also safety considerations, wearing protective clothing and so on, which we shall discuss later.

What do you allow? Do you set deadlines? What about absence? Or being late for class? Or failing to produce work? Students must establish *good practice as learners* to match *good practice as the teacher*. These include being organised, doing learning tasks, meeting deadlines, developing study skills and much more. Think about how to communicate their responsibilities as learners – to create working relationships. It helps to avoid disruptive actions by individuals who will upset the working of the class. The essential quality is leadership, not bossing. Perhaps, the teachers above had an image of the teacher as 'the boss'; and they were not sure they had the personality or the presence for such a role. They might remember a teacher they were afraid of. My father-in-law would say, '*You didn't muck about in her class*'. But do they remember anything else they learned in that class? Why not a class they found stimulating?

Adults generally don't muck about, although you may find occasionally the disruptive man or woman who seems determined to make things difficult for you. It is not true of youngsters, however. Teachers in FE are now finding increasing numbers of 14–16 year olds in their 'adult' classes. They are in specialist areas where the expertise and resources of the college are made available to schools.

Even FE teachers with long experience will find this unsettling. Youngsters come to FE with behaviour patterns in classes which may reflect their experience in school, or their feeling that since this is not school, they can behave as if released from discipline. The same considerations apply. It is essential to establish the rules and responsibilities that you expect in your class. But teachers who only require obedience will find themselves in constant conflict with some of their students. Being valued is fundamental to gaining a student's cooperation. It is very easy to start from a mind-set of 'they are the problem' rather than 'they have problems'. Left-handedness was a real problem up to 50 years ago: 'sinister' means 'left' in Latin. In 80% of Colleges at Oxford and Cambridge University being female was 'a problem' until 30 years ago, in 20% it was being male. Even more recently, being female caused headaches for almost all trainers and senior officers in the police and the armed services and in some traditional male areas like motor vehicle workshops. In nursing, it was more likely to be being male.

Tens of thousands of left-handers were made to write with the right hand, because it was the 'right' way to do it. If you did things with the left-hand you were being 'difficult', a nuisance. My wife was forced to do everything against her natural ability: to write, to draw, to play hockey or to play cricket, and no-one was able to teach her to sew or to crochet because the teacher could not do it upside down! It has stayed with her as a painful experience that for a child lasted a very long time.

For some it embedded a poor self-image because they were different. How a person of any age is treated is likely to be reflected back in their behaviour. In *My Fair Lady*, Eliza after her triumph at the Embassy Ball visits Professor Higgins' mother, who asks her, '*How on earth did you learn good manners with my son around?*' Eliza replies, '*It is not how a person behaves that makes her a lady, but how she is treated. Professor Higgins treats me as a flower girl and always will. Col. Pickering always treats me as a lady and always will …*' Of course, she knew Higgins was listening to her. Later we shall look at case studies where some teachers had bad experiences.

Managing teams

Good management, in industry and business as well as in teaching, consists largely in creating teams of people working well together to achieve things. This is done in various ways. It helps if people have set targets, schedules and goals to achieve. Managers can motivate them to accept 'ownership' of the targets, to harness their energies to work together for a shared purpose. To do that, they need to identify strongly with the group, to be part of the team, to see their own achievement as part of the achievement of others, and that includes the manager.

Will it happen if all the decisions are taken at the top? If managers want robots they can buy them. People need motivation, guidance and support; it must appear to them that they, their ideas, their talents, are valued and worthwhile. The leader is there to give all this shape.

Sensitivity: identifying needs and problems

Clearly, teachers have to work with the consent of students, especially adults. But we need more than passive acceptance, we want active participation and commitment.

In designing our classes, if we concentrate on what the students have to do in order to learn, in particular what barriers to learning they bring with them, the methods we choose will be student-centred and activity-based. The teacher in the class is relieved of a great deal of pressure to 'deliver the goods'. S/he can concentrate on the different role of supporter and guide, to act as a reference point to assist the learning. See Karen's class again (Case Study 10). The teacher can also watch the students. This ability to observe and to be sensitive to what is going on is most important. Case Study 13 describes an example.

CASE STUDY 13

Rob taught a GCSE History syllabus to full-time students of mainly 16–17 years in an English college. He was faced with trying to get them to understand the reasons for the partition of India after 1947. They had as much experience of conditions in India as John's Nigerian students (Case Study 12) had of an industrial revolution – none.

History is apt to take the emotions out of what happens, offering dispassionate accounts and analysis of grand movements, concentrating on key figures and political decisions. People are just not like that. No wonder most students find it boring. It seems to have nothing to do with them, and even if you can find film records that show violence and killing, there is such a constant exposure to violence on TV, in news reports or films, that young people are unable to respond any more. They just sit and watch without any emotion.

Rob's principal learning goals were purely descriptive; but he found he had to get over to the youngsters *what it was like to be there*: what religious fanaticism means, how ordinary people can feel so passionately about their faith that they will go out in mobs to massacre thousands of people who have other beliefs. In 1947, Indians were driven by the wildest of emotions. As it happened, there was a level of experience in the class that he could exploit; for a reason he did not know, the girls in the class appeared to hate the boys. The messages were clear in all their behaviour. They came to class in a bunch, separately from the boys, deliberately late. As they came in they challenged Rob and the boys, and they sat in a group as far away from the boys as they could. Rob did his best to make them take part in discussions, to get the class working together. But what an atmosphere, and what a conflict!

The problem had to be faced, and Rob adopted a strategy to tackle it and maybe turn it to his advantage. He had to get the girls talking to him to explain why they felt as they did. The powerful feelings in the class could be used to help them to understand 'partition', why it was thought a necessary solution in India.

They could be helped to see that reasoning with people whose behaviour is driven by hatred and fear or strongly held beliefs just will not work. He hoped they would find that their own emotions were trivial by comparison and that 'their problems' at least could be talked out without partition!

Discussion

1 Had Rob thought through what the students needed to learn and how they might learn it?

2 What was Rob's original approach and his learning goals?

3 Why were they less than successful?

4 If the conflict had not arisen in the class, would these goals still have been appropriate?

5 What other major difficulties were there?

6 How would you have tackled the conflict in this class?

7 What is going on in your classes? Can you observe it?

8 Can you use it to your advantage?

Comment

The History syllabus and the textbook were Rob's starting point. Perhaps, for a majority of teachers these appear to dictate what their job is and what the students need to learn. After all, they are there to pass an exam and it is the teacher's responsibility to ensure they do so. S/he will be judged by how many fail the exam rather than by success. This pressure can inhibit concern with the needs of the students as individuals or as a group. There is a danger that the teacher, students and institution will all see the purpose of the class as instrumental, the teacher's job is to deliver the goods as effectively as possible. This is true in all disciplines, not just in academic general education. Non-testable 'added value' from taking the class – even if that is really important learning and change – will be discounted if the students do not pass the exam or achieve passing grades.

There is an assumed starting point, which is in practice the end product, not where students are now. The result may be that no one has ownership of the learning, neither teacher nor students. It can turn into an elaborate game, the purpose of which is winning by learning good game-play; the content of the textbook is mugged up for tests and then jettisoned as so much lumber. It is justified by the argument that the process develops certain skills and confidence, transferable to any learning context. For those who succeed this is undoubtedly true; hence the persistence of the approach. But it can be so much more. A major effect is that most students see the whole of education as having nothing to do with them, nothing to do with their growth as people. There are winners and losers, that's all; an indelible self-image as one or the other. It is the old-world view of schooling. In new world countries generally emphasis is on the individual to discover his/her strengths and to develop a very positive self-image. The really important shift in educational policy now is to start by counselling each student to identify personal learning needs and a commitment on both sides to meet those needs. But in a class the teacher is still under the external pressure of examination results. How to marry both concerns is a major challenge. On the other hand, even the most unlikely subject may be turned into an exciting learning experience by a talented and enthusiastic teacher.

Rob revised his learning goals and his approach to achieving them. The students, by exploring their own emotions, could understand those of others and what drove them to behave as they did. In the class, the girls' anger could have destroyed any possibility of achieving the overall learning goals. Rob turned the anger into a tool for learning. It is likely that this learning will remain important for them as people, it is memorable because it happened to them; they will have gained some insight into human behaviour; it has become a part of their own knowledge structure, *they own it*. It is not just mugged up 'out there' information 'for a test'.

However well you prepare, you cannot predict how things will go in any particular class. All experienced teachers will confirm that you can prepare exactly the same material and work for two apparently similar classes; in one class the lesson goes tremendously well, with good commitment and excellent learning activity, in the other it dies. Why? It is very difficult to say.

It could be something in the chemistry of the class, the mixture of personalities, perhaps, or the time of day or week, or the way you or they are feeling. It could be something that happened in another class, or in the corridor, or the weather, or some other outside factor. Groups of people are in this respect like individuals: all sorts of things can cause mood swings or emotional responses that affect how they behave. You need to be sensitive to what is happening and adapt, change, adopt some new tactic.

Teaching is about complex human relationships: how groups (or groups within groups) form and feel about each other and about strangers, including perhaps the teacher. Without a relationship of mutual trust linking teacher and students, difficulties are bound to arise.

No doubt, for many people the prospect of teaching is daunting. There are memories of being in a class of difficult students who are making the teacher's life hell. For many, there is a stereotype image of the teacher doing battle with a class that is exploited in many films. But it is much easier to remember the sensational rather than the routine. Of the vast number of classes that happen every day everywhere in the world, only a very few become battlegrounds and not necessarily involving the teacher.

That does not mean that teachers do not frequently lose control of student learning or fail to manage class learning effectively. Some fail to get organised, to identify for themselves and students what they are trying to teach. They fail to motivate or stimulate their classes. Occasionally, students do rebel out of boredom or protest at what they see as a waste of their time or feelings of alienation. Teachers feel the pressure to deliver the goods. They can feel as if everything rests on them, that the students are waiting for the teacher to do it for them. Many students seem to think that all they have to do is be there, learning a foreign language, say, will happen by a kind of osmosis. Teachers can and do reinforce that view of how it happens.

Structure and links

REMEMBER! … It is much easier to understand the parts of a thing if you have a view of the whole of it first.

The most obvious evidence to your students of your competence in dealing with the class is how the lesson is structured. Share your structure with them. It is helpful for the class to have copies of your lesson plan, so they know what is going to happen and what they have to do. They will know what you are going to do, and what that has to do with their learning.

They and you need a baseline from which to start. If learning goals for the lesson are clear, at the end they can be invited to assess for themselves their achievement of their goals and provide you with feedback on how it was for them, as you did in the peer-group teaching. It will enable them to focus on their learning needs – what has to happen now. And they can consolidate the learning by reflection at home.

Whatever we set out to learn has to build into a structure. The same is true of a sequence of classes. They need to build and link learning into new knowledge and skills week by week; learning one week must help to make sense of learning from previous weeks. A student has to be able to see the links clearly. Your structure should make the links plain.

In order to make the links, the beginning and the end of each session are important. At the end of a class, students need to focus on what they have learned, partly to assess their own learning, but also to be able to do something with it. At the beginning of the next class, they need to 'revisit' previous learning to ensure that it links into what they are going to learn now. The first activity of any subsequent class should be to establish this linkage.

And what of the time in between? What happens to the learning in the time between classes? The left-hand graph in Figure 9.1 shows the rate at which what we have learned evaporates. Within 24 hours we have forgotten 75% of what we learned today. After a month there will be very little left. It explains why revision is so difficult: you are not really revising at all, but learning everything again from scratch. How then should we tackle the problem of recall?

The more often something is recalled, the easier it is to recall it. Consider again going to a department store. The more often you go there, the easier it is to find what you want quickly. If it is six months or a year since you went there, it feels as

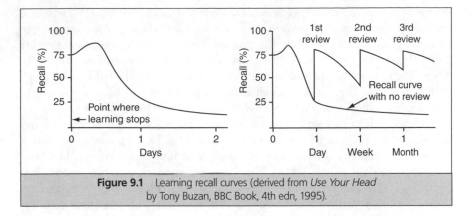

Figure 9.1   Learning recall curves (derived from *Use Your Head* by Tony Buzan, BBC Book, 4th edn, 1995).

if you have never been before. What is needed is some way of regularly revisiting what you have learned, reviewing it and refreshing your memory. It will also be processed each time by the brain to become part of understanding a greater whole, linking it to other learning. This processing allows you to take control, to have ownership of the learning. Reviewing is simple. The more frequently we revisit learning, the more easily we will recall it, it becomes familiar. Students should be encouraged to review their learning between classes. Effects of reviewing are shown in the right-hand graph in Figure 9.1.

Teaching and learning materials

You should assume nothing about your students' ability to cope. Students must be able to deal with the learning activities and materials you use. Similarly with your teaching: your style, your language, your visual aids. Whenever you write anything, come back and look at it again and again – to see it as others see it. You know what you mean, it is clear to you. Will it be clear to your students?

How complicated we can make things when we try! Particularly when we present a slide on an OHP or a handout to the class. The main criterion is that any material you use be as brief as you can make it. Get rid of anything that is not absolutely essential for your students to have. They need the bones, not the flesh; you can build up the flesh in class. When you write on a whiteboard, flip chart, or chalkboard, or put up a slide, or project an image from a computer, whatever, walk to the back of the class and look at it from there. Can they read it easily? Does it make sense? Is it easy to grasp?

Make your instructions simple, direct and easy to follow. Try to ensure that they understand why they are doing it as well as what to do. Make them positive like mine here and not negative as 'Thou shalt not …' What of your voice? Just as visual aids are of no use if people cannot see them, so a teacher must at least be audible. It really helps if your voice is pleasant to listen to, and if you speak slowly with lots of pauses, give it thinking time. Actors in a theatre have to wait for the audience to react, to give it space and time, especially if they are trying to be funny! That needs practice, too. Some rooms are difficult for sound, some full of distractions.

What matters is that the learning is successful, not that you feel pleased with how it was for you. Any teaching method may be successful with a particular group – in the right circumstances. You need to choose a method you feel comfortable with and can handle effectively. But watch to see how it works. There is no point in trying to be 'clever'. Think critically about what you are doing, and particularly what they are doing. There may well be alternative ways of approaching the learning that are no more difficult than the one you have chosen, and which could be rather more interesting and stimulating for you as well as for them. It is easy to fall into the trap of thinking that using some impressive technology will solve problems for you.

All teachers fall easily into repetitive methods. There has to be variety of activity in each class and between classes. No activity should go on for too long, whether it is the teacher explaining something or the students reading for information, your using slides or their watching a film, a video or a computer-generated presentation. The same is even more true of repetitive skills practice. There is a curve that relates to concentration as there is to learning and to forgetting, and the curve descends sharply after about 15 minutes. After that time, playing scales on the piano becomes totally mechanical. You must change the activity at least as often as that. As in the revisiting curve above, changes of activity keep the learning/concentration curve rising or steady.

ACTIVITY 5

CONCENTRATION CURVES

In Figure 9.2, the concentration curve (a) indicates a general tendency for concentration to fall away after 15 minutes. Curve (b) shows the effects of changes of activity every 15 minutes or so.

You can find out how you compare with the general pattern – discover what works for you. This is part of your development of Study Skills. Encourage your students to adopt similar *good practice*.

1 Find a book that requires concentration. Make sure you have suitable conditions for study. Note the time you start reading and the time at which you stop 'taking in' what is on the page.

2 Sketch your concentration curve on the axes (c).

3 Now, experiment with breaks or changes of activity, such as making notes, to see how your ability to maintain concentration is affected.

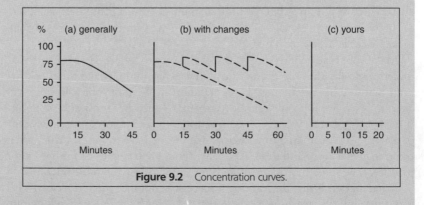

Figure 9.2 Concentration curves.

<table>
<tr><td>

CHAPTER 10

</td><td>

Communication

</td></tr>
</table>

In **Task 9** you evaluated the effectiveness of your lesson plan in a teaching context. In **Task 10**, we look at a particular aspect: *Communication*.

TASK 10

COMMUNICATION SKILLS

In evaluating your teaching in **Task 9**:

1 Consider how effective your communication skills were.
2 Use the criteria below to assess what needs improving.
3 What do you need to do? How can you do it?
4 What difficulties are you experiencing in communicating with your students?

Performance criteria

10.1 Interactions between individuals and groups are observed.

10.2 Groups as they form are noted. There is control of group behaviour.

10.3 A class identity is established that supports members of the class in their learning activity.

10.4 Learning difficulties of individuals receive help/support.

10.5 The teacher responds to student feedback.

10.6 There is sensitivity to problems students have in grasping information and instructions.

10.7 The teacher uses appropriate vocabulary and delivery.

10.8 Learning materials and aids take account of student readiness and ability in language, and are effective in promoting the intended learning.

10.9 Visual materials are well designed and distraction removed.

10.10 The teacher watches carefully and observes what happens.

10.11 The teacher makes use of feedback and evaluates honestly.

Messages

Communicating is not just about transmitting messages. No amount of improvement in transmission will help if the radio receiver is switched off. How will you switch it on?

This communication is two-way. Are you, as the teacher, switched on to receive the messages from your students? You can be sure that when they arrive in your class they will come with all kinds of expectations: about you, what they will be doing, what the other students will be like, what it is all for. How will you read their messages? How will they read yours? As they explore the new experience, they will take messages from the room and the furniture, from the behaviour and language of the teacher and of other students. They will tend to form groups, create 'territories' and 'private space', and do things to try to feel comfortable there. You will need to watch this behaviour carefully, alert to the messages. Sometimes rather worrying patterns of behaviour develop, such as hostility between groups and individuals. You need to interfere, to take control fairly early on, to ensure that a network of cooperative relationships develops.

You will probably notice that students choose a particular place to sit, where they will establish 'my' chair or 'my' desk. They will tend to return to their own 'territory' to stay with the friends they first make. This may be defensive behaviour, they need to feel safe and comfortable. But try to ensure that small groups do not become well-established, regularly create new groupings for group work. This is because groups and group behaviour, once firmly established, will resist change. A stranger who joins any established group will find it hard to become a member. You will probably notice how your class identifies itself as different from other classes, other groups of students.

Be alert to how it looks and feels to them. Try to manipulate the situation to the advantage of the group as a whole rather than just allow whatever happens. Try to think of ways in which you could get your class to talk openly to each other to remove the barriers we all bring to any new social group. Just talking may be ineffective, they need to have a specific task to do, something to give focus to the exercise. Look again at the ice-breaking ideas on pages 58 and 63.

Lesson Plan 1 (page 63) is a structuring of group behaviour: students are asked to interview one another in pairs and then introduce their partner to the class. This usually works well with all ages, and can become light-hearted fun. If you introduce yourself first as a model, it will allow you to be honest and open with them, telling them about you, your interests, what you have done in the past. All of which will help to establish a bridge.

But can they do it sitting in rows? How will you have to organise the room so that they feel able to talk easily? You might even want to move them into an open circle, as in the party game of Vivienne's class. But you have to move the furniture again if you change the learning activity because each activity requires a supportive arrangement of the room. You should be able to invent something that will serve. If the desks are screwed to the floor, of course, you're in trouble.

Once you have broken the ice, once they know each other and there are smiles, how will you maintain the momentum? It will help if they have other things to share. Perhaps they might be asked to agree in larger groups on their expectations and needs, which can lead on to agreement of learning goals. It is a useful technique to start with pairs or small groups and join those into larger groups. Or they can begin working on a small-scale project. That again is the thinking of Lesson Plan 1.

Your messages

Look carefully at the messages in your own behaviour. As people come into any new experience they explore it: they look for messages, or clues, to tell them what kind of place it is, what are the patterns of behaviour, what are the rules, dress and relationships there; what role the teacher intends to adopt, what their role is to be. It is your behaviour rather than your language which tells them how you feel about them. Of course, you have to tell them if you want them to call you by your first name.

Most of what we 'say' to people is transmitted in body language, the closeness or distance we create, things we do, things we get them to do, or allow them to do, or inhibit them from doing, or the way in which they see our value system. Watch your students and observe their behaviour. Are you creating barriers? Are you creating distance that separates you from them? How are students reacting to what you do? If they all sit at the back of the class – as is very often the case – will you go to them or invite them to come to you? You must try to bridge this gap very early on.

Look at what you do, and ask: Why do I do that? Some teachers like to have a large desk that forms a barrier or a protection between themselves and their students, or they create distance in other ways. Some teachers seem trapped at the front of the class and do not move to get closer to students. Your tone of voice matters greatly. Listen to someone dealing with a dog in a park. See how the dog is controlled by and responds to the owner's tone of voice, not to the words. Unconsciously, we do that with our students too. Is your tone of voice welcoming or hostile? Do you feel you need to command respect or to win cooperation? With some, particularly younger classes, you might feel you have to start fairly forcefully to make sure they know the rules – and then you can become warmer.

REMEMBER! … We have to show a genuine interest in our students
if we want them to respond well to us.

CASE STUDY 14

Gillian taught computing in a college in the United Kingdom. Most computing classes took place in a computing room, but a theory class was in another classroom. She had thought carefully about what she was going to do and how.

Gillian prepared well. The room had been set out in an open square to encourage her students to interact with each other as well as with the teacher. She was showing them the way techniques for computing had developed. She brought in things for students to handle, such as a large magnetic tape and perforated paper rolls.

The class, however, had divided itself into three distinct groups, each with its own territory. A group of girls, age 17+, sat along one arm of the square, out of direct eye-contact with Gillian. Boys of much the same age sat along the opposite arm (except two who had made a territory for themselves in a corner). Directly in front of Gillian sat about eight mature students, women of 30–40 years. The girls and boys took no part in the lesson. They gave the impression of disliking each other and the class. The women were eager and had got close to Gillian, who was of their own age. They held her attention, maintained eye-contact and responded to her questions. Things went very well there. Afterwards, her tutor, who had watched the class, asked Gillian what she felt about the lesson. She was sure it had gone well, that the students were keen and interested. Her perception of what had happened was conditioned by her interactions with the mature women. His, as observer, was different.

She had been unaware that the class had divided into three groups, two of which had taken no part in the lesson. This characteristic of student behaviour in the class was important: she needed to change her approach in order to deal with it. Her chosen method had been highly successful with the mature students. Why did it not work for the younger ones? Was it her unconscious messages about her preference for interactions with the mature women that seemed to exclude them? She needed to find some way of integrating the three groups. She had in fact been doing most of the work in the class. Most of the students, even the mature women, had been idle. Most of those who were not participating were not learning.

Gillian decided that the students had to be given learning activities, tasks to do as individuals and groups. She agreed to try putting them into sets of three, one from each divided group. No doubt there would be opposition because people hate changing once groups have formed so strongly. But in practice it worked quite well.

Discussion

1 Why do you think the behaviour of the mature women and the youngsters was so different?

2 Have you observed or experienced this yourself?

3 What unconscious messages was Gillian giving to her students? Why did she do that?

4 What activities do you think they could do in sets of three that would help to bring the divided groups together?

5 Why might there be opposition to this happening?

6 What is the best way to take control of group behaviour?

Comment

It is easy to fail to see what is actually happening in your own class. This is why it is so important to observe other classes and why peer-group teaching is especially valuable. This is also why you need an educated eye, a mentor/tutor, to share your class.

Groups have to be managed; it is too easy to just let your students get on with it. We have seen already how fundamental to learning activity group dynamics are, how people will identify 'territories' and collar 'space', develop defensive postures within classes, as the students did in Gillian's class. If, as can happen, all the women choose to sit together separately from the men, will you have the courage to ask why, to challenge both groups to look at what they have done – as quite unconscious behaviour?

Do not make it offence and defence; much better to get them to look at where they have placed themselves, what they have done, and ask them to think about it. Laughter, their laughter, is a better management tool than anger or embarrassment.

Can you see what you do, quite unconsciously, and how that communicates with your students?

Models

Your most important task is to establish a sense of belonging in the class, to include you. Help them to feel comfortable with the group and with you. They must agree a method of working together and cooperating (same meaning) with you. Good management is partly setting targets, motivating people to achieve them. This is much easier if there is a good team spirit and supportive behaviour. Getting to know one another by having social contact is helpful in breaking down barriers, too. Lesson Plan 1 includes a coffee break after they have introduced each other. It might be appropriate, at least for adults, to ring each other up when they are having difficulty with a learning task, so they may need telephone numbers.

You cannot help being some kind of model. Everything about you will be studied by students as you will be the focus of their attention. Be aware, but don't worry about it.

Your approach, how you come across to them in behaviour, distance or warmth, enthusiasm, interest in the subject and in them, your energy, your value system, even your state of health, will be communicated in subtle ways. The clothes you wear say a great deal about you. Students will look to see what is acceptable, particularly in workshops, wards and areas that require appropriate clothing. A famous lady, who has a great following as an inventive chef on TV, demonstrates her preparation and cooking with her long hair flowing freely and without protective clothing. What is she demonstrating? That you can look glamorous while cooking? That that is more important than hygiene?

People will adopt a pattern of behaviour, language, style of dress, or whatever, that belongs to the group rather than to any one individual. It is fascinating to watch what they choose to do, to wear in particular and you can learn from it.

An external examiner visited a course of teacher training in a college in the United Kingdom. There were two male tutors and 24 mature students from a wide range of backgrounds. The assessor wanted to find out if the tutors saw themselves as models for their student teachers. The two tutors were rather worried by the idea of being models. They felt that teachers had to develop their own personal style: teachers must be themselves since they taught in so many different contexts. And this of course was true.

But when the assessor asked the student teachers the same question, the answer was different. *'When Ray comes to watch us teach, we do as he does. We have it all neat and tidy. We have a structured lesson plan, time things carefully, all our visual aids set out, we have it all organised.*

CASE STUDY 15

But when John comes, we don't bother. It's "thinking on your feet" and letting it develop, jollying it along and seeing what happens.'

They reflected back to each tutor his behaviour in their classes; they thought he would want to see that in their classes.

Discussion

1 Consider your own use of models, especially your role models. How did they affect what you do?

2 Where did your model of 'the teacher' and what the teacher does come from?

3 What sort of role model do you think appropriate for your students to see? Would it worry you?

Comment

We cannot avoid using models. Sometimes they are not helpful. Many people come to teaching with models of 'the teacher' and 'what teachers and students do' that are barriers to understanding. Don't imagine that you can avoid being seen by the students as a model. An important aspect of teaching is to ensure that the model you present is one you would wish your students to adopt. You project a pattern of behaviour. If you adopt careless or perhaps dangerous practices in a workshop or laboratory, it is no good telling the students they must do things the 'safe' way. The same applies to the models they have in their places of employment; and it is confusing if the models they see and are told to adopt are in conflict. We have already noted the confusion caused by having different patterns of behaviour expected by teachers in classes.

This makes clear the nature of communication. We want to belong, to be accepted as part of our group. To do that we have to adopt the behaviour, language, style and so on that identifies us as a member of this group. You will be able to think of groups that exhibit quite bizarre special clothes or language or behaviour to identify 'belonging'. Some are antisocial in the sense of hostile to society in general, like graffiti writers and motor-bike gangs.

What about the groups you belong to? We all belong to more than one in various aspects of our lives. Do you change your language style, clothes or behaviour as you move from group to group? If so, why? Think carefully about that. How do you categorise people?

The student teachers in Case Study 15 had two models to compare and they took delight in the comparison. That was no doubt good learning.

Energy

Communicating is not one-way transmission, nor is it most of the time consciously done. Humans are exploratory animals. Most of the energy has to come from the receiver, who has to be actively wanting to find out. Unless the brain is actively processing information, no change will occur in perception or understanding.

Consider what you are doing now. The words simply sit on the page. The energy has to come from you to make them mean anything. In this book I, as author, must try to present what you, as reader, may think is important for you to read, do, think about. I have to try to communicate with you. I have to try to be interesting. I have chosen to do that by using case studies of real situations. But you have first to want to know, to want to communicate with me.

Convictions

There is the problem of mind-set. People arrive with fixed mental images and models that may stop them from seeing what we want them to see; just as I walked past the Adult Centre I was looking for because my mental image of it was wrong. We tend to select what we find easy or familiar and reject the rest. This happens if a new teacher has a fixed image of teaching behaviour, or students who are convinced the teacher wants them to do x, when in fact it is y.

We resist challenges to our accepted images, especially if they are part of our value system or our deeply held convictions. If the evidence is all against us, we just shout louder to drown it out. You must know people who do that. Some teachers may do it with students who challenge them. Bravura tactics belong in politics, not in the classroom or the workshop or the ward.

Many people prefer to walk away from things rather than face the possibility of challenge to their self-image or of failure. One of the most accurate measures of motivation is the readiness to come back from failure and try again. It is most clearly seen in individual sports. I gave up trying to ice-skate because I could not deal with the damage to me and my self-image when I performed badly! But if people are determined to succeed, nothing will stop them. What really helps is doing it with others having the same problems, so that there has been a huge growth in clubs for slimmers! If we are all learning together, there is excitement and energy in the system. There is also the incentive of competition. As with reading a map, you have to explore the area to understand the map fully. Group and individual learning projects are exactly like that.

Barriers

Often, people bring a history of painful learning experiences of the past such as mine in the skating rink. I've known graduates of famous universities declare, '*I'm hopeless at maths*'. What do they mean? Why do they believe it? Of course, it may well be true, but how has that come about? Such a strong conviction about oneself is a self-fulfilling prophecy; it may arise from past failure, or poor teaching, or the absence of any attempt to discover what the real learning problem was. People with a mind-set present some of the strongest barriers to learning. Not unlike phobias, the only way to overcome them is to face them squarely. They arise in the same way as phobias do, from traumatic or damaging experiences.

If you are to succeed, you have to believe there is at least a possibility of learning. It is even better if you think you will learn if you try hard enough. As the teacher, you will need to recognise the barriers that individual students present and help them to look at them objectively, and ask: is it really so? One of the greatest pleasures in teaching is to watch students do something they 'knew' they couldn't do. When someone who is afraid of heights is walking across a high bridge and you hear them say, '*I can't believe I'm doing this*'. Watch someone get a computer program do what they want it to.

REMEMBER! … We have to be genuinely interested in our students and the problems they have in learning.

The things we want students to do must be do-able. It is easy to give students tasks that are too difficult for them, or for anybody. I take the view that if I want students to do something I had better do it myself to find out how hard it is. Whenever I set a task I do it too; it is the only way I can find out what is involved. It helps me to assess their success properly, and to provide a model. How else will I know what problems they have to deal with to be successful?

It is important students do not set about trying to learn things with a distorted mental image, a mistaken idea of what kind of a thing it is. They are bound to fail if they don't know what they are trying to do or what they are looking for. Equally, they need to know beforehand how success will be judged. One advantage of stating 'criteria' is to give students a means of assessing their own success, and so to discover what they still need to learn. The new buzz-word is 'focused'. Everyone has to be focused. They must know what it is they are trying to learn and then by reflecting on the experience, focus the learning for themselves to make it part of their learning structure.

ACTIVITY 6

YOUR LEARNING BARRIERS

Look at your own learning barriers:

1 What are the things you find particularly hard to do or to learn?

2 Can you list them? Do you know what they are?

3 Why is that? Can you think where they have come from, the circumstances that led to them?

4 If students turn up in your class with such barriers, what can you do to help them?

Variety and pace

All your classes need a variety of activities (involving everyone) to maintain attention. We earlier discussed the difficulties of pace with individuals in a class. In group activities, only some students may be actively involved while the others are just there. Classes need changes of pace, including periods of high energy and periods of rest. Successful lessons reflect the concentration curves of the students. All athletes know how to conserve energy, to pace themselves. So do singers and pianists: to relax and just let the voice or the hands work as they will, then charge them with that extra vitality and excitement that grabs the listener. Otherwise, the overall effect is monotonous or exhausting.

Specialist vocabulary

In all subjects, vocabulary must be learned that enables specialists to communicate with specialists. It is as true of pottery and flower-arranging as of computing. I have been amazed at some of the vocabulary that has to be learned in a class on horse-management. In that sense, all teachers are teachers of language. Education is certainly no exception.

If this book is too full of jargon, or perhaps if my sentences are too complex, we will not communicate. We have to think about the readiness of students to work with these words, and of how they can link them to their own experience. Without such linking, the words will not make sense. It is not a matter of intelligence, it is where we are, you and I, or you and your students. If I were talking to you, instead of writing, you would use the expressions on my face, my gestures, my tone of voice and so on to help you to share what I am saying. I could use your responses to what I say, how you feed back to me, to shape what I say next and again. More importantly, you could question me, have me repeat things in other words, reframe them with you into your words. We cannot do these things through the printed page. But you can and must do them with your class. Feedback matters. You should recognise also that what you do may actually get in the way, make it harder for people to listen and hear. Please, think about that carefully.

Language and culture

Do you share a common language with your students? Groups develop shared language that helps to bind them, and to separate them from other groups. 'Language' includes body postures, vocabulary, value-systems expressed in words, cult words and jargon, and dress. Having different age groups in your class may present difficulties of communication, because much of this will separate rather than bind groups together. They may well belong to different 'cultures'. Some scream their differences at you with bizarre hairstyles, for example. Many problems teachers have with younger groups can arise from their feelings that they are isolated, even alienated, from the teacher and the experience of the class because of these factors. They feel they belong to a different culture from you or the older members of the class. You don't have to go to Japan or Africa or America, as I have, to experience divides of this kind.

> David's initiation into FE was to set up a General Studies programme for engineering apprentices in a UK Technical College in 1962. The government of the day had decided that all vocational training should be 'liberalized' by elements of general education in the curriculum. For apprentices on a day-release programme from industry and commerce, it meant including a period of General Studies. For these teachers the remit was dauntingly wide: they were expected to improve the linguistic skills of the students while at the same time broadening their general education in one period of an hour once a week. Many of the vocational teachers could see little point in it and the apprentices in the main resented being

CASE STUDY 16

made to do things again they hoped they had left behind, to get on with things they were good at and that they enjoyed doing.

There was a cultural and linguistic divide between most General Studies teachers and students. Not surprisingly, what happened in General Studies classes was as varied – and unpredictable – as the number of people involved. Some classes turned into English lessons, some into free activities, in some cases the students were engaged in projects, in others they were prepared for examinations. The problem essentially was that there was no clear statement anywhere of learning goals. Another obstacle for David was that the resources available were few and the rooms allocated for the classes were often quite inappropriate for what he wanted students to do. He had to teach some motor vehicle apprentices in a loft equipped with Dickensian high desks requiring high stools over a workshop where, from time to time, they were testing diesel engines.

For a young teacher, it was 'a baptism of fire'. But it was also accelerated learning; David had to survive. His principal decision was to find common ground where the students would see value in what he asked them to do and would be prepared to go along with him. He also had the opportunity to experiment with as many approaches as different groups seemed to need. What he very quickly discovered was that without winning their respect and cooperation, the experience was a battle. For each group he asked the vocational teachers what was important for the students to know or to be able to do, sharing the ideas with the students as they developed. Naturally, he had disasters but again important learning. Some motor vehicle lads were illiterate, as far as he could judge, not able to spell their own names. He had to do something about it, but that was to challenge their pride and their self-image as he painfully discovered. They didn't want to learn; they had had experience of so much failure in the past. David failed to help them and remained totally alienated. He knew he did not dare take his eyes off them; for weeks he taught from all parts of the room, often behind them. When, for the first time, he turned to put up a chart of the roads of Britain, an egg whistled past his ear to splatter on the chart. Had that lad brought it with him every week? He felt he could do nothing but go to see the Head of Department. David had no idea how to go about teaching adult literacy to a class of twenty 15-year-olds, whose role model was Marlon Brando in *The Waterfront*.

David had to understand his students; he quite literally had no idea what the world was like for them. Oxford and London universities had not prepared him for it, although he had grown up in a fairly working-class environment. He sat in on vocational workshop classes at the invitation of the teachers. He went to places of employment, mostly huge factories, to see their working conditions, he talked to the apprentices' employers and supervisors. He was astonished by so much of what he saw: enormous machine shops, the noise, the atmosphere, people the lads he taught worked with. It was foreign territory. In the end, he did feel he knew them and many, not all, came to respect him because he wanted to know about them.

Another important outcome was that cultural barriers between himself and most teachers in the vocational areas, either in the minds of the students or of the teachers, were broken down. One well-known book used widely by General Studies teachers was written by a man I got to know casually. He started from the conviction that you had to start from where they were and to see the world as they did. He decided to become 'one of the gang' and from there 'the leader' of the gang; he spent a lot of his own free time socialising with his students in youth centres and pubs. Very few other teachers wanted to use that approach.

Discussion

1 Why did the government in the 1960s want vocational apprentices to do General Studies?
2 What do you think would constitute a good 'general education' today?
3 What skills, knowledge, experience do you think your students need to cope with your class?
4 If some or all of them lack this level of readiness, how should the problem be addressed?
5 Do you feel you could help your students if they lacked basic skills in literacy or numeracy?
6 If you feel you really do not understand students in your class, is it because of a cultural divide?
7 If so, what can you do to bridge that divide?
8 What do you know about your students' world – how it is for them?
9 Do you feel you ought to know?
10 Would it help you in your preparation and teaching?

Comment

Classes can be a clash of cultures where communication breaks down because there seems to be little in common, little that is shared. The responsibility for bridging the divide is the teacher's. So long as there is little trust or understanding on either side, no positive learning is likely to occur. A way forward is to get the students talking to you to explain what they feel, although that in itself is hard without a level of trust. They must feel that you genuinely want to know. You can do much more, as David found was necessary as a young teacher 40 years ago.

Present government policy is to recognise that many adult students will appear in FE classes with inadequate literacy or numeracy skills so that all teachers should receive training in methods of helping adult learners to acquire these skills, without which students cannot progress, much more so than if people lack computer literacy and keyboard skills, for which there is a high demand. Yet it is hard for people to admit their lack of basic skills because it is damaging to their self-image. Some resent having to face facts, to do something about it. Just knowing methods is of no use unless you can win the cooperation of the learners.

The 14–16-year-old cohort

The early part of the new century has witnessed some fundamental shifts in the perception of the role of FE and a drive to overcome the separation of schools from adult colleges, defined as for 16-year-olds and over. There is a long history of over 30 years of cooperation to make expertise and resources in FE colleges available to senior school curricula (16–18).

Educational policies display cycles. What is new is in response to technological innovation. In my life-time the school-leaving age in England and Wales was raised from 14 to 15 to 16. Fifty years ago apprenticeships were entered at the age of 14 and boys, only boys of course, were articled for five years. And technical colleges expanded to provide training in vocational skills.

Employers in the 1990s were convinced by accountants and management consultants that it was uneconomic and unnecessary to train apprentices in skills areas. The result is a dire shortage of skilled craftsmen. Vocational departments in colleges, especially in engineering and building trades, have been reduced or closed. The image and the purpose of FE has totally changed.

The variety in talents and intellectual potential of pupils in schools remains pretty constant. There will always be many youngsters for whom the skills training provided in the past by colleges was right and that it was quite sensible to start it at the age of 14. It is also clear that our kind of society cannot function without people who have these skills. But it is much easier today to find a well-qualified plumber in Australia than it is in the UK with a population four or five times greater. How do schools cater for this kind of practical talent? What resources and expertise is now available, in schools or colleges, to provide training in vocational skills? What is there to motivate and interest them? For 14-year-olds with this bent, it would be appropriate to return to the kind of training available 50 years ago in vocational departments, where the boys in particular could have hands-on experience in machine shops, brick-laying, plumbing, car and motor-bike maintenance or many other occupations important to an industrial society. Motivation is no problem in workshop simulations. What is more generally available in colleges is training in more sedentary occupations, such as computer skills, where motivation is bound to be much more difficult.

Computers for many youngsters are machines to play computer games with rather than to search the Internet for information or to use adult world software. It is hard to convince them of a need to learn vocational skills. Some teachers meet the students half-way as it were, letting them do 'treasure-hunts'. Such activities using search engines can have a serious learning purpose. But in a mixed class with adults who are there eager to learn computer skills, the problem of meeting both sorts of expectations becomes acute.

Counsellors in schools and colleges need an appropriate range of options to offer youngsters if they are to benefit from attending college. What they do must seem purposeful rather than time-filling. When the youngsters arrive in a class they will have chosen something they are committed to learning; the teacher should be able to assume the same contractual basis as for other students. It does not always happen if there is a lack of varied appropriate provision to motivate them.

One way forward, if the students are there perforce rather than by choice, is to try to get to know them as in the General Studies for apprentices, to show them that they are valued as 'people with needs', 'they are not the problem'. Easier said than done. There will always be some, usually a few, who just seem out to cause trouble; they are in fact the problem. Without the cooperation of all concerned, including parents, little progress will be made. In the past Heads of Department in colleges were used to dealing with parents, employers and students and could make progress even in really difficult cases. Today, it is the role of counselling professionals. You can only refer your real 'problems' to them. My own experience is that it is a matter of carrots and sticks, with emphasis on the carrots. Everyone wants something and we have to find out what it is and use it to take them where we want them to go. It is how advertisers work: they don't talk about clean teeth, but sweet breath, beauty, attractiveness to the opposite sex, health and happiness, avoiding pain, halitosis. Interesting things to discover are much more effective than threats: cooperation rather than the need to control.

Game play

Many plays were written after 1960, after the success of Becket's *Waiting for Godot*, on the basis that everything in life is essentially a game, with sophisticated and very complicated rules. One of the most fascinating plays is *Who's Afraid of Virginia Woolfe?* by Edward Albee, available on DVD with Elizabeth Taylor and Richard Burton and well worth seeing. It is a study of games in a marriage in which the rules are constantly being reinvented. By transference we might learn to see our classes as complex games, in which the rules are usually steady but might be reinterpreted.

There are techniques that teachers or anyone in authority learn pretty quickly to maintain respect for the rules of behaviour necessary in classroom or workshop. Mostly, they are 'game-play', such as David's 'instinctive response' to his motor vehicle group, in Case Study 16. He did not turn his back on them, but stood while they sat, came close to them, walked among them, related with individuals, taught them from behind. It was only when he relaxed this control that one individual made his protest but taking care David did not know which one it was! Gamesmanship on their part as well as his. By experience, teachers come to recognise the games and the rules and how to win.

There is no short-cut here. Because the mix of students and so the pattern of behaviour in a class is unpredictable, and the context, the learning environment and the personality of the teacher are whatever they turn out to be, the best advice again is to look at all these things 'objectively' as far as you can. Try to stand outside the situation to see it as others might see it. View it as you might a play on a stage. Ask: what is actually going on here?

Above all, try to keep your sense of humour! Almost any disaster, even a real one, can have its funny side. A colleague of mine blacked out a whole district of a town by being utterly stupid and misusing electrical 'buzz bars' at the side of a stage. Amazingly inept, amazingly dangerous, but …. People usually only drown if they panic.

Presenting information

Attention

For anyone to assimilate and to be able to use newly acquired information they must be alert, wanting to know. They must be paying attention. Consider the things you have done in the last day. What can you remember? Why those things when all the rest has disappeared? Probably because you were paying attention to them. Questioning is an important technique in presenting information because it helps to focus attention. I have just done it and given you my preferred answer. Using questions to involve the class is normal teacher behaviour. Many teachers use questions badly, unfortunately.

A good way to improve questioning is to name the person you want to answer. If you just fire a question into the air, it will not challenge most students directly enough to ensure that they attend or concentrate. As the teacher you lose control of what is happening. If you want to engage your class in a discussion or even just want them to listen, make sure they are ready to listen and not distracted and still absorbed in what was happening before. They will not even hear you, let alone understand.

You have to use questions consciously in terms of what you are trying to do. Most teachers' questions are preparing students for the teachers' answers, to make sure they actually hear them, as I have just done. But students soon know if you are playing a game: 'spot the teacher's right answer'. Often enough, they will not want to play: '*Just tell us, sir!*' Of course, many students will give the wrong answer, perhaps an astonishingly wrong answer, or mistake the question. But the answers students give must be treated as valuable, worth exploring and developing. Any answer is better than none, and will indicate where they are starting from, their present level of comprehension. Students can only make progress from where they are, their level of readiness in their thinking, not from where someone else is – you for instance.

Listening usually depends on looking too. An experienced teacher arranges the class or will keep moving so that eye-contact can be established with every student. Communication is not just words, but the whole behaviour pattern that the words are part of. We communicate in a multitude of ways. If a student is not looking at you, held by your gaze sometimes at least, what you want to share is likely to be lost.

A group of students staged an adventurous production of Christopher Marlowe's play *Doctor Faustus*, with an ambitious set and mysterious lighting. They invited a famous actor, Leo McKern, to come and see the play and give them some comments. His verdict was: '*Everything was going for the play, the set was really good for creating the right feeling. The main trouble is the lighting. The curse of the theatre is audibility. And I find if you can't see it, you can't hear it.*'

In discussions, in group work, whenever people have to work together, they must be able to look at each other, to establish eye-contact, get close to establish group space rather than individual space. They need to have group territory in which they work. They cannot do that sitting in rows and talking to the backs of heads. They can only 'communicate' with the teacher.

REMEMBER! … If you want people to hear what you say, you have to establish contact with them first.

Eye-contact is important. Physical contact may be necessary, for example, grabbing someone, but only in an extreme case, maybe to protect them from danger. Generally, you would not touch your students in case your actions were misinterpreted. Today, even women teachers have been accused of assault after a perfectly innocent touch on the shoulder. Sometimes it is appropriate, to attract the attention of a student with a degree of deafness possibly.

A whole range of human relationships relates to the level of person-to-person contact which can be made. Students with special learning difficulties respond to touch better than to words, for example. So do young children, but there are obvious dangers. In Australia there has been a national campaign to raise awareness for young children of *good touching* and *bad touching* where you wear your bathers.

Think about your students' attention. Ask yourself at intervals:

- Have I lost them?
- What should happen now to restore their attention?
- Is this the time to change the activity or the focus?

Obviously, it is far better to change the activity, to involve them, to engage them actively in the learning process again.

Visual presentations

Try to present most information visually. To make it effective, eliminate unnecessary and possibly confusing detail. A picture is worth a thousand words, but not if it is a poor picture, or if it is detailed or complicated. People can only absorb and make sense of a limited amount of information.

For instance, suppose you wanted to show a projected image on 'performance criteria'. What you use as a visual focus cannot be the same as I use as description in a book or what you could put on a handout. A handout can carry much more information and detail, because a student will have time to study it (though it must still have a clear structure). You can hold it in your hand as you can a book and reread it if you fail to comprehend. You could use the format of Tasks **8** and **9**, with performance criteria attached.

You might try using this as a projected image, but there is too much to take in and it is in the wrong form for it to be usable in this way. The information is too wordy. A visual aid is meant to focus attention, not to present *all* the information. After all you are going to talk about it, amplify and explain it. What you need is a structure of keywords that you will use as you would notes for a speech and that the students can learn quickly and remember (Figure 10.1). The image might be designed to look more like this; it might be better as several images to talk about, with even fewer words on each. It could be improved even more by use of colour.

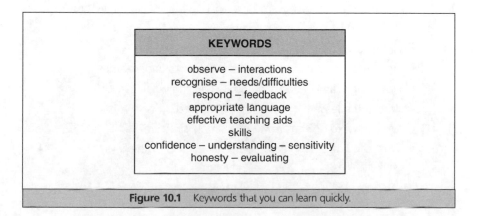

KEYWORDS

observe – interactions
recognise – needs/difficulties
respond – feedback
appropriate language
effective teaching aids
skills
confidence – understanding – sensitivity
honesty – evaluating

Figure 10.1 Keywords that you can learn quickly.

If you are using Powerpoint to produce computer-generated images to project, you can build up by adding ideas, but 'the whole' must finally be easy to grasp. The question is not how clever is it? but how easy is it to read and take in? to see the links between the ideas? to grasp it as a whole? to understand it?

Visual aids

The major purpose of visual aids is to create a change of focus. They help to create attention. If the class has to focus on the teacher all the time, the pressure on the teacher to perform is acute. And we all have distracting mannerisms; some teachers cultivate them deliberately.

If you switch on a projector (or indeed a sound source), attention switches away from your face to the screen. This is helpful in dealing with attention span and gives variety. But it becomes self-defeating if the projector is then left on. You must switch off again when you want students to concentrate on something else; otherwise it becomes a distraction.

We learn 70% by using sight, so that visual images and presentation are very powerful aids to learning. They are usually more effective than sound alone. Generally, seeing skills are more highly developed than listening skills. But this also presents a problem. What we want is attention, so that we should control all the visual images to ensure that they work to our advantage. A friend of mine can still recite a speech by General De Gaulle in French, which she learned 50 years ago, because she was bored in French lessons and this speech was posted on the wall near her desk. Most rooms are full of visual images. Many will divert attention and distract people. Teachers can never control what their students actually learn. Most teachers use a chalkboard or a whiteboard at some time or other. What does it have on it? Its purpose is the same as any other visual aid: to present information visually to focus attention. If anything on the board is irrelevant, clean it off. Try to ensure that work on the board is easy to absorb and to follow, that it has a structure. Don't use it as a jotting pad with no attempt to organise what you write.

Take control of all the visual stimuli in the room and make them work for you.

TASK 11

DESIGNING A VISUAL AID

Ask critically in designing anything to present visually or to project in whatever way:

- How much information is there on this presentation?
- How much of that actually makes it harder to understand?
- How much can I get rid of without changing what it says?
- What is the least that I need, that they need?
- Will one word do? an arrow? or a simple structure?
- What can I do to help them to see the structure? the links? relationships?
- What do I want them to take away?

CHAPTER 11

The learning environment

In **Task 9** you evaluated the *effectiveness* of a lesson plan in a teaching context, and in **Task 10** you looked at the *communication* taking place. Think about another aspect: *the learning environment*.

Control of the environment is so important in enabling the intended pattern of learning (and teaching) to happen that I have chosen to deal with it separately here. Nevertheless, it must receive due attention in your preparation for teaching as an integral part of the communication process.

CONTROL OF THE ENVIRONMENT

TASK 12

In completing Tasks 9 and 10, were you able to meet the performance criteria below?

Performance criteria

12.1 The effect of environmental factors on learning is noted.

12.2 Effort is made to optimise the use of the environment.

12.3 As far as possible it is made suitable for the intended learning activities.

12.4 Learning areas are set out to support the planned activities.

12.5 It is equipped to support the activities and structured to facilitate them.

12.6 A safe working environment is created.

There is nothing particularly difficult to understand here. You know how you react to colour, light, darkness, being too hot or not having enough oxygen in a room. You get depressed when it is always dull and raining – a winter of eternal grey. How cheering it is to see bulbs coming through on a lovely spring day! You have noticed children becoming excited and noisy in a high wind. You have gone to sleep in a darkened cinema or a lecture room. You have felt the atmosphere of railway stations and airports, the pressure of tunnels and the thrill of bridges.

Our surroundings have a marked effect on our feelings and our behaviour. Some people seem to be particularly conscious of the effect of colour; some even choose a car because of its colour, or it is said to match a handbag! But these things do not usually happen at a conscious level.

There is an extraordinary lack of apparent concern about this kind of thing when it comes to classrooms. They are painted (or not) in rather depressing colours and seem to be designed for some other activity than what is supposed to happen there. They are often badly lit, and badly ventilated, they are too hot or too cold. All have a bad effect on the students' ability to work: in airless rooms people simply go to sleep. Unfortunately, teachers fail to see the cause or take action to remedy it.

CASE STUDY 17

John visited a high school in Florida to talk to the students. He was asked to compare British schools with those in Florida. He started by asking them if they liked living in caves.

Every public building he visited was built without windows. People worked in artificial light and artificial air. The reason was simple. If you have windows you suffer from solar gain: the sun makes the room uncomfortably hot and therefore air conditioning is made even more expensive.

In more northerly states of the USA and Europe we try where we can to bring the outside inside through large windows. In Florida, they hide from it. It makes for a rather strange experience when you come to it for the first time: you feel chilled to the bone as you walk from a humid street at 90°F into the cool, dry atmosphere of a room at a temperature of only 70°F (a scale still used in the USA). You feel you need to put on an overcoat when you go into a department store.

Of course, the students who took windowless rooms for granted had not noticed the absence of windows. Almost anything can be 'normal' if that is all we know.

1 What do you consider to be 'normal' in classrooms here?

2 Given the opportunity to start from first principles, should they really be like that?

3 Look closely at the environment your students have to work in, how do they react to it?

4 What is it saying to your students not just about the credibility of a teacher expecting them to work there?

5 What is it saying about how they are valued as people?

6 What are the effects of the environment on what is supposed to happen there? Is it supportive?

7 If it is unsuitable, what improvements could and should be made to make learning easier?

Problems

There are many problems caused by an environment apparently hostile to the kind of learning activity and attitudinal changes you wish to encourage. Look carefully at your teaching situation, try to ensure that it provides an appropriate model of behaviour. In a computer room there may be unsuitable chairs or scanty workspace for the students to get themselves properly organised to work. The keyboard operator is expected to learn about the importance of posture and organisation, of having a ship-shape office. If a room is saying 'do as I say, not as I do', it will handicap both student and teacher. Where is the credibility in the learning?

Usually, the problems are more routine. When you observe classes, ask yourself:

- What are the messages in this room?
- How is it controlling what happens here?
- What learning/teaching behaviour does it assume?
- How much distraction is there?
- Does it make it hard for students to concentrate?
- How 'noisy' is it? what are the acoustics? and the lighting?
- Can the teacher relate easily with all the students?
- Can they all see and hear?
- How does the room control person-to-person interactions?

There are many other questions. Teachers will stop trying to do more interesting things with their students if it is too much hard work to get things ready. How much effort is required

- to get the things the teacher may need?
- to get a projector, a recorder, a DVD player, even chalk?
- to get photocopying done?
- to produce handouts?

Because of the out-reach programmes of FE colleges and the establishment of courses in all sorts of places such as prisons and homes, many teachers find themselves, as David did in his first FE job (Case Study 16), in unsuitable rooms with no equipment, and constant distraction and interruption. Often enough, matters can be improved, but not by you. You can only do as he did, go and talk about your problems with those who can do something about it.

Two teachers on a teacher training course near Birmingham reported to a tutor who was encouraging them to use a variety of approaches that their situation made talk of resources somewhat remote.

They worked in a prison for male offenders. They had a room with tables and chairs, that was all. They did not have access even to an OHP. They had to deal with individuals who came in groups but groups that were always changing. They could not predict the pattern of attendance, who was to be there, because there were so many other things in the prison regime which took precedence. It was not unusual for prisoners to be taken suddenly out of class for some more urgent prison business. The problems of discipline, however, reported by other teachers on their course did not occur – naturally!

The teachers had to negotiate an individual learning programme with each prisoner, trying to help each to come to terms with their learning

needs and make a commitment to the learning, which was partly instrumental about life-skills, information about finding a job, working, money;
and partly about coping as a member of society, self-knowledge, personal
relationships and so on. But they also did attempt some encounter activities as groups such as that described in Case Study 19 on page 124.

I suggest that you invent your own questions about this situation. It is,
of course, hard to say what might be appropriate as action to take in a
situation as constrained as this one clearly is.

Taking control

REMEMBER! … It is your responsibility to ensure that the environment
supports as far is possible what students have to do in order to learn.

When students arrive in a new environment, they explore it; they look for clues as
to how to behave there, as to what is expected of them. The messages are easily and
unconsciously read. People come to it with 'models in the head'.

If they see desks in a row facing a teacher's desk, they know it means: sit down,
be quiet and listen. Can they reasonably be expected to engage in group work, to
share ideas in discussion? They can only react with the teacher. Eye-contact is possible with no one else: they only see the backs of heads. We have to see people's faces
to talk to them, watch their expressions, to look for the subtle ways in which we
communicate: "*How did I know you intended to be funny?*" You can arrange the furniture the way that works best for yourself and your students.

So move the furniture. Set it up to do what you want to do. Remember that the
layout of furniture in a room tells people what is expected to happen there. Think
of a kitchen or a bedroom or a dining room or a laboratory.

Figure 11.1 shows four diagrams of possible layouts in a classroom using the same
desks and chairs. But there are so many other possibilities. It is useful to look at
alternative ideas for your own class, using plans of this kind. Think of interactions
you wish to encourage between individuals, creating groups, sharing; or of concentrating on private work as with a computer or in language work using machines.

What advantages or disadvantages do you think there might be of having students separated or grouped in the ways the different arrangements seem to dictate?
When would you use one layout, when another? Is it sensible to always use the
same layout whatever you want your students to do?

What if there are no desks, but comfortable chairs in a circle? What does that
say? Or a large table with chairs around it – a committee meeting? What if there is
gentle background music playing? What if coffee is set out ready on the table in the
corner? What if there are pictures on the wall, and a carpet? What if … like John
Lennon's famous song.

You can create your own environment with a little ingenuity. You are in charge.
Do not leave it to the caretaker, but please make friends with the caretaker; s/he can

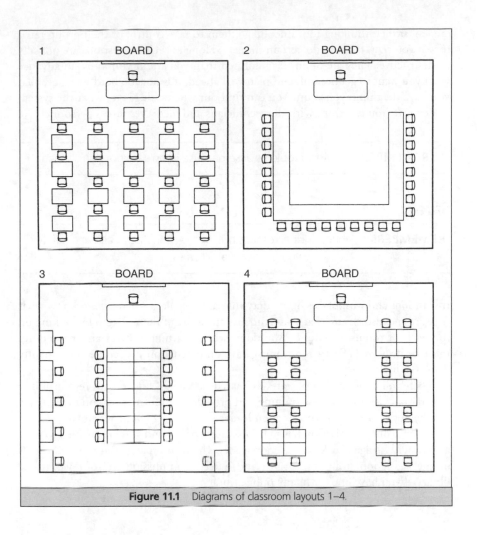

Figure 11.1 Diagrams of classroom layouts 1–4.

do so much to help you. It is polite and will improve relationships if you put the furniture back as you found it when you leave.

You might need to be quite forceful. How many teachers will have the courage or confidence to say, Hey! this isn't good enough for my students. If you want them to learn, help me to make it possible. But you may be surprised how much cooperation you do get if you make enough noise – in a nice way – about it.

There are, of course, many simple things you can do. Open the windows. Make sure there is enough light. Move chairs or tables around. Put up posters and learning materials. Plan the situations you want to create. Create space and territories and visual stimuli.

Overcoming obstacles

Quite often teachers fail to see the potential in the teaching environment or what can be done with a little imagination. Students may be more inventive than you are; enlist their thinking too. Encourage them to take control of their group territory if you want them to do certain things, so long as their suggestions are not silly or destructive. They are often less inhibited than you are. If you know in advance what you want to get hold of, and plan well ahead, it is not too hard to ensure that you have the things you want. You can find out where things are, what the system is – or isn't. You can work with the technicians and media resources personnel.

REMEMBER! … Most problems arise because people do not think ahead.

Safety

REMEMBER! … Your principal responsibility is to ensure the health and safety of your students at all times.

Institutions and workplaces have safety rules and regulations. You *must* know what they are and also ensure that your students are aware of them. Begin by looking on the walls of rooms, usually by the door, where warning notices and procedures must be displayed. Every room must have an evacuation procedure prominently displayed by law.

There will be a member of staff designated as 'Safety Officer' with responsibility to carry out checks, organise training and provide the information you need. Ask a member of your team or your section leader who this is in your workplace.

By law, your organisation has to have a safety policy and you are entitled to have a copy of it. So again, ask your section leader who to approach. You can find copies of the legislation from the Health and Safety Commission in your workplace library, if you have one, or in any public library.

CHAPTER 12	Assessment

Here, we are concerned with basic concepts and ideas in feedback and assessing learning in order to facilitate it. We shall explore the complexities of examining in Part 2 of the book.

TASK 13

ASSESSMENT

1 Use feedback and assessment in your planned lesson to promote the learning of your students.

2 Evaluate your success in meeting the criteria below.

Performance criteria

13.1 The teacher notes carefully interactions between individuals, with the teacher and in groups.

13.2 Learning difficulties are noted; support and help is given.

13.3 There is clear evidence of use of feedback and sensitivity to the problems that students experience.

13.4 Individuals are encouraged to take responsibility for their own learning and progress.

13.5 Assessment methods are identified in the lesson plans.

13.6 Assessment that is used is appropriate to the intended learning.

13.7 Assessment will provide good feedback.

13.8 Learning is assessed by students as well as by the teacher.

13.9 Learning is consolidated.

13.10 The session(s) and the outcomes are evaluated.

Feedback

Feedback enables learning to take place. How does it work?

The simplest example of feedback in a 'closed' system is a thermostat which controls a heating system to keep the temperature constant. It feeds back information about temperature to the boiler. If the desired temperature is reached, the thermostat cuts the boiler. If the temperature drops it re-ignites. Learning in classrooms is not a 'closed' system. It is 'open', dynamic, changes with time and experience. Feedback requires not just some way of monitoring change from inside, the assumption of pro-grammed learning in a computer, but additional input from outside, usually by the teacher. We all need a mirror to reflect back to us an image of what we are doing or what we are not – some means of judging how well we do, whatever we are trying to achieve, students and teachers.

When we work with other people, they are the mirror, but to use the mirror effectively we have to know what we are looking for, the responses we want or – more insistently – we don't want. Then we change what we do accordingly, to get the desired responses. Everybody knows how to do that. We do it in normal affairs all the time, otherwise social groupings and social interaction would be impossible. It is the way we learn. Learning activities themselves usually provide the feedback that we need. If I am trying to learn to skate, I know whether I am being success-ful or not! Other people, however, will be able to give me feedback to make me more successful. In formal education we have to invent complex systems of feeding back information. Learning activities we engage in are complex, so it is not sur-prising. If we attempt sophisticated tasks, we set up learning as a series of targets with *performance criteria*. Then we need to find ways to measure success. Usually, another person's perception, that of a mentor or tutor, is crucially important.

Evidence

We have to have some evidence and we must decide what kind of evidence; after that we must make judgements about the evidence, about what it demonstrates.

What really matters in assessment is the nature of the evidence. If we look for evidence, we must be sure that it is valid: that it actually relates to what we are try-ing to observe or to measure. For instance, does it make sense to try to measure how much skill I have acquired in skating by having me write an essay about it? Yet there is a strongly held view that exams are what matter, and 'an *exam is writing essays, isn't it?*'. What in fact will my ability to write an essay demonstrate? That I can write the essay, of course, but that is not what I wanted to find out.

If I want to show that I can write a good essay, however, the only proper evi-dence is essays I have written. It is unlikely that I shall succeed in writing a good essay at the first attempt. By using feedback – my own assessment of what I have done maybe, and what other people think about it – it is to be expected that my next essay will approximate more closely to a *model* of what a good essay is. I may read essays that are said to be *good models* to try to imitate them. I have to build up a mental picture of what a good essay is like if I am to be able to create a fair approxi-mation of it, and it may take me many attempts before I am happy with it. Whole books have been devoted to writing good essays.

In education we may provide feedback in an assessment process called *continu-ous assessment*, where there are many successive opportunities to grade work and provide feedback; the grades will be cumulative. Assessment at the end of a learn-ing programme is *summative assessment* (summing up). Assessment intended to shape learning by feeding back to the learning process may be referred to as *forma-tive assessment*, because it is intended to give shape or form to the learning.

We usually attempt to measure *change* or *achievement*. In both cases, we may use continuous assessment formatively in a learning process; or we may use it simply to record grades. When we are concerned principally with change as the student learns rather than grading achievement, we will use assessment frequently in a formative way to shape the learning, *self-referenced assessment*; and have perhaps a *summative assessment* at the end of the course to grade the students. One alternative will be *profiling* of achievements and change, which may be a more useful record of achievement.

A practical example

As a swimmer, I want to be proficient in life-saving. How shall I achieve that? How shall I know when I am acceptably proficient? How can I demonstrate it to others? What I have to do to demonstrate that I am proficient is the same as what I do to learn in order to achieve it. The difference lies in the judgements that are made about what I do. My standard of performance is judged against *criteria*: statements of what is to be judged and at what level. In this case I might be required actually to save someone from drowning, which is not designed as a test. Proficiency cannot simply be arbitrary judgements: either I save someone from drowning or I fail. The case is the same with most important learning that we do. The real test, the one that matters, comes when we have to do it 'for real'. The closer judgements made in training assess achievements that are transferable to 'reality', the more valuable the learning will be. The same is palpably true of teacher training.

All learning systems require proper feedback. We must try to see the purpose of assessment as principally to improve the learning. There is a view that assessment is the same as testing. Tests do come in many forms these days and they certainly have value. They are not restricted to essay-writing. But their use in providing feedback is limited unless they show much more than a numerical score; they have to be helpful in identifying what it is students need to improve or need still to learn.

A score of itself tells the student nothing from which s/he can learn. We must know in what way we must improve. In trying to find this kind of evidence, we have to look at what students have to do in order to learn. There are usually skills to be observed and/or products that can be evaluated. The essay is a product; so is a flower arrangement, a pot turned on a wheel, or a properly presented document using a computer. Products are tangible evidence of achievement. They can be compared to previous attempts by the same student and compared with those of others to identify factors on which we can focus our attention. We can identify what has changed as a student progresses and try to establish criteria for excellence. Like the cake that sags in the middle when taken from the oven, there is usually no difficulty in identifying what needs to be improved, but it is not so easy to tell the student how to do that.

Criteria

Clearly, I will progress more quickly if I do not have to guess by what criteria my success or lack of it will be judged. In most things in life, we learn by trial and error, gradually teasing out an idea of what we have to do to be successful. Often this can be a painful experience. We may ask: what are teachers for? In the driving test, we can read the legal and good practice rules set out in the Highway Code, issued for use by learners, instructors and examiners. It contains generalisations, minimal knowledge, to define pass/fail criteria. Driving a car under real traffic conditions is not like that. The judgements made by a driving examiner are of what the learner driver actually does under certain conditions. S/he has to decide if it is safe to let the person loose on the road, making judgements about more important things stated in the Highway Code: such as the ability to anticipate conditions ahead or the behaviour of other road users (and at speed), consideration for others, courtesy, aggressiveness. Unfortunately, test conditions make that judgement more a matter of guesswork than certainty, because the testee is not required to drive at more than 30 miles an hour or to go on to a motorway.

Unfortunately also, teachers frequently fail to tell students what they have to achieve, what they must do to succeed rather than fail. The learner does not know what s/he has to learn. Does the teacher know what the criteria are? Or is it just a feeling, a vague 'model in the head'? In the end, even when we have criteria, we have to rely on personal judgements, of course. Teachers should give feedback to students at every opportunity and obtain every scrap of information to assist both them and their students to enhance overall performance.

External examinations, set and marked by examining boards, are *summative assessments* against which an award could be made. They do not usually define a process of learning, but most examination boards do provide feedback for teachers of general achievement on exams, or for individuals if it is requested. Seek all this out, use it to improve your teaching programme.

As we learn, we change in so many interrelated ways: in knowledge and skills, perception and insight, development also of positive rather than negative attitudes. Very little can be measured as a statistical number; most of it is not accessible to tests that produce scores. A driving examiner sitting beside you with a check-box for ticks will not make better judgements than one who simply responds to what you do, though he may be able to provide more detailed feedback. Such a checklist is also a means of ensuring that all the criteria are assessed and every examiner is looking for the same things.

If, as many teachers are, you are required to use tests as part of a teaching programme, please look at the exploration of tests in Chapter 23.

Progression

The kind of criteria I have devised for this book are to be viewed as signposts, pointing a direction to establish good practice. They define a road and a journey, rather than points of arrival beyond which you do not need to go. A teacher who is fully satisfied with a personal performance in any aspect of teaching ceases to ask important questions.

As with the professional painter or musician, each product, each performance, will provide a critical evaluation so that the next one can be more mature, more fully formed, more impressive. No artist is ever satisfied; every performance is a learning experience to help the performer to improve. Your professional judgement will change with experience, insight and knowledge. Progress depends on using experience, reflecting on it to change your perception of what you are about.

It is the same with your students. They must be fully engaged in the process of learning, and that means also in the process of assessment. They need to reflect on their learning experiences, on what they achieve, in order to improve. Your criteria for them are signposts rather than goalposts.

When to assess

Surely, at the end of each learning experience, we need to know what we have learned, whether we have achieved the learning goals and how well: what we need to do *now*. On the other hand, where a teacher insists on a test at the end of each session, assessment may dominate the learning process to skew it from its main purpose. Frequency of testing is an important issue.

In designing learning experiences, we must have a clear idea of what students are setting out to learn and how we, and they, will know how far they have progressed towards mastery. There are long-term goals and short-term goals. Each lesson has its short-term goals. They should be perceived as part of those longer-term goals towards which they contribute.

Much of the assessment must take place 'on the wing', as it is happening. The feedback must be as close as possible to the learning for it to have any useful effect. It is not much use knowing that we need to do something differently once the point of need has passed; a week later may seem a very long time. If I am to improve my golf-swing, I need help on the course. Written assignments need to be returned promptly, with not just a letter grade but appropriate detail from you, before the student is expected to produce another. You need deadlines for returning stuff, just as students need deadlines for producing it and giving it to you.

The most useful feedback and help a teacher provides is when students are coming up against difficulties in doing things. That is the intention of the Tasks I have devised for this book.

EVIDENCE AND CRITERIA

TASK 14

1 In your own area of teaching, identify what evidence you would look for to measure the progress of your students.

2 How would you get your students to produce that evidence?

3 What kind of learning would you consider it would measure?

4 In relation to the learning goals, try to identify criteria you think the activity, or product of the activity, could achieve if it was well done.

5 Make the criteria as simple and as clear as you can.

6 Can you share these criteria with your students before they set out to undertake the activity?

7 How will you provide feedback to your students?

8 Will it be as written reports or comments on work?

9 Will it be through discussion or in a more formal way?

Self-evaluation

At the end of any learning experience we need to evaluate, take stock of what has happened, where we are now, decide where we go from here. What have you discovered so far? What decisions do you need to make?

There is no need to be highly self-critical.

A Try to answer the following questions as honestly as you can. Use your reflective diary to try to see what has happened, what has changed; and ask why.

B Where you can, try to identify evidence for your statements that you might show your mentor for comment or discussion.

1 Observation: What have you observed?

2 Lesson planning: How have you rethought your approaches, and why?

3 Communication: What do you now understand? or what has now come into focus?

4 Environment: What do you now have the confidence to do?

5 Implementing: Look again at the performance criteria. How far do you match up?

6 Performance: What still needs work?

7 Attitudes: Do you feel more positive? Can you relate better with students?

8 Confidence: Can you explore various methods?

9 Flexibility: How adaptable are you?

PART 2 | Developing the learning programme

Introduction

Part 1 focused on preparing and teaching individual lessons. **Part 2** is concerned with designing and implementing a teaching programme over a period. For further growth, just relying on learning from experience takes too long. To accelerate the process, you need information, ideas, further practical advice as well as extended experience, and that is what Part 2 provides. You will find varied strategies and methods, ways of developing attendant skills, with Activities and Tasks to explore your role. Tasks are those that enable the development and implementation of your teaching programme. Activities are those that promote your own personal insights and understanding.

All the Tasks are important; you should do them in the order set out here. But select those Activities that meet your requirements, addressing the material with your own questions from your perception of what you need.

Where Part 1 is a learning programme, the Tasks in Part 2 define that process further, but it is principally a resource from which to select information and advice. It is not intended you choose one of the teaching strategies here as the 'right' one for your purposes, nor that all the methods might be effective in your situation. You must select what is appropriate to the learning of your students where they are. No author can know, or attempt to predict, the context in which you are teaching, your students or your needs. Ideally, you will be able to use these Activities and Tasks in a context where you can receive tutor support. It is perfectly feasible to learn on your own but it is much better to work with a mentor and your colleagues, sharing your reflections with them. In order to learn you will certainly need feedback, we all do; and to articulate your feelings by reporting your learning experiences to others in order to reveal your discoveries to yourself. Writing a Reflective Diary is necessary to bring learning experiences into focus.

Part 2 repeats – of course it does – what you have begun in Part 1, but in greater depth. You have to explore the same experiences over and again to learn more by repetitive activity, which continuously advances and broadens your perspective. Revisiting is the essential activity of any learning, since doing something once will have little lasting effect. Repetitive activity in teaching, however, must not become a matter of routine, because you carry responsibility for the learning of others every time you teach them. You must tackle each experience with an alert, enquiring mind in order to learn from it and so do better.

Tasks in progression

The Tasks for Part 2 are set out below as an overview of progression:

<table>
<tr><td>**CHAPTER 13**</td><td>**A case study approach**</td></tr>
</table>

You have already become familiar with case studies. It is normal to deal with problems by reference to what happened on other occasions, usually as anecdotes ('I remember when …').

Case studies are different in that we try to impose a discipline on them. We give them shape and form so that we can learn by interrogating 'the experience' with questions. We can then apply that learning to find a solution to a present case or to future cases. Or we may compare several case studies to look for similarities and differences. It is the principles we learn from studies that matter. The same is true of a Case Study of your own learning.

Your learning

Your principal responsibility is to your students, but you are also a learner. In your own classroom, wherever you are teaching, you will be exploring your own learning. When you carry out the Tasks in Part 2 as you design, prepare, implement and evaluate a teaching/learning programme for a group of students in your own context, you will be making an extended Case Study of your own learning. The Case Study should enable you to bring into focus what occurs to monitor your growth and change throughout the experience. The purpose of the Reflective Diary you are encouraged to keep is to record learning. It may take any form, as suggested earlier; its purpose is more important than what it looks like. What matters is what it contains: how much information and of what kind, your reflections and how they are organised. Those who are comfortable writing text with a computer will be at an advantage. The Case Study will also contain the evidence in completed Tasks and materials you have produced in relation to them.

Part 1 adopted a linear approach to designing assignments and supporting ideas and activities. There is a sequence within which good practice in teaching must work. You cannot plan in a vacuum, you need sufficient information of the right kind.

In designing your own Case Study the same sequencing is required because it will develop over time and within a context. Tasks have to be undertaken in order. You cannot implement what you have not designed, nor evaluate it until after it has occurred.

A useful structure for any design project such as a teaching programme is to follow the stages:

Explore → Formulate → Design → Make/do → Evaluate

In order to design any programme you have to discover the questions and attempt to answer them. 'Explore' invites you to discover helpful questions, then structure them to find a useful, practicable approach. I have set out a brief survey of strategies and methods of teaching. They are not 'fully comprehensive' nor 'third party' to insure you against risks in setting out on your journey, but they are intended to give you a view of the possible roads you might choose to follow.

Strategies

One area of 'exploration' is to discover alternative strategies for your teaching/learning programme. You have to have some view of the curriculum model you wish to use. A curriculum (little running track) is a path designed to integrate learning experiences. Parts 1 and 2 here form such a curriculum. Think about a design project you are familiar with: a menu for a dinner party, a holiday, or a day out. There are appropriate and inappropriate ways of setting about doing such things. You could just open the fridge to see what is there, or put a hat on, go out the door to catch a bus to anywhere. My wife's mother once got so impatient waiting for a No. 14 bus in London that she said, 'Let's get on the next bus, it must be going somewhere!'

There is a wide range of alternative ways of setting about learning. You must choose one that is appropriate for what you want your students to learn. Far too often students and teachers grab at unhelpful methods of learning because they have not thought them through. They do not have enough information of the right kind, nor have they discovered helpful questions. You need a clear overview of what you and your students are supposed to be about. Once you have that, you can formulate an action plan, a strategy. You can then begin to design a programme. This book is a model of how to set about it. All this has to be done before classes can begin. Your Case Study starts with your thinking and your planning, although the bulk of it will be a reflection on what actually happens in your teaching.

You could usefully start with the Who, What, Where, Why, How questions in Part 1, or in summary:

- Who are the students, and what do they need to learn?
- What age are they? male/female and so on. Are they all the same?
- Why are they here? Is it for an exam? a qualification? or just for enrichment?
- Are they going to do it alone or with other students?
- What do they have to know, to understand and/or be able to do?
- What do they know, what can they do already?
- Where are they all starting from?
- Where are they all going? Are they all on the right bus?
- How will they know what they have to learn?
- How are they going to learn?
- What do they have to do in order to learn?
- Where and when are we going to be doing it?
- What is the time-scale?
- How quickly can they learn?
- What do they need in order to achieve this learning?
- What support do they need?

- How will they know when they have learned it?
- How is learning to be demonstrated and tested?
- What standard should it be set at?
- What conditions will affect the learning?

Make a list of helpful – and simple – questions and structure them. You need the list in order to know where to look for the answers, what helpful answers might look like. You can then make decisions.

The strategy chosen in this book is experiential learning – doing it and learning from doing it. You will have considerable experience to build upon, but in order to learn through experience you will have to be able to stand back from what happens and reflect upon it; and it will help if others provide the mirror.

STUDENT GROUP

1 The first requirement is a more detailed study of your students. If they do not form a coherent group meeting for a programme of study, it does not invalidate the exercise. You must design and plan for your students as they really are. If they are on a programme of individualised learning or you are to teach on an out-reach course in a community hall, or wherever, it is the same task.

2 Teachers have to do preliminary planning to design a programme before they meet students. When you meet the students they will be full of questions of their own, and you need answers.

3 The purpose of information is to assist you in designing a learning programme. Don't overwhelm yourself with information you cannot use. Decide what is relevant and useful, what you really need to know. Identify any information that is not particularly useful, and ask whether it is worth having.

4 Set down clearly for yourself what you need to know. Validate it with your mentor and/or your peers. Then you can decide how you are to discover the information. Again, the experience of what you did in Part 1 should help you.

5 Agree the form the study should take and the time by which you must have it ready – the sooner the better in relation to planning. If at all possible discuss various ways of setting about it with your peers and/or your mentor. There are many ways of setting about it.

6 One way is to create a questionnaire for yourself, or students, to complete perhaps at an enrolment or pre-course meeting. When you meet them as individuals, you will have a structure of questions to give shape to the interview. Of course, you must be prepared to answer their questions, too. To say you have not yet decided what the course is about will have quite the wrong effect.

7 What matters is that you actually use the information. Students may not be happy if they are asked and then ignored.

CHAPTER 14	Identifying needs

Considerable emphasis has so far been put on 'identifying needs'. It will by now be clear that this is not a simple matter. We may distinguish certain needs that arise from practical considerations and are similar for most people within the same situation; for example, to create the right conditions

- for individual learning and study
- for groups to work effectively together sharing the same learning programme.

Most needs people have are not so much 'out there', observable, in common, but 'in here'; therefore, much more difficult to predict and analyse: such as confidence, development of a positive self-image, psychological barriers to learning, pressures in the workplace.

Creating conditions suitable for learning and study are discussed in other parts of this book. Some may be physical, some psychological, some a matter of structure or priorities, managing time, space, oneself and so on. Here, I want to look at some needs that affect groups of students and more personal needs of individuals. Naturally, labelling a need as of this or that kind may not be particularly helpful in terms of doing something about it. We cannot isolate one need from the whole of a person's psychological make-up. People's needs are complex and largely unknown to them; often there are feelings that are hard for them to express and what they say may not be a safe guide as to what is really important for them. Think again of a patient with a doctor. But students should always be encouraged to articulate their own perception of need.

You were asked to do it for yourself right at the beginning of this book. You may have found that your perception of your needs has changed quite a lot through the learning experiences you have already had. Learning is always mainly learning about yourself. Indeed, all teachers who follow this learning path discover more about themselves than about anything else, and that includes their needs.

Groups

Adults must be consulted, to agree to what their goals are and what is to be learned, what their roles and responsibilities in the learning process are to be. Students ultimately are responsible for what happens for them. This may be affected by:

- bad feelings between individuals (or with the teacher)
- a failure for the group or working groups to 'gel'
- poor working conditions that do not value them as people
- pace of work, time of day, tiredness
- lack of comprehension of the teacher or of what they are to do

- lack of commitment if the work seems boring or pointless
- demands that are too heavy or that fail to stimulate or challenge
- lack of relevance to their perception of what the learning is for.

This list is merely a guide to help to shape your thinking about what group needs might be like and most of these could be within the control of the teacher.

In identifying group needs, you must carry students along with you. It requires sensitivity as the teacher to see it from the point of view of your students, to experience what it is like for them. To do that you must watch, observe carefully what happens, how students respond to what they are asked to do, how they react to what you do, and how the social context of the group develops.

When a class goes well it develops its own momentum. If it dies as groups do, you must know it has died and try to discover what is not going well. Students might feel undervalued, let down, or badly treated; individuals, even whole groups, might exhibit withdrawal behaviour as in Gillian's class (Case Study 14).

As group leader, you make the decisions on behalf of your group. You must win commitment to the programme of work, establish common goals and good working relationships to achieve them. You are responsible for creating supportive conditions for the learning activity. To do that you must know what it is for, what is the purpose of the whole enterprise. Asking students what they want to learn may be ineffective: they will come expecting you to know and to tell them. You must have your own programme to present to them. Negotiation needs a baseline. To arrive with a blank piece of paper and say "Well, what shall we do this week, this term?" will usually cause dismay. Even where you have a long-established relationship with a group of adult students, they will still want you to lead from the front. When I offered such an adult group in Japan the chance to choose an English novel to read from a list I had given them, they insisted I make the decision for them. After all, I know the novels and the writers and they don't.

Learning goals

Consolidation and assessment both require that learning goals are stated and agreed in terms that the students can easily comprehend and agree to, and which make it easy for them to assess progress and achievement for themselves. Negotiation of goals must begin from the teacher's learning goals and a programme to achieve them.

But negotiation matters. Flexibility matters. You need a rationale for your programme. And you should make it clear how flexible you are prepared to be to meet your students' perception of what they need to learn. They will trust you so long as they see that what they are asked to do is stimulating and interesting, and they feel they are making progress in their learning.

The better organised the teacher and the easier it is for students to do the learning activities, the more success there will be within the programme as a whole.

Personal needs

As social human beings, we all have personal needs. Most people are shy of talking about them, though some have no inhibitions. Encounter groups in the UK and the USA encourage people to express their anxieties and their needs. Many people come to adult/community education as a way of satisfying deeply felt needs they often find hard to express even to themselves. Every student is dealing with a host of conflicting emotions and pressures, which may bubble to the surface occasionally. Some techniques allow this to happen, such as role play. Teachers should not attempt to be counsellors to deal with students' personal problems, although the relationship with individuals might allow it to happen. Nevertheless, they must be sensitive to what individuals bring to the class. Much of their behaviour relates to such feelings.

We all need to maintain a good self-image, self-esteem and a sense of achievement. We all need success and find failure damaging. We need to feel that other people value or respect us. We are all sensitive to rejection. We need social contacts and friendships. People come to classes looking for these things. Others, women particularly, feel themselves constantly under pressure by demands of others, and are trying to identify goals or interests peculiarly their own.

There are extrinsic pressures, too, such as the need for qualifications and to get or keep a job. Students may feel threatened by what is happening in their working environment, their need to keep up as technological change or organisational change makes old skills redundant, and demands new skills. Lack of progress in learning activities may be caused by factors too personal for students to express in front of a large group, or even in a small group they work well with. It is easier to deal with personal needs as part of a learning programme through individual or small group tutorials (cf. Chapter 17). Being forced to face emotional hang-ups in front of a group can be counter-productive or might have a liberating effect, it is hard to predict which.

CASE STUDY 19

Evelyn wrote:

I teach an OCN (Open College Network) Social & Life Skills course at Levels 1 & 2: Drug Awareness, Alcohol Awareness, Healthy Living, Family Relationships and Parentcraft; the case is in Parentcraft.

I work in an adult male prison with ages ranging from 21 upwards. Those who choose to attend my course might be a father, great grandfather or not a father, but they have all been children so this qualifies them. The aim would be to give them an understanding of being a Parent and this would be covered in Parental Roles, Children's Rights, Child Development, Behaviour, Family Learning and Interaction.

I have a class of 10 students of mixed abilities regarding literacy, very different backgrounds, varying ages (22–56) and a range of different cultures. The Unit I covered was the last unit of a 5-week course.

7 AIM: Be aware of how positive parenting builds self-esteem in children. Give examples based on discussion of positive interactions with children to build self-esteem.

Self-esteem

I used an activity to demonstrate what it **'feels'** like to be given praise. I would link this with what it **'feels'** like for the child.

I had 10 students and started with student 1, going round the room in turn giving them feedback on how they had been over the past 5 weeks of the course (every afternoon) and what they had given to the course and shared with others. It was positive feedback, but always remembering to personalise it regarding their role in the family, class and course work. When I reached student 4, who had from the beginning of the course been diffi-cult on several occasions regarding behaviour, especially '**boundaries**', he immediately said, "skip me, go on to the next man", desperately wanting to leave the room. I asked him to stay and allow me to feed back what he had contributed. He was a father of four and brought up his children by himself as his wife had left them due to her drug problem. Although he was in prison their paternal grandmother, his mother, had taken over the role. Continual contact and visits with the children were very important to him and he requested the course in helping him with his parenting role. He was very attentive and took a lot on board. His contribution to the course was valuable with open and honest comments. In a strange way he presented himself as a '**responsible**' father – which does sound weird.

When I gave him my feedback and his contributions – **all positive** – he felt uncomfortable, embarrassed and was physically holding on to his body. I continued going around the room then asked them in turn to feed back to me what they were '**feeling**', i.e. physical/mental. Some described the '**feeling**' as if they were blushing inside. Another, butterflies in their stomach, a rush running through their body, sick, uncomfortable, wanting to leave the room quickly, tears within, something stuck in their throat, flushing of the face, ears, etc. Some of the '**thoughts**' were 'what does she want, why is she saying this, it isn't true, I don't trust or believe her, I bet she says this to everyone'. I let them hold on to the '**feeling**' for a couple of minutes and then repeated that everything I had said was true, reinforcing. I then said if you get all those feelings from what I have just given you then imagine what it must feel like for a child getting positive feedback from a parent and how that would build on their self-esteem. I had achieved the aim of the lesson through one activity – powerful experience.

Comment

Few teachers are likely to find themselves dealing with a class as psycho-logically complex as this one of Evelyn's. Many people in prison are hostile to society because society has been hostile to them at least in their own perception. They have suffered failure and rejection that has led to very poor self-esteem. Prison regime can only reinforce their sense of their own inadequacy, especially if they lose their family. One can only speculate on the conflicting emotions. Evelyn's 'powerful experience' led to pain in try-ing to interpret comments. Clearly, it was a major learning experience for them and the teacher: what each actually learned is difficult to say. Evelyn was sure that this experience had achieved the aim of the lesson: be aware how positive parenting builds self-esteem in children.

There is a wealth of discussion material in this case study, but I do not wish to lead it by any structured questioning. From the information here, what do you think the men in this class learned?

Costing time

What students (or employers) pay for in teaching sessions is expertise and time; the effective use of time is what the planning of programmes is mostly about. It is impossible to do everything in class time. Whatever programme is set up, most of the learning has to take place outside class time as the students work on their own or in group projects. You might well have to help them to do that. It is not enough just to send them out of the door and tell them to get on with it.

Setting up the learning as individual and/or group learning activities releases time, which can be used for individual tutorial support and reflection. In designing programmes, teachers will need to cost the use of time in some way. To be effective, students must be actively involved in all aspects of their learning. So, everyone requires opportunities for supportive individual feedback.

Motivation and tasks

Herzberg, in *The Motivation to Work*, saw 'motivators' as largely arising from tasks: what individuals or a group were expected to do. Many women, for instance, complain of the menial character of the kind of work they have to do and how this defines their role; such feelings tend to demotivate. Some highly qualified people who come to the UK cannot get posts commensurate with their qualifications and experience and have to take less prestigious and lower paid work. Redundancy above a certain age is a well-known cause of loss not only of prestige and income, even if they can get a job at all, but of their self-esteem.

Our perception of role and the tasks we have to do can give rise to satisfaction and excitement or stimulate hostility or even despair. Bear this in mind as you identify roles for students in groups and as you design tasks for your students to do. Try to avoid any possible stereotyping, especially if any in the group impose it on themselves. Adult students tend to have embedded self-images.

What roles do the students perceive? How does it look to them? For example, what effect is it likely to have on apprentices, who are expected to take dictated notes in class for three hours and practise for hours in a workshop things they do every day at work, if they are then told by the boss, "You can forget that – we don't do it that way"? Things like that may still happen if employees are seconded to a training course. It used to be, maybe still is, a big problem for teachers, too.

Motivation has been studied intensively. What makes people want to do things? to put in the effort? to overcome pain? Most people find they do much better, will keep going against the odds, if they have the support and challenge of others. There are many examples. It explains the enormous growth of clubs for slimmers, cyclists, those trying to shake alcohol dependency, or people rebuilding their lives after emotional trauma. We all need others to share what we do, the pain and the thrills. It is so hard to keep going on your own. We need competition as much as we need support, we need others to make us try harder to keep up with them or with the group.

From this stems the importance of groupwork and group tasks. Individuals will often achieve a great deal more through peer-group support. But peer-group pressure may level down as well as up, so that the teacher needs to monitor carefully what actually happens. One of the problems of putting students of all abilities into the same classes (in school or college) against streaming, is the tendency for the achievements of everyone in the group to find a level that fails to realise the potential of the more able among them.

Success breeds success, failure demotivates. Ensure that the tasks and the learning programme you set up are likely to be achievable by your students. If they are too hard (equally if they are not challenging enough) or are incomprehensible or seem to have little to do with what the students feel they are actually trying to learn, little real effort will be put into doing them.

In designing learning programmes, designing the learning tasks will be the most important part of the preparation. As we read in Case Study 19, you may have to devise tasks in a way that enables all the students, of whatever level of ability, to achieve their potential. You will have to modify tasks as they are attempted by your students; your students will certainly modify them to match their ability and needs.

The cost of failure

Motivation can be calculated by the cost of failure and how well people are prepared to come back from failure. Perception of the cost of failure to achieve goals set by oneself, by parents, by one's employer or peer group, is vitally important in what people are prepared to do. In some societies, the cost is very great, can lead to high suicide rates; it persuades people to play very safe, to look over their shoulder for approval of what they do and be unwilling to take personal responsibility. Japan is such a society, where almost no one will take responsibility for making a decision; indeed where it is very hard to get a decision at all by anyone.

In other societies, such as the USA, individuals are encouraged to take risks, failure is tolerated and there is always a second chance to do it. But when all pressures are removed, or failure is over-indulged, the tendency is to drop out and take it easy, because it just doesn't matter. This is why it is important to establish clearly the rules and expectations within the learning group. Teachers can use the natural competitiveness of groups to good effect. Peer-group pressure not to let the group down is a powerful motivator. Individuals, too, need to know what is expected in their personal learning programme. They need to have an action plan and time schedules, dead-lines and performance models, which can be monitored in tutorials. Good practice as a learner in any field involves goal-seeking behaviour.

Counselling services

One of the features of FE in the new century is the sophistication of counselling services available to students. Counselling is intended to cover the full range of need. For a full discussion see Chapter18.

Suggested reading

Ardrey, R. *The Social Contract*, Fontana (London), 1971.
Bloom, B.S. (ed.) *Taxonomy of Education Objectives, The Classification of Educational Goals*. McKay (New York), 1956.
Herzberg, F. *Work and the Nature of Man*, World (New York), 1966.
Maslow, A. *Motivation and Personality*, Harper & Row (New York), 1954; Addison Wesley Longman (New York and London), 1987.

| CHAPTER 15 | Devising a learning/teaching strategy |

A strategy is an overview, an action plan, a model in the head of the course you are setting up. You must know what you are trying to do, how you see it happening. Although there are many strategies that may be used in whatever you set out to do, some are much more successful than others; and what works well in one context may not be quite so effective in another. You have to choose the one that works for you and your students and for the kind of learning you hope they will achieve.

Strategy is a word used originally in a military context and comes from the Greek, which may be translated 'military leader'. It is an overall plan for winning – anything from a war, to a game of hockey, to a successful business venture. As 'leader', first you have to win the cooperation of 'your team', but yours is the responsibility for the overall plan: where you are going, how you will succeed together.

Clearly, it is 'the team' who must make the plan work. What the leader does on his/her own is not likely to achieve much. It is not enough for teachers to adopt a teaching strategy; it must link clearly with the learning strategies devised for their students, which should be the ones most likely to succeed. It is irresponsible to send students off to do things that have not been thought through as to where they will lead. It is extraordinary how groups are still sent off to do a mountain walk, say, in skimpy clothes on a hot day without proper equipment and have to be rescued when a mist comes down. Who is to blame for not devising a strategy for the trip, taking into account what the hikers must wear and carry, what they must know and what training they will need to cope with difficulties or with emergencies? If we plan a journey of any kind, say the journey I have devised for you in this book, we need to anticipate how it will be for those who undertake it.

What is good for your team is good for you. There will be added benefit for anyone working with colleagues in groups or as teams, especially if the tasks involve problem-solving. Learning is change in many things. Teachers should have an overview of the kind of changes that the teaching/learning programme they design is intended to promote, how the changes will occur and how they will be managed and assessed.

Any course or programme may be judged on:

- **cognitive changes** it is intended to facilitate
- **behavioural changes** that will be observed
- **attitudinal changes** that are needed
- **enrichment** it provides through learning experiences
- **effectiveness** in achieving the learning goals.

Courses are nearly always designed with emphasis on cognitive or behavioural change because they are the easiest to observe and assess. Enrichment is just as important because attitudinal change is usually a prerequisite of other learning and results from the nature of learning experiences: that is, the tasks students are asked to complete and the intended roles they perceive in learning. In adult and community education, enrichment is frequently the major purpose of a course.

You cannot plan a teaching strategy to facilitate the students' learning behaviour before you know what it is. The appropriate way forward is for you to identify:

- what your students are setting out to learn and the changes that need to happen
- what learning strategies and behaviour are likely to succeed best.

Many teachers will say that the strategy is decided for them by awarding bodies or others such as employers or the college. In the present climate of accountability in FE, everyone is looking over the shoulder for the approval of those to whom they are accountable. Pressures to conform, to play safe are strong. Results tables and strict assessment procedures have an inhibiting effect on how far a teacher feels free to choose not just the content, but the methodology for teaching a course. On the other hand, decisions teachers make that are intrinsic to the learning process need not be determined by instrumental questions arising from external assessment procedures. There is much more emphasis now on negotiated curricula; and teachers really do have a great deal more freedom to choose the design of their courses than they might think.

Any strategy, yours or the students', may be more or less successful. Few people consciously decide how they are going to learn, they just set off, as unprepared hikers do; they put on a hat and go out the door. Because their chosen learning strategy is inappropriate to the intended outcomes, they run into trouble. Observe the students in your classes who have not grasped the nature of a task they are asked to do; if they thought about it they could do it more efficiently – or if you gave them better guidance. Discovery learning can be exciting and effective in terms of motivation, but has to be managed to ensure that it is effective in what is 'discovered'. The important questions about a learning strategy are:

- Does it work? Will it work?
- Is it the most effective way of learning this?
- Is it efficient in the expenditure of time and effort?
- Are there other strategies? Would they be more effective?

PLAY THE GAME

Here is a game, a teaching strategy used in management training. Play the Murder Game to see contrasting learning strategies in action. The same patterns emerge whenever groups play this game. They won't work for you because you will have read this description first!

Murder game (bottom-up/top-down)

It is a leaderless game. That is important. Everyone in the group has equal responsibility for solving the mystery and deciding the methodology for doing so. No information is given that is not on the cards dealt out. No instructions are given. The group has to make up its own rules of play. The purpose of the game is to extract information about a murder in a country house: this is something most people feel comfortable with. Information ('clues') is printed on individual cards. The cards are shuffled and dealt to the participants, so that each has a fairly even number of 'clues', but each 'set' is completely random with apparently unrelated facts.

Two observers make notes on what occurs: how the group sets about it, what individuals do, what they decide, how the mystery is eventually solved or not. The final debrief is concerned with the strategies of learning each group has chosen.

People usually try a **'bottom-up'** strategy first: 'Let's have everyone read out what's on the cards they have, I'll start.' 'Let's put the cards on the table so that we can see all the information.' It soon becomes impossible; there is too much information to take in, with no shape or order. There is a moment of hilarity or panic.

Someone will probably suggest that they should look for patterns. 'I've got something about a knife on the floor. Has anyone got anything to add to that?' This looks promising, and confidence rises. Eventually, someone is likely to suggest they write down specific questions and then see who has information to answer them: who was killed? when? where? what with? are there red herrings? It begins to look and feel like business.

It will be successful if they identify helpful questions. This is called a **'top-down'** strategy, it starts with questions: Who has any information about the weapon, the room, the time? It is proactive. It imposes a logic, a structure and a pattern on the proceedings, which pays off immediately. All is quickly revealed.

In the debrief, it is important to ensure that people talk about their feelings as well as lack of comprehension. How did it feel to be frustrated? to be overwhelmed with information you could not use or make sense of? How did it feel 'when light began to dawn'? How did they reach their result? Was it by little steps, or did it suddenly all 'fall into place', like solving a jigsaw puzzle?

The game is 'experiential', about 'feeling it'. We have to feel these things if we are to know how it frequently is for our students, many of whom 'experience' frustration, bafflement, despair at what seems to them to be totally incomprehensible in what they are trying to do.

Pattern recognition

The human brain is enormously gifted in recognising patterns. The above game was won by doing it. Pattern learning and recognition is the principal brain function in all learning. Social interactions, language of all kinds, art and music, business, all our life experiences depend on our astonishing ability to discriminate the most minute differences in patterns. A sheep farmer has little difficulty knowing individual sheep. Out of a million faces you will easily recognise one you know, even if that person has changed in many ways with age or injury.

How do we do it? No one knows, but this learning is unstoppable and totally effective; we do it easily without trying. We learn new patterns to come to terms with every new experience. It is a powerful tool, therefore, to use in teaching. As a learning strategy, there are a myriad applications.

One is in learning to spell in English, which is notoriously maverick in its use of Latin, Greek or other languages, so that we cannot be certain of the spelling of words by derivation. Monosyllables from Anglo-Saxon are spelled as they were spoken centuries ago, and still are in Lincolnshire or London: 'boat' pronounced 'bo-at', 'pea' pronounced 'pe-a', 'say' pronounced 'sa-ee', as exploited by G.B. Shaw in *Pygmalion*, who advocated spelling 'fish' 'ghoti' as in 'tou*gh* *wo*men in posi*ti*ons of power'. Listen to any regional UK accent or the English speech preserved in the Appalachians in the USA to 'hear' why English words are spelled as they are. But spelling is no longer phonetic. Words are not said as they are spelled or vice versa. People learn to spell by pattern recognition, just as they learn to drive a car and cope with traffic conditions and a million other activities by recognising repetitive features. They don't have to think about it. If you try to remember the things you do by recognising patterns, there are so many that you will quickly give up.

Patterns that are predictable as related phenomena (things we see or hear) are labelled 'rules' and explained as cause and effect. Grammarians discover 'rules' in language use, though in English the 'rules' are instantly 'broken'. Consider any 'rules' for spelling, grammar or phonetic sound of letters of the alphabet. How do you pronounce 'a' or 'i' or 'ei' or 'ough'? Or homophones, pronounced the same way but spelled differently: "*None of your rough stuff here!*"; and allophones, words spelled the same but pronounced differently: 'I *have* a *shave* in the *morning*'. At a London station my daughter was asked by an Australian, '*Does this train go to LoogaBorooga?*' (Loughborough). Why do we say it that way?

In the end, we recognise patterns according to their use. Pattern recognition is fundamental; is it 'a *desk*' or 'a *table*'? it depends on *use* not *design*. *We fast, go fast, make fast*: it is clear that we distinguish nouns, verbs, adjectives, adverbs by use not form; we easily turn nouns into verbs, verbs to nouns: '*to dial*', or '*make-up*'. The more patterns we can discern, the more words we need; the more words we have, the more we discriminate patterns.

Language is of fundamental importance to all learning. But language is not words alone. We recognise subtleties in body language, facial expression, eye movement, tones of voice, sensitivity to space, speed of utterance and movement, everything: aggression, love, fear and delight. They are the same in human societies everywhere on earth. All constitute a universal language. Social interactions depend on recognising subtle patterns. We are not alone, it is the reason gorillas have large brains.

Holistic learning as in theatre

I have strongly advocated in this book learning by doing it, learning as a holistic experience in which *the whole person is engaged* and in which the experience is learned as a whole, as in the learning of lines in a play, an approach called *somatic* (through the body as against with the mind only).

I have found it is helpful to imagine classroom interactions also as theatre. If we think of the room as a stage, we should design the environment to facilitate the activity that is to take place there with an awareness of the effects of spatial relationships and interactions between the characters. It is a way of distancing oneself from the experience also, to view it as others might see it. Learning to teach is a holistic learning experience – as intended in this book starting with peer-teaching.

Research last century analysed the great variety of ways meaning is conveyed. Body language, movement, spatial relationships, as visualised on the stage, are all *signifiers* in the jargon of *semiotics* (the study of how meaning is conveyed/read – in signs, signals and actions as against words), as are the props, costumes and stage settings. All must work together to make the same statements. In rehearsal, text is learned as part of the action so that all become integrated: to *feel natural* to the actors. John Barton at the RSC asks his actors to *discover* the words *as if they are expressing their own immediate thoughts*. I have found in directing Shakespeare that students understand the meaning of what they are saying only by expressing it as action, gesture and voice and spatial relationships, distance and physical contact. They must go for the meaning *expressed in all they do*, and the verse takes care of itself. It becomes easier once they put on costumes and make-up: *On with the motley!*

Adopting *persona* (another *being* originally as a *mask*) is the most primitive of human actions as witnessed universally in traditional dances and rituals from the earliest cave wall paintings; in which the whole person changes. Training in all areas of human activity, especially in our specialist world, is conducted in uniforms or 'appropriate dress', as in the military, nurses, policemen, workshops, and a myriad other areas, including the business suit, shirt and tie. Dress becomes *associated* with behaviour as a whole, a form of *operant conditioning* (see 'Behaviourism' on pages 299ff). The environment is also designed to reinforce the activity required there – offices and classrooms as much as workshops.

Behaviourism originally derived from the conditioning of higher mammals like dogs and rats. The whole behaviour can be *conditioned*, so that when a horse is saddled or wears a harness it *knows* what to do and does it. Highly intelligent dogs can be trained by cues such as a harness to adopt human behaviour – as a guide dog, say, to respond to needs, even to summon help by hitting an alarm button if their 'charge' is ill. Take off the harness and the horse or dog reverts immediately to their natural behaviour.

Humans change their clothes. People in all walks of life adopt several roles, each recognisable by a pattern of behaviour and speech, exhibited in dress and appearance. Everyone 'makes up' (male and female), 'dresses up', chooses the persona they want to present before they go out in the morning and change it as occasion demands during the day. It is party with our pattern recognition in all we do. Theatrical myth has it that actors start with Stanislavsky's *cerebral* approach: an actor has *to be*, has to avoid *mimesis*, has to think the thoughts and feel the emotions of his character, to live that life off-stage and on, to bring on-stage that person's off-stage experiences. It is an approach satirised in *Chorus Line* Morales' song: *I had to feel the motion … be a sports car … be an ice-cream cone. But I felt nothing!!* It is a psychological fact that the more you concentrate on *how* to do a thing, the harder it is to do it. Even walking becomes unnatural on or off stage. We are reminded of Hamlet's advice to the Players: '*Let nature be your teacher.*'

Stanislavsky himself found that a cerebral approach raises the wrong kind of self-awareness and it can happen in teacher training. Actors become false, stilted on stage. He found that it was more effective to let *the body* express the character's emotions and intentions. The *somatic* approach enables actors to discover the emotions in themselves. Thus make-up and costume have more power to create a new *persona* than cerebration, as children know who play soldiers, nurses, policemen.

Children learn a second language more effectively if they use it just as they learned their first, if they explore social interactions as a whole in an environment which simulates the context in which the language is spoken.

Chanting/singing under trees!

Many strategies in teaching make use of pattern recognition because it is much better to work the way the brain works. One form of pattern peculiarly human is music, a function of a different part of the brain from speech, since many people when their speech and understanding of speech is atrophied by a stroke can still sing all the words and tunes of songs they have learned, particularly when young. The fact that the brain retains musical patterns easily is the reason story-telling originated as a holistic drama expressed in words, singing and dancing universally in human groups. By 1970 the most innovative theatre director last century, Peter Brook, was starting with *sound* and *rhythm*: his actors had to *sing* a Shakespeare text. Poetry is tens of thousands years old, its forms derived from dancing and singing. Traditional story-telling and all religious books were originally in the form of poetry: they were chanted to be learned by heart thousands of years before writing was invented, and are still learned by ear today by many who cannot read. Folk tales and songs disappeared at the end of the nineteenth century in Europe with the advance of literacy.

Latin chants and the litany, hymns in the Lutheran, Anglican and Methodist churches all serve the same purpose. In traditional cultures, priests, who are not distinguished from poets, spend 20 years memorising with perfect accuracy of recall tens of thousands of verses by singing. Anglicans too learn The Lord's Prayer, the Responses and Creed by chanting, and it is unusual for any to ask or any to explain what they mean. In Moslem countries, Mullah schools teach children the Q'uran sitting under trees swaying backwards and forwards chanting passages over and over until they are embedded. In English schools multiplication tables were learned as chants till 'fixed' for a lifetime. It suggests one way of learning mathematical and scientific formulae, but examiners might be a little surprised if they were chanted in an exam.

Chanting (French for singing) must be among the oldest strategy for learning in every society in the world. The ability to learn by heart a play by Shakespeare, and even a play in Ancient Greek by Sophocles, as is still done in a few English schools, is explained by the fact that the actors are learning verses, musical sounds as patterns. But it is made much easier by learning with the whole body, *somatic* learning. Language which is integral with gesture, movement, intention, emotion, voice, is embedded. That which is simply words vanishes unless it is chanted. In the former, the words are part of a pattern of behaviour, in the latter there is no pattern to learn without sound.

Rote-learning

Chanting is a form of rote-learning. The children who learn the Q'uran this way, Catholics who learn Latin hymns, many Anglicans and Methodists who sing English hymns, give little thought to meaning. They don't know what the words mean in many cases. The English Church insists on children reciting a Catechism if they wish to be admitted to the Church. Questions and right answers are learned by rote, often as a chant. The fact that the children do not understand any of it is irrelevant.

Rote-learning is very powerful and lasting, as all who learned their Tables will affirm. So, what is wrong with it, one might ask, if it is effective? Teachers of science and maths used to be content if students remembered and could apply formulae. But today, it is felt much more important for students to have an insight into what the formulae represent. Unfortunately, for many students who in the past could do calculations and apply formulae blindly but successfully, achieving insight inhibits their ability to do these things well or quickly, if at all.

It hardly matters, perhaps, as being able to use a calculator is a sensible way out. One problem is that students can no longer spot when the calculator comes up with an impossible answer. A physics teacher told of a student who was happy with his result when he had discovered that the circumference of the earth was 1.5 metres! Fifteen years ago in Japan, all answers arrived at using a calculator were checked on an abacus to ensure they were correct!

Kanji strokes/look and say

In Japan, 'worpro' in computers (Japanese language shortens words like this) offers Chinese characters or 'kanji' for each phonetic input on the keyboard; the writer chooses the right one for the text. Tens of thousands of homophones in Japanese, spoken syllables with exactly the same sound, can be written each by up to a dozen kanji, the meaning determined by the kanji and not by the sound. Japanese have to visualise spoken words to really understand their meaning, and they often get it wrong. You cannot conduct business by telephone in Japan; it is much safer to do it by fax.

The kanji are recognised by their pattern of strokes. They are taught by repetitive practice of drawing each one as strokes, which have to be done in a patterned sequence in one way only to embed learning. A huge amount of time in Japanese schools is required for this practice. But today, the use of 'worpro' makes writing kanji unnecessary, the skills disappear rapidly. All that remains is recognition. Chinese characters are in fact constructed of elements which contribute either meaning or the phonetic sound. To use a kanji dictionary you need to know some of these elements, but they are not taught. Teaching is simply embedding patterns. But it is hardly different from teaching reading in our alphabet, where the learner is simply required to recognise a word and is not shown how it is made up of elements that give it meaning. In one extreme case, it used to be a policy to teach words to infants by 'look and say', where words on flash cards had to be recognised and spoken by the infants. This was not ineffective rote-learning, but it quickly taxed the memory capacity of the children. And they had no way of correcting errors they made, nor of making the sound of new words as they met them. With no teacher they were lost. It was not a good way to make for independent learning.

In some strategies to learn a foreign language emphasis is placed on patterning. Many patterns of sentences receive repetitive practice using substitute words as nouns, verbs, adjectives and so on. It is tedious but not ineffective for embedding patterns. The application of these patterns to interactions using creative speech, however, demonstrates that much of the learning is not easily transferable.

Some language learning consists of memorising pages of vocabulary for tests as 'look and say'. This technique tends to assume a one-to-one equivalence between the learners' native tongue and the target language. In practice, words have *uses* not just *meanings*, and so the words are likely to be more often misused than meaningful in context, indeed, will have a comic effect. But that is considered to be a second step to the acquisition of vocabulary by simple recognition. A group of English choir boys in Germany were shown a huge grandfather clock and told, '*This is Goethe's watch.*' I heard someone remark, '*I see no reason why I should be kept at your convenience.*' The strategy is not ineffective in words written as Chinese characters, but it requires 'hearing' each word pronounced as you look at its kanji group. In the primary school use of 'look and say', the same was true. As with the Midland town above, names of Japanese towns and people have to be spoken before even a native Japanese knows how to pronounce the kanji.

Subliminal messages

Other strategies, particularly for learning foreign languages, have been advocated. At another extreme is use of subliminal suggestion. It is argued, it is demonstrably true, that most people learn best when they do not know they are learning, when they are not trying to learn, when they are doing something or looking at something or when they are playing, having fun. Watch how quickly a child will learn to use a computer game. We learn all the time, especially when we don't think about it. We learn when we are looking out of the window in a train or bus. So why not use this as a strategy?

Another related approach is the use of mnemonics to pattern recall, as used in Case Study 11 of Vivienne's class. The learning of names is unconsciously fixed by recalling some unconnected idea as part of a game. There are many books devoted to such techniques.

Subliminal means between or behind the lines and refers to images flashed for a minimal time in a visual projection on a screen or on TV. The viewer does not 'see' the image consciously and yet it is perceived and stored by the brain; it can be recalled under hypnosis. The fact that the brain does this may be the explanation for amazing things 'recalled' under hypnosis, which have been 'explained' as memories carried over from a former earthly existence. One person, for example, who could 'read' a papyrus manuscript was eventually shown to have seen the papyrus momentarily in a museum looking over another person's shoulder.

As an extension of look and say, it is argued that flashing images and saying the word while the learner is in a vacant state of mind is effective in embedding the word. Wordsworth would agree in *To Daffodils*: '*When upon my couch I lie / In vacant or in pensive mood / They flash upon that inward eye / Which is the bliss of solitude.*' It is certainly true that for most of the things we remember, we cannot say when or how we learned them. Perhaps, they did just flash by the eye as on a train journey.

In a strategy based on learning by non-attention, a learner is invited to relax, to leave the mind vacant of thought. Images are then flashed on a screen together with cue sounds or words; the learner is later asked to recall the learning by a similar patterning.

I have advocated above the need for a learner to 'pay attention' in order to learn; and for the teacher to ensure that the learners are 'paying attention' when s/he wants them to hear or see what s/he is teaching. Perhaps we should modify that. For learners to *know* they are learning, to do it consciously and be able to recall it, they need to be paying attention. Clearly, learning will happen whatever we do. The trouble is that it is likely to have no pattern, no structure, and be impossible to recall unless we are in fact conscious of doing it. Students learn in all classes, but very often not what the teacher had meant them to learn. It does not mean that all such learning cannot be integrated, it can by using it to bring things into focus later. If we fail to do that, we will probably fail to make sense of most of the learning we do pay attention to.

Other strategies

Here are a number of consciously chosen teaching and learning strategies to think about. The brief summaries here are of approaches to learning that, in practice, involve a great deal of thought.

Closed and open strategies

By 'closed' we mean that the learning outcomes are predictable, there is little room for creativity by the learner. By 'open' that outcomes are unpredictable, the process is dynamic, changing with time. Strategies may be more or less open, allow of more or less control of goals and processes. 'Indoctrination' and 'Travelling hopefully' are at opposite ends of the continuum from total control by a teacher to no control. The latter is an open strategy, unpredictable in its processes and learning outcomes. Indoctrination is a closed strategy; all decisions are made by the instructor; every aspect is to be predicted, content, process and outcomes. Some strategies employ 'conditioning' as a means of controlling and 'shaping' learning, based on a teaching theory known as 'Behaviourism'.

In Part 3, I explore arguments for adopting particular approaches; and I discuss theorists who have researched and advocated them. Behaviourists believe in 'closed' programmes of 'instruction', teacher-centred in all decision-making with predictable learning outcomes and structured programmes to achieve them; assessment is the prerogative of instructors, who uses it to 'shape' student learning. It is the most influential theory in American education where teachers are all instructors and classes are mostly teacher-centred. Cognitive philosophers, those who are concerned with 'thinking' processes, advocate 'open', dynamic, student-centred learning.

Deductive/inductive

Deductive approaches to learning/teaching are closed strategies. In them rules and concepts are stated that lead to predictable results. Once the initial parameters are stated, all else follows, as in 2 + 2 is 4. There is little room for creativity. Even in student-centred maths workshops, students must get right answers by correct methods. Nor is it any good trying to beat or out-guess a computer program. You must learn to use it 'the right way' first before you can do anything creative with it.

Inductive strategies are open: 'we're going to mess about in this area for a bit to see what we can discover'. They are about generating questions and problem-solving. Answers lead only to more and better questions. Discovery learning is of this kind; it is a more exciting and stimulating approach to the learning of science than traditional instruction. But students must 'discover' right answers and correct formulae or they will fail to learn 'science'. In almost all cases, discovery learning has to be 'managed' to avoid reinventing the wheel or designing a bicycle with five wheels; or if you 'discover' that the circumference of the earth is 1.5 metres!

Exploring/discovery learning

Exploring as a learning activity is fundamental to all higher life forms; to use it as a learning strategy requires a great deal of planning and organisation. Discovery learning has the excitement and fun of exploring, but it is much better, much more successful if we know what we are looking for or what we are hoping to find or to achieve, rather than rely on serendipity. In controlled situations with proper feedback, very exciting things can happen.

We should make learning fun. In the early years of schooling, learning through play is very effective. Discovery learning, however, is not play. The less control teachers have of the process, the more carefully the activities need to be designed to ensure more comes out of it than fun. Many projects labelled 'discovery learning' are serious, in a science laboratory for example. They have to be carefully 'managed'.

Travelling hopefully

This is the strategy most people use most of the time: it is mainly trial and error learning. It is how we deal with life, a Micawberish optimism that 'something will turn up'. It is painful and ineffective, an inefficient way of learning. No doubt, the mountain walkers above learned what not to do, about dangers, about survival, but possibly at the cost of deciding never to do it again. Painful experiences are memorable but can be demotivating. To keep going, you have to really want to know.

In acquiring skills, 'getting the feel of it' by trying, failing, trying again is unavoidable; maybe it is the only way to learn to ride a bicycle or to skate on ice. But learning is much easier, certainly much easier to assess, if given shape and structure; and made much more effective by use of feedback in achieving identified goals. Teachers are not usually dealing with 'real life' learning. After all, what are teachers for? They can at the very least provide a model of how to skate or how to ride a bicycle or whatever.

Indoctrination

Institutions such as the army, the church, paramilitary organisations, and very many others, ensure that trainees, members, learn the right answers, the accepted codes, obedience and discipline. Many will argue that these are the true aims of education. To challenge or even question what is taught is strongly discouraged, usually suppressed by punishments. Well-tried techniques exist to indoctrinate learners to achieve very high pass rates in tests of acquired 'knowledge' and 'skills'. Even when the methodology of teaching appears to be inductive, it can still be part of an indoctrination strategy, as in Case Study 31 on page 251.

In FE, too, teachers may wish to avoid risks altogether, making all the decisions themselves, avoiding any challenge and discouraging independent thinking. Where demonstrable high standards of performance weigh heavily in importance, there is strong emphasis on using the right techniques and 'knowing' in the sense of being able to repeat right answers in tests. These are achieved by repetitive practice and rote-learning with little understanding. Many forms of training have used such strategies, but they have no concern to develop skills in problem-solving or using intelligence in decision-making. Which involving students more actively in the learning process to give them some 'ownership' is intended to promote.

Read Chapters 24 and 25 on Behaviourism and Neo-Behaviourism. Use of conditioning or structured linear programmes to embed instruction are sophisticated. In America many programs of instruction occur which can be described as Tell and Test.

Tell and test

I once said to an American friend that I had observed in America a tendency to use this approach. He said, "Yes, but it's like this. First, you tell 'em you're going to tell 'em – then you tell 'em – then you tell 'em you've told 'em – then you test 'em." This strategy appears to be most efficient in terms of test results, but testing dominates every aspect of the learning process. The whole business belongs to the instructor, the student has no ownership of learning whose purpose is purely instrumental: to pass tests to obtain a sufficient number of grades on a computer printout to be awarded a qualification. It appears to have little to do with 'education' as interpreted in the UK. Present emphasis on results as the principal measure of accountability seems to deny this. This strategy might seem to be little used in the UK until one thinks about what many teachers actually do with their classes.

Cram it all in

Students faced with examinations which are essentially memory-testing frequently adopt the strategy of 'memorise it, don't try to understand it – that will come later if at all'. Teachers succumb to it in despair at the size of syllabuses they and their students have 'to cover'. I have known some students memorise a textbook in Human Biology and retain it long enough to gain a good pass in an external exam, and the next day be unable to remember any of it. It was in fact a standard practice in schools for GCE exams, one of the arguments for adopting a different approach in GCSE where students have to show their ability to apply knowledge.

Beat the system

Examination practice is often a strategy for beating the system. In fact, such practice tends to take more time than learning anything else. In Japan, there are thousands of Juku, private schools, which charge high fees to 'train' students to pass university entrance exams. Such schools start even before infant school entered at age 6; infants have to pass entrance tests in Japan. The school a child starts at will determine the next school and the next; getting kids through entrance exams at all changes of school is a hugely profitable business and very expensive for parents.

Any system based on selection and/or grades achieved on exams for advancement is bound to generate an exam-busting industry. Beating the system is not about understanding content or learning skills, it is about getting a good grade. Even in America, the first question a teacher will be asked by students is, 'What do I have to do to get a C?' – to pass the course, because instructors do their own grading. Students often have no interest in the course or what they are supposed to be there to learn.

In the game of beating the external examiner in the UK, the most important part is question-spotting so that students can ignore everything except what is necessary to answer the questions they know are most likely to be asked. Teachers and students spend a great deal of effort analysing papers from previous examinations. It is a strategy that has paid off for the last 50 years or more.

Another is knowing what examiners are looking for. Pressure on examining boards in the last few years to publish criteria used by the examiners for grading has had the intended effect: candidates now achieve high pass rates and high grades, because they know exactly what they have to do to get them. The government and society watchers, employers and university dons, express horror at this success: 'Standards must be falling if so few actually fail, how can there be selection if everyone gets an A or a B?' What are the exams for? Clearly, they are perceived as principally a mechanism for selection. They used to serve as predictors of future ability to cope with demands of advanced courses or in employment. But this syndrome is not limited to external examining.

CASE STUDY 20

Sarah undertook a 'distance-learning' first degree course from an Australian university in Queensland in Asian Studies. One Unit required her to take courses in English Literature, which made clear to her the strategy she needed to pass all Units of the course. She was 38 years old, she loved reading, had read widely, had good understanding of British writers, and was prepared to write out of her experience in assignments she was given.

She had to buy reading materials and texts prepared by the university tutors and study them to write essay assignments on topics. She quickly discovered that the assignments, which appeared to be 'open' inviting a creative response, were actually 'closed' and intended merely to test whether she had read and could repeat what was in the papers written by the tutors. If she paraphrased and précised the papers, reflecting back to tutors what they had told her, she received A+ grades. If she wrote anything creative, or seemed to be challenging the opinion of a tutor, particularly if she produced evidence from any other reading, she received no more than a C grade.

The university had adopted an American model of Units, which were each graded according to their own criteria. Each Unit was tested by assignments plus exams to be taken at a designated centre. Grades for completed Units would, over time, cumulate, using a computer printout to certification for a degree.

Discussion

1 What is a university for?

2 What is a course? How is it defined?

3 What is 'distance-learning'?

4 What is the purpose of setting assignments in a distance-learning programme?

5 Are courses and assignments about acquiring content or about learning how to learn?

Comment

Obviously, it was in Sarah's best interest to conform and just reflect back to tutors what they had set down as right answers. The university appeared to have little interest in stimulating wider reading or in encouraging independent research or thinking. Unfortunately, many university courses appear to be like that. Even in subjects like literature, the assignments are about grading and testing accuracy in the acquisition of prepared materials. They are principally concerned with content, not learning how to learn. Tasks and assignments are designed as tests, not as a learning process. In many universities, even post-graduate courses are 'taught' courses for MA, and it is certainly not unknown for PhD.

Teach the textbook

'Teach the textbook' is the strategy for control of classroom instruction by administrators in all the educational institutions in the USA and in Japan, and it is frequently a practice in the UK. It used to be said that the Minister in Paris knew which page of every textbook every pupil in every school in France was reading on a particular day. A friend of mine who was an inspector of schools in Northern Nigeria when under British administration, told of visiting a village school to find it empty, with the teacher asleep under a tree. He proudly said that he had read the pages allocated for that day to the pupils and sent them home! He had done what he was told to do.

It is not unusual for teaching to become a boring regime doing pages of the book. Textbooks in every subject area are chosen by an institution, teachers have no 'ownership' of the teaching. The book is usually chosen as 'content' with little concern for 'process'. But even under such constraints, an inventive teacher can use the textbook as a resource – and design a process of learning around it, bringing in other resources and visual material, encouraging students to find out things for themselves in resource centres or libraries or on the Internet or by using their eyes.

Textbooks are often allowed to control the process of learning even when they are 'content' to be learned for tests as in most academic areas. Even if a book is designed as a process, as often in teaching a foreign language, and it is made supermarket-style 'come hither' by lots of colour pictures and amusing dialogues, the teacher who simply has students read the dialogues does them no service. It is possible to invent all kinds of learning activities around the book. All subjects lend themselves to inventive activity. The textbook is often used as preparation material or reading at home, which if thought necessary can be monitored by 'quizzes' in class.

No textbook writer can do other than guess the context where the books will be used and very often miss their target. Often they are selected by the institution for a 'wrong' reason, like prestige. But teachers have to be responsible for making sure that students can learn. If students find the textbook impossible, for whatever reason, it is irresponsible to go on using it without addressing the problems. Yet that is what very many teachers do.

There are still many single sex schools and colleges in Japan. Sheila taught English Conversation in a Women's University, where it was a requirement for all students regardless of their 'major'. Most had not enjoyed it at school and saw little point in doing it any more. The university was conscious of its prestige as an academic institution, so that the policy was to use American textbooks set at a level of competence way beyond where these students were. The books were intended for use in an American university for students learning English as a second language: that is, living in a society where English is spoken as the native language, where students could be assumed to hear and use English all the time. This was not so in Japan for these students. The topics assumed knowledge as if living in America.

Sheila complained that her students could not cope with such a book, to the astonishment it seemed of the Japanese faculty. She took the 'topics' from the book and designed her own material to cover them at a level of language and experience the students could understand. The students made progress in English and enjoyed the course. But the university was much better pleased with American teachers who simply 'taught the textbook', making students plough solidly through page after page, exercise on exercise, with little or no understanding.

John was seconded for a year to teach in a Community College in Florida. He was required to take a class called Humanities 2. Teachers in American colleges have freedom generally to run classes any way they please, but Administration wants to control Faculty. Their preferred way is to insist that all teach an approved textbook for identified classes like this one. At the end of each semester students must complete an evaluation sheet. The first question for John's class was: Did the teacher teach the textbook? The books are entirely 'content' for memorising. Few are concerned in any way with the process of learning to facilitate 'finding out'.

John's textbook was enormous. 'Content' covered briefly all aspects of Humanities from the Renaissance to the twentieth century across Europe and America: religious issues and conflicts, movements in art, styles and developments in painting, sculpture, architecture, music, musical developments and styles, political figures and movements, literature of all kinds, social changes, and so on and so on. It was impossible! The course was for a semester of 8 weeks with two 3-hour evening classes a week.

John complained to his head of school, but he was told, 'It's only a survey'. John wondered what for? was it the 'naming of parts'? American education values breadth, knowing a little about a lot even if it is only names, to a lot about a little on the English model. T.S. Eliot parodied this in The Love Song of J. Alfred Prufrock: 'About the room the women go Talking of Michelangelo'.

The group, 15 adults, was not motivated to learn. Most had not yet done Humanities 1, and those who had had hated it. It covered the earlier period from Ancient Egypt, Palestine, Greece and Rome, the mediaeval period in Europe and so on over the same range. All said they had to come to Humanities 2 to complete 'a requirement' to fill space for the required 24 credit hours; they would not be there otherwise.

What on earth could John do to make the experience tolerable, let alone exciting for them? He decided he would set them to read sections (small sections) of the textbook week by week. Class time was to be about stimulating their interest. He found a large store of colour slides of art for the whole period, and used them to focus on the way ideas developed over the centuries. Classes were planned with 'an input session', time for group work he assigned, for reports, and finally question and answer sessions. John also varied the input: some evenings he played recordings of music of a period or read passages from certain authors.

He divided them into three groups of five, as seminar groups, to research particular topics to report back first to their own seminar group, then to the whole class. He sent students to the library for research and agreed with staff there to help them. He insisted that they each produce a number of written reports to hand in over the semester.

The enthusiasm for the art slides, each showing no more than 45 minutes, and for the music was very marked. They enjoyed the chance to explore in the library, bringing back really interesting things to tell.

John did not, however, appreciate how novel all this was for them until he managed to upset one girl of about 25 who produced an exuberant essay on Renaissance sculpture, but illustrated it with Greek and Hellenistic statues, in particular the wonderful Laocoon that inspired Michelangelo. In his comment John pointed out that they were 1,500 years earlier than the Renaissance. She was so angry. She said, 'Look! This is the first time anyone has ever shown me pictures of art or anything. I just thought that statue was wonderful, I really did, and now you tell me I've got it all wrong! When I was at school we had to learn from a book for tests. And we did the same thing over and over – for three years we started with Christopher Columbus.' That is what they had expected to happen in this class.

At the end of the session, the evaluation expressed how much they had enjoyed researching in the library and finding out so many interesting things. What they had discovered mattered much less than the pleasure and excitement of doing it, bringing it back and sharing it with others.

Discussion

1 What does 'teach the textbook' mean?

2 Some teachers allow the textbook to run their class. Why do you think they do that?

3 What are the dangers of handing over the decision-making to a textbook?

4 What did John do to change the textbook into a resource to be used with other resources?

5 What was the advantage of doing that?

6 How would you create a variety of experience for long evening classes of two or three hours?

7 What would you do to ensure that students enjoyed the learning – that learning was fun?

Comment

Three hours in an evening twice a week, even two hours once a week, can seem an awful long time. It is essential to bring in as much variety as you sensibly can. John planned 5 minutes of questions to link to previous classes, 45 minutes input with varied visual or audio stimuli, 90 minutes seminar sharing, including time each week in the library or resource centre, 30 minutes class sharing for consolidation. Each week there was a programme for individual reading of sections of the textbook and research for seminar projects and writing-up. There was far too little time each week. John did not actually teach the textbook, but the students gave a very positive evaluation.

Laboratories for learning

There has been a tremendous investment in 'laboratories' (work places) for participative activity by students. They used to be confined to science subjects, where it was realised early that theory had to be seen in action. In the past, these were more often used for demonstration by the teacher than as places of discovery by students. A teacher would demonstrate an 'experiment', students would repeat it. For the last 40 years teachers have set up structured experiments in kits, for individuals and groups to learn both how to use the equipment and to use it for discovery, some 'open' in terms of what is to be found.

Now laboratories exist in all areas, like physical training laboratories for theoretical insight to sports, language labs expensively equipped with sophisticated interactive work-stations. Others under different labels: workshops for maths, literacy, numeracy; resource centres; computer bases to 'drop into'; media centres with TV cameras, audio equipment and control panels; drama studios with stage boxes, projectors and lighting; music studios equipped with electric keyboards and computers as well as traditional instruments; photographic, painting, sculpture studios and pottery workshops. All are laboratories to encourage exploration, self-awareness, confidence, interactions. Many are also meant to simulate professional facilities.

The strategy is learning as a 'holistic' experience, to explore with one's whole body and mind and to integrate (make into a whole) what is otherwise learned as unconnected bits. It is not new. No one ever learned to swim in a classroom, most schools used swimming pools. Most had playing fields, running tracks or gymnasia. What is new is technology that makes possible many many things hardly dreamt of before, but which are now more and more affordable and taken for granted. Video cameras are small, versatile and cheap, as are printers and scanners, laptop computers that may be linked to a radio hub to be used anywhere in a resource centre. 'Palm' size computers can be used to make notes on the move, as can tiny voice recorders. People access the Internet on mobile phones. My book is going out of date as I write.

Learning is fun and exciting. The interaction of teacher and students is what makes strategic resources like these work well. Teachers need to develop different skills. Equally, students cannot be expected to just walk in and use the resources without proper training and support.

Work simulation

Nor is there anything new in work simulation, it was ever a traditional strategy in vocational training in workshops, equipped as far as possible with the latest machines and facilities found in real working environments; but usually with a greater variety of machines to enable students to acquire techniques, insights and skills to enrich what happened at their places of work. It was far from cheap to buy all the latest machines, even more so when they became computerised. Office environments were also simulated and often had to be re-equipped at considerable cost to keep up with technological changes.

Up-to-date machines had to be matched by up-to-date teachers. Replacing type-writers with computers should not mean replacing staff. Teachers must up-date their own knowledge and skills as constantly as doctors do. You cannot teach what you do not know or cannot do. Nor is it unusual to find a student in your class these days who is more experienced, more skilful, than you are.

Generally speaking, work simulations in workshops tend to be serious stuff, with worksheets and schedules and carefully designed parameters. After all, it is supposed to be 'real'. Many teachers, however, do bring excitement and even fun into the activities by inventive, creative project work.

Interactive and group-based projects

It is normal human behaviour, as social animals, to produce better results when they work effectively in groups. In addition to the stimulus of competition, there is also a richness in the experience and expertise of the group members. This is an invaluable resource that should be exploited by the group and by teachers.

Generating and sharing ideas are important in problem-solving, but control of group activities and organising them require special skills. I have advocated use of this strategy for the development of interpersonal skills and the enrichment it can promote.

Competing groups

This strategy is frequently used in business, on playing fields, even on the factory floor. Many games used in education and training programmes are of this kind. Properly managed, they generate energy and motivation, but when badly handled they can destroy good working relationships. The use of games is discussed on pages 197–201. All the greatest human achievements have come about through competition, when creative people challenge each other, as in Athens in the fifth century BC or the Renaissance in Italy in the fourteenth and fifteenth centuries, or in Europe, Japan, China and America today.

Problem-solving

Challenging students with problems to solve is a well-established procedure in maths and science. It is integral to understanding in all subject areas where theory has practical application. Thinking through a problem to a solution is an effective way of learning and can lead to insight. It can be exciting, but it can be frustrating. It will expose elements of theory or principles that have not yet been grasped, and it will identify what still needs to be discovered and learned. The strategy can be used most effectively in group work as well as for individual projects.

Research and report back

This strategy is used effectively with students who are well motivated and work without supervision. Clearly, they have to develop the skills and expertise needed to find information for themselves. If individuals report back to a group to share what they have discovered it is valuable for enlarging the information base of the group. It encourages students to take responsibility for their own learning.

The strategy cannot be used without a great deal of preparation by the teacher both to ensure that students have the necessary skills and training, and that there are appropriate resources – which means working with staff in resource centres or wherever students will be looking for information.

Teaching as learning

One of the most effective strategies for learning is to have students teach others, what you are doing now. You have to learn it to teach it. You discover quickly how much you do not know, the gaps in your understanding, what you have to find out and quickly. You frame 'information' into language and forms you are familiar with and which students will understand. Doing so shapes it and integrates it to your own structure, your insight and understanding. To teach skills you have to rethink what you do and how you do it. Students will challenge the teacher and provide feedback from which to learn more.

Teams

One effect of a strategy of learning that involves working in a team, or competition between teams, is that it produces a lasting effect on social behaviour as an adult, so long as one can avoid the effect of 'stardom'. The way it is used is as important as the approach itself. One can see it in two cultures that are both committed to the team and the group, Japan and Australia.

In Japan, the team is of prime importance especially in companies. Individuals do not expect and do not receive rewards for individual contributions to the over-all achievement of the company; key workers live in what for Europeans are poor conditions, with few personal incentives but a heavy expectation of commitment of time to group, usually single sex activities in and after working hours. Advancement and promotion is on length of service, not talent or merit. Younger doctors in famous teaching hospitals, who have an international reputation and have studied abroad, must wait patiently in departments for many years for dead men's shoes, for promotion or status. The disadvantages of any apparent group disloyalty means that there is little voluntary movement to other hospitals to look for promotion. The same applies to all institutions and companies. Change is painful and slow.

Conformity to group decision-making affects all levels in society. One effect is an apparent inability to make decisions at all, which shows itself where decisions matter, such as driving in cities; and an inability to 'put yourself in the other bloke's shoes'. You can watch the way drivers react to other cars, going head on into situations that with just a little thought or just a little feeling for what it is like for the other driver they would avoid. The teams, however, prosper enormously well.

There can be few countries so committed to team games and sports, to competition and to do your best for the group than Australia; the facilities for sports are astonishing. And there are constant reminders on TV about being proud to be Australian, of Australian achievements, that you live in the best country in the world. Everyone's 'a mate'. If you get on and you get rich, 'good on you!' The learning strategy adopted in the schools is, however, entirely centred on the individual, to discover and nurture each person's strengths rather than impose academic goals uniformly on all. It is about social responsibility and challenging one's own potential and talent, saying what you think and 'going for it'. Of course, there are misfits, antisocial elements and groups; freedom means that things can go the wrong way. But overall, individuals do 'go for it', and not at the expense of others. There is a high level of caring for others in Australia. But they say what they think and do it without animosity or fear. They are at the very opposite end in terms of social behaviour from the Japanese.

The way teams work can be seen also in the arts. If you watch a performance by an orchestra under Herbert Von Karajan, all the bows move in unison, the phrasing, tempi, dynamics are 'studied' and precise. German conservatoires of music turn out players who have been trained in the standard repertoire and can instantly join a professional orchestra. By contrast, Sir Thomas Armstrong, called Tommy by all, said that what he did was to hire the best players and let them play. Presumably, that is the policy of Chelsea, too. English conservatoires turn out players who are in demand because they are terrific at sight-reading and can play instinctively, listening carefully to what others are doing. I was once involved in a performance of Verdi's Requiem in the Festival Hall conducted by André Previn. The choir was trained by a choir master, the maestro had one afternoon rehearsal. This was remarkably short. He started movements, practised changes of tempi, some phrasing and dynamics and then said, "We'll leave the rest to the performance." Leave it to the excitement of the moment, to what the shared experience will evoke without trying to predict or constrain it.

I prefer to drink Australian wine because it is predictably good, as long as you choose good makers of course, and if you know where in Australia the better wines come from! Wine-making is a science in the new world vineyards. French wine-making is still an art; you have to take a chance when you buy and you may have to put up with the disappointments of mediocre wines, but you can experience from time to time an elixir of delight no science can match. The same is true of music. It is true of any creative activity where you 'get good players and just let them play', as long as they are ready to ensure that it is the team that gets the glory. A Japanese orchestra is astonishingly brilliant in team-playing, but it is rare for a performance to thrill.

STRATEGY AND YOUR LEARNING PROGRAMME

TASK 16

You must develop some overview of what you and your students are about: what the relationship is between your activity as teacher and theirs as learners.

1 Try to clarify for yourself what you consider the responsibilities and roles to be, theirs and yours.

2 How far are you willing to involve them in the decision-making?

3 What are the constraints?

4 How will you communicate with them to share your thinking?

5 What kind of learning/teaching strategy is most likely to help them achieve your learning goals?

6 How would you justify your choice of that particular strategy?

Design a learning/teaching programme for your student group. The strategy you choose will give it overall shape. This programme will clearly develop and change over time since it covers a series of teaching periods. Within it there has to be a variety of learning experiences to match the learning needs and goals of the students.

The performance criteria below are intended to outline what is good practice in such a design. The statements build on those in Part 1, but are to be understood to imply greater depth. Feedback from reflecting on your experience, especially if you use a variety of approaches or methods, will ensure that there is development both of the strategy and methodology throughout the programme. Lesson plans and evaluations with consequent rethinking, getting together of materials and resources, all cumulate into the Case Study of your learning.

Performance criteria

16.1 Students in the group are known in relation to their educational and/or employment background, personal learning goals and motivation.

16.2 There is shared perception of learning goals in the group and with the teacher, both overall and within each lesson.

16.3 Teaching sessions are planned and sequenced to meet specified and/or negotiated goals known to all. Links are clear. Students understand how the activities and sessions are intended to progress towards achievement of the overall learning goals.

16.4 There are clear links with prior learning, conscious and unconscious learning, in the process.

16.5 Where appropriate, the learning is consistent with requirements of external examining bodies.

16.6 Teaching methods and learning activities planned are appropriate to promote intended learning.

16.7 They are also appropriate for the students in terms of their background and ability.

16.8 Lessons will engage students in learning activities consistent with their readiness to learn.

16.9 Sufficient flexibility will allow for different pace and styles of learning for individual students.

16.10 Learning materials and aids designed/selected will be effective for the intended learning. Materials and aids will be of a presentable standard.

16.11 Assessment of the learning is clearly identified in planning sessions and activities and consistent with requirements of examining bodies.

16.12 There is evidence of critical evaluation of the effectiveness of the materials, the activities and the overall strategy in the learning programme.

DESIGNING AND IMPLEMENTING INDIVIDUAL LESSONS/SESSIONS

The good practice established in Part 1 should inform what you do. Each learning session requires a lesson plan to define teaching/learning activities, with appropriate resources for teacher and student. Links between sessions should be clear, what is planned is relevant and stimulating.

Because you will be using these sessions as the main substance of your Case Study, good variety in methods and approaches will ensure that you have wide experience to learn from. Nevertheless, it is of importance that they make sense to students, what they feel they are about, and not just to help you to gain experience.

You should make your own assessment of progress towards satisfying the performance criteria set out below, but also evaluate sessions with a mentor to match your view of what occurs with theirs. There should, therefore, be clear evidence. Your thinking as well as your teaching will develop and change through the teaching programme.

To summarise:

- plan and use a variety of approaches and methods
- evaluate what happens thoroughly and honestly.

Performance criteria

17.1 Each session addresses specified learning goals.

17.2 Teaching methods/techniques are appropriate to these goals and the characteristics of students.

17.3 Sufficient skill is demonstrated in using the chosen methods.

17.4 The duration, sequence, structure and content of each session is properly controlled.

17.5 The teaching/learning content and methods are consistent with examining board requirements.

17.6 Learning problems and opportunities for further learning are identified during the session.

17.7 The programme is sufficiently flexible and adapted to needs as they arise.

17.8 Learning and teaching aids are used effectively.

17.9 The health and safety of the students are assured.

17.10 Individuals and groups are managed effectively. Control of the learning is evident.

17.11 Learning is linked, consolidated and assessed.

17.12 Each session is properly evaluated.

Suggested reading

Belbin, R.M. *Management Teams: Why they Succeed or Fail*, Heinemann (London), 1981.

Berne, E. *Games People Play: Psychology of Human Relationships*, Grove Press (New York), 1964; Penguin (Harmondsworth), 1970.

Bligh, D., Jaques, D. and David W. *Seven Decisions When Teaching Students*, Intellect Books, 1981.

Brady, M. *What's Worth Teaching?* SUNY Press (New York), 1989.

Daines, J., Daines, C. and Graham, B. *Adult Learning; Adult Teaching*, Univ. of Nottingham, 1993.

Davies, I.K. *The Management of Learning*, McGraw-Hill (New York), 1971.

Goldner, B. *The Strategy of Creative Thinking*. Prentice-Hall (New Jersey), 1963.

Harkin, J., Turner, J. and Dawn, T. *Teaching Young Adults*, Routledge–Farmer, 2001.

Jacques, D. *Learning in Groups*, Kogan Page (London), 2nd edn, 1991.

Joseph R. *Stress-Free Teaching*, Kogan Page, 2000.

Moseley, D. *Helping With Learning Difficulties*, Open University Press (Milton Keynes), 1976.

Sotto, E. *When Teaching Becomes Learning: A Theory and Practice of Teaching*, Cassell (London), 1994.

Wisker, G. and Brown, S. (eds) *Enabling Student Learning: Systems and Strategies*, Kogan Page (London), 1996.

CHAPTER 16 | Teaching methodology and skills

The methodology from which teachers may choose ranges through a continuum, from total control by the teacher to total control by the individual student of his or her own learning.

Where, over this range, teachers choose methods in relation to retaining control depends on many factors, not least the teachers' confidence in their own ability or how far they feel able to trust their students. Teachers and students now have access to an array of new technology, including ICT, which it is hoped will improve the quality of learning. New technology changes the context within which the learning occurs, but on its own does not affect the interactions of teacher and students. It is essential to understand the principles of learning and teaching that inform its use. Over-reliance on ICT might confuse students and inhibit progress, if in McClure's famous phrase: *the medium is the message*. Figure 16.1 summarises the *teacher control – student control continuum*. In all of these, developing technology may be used to enhance the learning process.

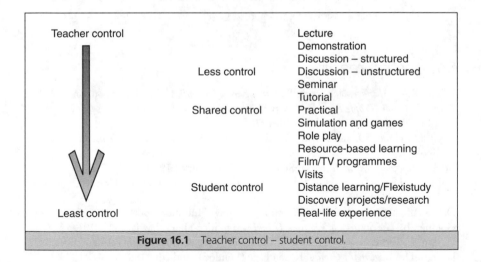

Teacher control		Lecture
		Demonstration
		Discussion – structured
	Less control	Discussion – unstructured
		Seminar
		Tutorial
	Shared control	Practical
		Simulation and games
		Role play
		Resource-based learning
		Film/TV programmes
		Visits
	Student control	Distance learning/Flexistudy
		Discovery projects/research
Least control		Real-life experience

Figure 16.1 Teacher control – student control.

Who makes the decisions? Who chooses content, learning materials, the learning goals? Who controls sequence or pace or interactions, the assessment procedures and criteria for success? Teacher or students? It depends on so many things:

- the teacher's ability to cope with demands that students may make if they make the decisions

- the students' ability to cope with the responsibility of choice if they are conditioned to a passive role in learning
- whether students can cope with being allowed a greater degree of control
- whether they have the necessary skills or how quickly they can acquire them
- whether they have sufficient motivation and commitment to the learning
- their sense of ownership of the decisions that are made.

Effectiveness depends on

- the teacher's making a conscious choice based on experience of the alternatives available
- the suitability of the chosen method for promoting the intended learning
- sufficient skill in exploiting the chosen methodology (both teacher and students)
- variety, both within learning sessions and in a full programme
- economy of effort relative to learning benefit, how hard or how straightforward it seems
- proper control and management of the learning process
- proper use of feedback, monitoring and flexibility within the programme
- assessment of the learning which informs both process and outcomes.

Appropriate methodology

No learning/teaching methodology makes any sense until teachers and students have *agreed learning goals*. No one should set out on a journey with absolutely no idea where s/he is going or of how s/he will get there. Hence, the need for negotiation of short-term and long-term goals, and structured programmes to achieve them, and not just with individuals. There is the same need within classes and for groups.

The appropriateness of chosen methods of teaching and learning is vital in attaining agreed goals. The method may hardly be 'chosen' at all. Teachers and students go for a familiar behaviour pattern without thinking it through. 'Old and tried' usually means 'easiest, least bother'.

Learning activities may be chosen with little thought to the skills, let alone understanding it requires to undertake them, with the result that many students become demotivated and confused.

Teachers cannot *assume that students can*:

- listen effectively
- take notes
- interpret graphs or symbolic forms used to present information
- explore resource bases or websites

nor that they have *acquired* the necessary

- study skills
- reading skills
- numeracy skills.

All the skills have to be acquired through experience and practice. In recognition of this, guidelines for teacher training/qualification require all teachers to have expertise in developing literacy and numeracy skills. You should check, where possible, your students' level of readiness in any of these fields. The range of skills required of students and teachers has increased with advances in ICT, while they also have to acquire all the new words and symbols that ICT constantly invents.

The problem of motivation to overcome barriers that occur in 'on-line' learning if 'on-line help' is not constantly available can be serious. But to ensure proper and timely response to student needs 'on-line' is expensive to resource, even though without support and instant help at a point of need, mature students especially are likely to give up trying. ICT is a frustrating experience much of the time. Learners need great perseverance initially to overcome this frustration.

Competence in teachers

All learning by teachers is experiential. Competence in the use of any methodology involves being able to choose intelligently, with the knowledge, experience and skill to make chosen methods work effectively.

This can only be acquired by experience. It also requires confidence, risk-taking, reflection on what actually happens, and the will to learn from that experience. But it also needs a supportive environment. Where the risks of failure are too great, everyone at whatever level will play safe.

Learning is the result of some risk-taking, from a baby's first exploration of its environment. In formal learning, risk-taking is controlled, usually by the teacher. How far control extends in Figure 16.1 depends on confidence in managing the process. Hence, the need for Managed Learning Experience (MLE) alongside Virtual Learning Experience (VLE) below. Methods of teaching and learning must be matched to what is to be learned. We need to ask: 'What are we/they setting out to learn?' 'What is the best way to do that?' Yet the conditions and constraints under which learning is to take place will affect both decisions and outcomes. It is hard to specify too closely what the performance criteria should be for success in the use of any method chosen by teachers.

The measure of success is how far the students achieve intended learning goals rather than an evaluation of the performance of the teacher. Nor is it easy to match one to the other. In all group-learning situations, all sorts of factors that are not within the control of the teacher affect success. Some of these factors are explored in case studies or elsewhere in this book and include:

- commitment to the experience by the students as a group, or as individuals
- reluctance or resistance if attendance on the course/programme is not voluntary
- conflicts between student groups or individuals, or disruptive behaviour by individuals

- unsuitable classroom design and equipment (often intended to promote an outmoded methodology)
- external pressures from employers or from examining bodies
- the weather, which affects mood and attitudes
- most importantly, established attitudes and ingrained traditional practices.

Teachers spend much of their time trying to overcome established patterns of behaviour in classes, which may be in conflict with the teachers' perception and intention of how the learning is to be achieved. With younger groups presently being encouraged to undertake FE courses alongside more adult learners (there is a growing cohort of 14–16 year olds in FE), even experienced teachers are becoming concerned with issues related to classroom management and to motivation of a kind they have not experienced before.

Improving performance of learners

Any method can be made more effective by careful preparation and thinking it through. None will be effective unless teachers and students have developed the necessary skills and are committed to the learning. Hence, the central importance in learning programmes of tutoring and monitoring.

Watch your students carefully to try to discover what is affecting the way they cope with the teaching/learning programme. Invite them to talk about their difficulties. Consultation can help to alleviate problems; and so you should talk also to those responsible for the provision.

Decisions about which method to use and what then happens must be carefully evaluated. This should include the students' perceptions, but how many teachers have the courage to ask students how they feel or react to what they as teachers are doing? Are they prepared to change what they do?

Teaching is as much a learning experience for the teacher as for the learner. Observing what happens, reflecting on what happens is a life-long learning process. A mentor matters: to share the experience with you as you progress in your own learning, to be your mirror.

Negotiated learning programmes

It is government policy to promote learning programmes negotiated individually with providers of education. Life-long learning on the American model is to be encouraged, with removal of barriers that prevent access to learning resources and opportunities.

Please compare the discussion in Chapter 18. Reasons are not hard to find:

- technological change in commerce, industry and society in general
- constant flux in working patterns and in employment
- constant need to up-date skills, to retrain, to rethink, to re-educate at all levels of society
- the need for institutions to provide a service which matches demand wherever it occurs and at times that suit the learners rather than the institution

- many colleges are run as businesses marketing their expertise through negotiated contracts.

All this impacts not least on those who must implement educational provision. The implications for teachers and institutions are profound. Institutions now have sophisticated guidance and monitoring programmes which are linked to computer profiling of individual students.

What has to be decided is a national method for accumulating credits. The American model ignores the process of learning in favour of administrative efficiency. Each semester a student must choose to attend a certain number of classes, for each of which s/he earns a 'credit' at a certain grade and this is recorded in a computer profile. Credits are gained in almost any order over any number of semesters. The number of credits alone determines the award of certification.

An advantage of such a system over the English all-or-nothing awards is that credit is given at least for what students do achieve; if they fail to complete a full NVQ, for example. However, loss of an integrated whole within a learning process is surely not an acceptable outcome for most students. Others might argue that it hardly differs from the present non-integrated curriculum leading to GCSE.

Negotiation requires:

- non-teaching skills in tutoring and mentorship
- a new view of one's role and a positive attitude to individual needs
- reallocation of resources
- relationships between learners and teachers different from those prevalent in the past
- new methods of assessment and the recording of achievement, of monitoring and progress-chasing.

The most obvious effect within institutions is investment in ICT and resource centres, development of on-site, out-reach, on-line and distance-learning programmes, websites and aggressive marketing. All imply a need for a new perception of roles. Teachers are much more obviously managers of learning.

This has been referred to as CAL, Computer Assisted Learning, which is a broad title to cover a wide range of ways in which learners interact with computers to access computer-based information which may in turn be linked to learning programs.

New developments are also known as VLE (Virtual Learning Environment) which is linked to MLE (Managed Learning Environment). Students access on-line interactive learning materials; and tutorial teams monitor and manage both access to the materials and individual student progress. The tutors can construct profiles of individual student interactions with the materials, and their levels of success in using them.

What appears to be missing is the contribution to the learning that students themselves can make. In addition to pathways and loops to facilitate acquisition of information and websites, there needs to be a mechanism for two-way or multi-way interactions, with tutors certainly, but also with groups of students working together on projects. Feedback on individual students, on their acquisition and processing of tutorial materials, should also help to refashion the on-line learning materials by using student input.

I remember visiting a school in Reading in the mid-1980s, long before the development of www, the World Wide Web. The school had invested heavily in Apple Mac computers, which at that time were the only 'user-friendly' models. Pupils of 15+ were using computers to work on group projects with counterparts in Canada and New Zealand. They shared ideas and information interactively by using electronic mail. It is much easier to do today, using Internet, databases, broadband and the rest, but those pupils achieved remarkably successful results with their much more limited facilities.

Discussion

1 What is the purpose of the Internet?

2 What creative ways of using e-mail and websites can you imagine?

3 What kind of projects would you like to share with others using this IT?

4 Who would you like to share with?

5 How should that be different from 'chat rooms'?

Do you know of others using the Internet in this way, perhaps notorious cases like chat rooms?

Comment

Why this innovative approach to use of Internet on-line learning, linked to projects, has not become mainstream practice in most schools and colleges is not easy to understand. Maybe, the educational image of the Internet is that it is about accessing information, treasure-seeking using search engines, and down-loading to databases. There is enormous investment in Resource Centres designed for this purpose. Students are encouraged to concentrate on individual project and presentation work. A one-way view of communication inhibits perception of the electronic medium as the means of promoting multi-way interactions between learners. The growth of 'chat shops' is evidence of the excitement and desire for this kind of activity. At present they have acquired an image of exploitation, however.

Providers of on-line courses spend hundreds of hours designing websites, writing information bases and programs, when there is excitement to be generated by involving students in development, research and problem-solving projects. There is no reason for it to be limited to institutions; it can be nationwide, even international. VLE/MLE is used by some institutions to monitor the work done by students on widely dispersed campuses.

Yet the experience of most teachers and institutions is that, however good distance-learning and interactive ICT materials are, or however much support students receive individually in accessing and using them, students respond much more effectively to group interactions. It is evident in their need to be able to access help-lines whenever they need them. We noted earlier how important it is in communication for people to 'read' each other in all forms of language; the most telling are non-verbal.

Developing technology will surely overcome this as the use of video-links via the Internet is set to become standard practice.

Institutions provide formal classes or workshops, and seminar or small group sharing/support. Students welcome the opportunity to enrol on structured courses, to attend classes and lectures. The institutions have recognised, however, that they must be prepared also to send teachers to out-reach venues for particular groups of students and to be flexible in all their provision. The implications for such teachers are discussed below. People react much better with people than they do with machines. ICT surely can be designed to facilitate VLE interactions. In contexts dealing with personal relationships, in environments such as teaching – indeed in most contexts – there is no substitute for personal interactions face-to-face.

Lectures

This is a general term covering a range of activities. Some lectures are very formal, given in spacious lecture theatres to large audiences at a safe distance, even requiring use of a microphone. The method is 'the norm' in universities worldwide, but it is demonstrably ineffective, perhaps most of the time. One major obstacle to student learning is that the responsibility for the learning lies entirely with the lecturer. The students have no part in decision-making, content, sequence, pace or structure, and so no ownership of the learning.

Lecturers usually start from where they are and not from where the students are. The lecturer must make untestable assumptions; that all these students are at the same point of readiness and skill, that all have the necessary foundation of knowledge and understanding, with appropriate vocabulary and knowledge of symbols, to follow the lecture.

Clearly, it must help if you check the accuracy of these assumptions as the lecture proceeds. Lecture-style, or didactic methodology, is necessary with ordinary classes. Teachers must use presentation techniques some of the time even in informal classes, for all lessons have input however brief (as it should be). And it does need to be done well. Peer-group lessons will turn into mini-lectures often enough because the skills involved do need practice.

Many teachers will point to the advantages of lecturing. It is economical in time and teacher costs. Teachers can deal with large amounts of content relatively quickly and efficiently, with many students. Lecturing allows for the efficient transmission of accurate and up-to-date information.

Lectures may be effective not just in ensuring that students acquire information, but in stimulating them to want to find out, to become active, enthusiastic learners rather than passive listeners taking little part in the learning process. But how can we ensure that happens? In some contexts, students may appear to be expected to do little more than occupy space for a statutory period of time. See Case Study 21.

Preparation

Know your stuff. You cannot teach what you do not know. You must always arrive at a class of any kind with much more material properly prepared than you expect to use. It helps if you exhibit enthusiasm and excitement about your subject. Too often, lecturing is a matter of routine. Technique is no substitute for enthusiasm. Take control of the learning environment. Move your students, chairs, tables, if they are not screwed to the floor, that is. Make it easier for them and for you. Test for visibility and acoustics. Impressions count. Practise. Appear – and be – organised. Take control. Lecturers need things to hand such as slides and handouts, in order and in sequence. You should give yourself a checklist.

Leave nothing to chance. Prepare properly. Set up any AVA beforehand. Test equipment, if you are relying on IT especially. A failure of equipment leaves the lecturer stranded, especially when there is no prepared back-up. IT is notoriously unreliable. Nothing is worse than the embarrassment of appearing incompetent and unable to find things such as handouts as and when you need them; showing slides upside down, for example, or in chaotic order or back to front. Computer-generated presentations, as long as they work, will ensure that such chaos is avoided, but too often it has the disadvantage of lack of flexibility.

Presentations need to allow for modification, loops and leaps when it becomes clear that that is what is needed if you realise that your students have not grasped some essentials, or lack assumed knowledge, or are unfamiliar with the symbols, vocabulary or data-presentation you are using.

The most obvious trend is for lecturers, whether on a large scale or within a classroom, to use Microsoft Powerpoint or similar presentations. Where in the past lecturers prepared projector slides or acetates for an overhead projector (OHP) or other visual presentations, now they use a computer linked to a projector, and perhaps to an interactive whiteboard.

But can the new technology improve the quality of the learning? Whatever we use, it has to be worth the considerable trouble involved in producing the material; and that is measured by how far it improves the learning process.

There are principles that all teachers should be aware of in relation to learning acquisition and barriers to communication. These apply equally to new technology and new presentation techniques, perhaps even more than to those now considered outdated. This is because there is a mystical belief that somehow ICT will solve all problems. Too often ICT distances the lecturer from the students.

Recent research in Australia and the UK has shown that in most cases use of Powerpoint has decreased the effectiveness of presentations in motivating students to want to learn, and has certainly done little to improve the learning curves of students. It is most effective when students themselves have used the technology for their own presentations and research.

Structure

Learning from lectures can be improved if we ensure that the students know the structure beforehand. One appropriate method is to give your students a handout with a key-word outline. It should include your learning goals and, if appropriate, your method of assessing the learning.

Tell them whether they are to take notes, and in what form. Note-taking can aid concentration, but it is hard to write and listen at the same time, and notes usually become chaotic. You may decide to provide a summary note-structure for them as a handout, with spaces for their own notes. IT has the great advantage of making printing simple. Note-taking is discussed on pages 225 and 229.

Bear in mind the students' attention span: about 15 minutes, and less if things are physically uncomfortable. Change the focus frequently with visual stimuli. Think two-way. Use opportunities for feedback at intervals, such as taking questions. This is often done at the end of the session, but I find it better to take questions as they arise. It wakes them up and involves them in the process, but as under the discussion of questions on pages 247ff, it is best to direct questions to named individuals.

Consolidate by recapping and making links between each section. It removes strain and gives students confidence that they do understand the information. Use your key-word structure to check you are not straying.

Another approach is to take questions at the beginning. Students who come to a lecture alert and ready will have their own questions. This is a good way of knowing where they are starting from, their mind-set. It can help you to direct your input more accurately to their needs. It is very easy for teachers to 'miss' their students partially or even completely. Your alerting structure must address questions, yours and theirs. Leave time at the end for a final consolidation. Link your input to what they must now do to ensure they use the new information. And at the beginning of the next lecture review this learning.

Personal contact and feedback

Watch and check that you can be heard, and that your visual aids can be seen by all. Ask people at the back; tell them to keep you up to the mark if they can't hear you. A good strong image is useful to grab attention, like the cartoon at the beginning of this book. Visual aids that cannot be seen are a distraction rather than an aid to learning. Pitch your voice low, but think of talking to the person furthest away. Talk slowly. Leave gaps for them to think about what you have said. Watch! If you see attention drifting, consolidate and recap. Consider 'noise' and distractions. Don't just ignore them and hope. Use personal names if at all possible. Humour helps too! Get your audience on your side.

Language register and use of symbols and vocabulary must be at a level of shared experience with the audience; if not, you must explain. See 'language registers' on pages 253.

Try to establish eye-contact with members of the group. Don't get trapped by the situation in the lecture-hall or the classroom. Move around when you can, even go behind them to teach from the back if you want them to concentrate on visual material you are showing so that you can see it as they do. Consider Case Study 24.

Enter a closer space zone. Become part of the group, discussing rather than talking at them, so that you can understand how it is for them, and be aware of any difficulties particular students may be having. Ask individuals (by name if possible) to explain things – for feedback. Encourage two-way exchange. This is not intended to be a sermon in a church. Distance matters. Lecturing can too easily create barriers.

> **REMEMBER!** … The students will be watching you much more than they will be listening to you.

What is your posture saying? What are your signals about personal space, physical distance? behind a desk? on a rostrum? in a pulpit? What are your messages about roles and relationships?

What have they learned? How will you know? How will they know? You need to consider what is appropriate in terms of assessing learning from any input in whatever form.

For it to become part of their knowledge structure they need to do something with it. They need to review the learning. What will they take away in order to do this? You should consider that carefully in your planning.

What follow up is needed to consolidate the learning?

Unless your lecture is a one-off occasion, it should have an effect on the learning process you have devised overall. What part is that? How does it link to other input or other learning activity? So, what is to happen after the input/lecture? What do your students need to take away to enable them to use the new material effectively? How will you link this learning to the next class?

Evaluation

All this forms part of the evaluation of the lecture. What should the evaluation be about? If only the teacher's performance is evaluated, what has that to do with student learning? This is the most important question. The answer includes the factors above, clearly. But most importantly, was it effective for its major purpose? How did it affect and accelerate the learning you intended? Or indeed, what unintended or unconscious learning occurred? How can you find out? The performance criteria for competence in using the lecture method are not different from those for other approaches and are set out in Task 17: Designing and implementing individual lessons/sessions.

Please read also the advice in Chapter 20 on interactions in classrooms.

Audio-visual aids

The chalkboard or whiteboard is your most valuable audio-visual aid, but it is often very badly used. A board is often replaced with an OHP or a flipchart of large sheets of white paper. The skills you need to use AVA effectively are discussed later under 'Barriers to communication'. The major purpose of AVA in the lecture room or the classroom is to focus attention. If you switch on a projector of any kind, attention is diverted from you to the screen. It helps because 70% of what we learn is with our eyes. It also provides variety and regenerates interest, for the 'attention span' of students is normally no more than 15 minutes. But this is obviously self-defeating if the projector or OHP is left on. We must use it only when it is needed, otherwise it is 'noise'. Students need to concentrate on the teacher when s/he wishes to engage in two-way exchange.

Projected material, however well designed, is likely to become less effective the longer it is used. Variety of experience for the students will include a mixture of such material and other forms of presentation, with question and answer and other interactions with the lecturer/teacher.

159

Visual stimuli are in the control of the teacher and must be used effectively. Clear the board of distracting material, especially work from previous classes. Don't inflict your material on others by walking away and leaving it for others to clear away.

The principles that apply to AVA in general apply equally to presentations with Powerpoint. Since visual stimuli are particularly powerful, they must be chosen and designed with care. A picture can be worth a thousand words, but not if it is a bad picture or misleading or irrelevant or difficult to interpret or excessively clever and verbose – or if people cannot see it!

Pictures are extremely rich in information; simplified diagrams are often clearer and simpler to grasp. They allow you to eliminate everything except what you want to show. You can also build up the structure impressively with your computer or by using overlay techniques on an OHP. Look at some of the cartoon sketches in this book.

REMEMBER! … Whichever AVA we use, we must focus attention on essentials and select out 'noisy' detail.

Design factors

In choosing any visual stimulus you must appraise it for what you want to achieve by using it; how effective it is for the specific purpose you intend. You may intend to show how the parts relate to the whole, for example, or you may want to concentrate attention on fine detail. Both are needed for understanding. Good diagrams or pictures can make understanding very much easier. Or you may use quite sophisticated animations.

In constructing images, certain factors improve effectiveness:

- *Simplicity*: The brain simplifies and searches for patterns. To help we too should simplify our images as far as we can.
- *Closure*: We like to perceive things as 'wholes' rather than in bits. We should ensure that the whole is clear even when we *want* to concentrate on details.
- *Clarity*: The brain tests hypotheses about figures and images and will test out different ones. We must try to avoid ambiguity or lack of clarity.
- *Boundary*: To see we must differentiate things. We must ensure that clear boundaries define differentiated areas: words and symbols. For this purpose the use of colour can also be effective.

This last is particularly important in work we put on the chalkboard/whiteboard, which is often used as a jotting pad. Students cannot learn from an undifferentiated jumble. Draw lines, circles or boxes round groups of words and symbols that belong together. Show the links with arrows. A good example to visualise is a child's wooden train; simplification of the complex engine to horizontal and vertical cylinders, cubes and circles, especially if differentiated by contrasting colours, makes it easy for any child to 'see it'.

The Shannon–Weaver theory

In 1949 the Shannon–Weaver mathematical theory of communication was published. These theorists made the distinction between 'information' and 'informational channels': between what information is about and the way it is transmitted person to person, the medium used. Shannon and Weaver were concerned to improve radar and radio transmission: *we want to maintain a high-fidelity transmission so that messages don't get garbled on the way. We also want a lot of redundancy and clarity: for we don't want 'noise' interfering with the transmission.*

'Noise' and 'redundancy' are technical terms. 'Noise' in radio is the hiss of background sound that may prevent us hearing what we are trying to listen to. We have all had the frustration of noise when trying to listen to a concert or a talk on the radio. It is worse when television pictures break up or develop strange images or disappear. The phenomenon is often referred to as interference. 'Redundancy' refers to an excess deliberately put into the signal to ensure that important parts of the message get through. The S–W theory is about effectiveness in sending and receiving signals. We are dealing here in metaphors, so this account is not to be taken too literally.

Problems in teaching environments that affect information transmission, whatever the source of signal, increase with distance. If we are communicating directly with people, the farther they are away, the harder it is for them to read our signals, and for us to read theirs. Since much of what we communicate is to be read in our body language, *distance matters*. So much of what we wish to share is to be read in the way we say it or demonstrate it. Where these cannot be read, subtleties and nuances are lost. If we hand over everything to a machine, none of these can be read.

The problem exists even when using the chalkboard/whiteboard – or even an OHP intended to overcome problems associated with loss of personal contact between teacher and students. From the point of view of students, the teacher turns to the board and away from them, so that all eye-contact is lost; the teacher concentrates on the board rather than on the students.

Frequently, the teacher obscures what s/he is doing on the board for most of the students, and unless boardwork is planned, it is not easy to avoid as much 'noise' as light as the board becomes too cluttered. Projection from in front of the board makes matters worse, the image is partly projected onto them. Lecturers need a long stick to point to information projected onto the board, to avoid getting between the projector and the image. Sometimes technology becomes rather comic. Think of the way in which TV weather presenters have to deal with maps projected behind them; or are they?

The OHP was intended to overcome loss of eye-contact between teacher and students. What is most important is the ability to be part of the learning group rather than isolated at the board.

The interactive whiteboard is technology linked to a computer. Images apparently written on the board in much the same way as with pens on an ordinary whiteboard are transmitted via metal netting under the white surface to a graphics program in a computer, then projected onto the board. 'Tools' of the computer graphics program are used by touching symbols at the edge of the board and by using a variety of graphic pens. Clearly, to learn to use this technology, it is necessary to practise on a computer to achieve a reasonable level of confidence. You cannot learn in front of the class.

Those with skills in the use of such graphics programs find the freedom of a large-scale board exciting. Others may find that they need to concentrate on the board to avoid appearing to use the technology less than perfectly. And this tends to divert their attention from the students. Unfortunately, the designers of the interactive whiteboard have perfected the technology, but have ignored the advantages of the OHP over the whiteboard in classroom presentations. One main advantage was the ability to cover and reveal information as required and to point or highlight items on the slides without coming between the learners and material on the board (see Figure 16.2).

Figure 16.2 The many faces of ICT: where are you?

> **REMEMBER!** ... You make the decisions. You don't have to use something just because it is there. But do so if there are significant added benefits. Teachers learn what works and how much effort it takes to make it work well by critical evaluation.

A computer projection does better what an OHP does: it removes one set of work to replace it with another slide. It avoids noise and confusion where a static board becomes cluttered. It uses prepared slides, demonstrates and builds up information and structures, without the lecturer obscuring work or the process from the students. It is easy with an OHP to build up work by inductive methods within the classroom, and only marginally more difficult with a computer. Pointing and highlighting is easy with a pen on an OHP or by using the cursor on a computer screen as the source of the image.

With the use of a remote control mouse, as illustrated by Carina in Case Study 24 on page 180, the teacher has freedom to move among the students in the class. You need to face your students, or mingle with them as part of the learning group to observe their reactions to the material that you are presenting. To understand their difficulties, you need to get close to them to see it as they see it.

Because all this can be achieved while facing your students using a laptop or a keyboard with a monitor, to use an interactive whiteboard appears retrogressive; the teacher is isolated again and may obscure the board s/he is working on.

Laptops and computerised writing tablets linked to graphics software work like the OHP, and with significant advantages. They are much more portable, and they have large storage and retrieval functions for databases and prepared materials, so that they can access many software programs that may be linked together to produce video sequences, animations, text and graphics. Naturally, there is a pretty huge cost in time to prepare such presentations, so cost has to be matched to benefit. If you are to use all this sophistication, you must be prepared to put in the hours to learn it properly.

By linking to a printer, you can produce handouts to supplement your presentation materials. Nowadays, manufacturers are producing easily portable projectors in carry-bags, which, coupled with light portable screens and laptops, can overcome the recurring problems of ill-equipped premises, or the difficulties and expense of large permanent installations.

The manufacturers have in mind the needs of salesmen making presentations to companies in committee rooms. It is a useful model because the presenter has to engage in two-way exchanges and be very much part of the group, taking questions and explaining where there is confusion.

Unfortunately, students are conditioned to sitting in front of a screen, usually a TV, switching on and switching off their brains. Very few have developed an alert, exploratory mind – or the ability to throw questions at the screen. And there are few teaching programmes which attempt to develop such skills.

Even if the use of this kind of portable ICT equipment involves trouble in setting it up, the big advantage is its flexibility, which allows you to control your learning environment.

Noise and redundancy

Noise

'Noise' is a problem affecting all forms of communication, because it diverts the learners' attention. Learners need to concentrate, and anything that interferes with attention is 'noise'.

Conflicting messages, emotional stress, aggressive behaviour may act as 'noise'. Monotony in delivery, or excessive amounts of information, verbosity in the material presented, lack of variety in the learning activity, distracting information on the walls or on the chalkboard are all 'noisy'.

Excessively clever presentations are 'noisy' also. The medium is not the message. Sheer volume of information is 'noisy'. An overloaded channel or receiver obviously cannot cope. Look at the visual material you use, what you write on a chalkboard or an OHP transparency, what your computer charts or animations are presenting. How much of the information can possibly get through? How much is 'noise'? Even if it is brilliantly conceived and presented, anything that is a distraction from 'the message' should be cut out. Lack of clarity in the signals and messages you wish to convey interferes. Your tone of voice, perhaps, the words you speak, or the visual materials used – the means of transmission – all need to be clear and easy to understand.

Monotony of delivery becomes 'noisy', rooms with difficult acoustics, and rooms that are too hot, lighting conditions that prevent proper vision, seats too hard (or too soft) can all get in the way of the message. You must try to experience it as your students do.

Any distraction is 'noise'. For example, after one seminar I was running with a group of adult students, a colleague remarked that he had had great difficulty in concentrating on what I was saying because a woman sitting opposite had such 'noisy legs'. In another session some female students told me they found the design of an Aboriginal Corroboree on the sweatshirt I was wearing so fascinating that they simply couldn't follow my words. As I remarked earlier, students are watching you more than they are listening to you.

Unfortunately, many teachers do not make any attempt to observe what students are doing, they talk to the wall or the ceiling through a microphone. When handing over to a machine such as a projector, they will sit apart and let the machine get on with it. Or they may concentrate entirely on controlling what the machine is doing, oblivious to the 'audience'. It has ever been so when using professionally produced film material or video material. The use of ICT can make it worse. How can you ensure that it enhances the learning?

Redundancy

Redundancy implies that a message is so strong that it overcomes all noise likely to be round. A tale may be so absorbing that listeners ignore everything else; people 'lose themselves' in a book or film or a computer program. The content of a lecture, or the enthusiasm of the lecturer, is so fascinating that even if everything they do is 'wrong' in terms of technique, their audience will want more.

Most people are actually quite good at shutting out the world. Clearly, if the material is good enough, the problem is at least partly solved. That, however, is no excuse for a teacher's abdicating responsibility for ensuring that the intended learning occurs, rather than much that is unintended. It is remarkably hard for teachers to control what their students actually learn. Control of the learning is the teacher's responsibility, more than perfected lecturing techniques.

Structure: ambiguity and selectivity

Chaotic presentation of information with little or no structure produces a great deal of 'noise'. You must ask: How hard is it for students to understand this? What exactly do I want them to take away? What can I get rid of so that they can grasp essentials?

Less is frequently better. Structure matters in all learning activity and materials. For example, it is notoriously difficult to write instruction manuals. There has to be a clear learning path and action plan. Often a simplified diagram helps. A correctly sequenced structure is vital. But in one jet aircraft, the instructions to the pilot on how to eject in an emergency were printed on the pilot's canopy. The first instruction was: *Eject the canopy.* Think about that.

Ambiguity. One source of noise and confusion is ambiguity. Look round you, you will often see examples of hilarious road signs. *Crematorium Pedestrians Only* (Figure 16.3). Drivers in WA agree whole-heartedly with *End Roadwork*, or may be puzzled by the sign at a level crossing: *Do not cross when bell ringing* (Figure 16.4).

A head of department in a college once wrote a memo to a colleague telling her to arrange a week's leave with her team leader. '*Do you think Corfu would be nice?*' she said. Much of the problem can arise by punctuation, actual or assumed, which implies stress in the sentence. *A woman without her man is nothing/ A woman; without her, man is nothing.* Many times it depends on how we read it to ourselves or aloud. Exam papers are a rich source of humour. I read, *The women sat around the room balancing cups of tea in protruding places. You can see the breath he takes and hear his pants. The time struck a few shops away. Some of the children came from very disturbed backgrounds and others were not so lucky. One of my neighbours husbands*

Figure 16.3 'Crematorium pedestrians only'.

Figure 16.4 'Do not cross when bell ringing'.

has to be at work at 8 o'clock. It seemed strange, appearing from the top of a tall building I could see the village (Figure 16.5).

Word order is among the most difficult things to learn in any foreign language, particularly in English, where along with punctuation it has a profound effect on meaning. *Leaving the cricket field the sun casts its sleepy eye over the play park. Did you put the chicken out in your nightdress? A frenzied goose – massive in size – began to chase me. Quacking non-stop I ran for all I was worth.* Of course, we need to choose our words; Shakespeare had great fun with those who used words for an effect, but for the wrong effect. *Many of our entertainment buildings are plagued with wet and dry rot and suffer from melancholy effrontery. Her eyes were misty and her eyelids carried heavy lines which showed a chain of sleepless nights.*

You might have some fun making cartoon sketches of these or similar errors in English!

Sometimes ambiguity is dangerous. Which switch? When? In what sequence? *'I didn't mean you to plug it in there!'* Whose fault is it if there is an explosion? It is essential to get a third party to validate any set of instructions, to eliminate ambiguity.

Selectivity. The brain also selects from any experience. However hard we appear to be concentrating, we select a few things, perhaps 10%, and ignore the 90%.

Figure 16.5 'It seemed strange, appearing from the top of a tall building I could see the village'.

The human brain has a limited instant storage capacity, and in most students that capacity is used for temporary storage of information, especially where they are conditioned to input–output testing, and where accuracy of recall is all that is required. They are not expected to use new information by applying it to an unfamiliar context, which is the only way to ensure that new information is processed into useable knowledge by individual students. Once the point of need is past, the information is likely to be jettisoned, just like the jet pilot's canopy. Teachers who recognise this selectivity ensure that important information is not selected out. Repetition and redundancy are important.

A reasonably effective way of doing this is to invite students to explain what they understand, or what they have to do, what the thing is about, how it works. In trying to explain to someone else there is not only an alerting of the brain, but processing in a student's personal knowledge structure, and formulation into terms, words and symbols, that are the student's own.

Information only becomes knowledge through this processing. Knowing is a learning process, not a storage facility. You can only transfer information, other people's knowledge, perhaps. The present analogy with computers is misleading. A computer may be stuffed full of information or data, but it knows and understands nothing. A computer does not 'think'. Asking students to reformulate information makes good sense when dealing with presentations in ordinary classes, but in a lecture room full of students it is only practicable to select a few of them to provide this feedback. Do not just throw questions into the air. Choose one individual – and if you can, by name.

Follow-up learning activity in seminar work or assignments is essential to ensure that the new material is used and is not quickly ejected.

It is hard for students to grasp something they are only exposed to once. Repeat material, in various versions preferably; this is necessary redundancy. Make presentations using different media, computer-generated or OHP slides, discussions, handouts, perhaps on-line materials. You will have realised by now that this book is full of repetitions. Students need to take away a pattern, a structure, in order to learn it. If they try to listen and copy out, they are likely to select and distort information and so embed misunderstanding. If you are lecturing, it is best to give them the structure so that they can use it to follow the lecture, as headings with gaps for their own notes, with keywords and patterns to make sense of them.

They will then take away accurate notes to revise from.

If the method is intended to be inductive (see pages 136 and 251), you must genuinely build up – on the board, simple or interactive, on the laptop or on flipcharts or the OHP – whatever they discover or suggest. You must value everyone's ideas, not just those that suit a prearranged summary as in Case Study 31. The result of the 'brainstorm' must be written up into a comprehensible structure to ensure that it makes sense as a whole. The computer version can easily be printed as a handout.

This will enable you to make the appropriate links to the next class. ICT can assist here, but the principles remain the same.

Clarity and simplicity

What about the teaching material we use? Is it clear? Could we simplify it to make it easier to grasp? Could we structure it more clearly? How much is essential? How much is distracting padding? We need to be constantly alert to the need for clarity and problems of distraction, ambiguity, lack of structure and so on.

It is so easy to believe that the more that is said, the clearer it will be. Frequently the opposite is true. Teachers tend to be verbose, they use too many words, too many symbols. Structure with keywords matter more than the information it contains. The message is: *simplify it.* The new technology tends to value richness and cleverness above clarity and simplicity so the movement away from direct communication also becomes a move towards complexity. Students are to be fascinated, their attention held, by cleverness in graphics and animations. The content takes a back-seat to the rally driver as we import into the classroom and lecture theatre the forces that are driving the mass media.

The opposite problem can arise. Students are not given all the information they need by the teacher, or the instruction card, or the worksheet or other task guidance. After I have jettisoned my canopy, what do I do then? Which lever do I pull? Which button do I press? Help! Teachers do make unjustified assumptions about what learners already know or will bring to the activity, so they fail to think through what it is that students need to know in order to understand what they are now presenting.

Nor do we check whether students are ready, have sufficient understanding or levels of skill.

NOISE

Before you start a teaching session, remove distractions.

1 Check for 'noise' in the environment.

2 Check for 'noise' in the way you present information:

- is it clear?
- easy to comprehend?
- at a level appropriate for the students?
- is there too much?
- could it be restructured?
- could it be divided up into more easily assimilated parts?

3 Use keywords and indicate direction clearly.

4 Sequence any instructions you give, ensure that they are complete.

5 Validate your materials for ambiguity and omission.

6 Be positive, not negative (The Ten Commandments fail this test).

7 Watch out for jargon.

8 Use short sentences and active verbs ('Do this … ', not 'It is best to … ').

9 Use a variety of presentation of the same material to ensure useful redundancy.

Lecture-demonstrations

Lecture theatres and science laboratories are often equipped with demonstration benches, designed to enable lecturers to demonstrate practical applications of principles they are teaching. In science, the lecturer may demonstrate an experiment which students will then also do on their benches. This is an advance on what used to happen in science classes when the students' activity was confined to taking notes. The modern trend is to use film and projected material and animated drawings perhaps without the 'actuality'.

Your purpose is to enhance transmission of information to the group by the use of tangible, sometimes sizeable and sophisticated equipment. It is better to see 'real' things actually working than to be told about them. But the ergonomics of seeing from any considerable distance, or as a group around a bench, are the same as in any other demonstration. Lecturers often need to ask, '*Can you see what happens when I do this? or how this part works?*' The answer almost equally often is '*No*'.

When teachers wish to use demonstrations as part of lectures they must consider such factors seriously. No visual material is any good if students cannot see it. Nor is there advantage in tangible objects, as against perhaps a video presentation, if students cannot touch them. Film or video may indeed be much more successful where presentation is to be made to a large group. The ability to focus attention, to enlarge the image of small parts, to stop and repeat, adding to the explanation or in two-way discussion, will ensure that what is presented is seen and understood.

For smaller groups there may be much greater advantage in using tangible equipment. Enhancement of the images using a video set-up in ways described below is better. The group can see both the hands-on experiment – the equipment on the bench and the person making it work – while the camera can focus on the whole or on parts, enlarge images and so on, to ensure that everyone gets a first-class view. This is a very positive use of new technology, affordable, versatile and very 'user-friendly'. But it is hardly a one-person show, you need someone to handle the camera.

If the demonstration is also recorded, the re-run can be used along with previous recordings.

Demonstrations

All teachers are role-models. We inevitably demonstrate to our students what we truly believe to be appropriate behaviour, whatever we are doing, wherever we are working. It is easy to signal '*Do as I say, not as I do!*' Bear this in mind, if you are working in areas of danger, or where proper working practice and safety precautions must be a matter of habit. A teacher's overriding, inescapable major responsibility is the students' health and safety. In that sense everything we do is a demonstration.

REMEMBER! … If it is unsafe, you must not do it.

More particularly, we need to consider formal demonstrations of a skill or a technique. Here we are concerned with practical or motor skills. The present emphasis in FE/AE is on learning to use ICT (Information and Communication Technology). It needs an approach more like that discussed later. Many occasions arise in ICT for the demonstration of software programs, computer shortcuts and so on. But these are only partly a matter of skill.

Preparation

REMEMBER! … To be effective, a demonstration has to be short and highly focused.

If your students are to attempt to master the demonstrated skills afterwards, you can only use small-scale techniques. Students cannot take in the whole of a long presentation from one exposure. They will select what they feel they need or what they are alert to. Plan to provide the essentials; never mind the frills. Much more time is required for adequate preparation than for the demonstration. *Think it through*.

Models

Think about models. If students know where they are going, or what the finished product will look like, they have a model in the head to work towards. Whether the product is a gateau, a dress, a machined part, a step in ballet or a passage on the piano, the model had better be a good one. Arthur Cranmer, in his book *The Art of Singing* relates how Sir Thomas Beecham did not like the way a singer sang a particular phrase. '*Not like this …*', he said, and made an awful noise. '*Like this …*'. He made the same awful noise! Support the learning with an additional model in the form of written instructions (clearly and sequentially as 'do this' statements), possibly supplemented with a diagram or a flowchart.

The whole and the bits

If you plan to give your demonstration only once – unless it is very short and/or immediately followed by their doing it – it will be hard for students to grasp.

One way of overcoming the problem is to have what you do recorded on video. This is not to replace the actuality of demonstrating in an appropriate context with the group observing you. That is necessary, but a video-recording of the same demonstration has advantages:

- You can do it at normal speed, using your practised skill.
- You can watch with them and explain things clearly.
- You can replay the video at half-speed (it is very hard for a skilled person to do things half-speed).
- You can put the video-tape on 'hold' at any point to look at details and to take questions.
- The students can always replay the model or those bits they can't quite remember.

This last is vital. *Learning is most effective at a point of need.* You cannot know what you have failed to see or still need to grasp until you find you 'can't remember how to do this bit', or what the sequence of steps is. If you have ever tried to learn Old Tyme dances or a barn dance, you will know what I mean.

In practice, when the students' turn comes round, they will go through the experience a bit at a time. It is easy for the teacher's demonstration to pass over the bits or to fail to present the whole properly. So, it is important to analyse the various steps and skills needed, the tricks of the trade, to show clearly how each is done. But they are to be seen as part of the whole conception, like phrasing in music or brush-strokes on canvas.

How and why

Although you are demonstrating 'how' to do something, you are also telling the students 'why' this rather than that. Your demonstration is about knowledge as well as about skill. Therefore, you must explain clearly, as well as show, the skills or techniques they are to learn. This is the part that is easy to ignore or to do badly.

Make sure you understand what it is the students need to know, and how you will ensure that they learn it. It is much more effective to make the theory part of the 'doing' and not teach it separately, although that has been normal practice. Even if it is taught separately, the link can only be made by the students in a practical context.

Again, video helps, because you can pause and repeat and so involve the group in question and answer to ensure that they understand *why* as well as *how*. It is standard practice now in improving team performances in games.

Where

The place you use for a demonstration should be properly designed for that activity, because you are modelling good practice. Everything must be right. Set up everything to hand and in order. You can't be hunting for something at a critical moment. Improvising is wrong: you do not want your students to learn it 'wrong'.

Check that equipment is working and is what it should be. If you are using knives, say which knife and why and ensure that it is sharp.

Wear the right clothes and the right protection. Are special safety precautions involved? Do things need to be sterile, for example? Students must see things done properly. They must learn to do it 'right'.

Human factors

Nor can the students learn if they cannot hear or see the demonstration. Afterwards, it is important for them to explore the experience with all their senses, as only then will they fully grasp it: the weight of the knife, the pressure to exert and so on. But in your part, you can get them to handle a piece of equipment, to feel the texture of, say, clay, or a fabric, so long as it serves to concentrate attention rather than to distract. This is what I mean by tangible objects.

How can you ensure that every student can see the demonstration? It can be a major problem if more than 10 students are crowding around you. Practical work is often done on flat surfaces, and uses small hand movements rather than large gestures. What angle of view do they need? Even in the round, how can a group of nurses, say, crowd around a bed and all see the same thing? Or novices in a workshop around a lathe, or caterers around a bench?

Some cookery rooms have large mirrors over the bench. But most teachers have to solve the problem in other ways. One way is to show the skill/technique repetitively to four or five students at a time. This is an excellent use of personal space, but what will the other students do meanwhile? You need to plan an activity for them, otherwise they will lose interest.

A video camera may be the only practical solution (but you need a technician too). A camera can focus to cut out distracting detail, and let the students see things exactly as the demonstrator sees them. It can view things from odd angles, from vertically above, say, with the images projected on to a large screen.

The video camera can be linked to a microphone. This overcomes the problem of trying to talk to students through the back of your head, too. If you are working at a lathe, say, how can they possibly hear your explanation? Do you talk as you do? talk first? or do, then talk about it? You cannot maintain eye-contact so you have no feedback, while many of the group may neither see nor hear properly.

Time-management and structure

Structure is sequencing within a time-plan. You need to plan how much time to allow for the various activities. The students need to practise themselves, and as soon as possible after a demonstration so that your part and theirs is linked into the learning process.

Time needed relates to the content and complexity of what you and they are setting out to do. Since doing it well has to be properly planned, that needs costing in time too. To plan properly you must decide before you begin what students are going to do to acquire this skill/technique and make it part of their competence. Where do you need to put the emphasis? on what they see or on what they do? Indeed, what are they to do while you demonstrate? Many a teacher discovers that some of the students pay little attention to the demonstration because s/he has to concentrate on what s/he is doing and so loses contact with the students. The problem becomes more acute the larger the group and so the easier it is for students to be excluded from the experience – to be at the back of a group around a lathe or a bench or a bed or an engine, or wherever there is a hands-on job to do. You must try to ensure that all can see and all are involved. Students at the back of a group almost inevitably are bored and misbehave, even 'grown adults'. Experience it the way the students do.

Speed and dexterity

You find it easy. Try to remember when it was hard. That is where your students are now, and where you need to start from. Their newly acquired ability will be the measure of your success.

A skilled performance is characterised by speed and dexterity, not having to think about it. It is often called 'memory in the muscles'. It doesn't just happen, it comes from doing it many times and doing it successfully. This is true of all skills at whatever level.

It is very hard to teach something slowly which you don't think about at all when you do it. Thinking about what you are doing often makes you clumsy. If you try to think how you ride a bike you may well fall off! If you try to analyse how you balance going down every step of the stairs, or how you hit a ball with a racket, you will come to realise how complex these actions really are. It requires practice to do them slowly and to be aware of each step. Practise demonstrating a skill slowly – but not in front of students.

Skill in the end is about what it feels like to do something well; this is an internal experience which leads to externally observable behaviour. The teacher provides the mirror to enable a student to do it well, and to know how it feels when s/he does it well. For this reason, it is not helpful to analyse complex skills into simpler skills to practise them separately and then hope to synthesise them into a 'global performance'. Unfortunately, such ideas have bedevilled much training in skills, especially in teacher training.

Evaluation

You need feedback from your students. It is not enough that you feel good about it. Did it help them to gain insight? Do they now understand what is involved? and why? as well as know how to do it?

Practicals

Skills practice

The essence of a practical is 'getting the feel of it', to feel the weight of a knife in the hand, fear of the danger of cutting your finger off; or the wetness and smell of the clay, the near-impossibility of drawing it up off a wheel. '*Why won't it do it for me when the teacher does it so easily?*' '*Why does my cake sag in the middle?*'

Handling a practical is handling frustration for both teacher and student. Oh! the temptation to be able to take it out of their hands and just show them again how easy it is! Why is it they can't understand? It is individualised, resource-based learning: all the 'good' words. So, what can we do to make it easier and more rewarding for them and for us?

We can improve performance once a minimum competence is achieved by understanding the how and the why. No amount of knowledge about balance or moments or forward velocity will help you to ride a bike until you have mastered the ability to stay on it. You must know what it feels like to pedal, steer and balance, to go much faster on the bike than you expect to, without panicking.

Barriers

The teacher cannot be totally in charge of what happens, even if the class 'do it by numbers', army training style. Individuals adopt their own learning pattern and strategy, and they bring attitudes and learning barriers to the experience as well as previously acquired skills.

Clearly, they must *believe* they can do it. If your demonstration makes something look too magical and amazingly perfect, it may convince some people that they never can learn to do that. We have to deal with confidence; success breeds success, repeated failure demotivates. Having a positive attitude is essential. You must try to experience it as each individual does.

At what level of difficulty is the skill/technique? What level of skill do they need before they can even attempt it? The learners may have learned behaviour that needs unlearning. It is so hard to unlearn! The teacher may need to analyse what is getting in the way. Established patterns of movement may not help in what they should be doing here. They may have a completely wrong 'model in the head'. Some students have problems with vision or hearing or balance, particularly if they must wear eye protection. Some are clumsy in everything they do, not very skilful at anything: they may need help just to develop eye–hand coordination.

Preparation and tasks

Students as well as teachers must come properly prepared. They need to be clearly informed of what is required: what clothing, what materials they have to provide and so on. Tasks must be agreed and set out on worksheets, which also show equipment they are to use and their responsibilities.

If the learning is to be at the pace of each individual, each will complete an agreed number of tasks in a sequence at their own speed. How will you 'keep track' of where each student is? One way is to have a 'tracking sheet', on a pin board, say, which can be checked off as tasks are completed. See Case Study 25.

Performance criteria for successful achievement of each task should be agreed and stated, so that everyone knows how to evaluate their own performance. It is hard to find you have failed to do something in the way that was expected, but which no one told you about until afterwards. Equipment and materials must be properly organised, in good working order and of the right quality and quantity. Thought must be given to establishing good working practice.

Rules and safety

It is vital that students establish at once right ways of setting about a task. Unlearning ways of 'doing it' once it is embedded is so hard. Try teaching an adult to sing. Rules must be framed accordingly. You cannot allow your students to work without the proper equipment and clothing. And they must take responsibility for their own organised work-station. They must be properly organised.

The environment must support the learning activity. This may require planning, particularly if person–machine ergonomics are involved. If you are training students to use visual display units (VDUs), for example, you need to make sure that table heights are appropriate, that chairs support the base of the spine, filters shield the user from glare and possible radiation, and so on. Better, of course, to replace known hazards such as these with screens that do not radiate harmful rays at all. The students need to sit as directed and observe safe time periods in the use of the machines. You will find pamphlets and guidelines on this and other safe uses of machinery issued by the Health and Safety Commission, available from your organisation's Safety Officer, or in a public library, or from the Consumers' Association or Citizens Advice Bureaux.

Students must know what the rules are because:

- we are about establishing good practice
- we must ensure that risk-taking does not lead to danger
- disorganisation is costly and inefficient
- there are well-researched physical illnesses that occur through bad posture and bad working practices.

Plateaux and readiness

A practical following a demonstration only makes sense as a part of an extended programme of skill development. Research into skills learning found that learning curves generally rise quickly, and then flatten into plateaux for a period of embedding and consolidation. Everyone is different, however. Teachers need to look for challenges to shorten this embedding period.

Readiness to take on further challenges or greater tests is for teacher and learner to judge. As a teacher, you should be able to recognise and use rhythms in an individual's learning. Much learning is a matter of repeated cycles. There is a need to build up the whole together – the teacher can take part by creating more interesting tasks for the learner to undertake. Too big a challenge too soon undermines confidence; too few challenges, too much repetitive practice which the student considers unnecessary, will demotivate. You must judge for each student. Individuals learn at their own pace, make their own leaps in learning, lose confidence, get stuck over things, have their own insights, and their own barriers to overcome. Practicals are inevitably one-to-one support in learning.

Action plans: attention, frequency and practice

Attention is a real problem. Because skills learning is so repetitive, it can easily become tedious. But students need to concentrate, to be alert in order to learn. More practice, if it is highly monotonous, will not necessarily result in a significantly improved skill. Tasks must be designed that give purpose and demonstrable outcomes from the learning activity while also demanding improved levels of skill. Concentration on achieving tasks is necessary to give meaning and direction to skills. Look again at Case Study 10 where Karen found that it was interesting tasks that encouraged her students to practise and improve their skills. Unless you know what it is for, practise may just be tedious.

This is clearly what happens in learning to play the piano. A learner attempts more and more difficult piano pieces. While developing the technical skills to play them, s/he is trying to recreate a 'musical' performance. But there has to be a pattern involving frequency of practice. It is no good someone turning up for a piano lesson once a week and never touching a piano in between lessons. Teacher and learner have to agree a learning programme; this is an action plan that identifies frequency of practice and study – a contract that identifies responsibility, goals and schedules. Skills are best learned by practice involving plenty of variety. This is how my book has been designed. In devising learning tasks, you must identify the skills to be practised and how they are to be developed and demonstrated. It helps if there are clear performance criteria also. Without feedback, practicals make little sense.

Skills have to be seen as meaningful by students within their context and important to them. Tangible products, cakes or pots or whatever else they may be, assist assessment and evaluation and maintain motivation. So do observable outcomes – as in a performance of a play or on the football field in group practicals (page 177).

Perception and insight

Most problems for students lie in the complexity of what they are attempting to do. People learn skills experientially and do so better when they have role-models as well as clear 'models in the head'. Knowledge, belief and attitude are the basis of skill. In the early stages of skill development learners must be aware (often painfully) of what they do, and take conscious control of their actions. My own prime example is learning to skate on ice.

We cannot begin to be inventive till skills are so embedded that we can think of other things. This implies that skills may be at different levels of conscious control. Once the brain has set up a pattern of behaviour, the skill itself needs less and less attention, less conscious control. Eventually, and as soon as possible, our thinking can be concentrated on what that skill allows us to achieve. For example, a driver can concentrate on the road ahead, rather than on how to coordinate clutch, gear change and accelerator.

Skill is a means to an end, not an end in itself. Much skills teaching in the past focused just on learning the skill rather than using it. More recently, the demands of examinations have shifted away from skill-testing to using the skill effectively, with criteria for success defined in terms of a context and products and the completion of tasks with performance criteria. What matters is the evidence.

Hence, skills learning must be related to individual needs, tasks designed as programmes. The students determine their own pace and readiness by feedback from the teacher, using the performance criteria agreed for the tasks. Action plans need frequent renegotiation because the pace of learning, even of individuals, is unpredictable.

Knowledge becomes increasingly important. The increase in overall ability in athletics is a consequence of extensive research into what makes for a better performance, as much science as art. The same is true of wine-making. Wines from 'the new world', such as Australia and Chile, compete with the best in 'old world' Europe because they rely on science rather than the winemaker's art.

Monitoring

The intention is that all the students will achieve mastery as defined by the performance criteria. Monitoring is an ongoing tutorial function and it depends on establishing relationships. Your main role in the practical, therefore, is

- monitoring the progress and pace of learning of individuals
- insisting on repetitive practice
- finding new ways to tackle it if there is a blockage
- intervening when the student is in difficulty or getting it wrong, or to avoid disaster of some kind
- adjusting or renegotiating action plans and completion of tasks.

Seeing what everyone is doing, while ensuring that each makes progress, requires skills in

- observing
- listening
- communicating one to-one.

Assessment

The purpose is mastery, so that assessment is based on achievement of performance criteria for each Task, not for each skill. This is more complex than it sounds. No progress is made without cognitive and attitudinal change in a positive direction. It is easy to observe 'can do'; 'can't do' requires analysis of what is going wrong and remedial action. This may be dealing with problems of knowledge or lack of confidence, or removing barriers to learning. It certainly involves understanding what a person has to do in order to do it right.

Designing the performance criteria

Performance criteria for each Task will state clearly what you believe to be good practice. Achieving the criteria identifies to what extent that good practice has become a matter of habit.

Group practicals

Practicals are about individual learning, but in some contexts group practicals are essential – in drama, music, languages and team sports, for example. The skills and insight of individuals need development, but they are expressed in a context of a group of people working together to achieve agreed and shared learning goals. Group projects (say, to put on a play or a concert, to perform together, to create a winning team, or just share a learning experience – language learning has to be in a social context) are essential to promote these learning goals.

The whole is much greater than the sum of the parts. To become part of effective teams, all the individuals must learn quite different skills, insights and behaviour than when they are learning by themselves. Responsibility in a role, commitment to the team and to the team goals become vitally important. An orchestra consisting of soloists will make a poor showing in a symphony. Having too many stars on the football field is a recipe for losing.

This is a major problem in drama-training and in the development of sports teams where role models are the 'stars' idolised in the media. Their debt to the large number of unknowns who make their achievements possible is hardly ever publicised.

As a teacher, your role cannot be largely didactic. You will have to lead, to shape, to manage and inspire. You will need excellent skills of organisation and management, the ability to win people over. You will provide the model in the head; and you are often the role-model of what the group is to achieve. You must ensure that this is communicated clearly, and that all show the commitment which binds a group together. Practical tasks achieved together are the only means by which it can happen. One major teaching activity is evaluating with the group how well they achieve the tasks and what they need to do as a group and as individuals to progress towards agreed goals. In practical situations, when your students are working together, your skill is in observing and analysing what is happening and why: what needs to happen next and how to match the model in the head with what actually occurs. You must communicate that understanding and insight to the group.

At the beginning of this chapter we discussed the continuum that ranges from teacher control to student control of decision-making/learning activity. How far along that continuum you progress depends on the extent to which the team develops its own momentum, where the sense of ownership resides. There is no short cut here. You will have to learn how to work with such groups, not only to get the best out of them, to set standards and to ensure that they achieve them, but also to avoid teacher-dependence. In the end, the team has to play the game without the coach.

Nor should you attempt to be a one-person orchestra playing all the parts; this is a team effort. Individuals must agree to take on roles, be responsible, make sure that things happen when and how they should. Occasionally, you will have to intervene or take over to ensure that it happens, but should do so reluctantly. It is your role to provide the overview to maintain proper control. The director of a play in a theatre has to designate roles on-stage and behind-stage. When all is ready and the performance has begun, s/he can only sit and watch. The stage manager runs the show.

Performance criteria and assessment are concerned with how far the team achieves its goals as a team. It is hard to identify how individuals are to be assessed in relation to such activity.

Human factors and responsibility

Students cannot learn either individually or in groups without the right, well-maintained equipment. Work simulation demands the right materials to work with to establish good working practice. Individual learners need to 'own' a working territory, though there is advantage in computing or engineering, for example, in experiencing a variety of machines.

What of supervision? How many students can work safely in a workshop or a craft room or a kitchen supervised – let alone be tutored – by only one teacher? How should the room be designed or set out to enable the teacher to see the students, either to spot where help is required or to intervene if it is clearly necessary? In some situations teachers just cannot see what the students are doing: who takes the responsibility then?

The legal position of teachers in relation to their responsibility for the safety of students – or of themselves – and of equipment has become a major concern with growth of 'out-reach' courses conducted on premises away from the parent institution. See 'out-reach courses' in Chapter 18.

Demonstrations in ICT

ICT is unique. There are similar situations where individuals sit at machines and demonstrations of their use must be one-to-one, but such tools are relatively simple to master, whereas a computer is enormously complex in the information stored in it and the sophistication of Applications Software. There is an ongoing need for demonstration of how to use new applications, that are not easy to master because of their very cleverness. Apart from which, older software is constantly updated and reinvented.

ICT needs an initial induction into keyboard and operational skills, but this appears to be the easy part, learning OS, the Operating System. No OS systems remain constant for much over a year, however; after all Microsoft has to stay in business. No one wants to market a machine that will not need replacing, or if they do, they will spend enormous amounts of money to ensure that people throw it away in favour of a new model. The skills of ICT appear simple, more a matter of repetitive practice than of demonstration. By far the most important are keyboard skills, and ability to move the cursor with a mouse. Without these skills the operator is painfully slow. *You learn it by doing it.*

The main barrier is a tendency to panic in face of the huge amount of 'know how' needed to do even the simplest of tasks. Even 'user-friendly' operating systems demand knowing precisely and sequentially which commands the operator must select in order to make things happen the right way. There are no margins for error as with most tools that will still work even when used inefficiently. It is either right or it fails completely; worse, the whole system can 'crash'.

Even with clear instructions people learn computing by passing through many experiences of frustration. The problem does not get easier with time for there are always new software programs to learn. The computer is always in control, you have to learn it, often by annoying failures. Programs such as Microsoft Word are annoyingly designed to make decisions for you which you usually have to cancel. Teaching ICT, perhaps more so than any other skills, is dealing with demotivating failure and frustration. Students easily become convinced that they can't do it. There are also sudden huge leaps when a student discovers they can do it after all.

Within groups, individuals progress at greatly differing speeds, so it is very hard to implement group demonstrations. Some are way ahead of the point the teacher is dealing with and others are no way near being able to cope with it. Both sets are worried, frustrated and annoyed. The teacher has to find ways of dealing with individual needs and individual pace in learning. This is easier to understand in an illustration.

Carina taught on a nationally funded training programme in ICT for adults in Western Australia. Her room, in a facility run as a profit-making business, was equipped with a ceiling-mounted projector on to a white screen linked to a monitor with a keyboard. The computer's cursor could be operated by a remote control, so that she could point to commands and click on them from anywhere in the room. It enabled her to be completely mobile. She could experience the projected image of the Desktop the way the students saw it. She needed only occasionally to use the keyboard, which she also did facing the screen, with her back to the class.

The room was small, without windows, lit by electric light and air-conditioned, like teaching rooms in Florida in Case Study 17 on page 106.

The students, about a dozen aged from 25 to 60, women 2 to 1 to the men, sat in three rows facing the white screen in sets of three each with their own monitor, keyboard and mouse. The aisle down the centre and a space between the rows allowed Carina to come to each student to check what each was doing – to stand behind some of them and lean over to provide individual help. This proved very necessary.

They were beginners in ICT learning the Desktop layout, the symbols and commands of the latest Windows OS. Many, but not all, were new to keyboard skills and use of a mouse. The purpose of the class was to familiarise the students with the commands and the use of the mouse. Operations had to be learned in sequence. It was clear that some found the most simple functions difficult to use or comprehend. They were clumsy with the mouse/cursor and could hardly find their way around the Desktop.

Despite having a step-by-step instruction manual designed to facilitate learning at home, and a demonstration by Carina of individual operations with the mouse, several students could not move the cursor to the appropriate symbol on the Desktop, nor click on it, nor draw down menus. Carina often had to stand over them and do it with them.

Progress was painfully slow and required great patience from Carina and most of the students. Several, who were already familiar with all Carina was teaching in that session, did each operation as she demonstrated it, some before Carina did it – then sat with arms folded for up to 10 minutes while she helped those who could not do it. She had to repeat each demonstration, sometimes more than once, and then take questions to clarify what she was doing. She could do that alongside any of the students using the remote control mouse to show each operation again on the screen.

The class was for 90 minutes and the students welcomed a break for coffee after 45 minutes. They clearly needed the chance to get up, walk around and chat together about what they were doing.

Discussion

1 Why were some of these students apparently unable to use the mouse, let alone a keyboard?

2 Why did they find it so hard to comprehend what they had to do to make commands work?

3 Would it have helped them if they had understood how the OS worked? Would an insight into the way the commands were designed – how they worked – have made it easier for them?

4 Each student had the step-by-step instruction manual. Why could some apparently learn the operational steps from it, while others could not do them even after Carina's demonstration?

5 What are the problems of learning from a manual or from on-line instructions?

6 What barriers to learning did some of these students bring to the experience?

7 Why did they need a break and the opportunity to chat together? Would it have helped at all to have had some chances for student-to-student interaction in the class?

8 Why was it so important for Carina to get close to individual students? What advantages did she gain by having the remote control mouse?

9 What problems could Carina have had if she had not had the remote control? How might she have dealt with them?

10 Many other teachers across Australia used the same programmed instruction manual. Why is that appropriate when dealing with ICT instruction? Would it make sense in other contexts?

11 The class was controlled by the manual and operated at the pace of the slowest learners. A 'lock-step' approach to instruction was normal in teaching keyboard skills in the past. But what difficulties does it pose for the teacher and the student group?

12 What alternative methods might be tried to overcome these difficulties?

Comment

Clearly, a computer is a tool, and like any tool has to be mastered by using it. The same is true of a mouse and a keyboard. They are tools. The only way to learn them is the same way you learn to ride a bike: to use them.

But a huge problem with computers is that there is so much information, so many commands. Windows OS, though it is becoming much more like the Apple Mac in simplifying actions, still seems tortuous in accessing Applications. It is easy to forget how to make something happen or where to find the command you want.

Without an understanding of the principles that underlie the way commands operate, you can only look for 'do this' instructions. In recognition of this there are HELP menus available, but these are frequently complex and hard to work through, because there is just so much information and the instruction sequences appear complex even in the HELP menus.

Manuals are complex, even those dealing with simple operations. The approach is to write a sequence of commands: 'do this – this happens (a reassurance that you have done it right)' then 'do this – this happens' in a chained program. A learner has only to get the sequence right, remember it and repeat it until the learning becomes embedded. There is no explanation of 'why'. It requires no understanding.

Since this program is only a means to an end, it makes sense to learn it while using it for the purpose for which it is intended rather than 'as a program'. Like other skills, the use of Applications is best learned in the achievement of tasks. Similar manuals exist for learning Applications such as Powerpoint. Often, they have all the examples ready prepared; the learner has to follow instructions with little chance for inventive thinking, which is assumed to come later.

Eventually, a learner begins to gain some insight into what the computer is doing, how 'drop-down menus' work or whatever. There is no substitute for learning by interaction with the computer, but there is a great leap in the ability to use a program when the learner understands what it is doing, s/he is not just blindly using commands. This usually happens when s/he has a purpose for using ICT.

Good programs are designed as programmed learning with branching paths and feedback loops when failures occur – to ensure mastery overall. They can be learned to levels of use, or application, from simple and straightforward to very sophisticated. Most people, for example, do not use more than 10% perhaps of the potential built into text processing programs or the 'functions' of a digital video-camera. They don't want to make professional films, they are content to record some family occasion like a holiday. The same is true of most technological wizardry. Maybe, it would help if the HELP menus were rewritten as beginners/minimal users, intermediate and advanced users sections.

Most people have practical reasons for learning to use a computer: they cannot use a college resource centre without achieving a level of computer literacy, just as in the past illiteracy inhibited the use of libraries and magazines. Since learning is most effective at a point of need, it follows that many people learn to use a computer in a resource centre, with individual help and support from the staff there. We must exploit, if we can, the perceived needs of our students at their points of need.

Might we accelerate the learning for most students by making sure they have an insight into *why* as well as *what* in courses for those who want to achieve mastery? That they understand how the program writer expected the program to work? It is not easy to find manuals that approach learning in this way.

Carina's room was equipped on an assumption that the teacher will model for the students the operations in a sequence set out in the manual. There appeared to be no need for them to understand what they are doing. Clarify by demonstrating the instructions and the learners will be able to master the commands and the skills.

For many if not most of the students, the pace of learning was seriously impaired rather than accelerated, while they waited for the slowest to master each action. Perhaps it would be effective to treat the class more as a clinic with the teacher supporting individuals working at their own pace with the manual. Or better to rewrite the learning program at different levels of need.

There could well be value in encouraging students to support each other, since trying to teach something to someone else is the best way to learn it yourself. The danger is that they could teach it wrong! The teacher must check what is being taught/learned. Would the teacher then need such a sophisticated set-up for demonstration? What could she use it for instead of modelling actions set down in the manual?

There is a case for teaching 'principles' by showing them in action, particularly fundamental operations: how the cursor works, how left and right hand clicks on the mouse work, how drop-down menus work. Students learn all this eventually, but it could be taught. There is also an ongoing need to demonstrate Software Applications, which can be done as class activity. It is likely that the same great differences in the pace of learning will occur at all levels of Applications.

The basic learning activity of the brain is exploring, discovering patterns. The problem with rote-learning is that it closes down enquiry, you just have to learn right answers; the test is whether it works or not. Unfortunately, if it doesn't, you don't understand why or what to do about it. All you can do is scream for help or go back to the manual and start again. It is what everyone does. If your car stops and won't go, you phone for help. Do you even know how to open the bonnet?

Teaching ICT as against learning by exploring tends to create teacher dependence in place of the confidence to learn on your own. Of course, there are hundreds like me too impatient to plough through the manual. They soon find it doesn't work. They are forced to admit: *When all else fails, read the instructions!*

But we should encourage students as soon as possible to become independent learners, to have the confidence to read the instructions and become adept without someone to hold their hand.

Gaynor was teaching computing. She was in her third year of part-time teacher training on a CGLI 7407 Stage 2 course. She recorded this teaching experience of when she was expecting her tutor to visit her class for an observation. She wrote: *We don't have to be a performer all the time!*

I had a lesson observation booked, but I felt quite ill. I did not want to cancel as I would have preferred to get the observation out of the way (they take a long time to arrange). The students were working on pre-release material and had all the input previously.

I had a tracking sheet that I displayed on the wall so that all the students knew exactly where they were. I started the session explaining that by the end they should all have completed at least one task and possibly two (differentiation). They had the tracking sheet to look back at and as they came to me with their work I gave instant feedback and put a tick on the tracking sheet when the task was complete.

This turned out to be one of the best sessions I had had to date even though I felt ill. All the learners knew exactly where they were and I could just sit at the back of the room facilitating and giving feedback when necessary.

Discussion

1 Gaynor did not prepare this class. She was surprised at what happened. What surprised her?

2 She had set the tasks earlier for individuals to do at their own pace, how did she monitor that?

3 Does it matter that you and I do not know what the students were actually learning in terms of content? what *'pre-release material'* or *'differentiation'* means or what the 'tasks' were?

4 What were the students actually learning in addition to the content?

5 What was Gaynor learning from the experience?

6 What form do you think the 'input' was in? How did the students know 'exactly where they were' and what they had to do to complete each task?

7 What was Gaynor's role in this class? How did the students react to this 'new' role?

8 Why do you think Gaynor felt *'This turned out to be one of the best sessions I had had to date even though I felt ill.'* ? What was good about it?

9 What can we learn about the role of the teacher in this kind of ICT learning experience?

10 What was important to do earlier that made it possible for the class to operate in this way?

11 What lessons could you learn from Gaynor's experience for your own classes?

12 Would it be possible to run all the classes this way? If not, why not?

Comment

Learning ICT can easily reinforce teacher dependence when what is needed is the confidence to learn on your own. The teacher also worries about losing control of the learning. *'They need to be told so that they get it right.'*

Letting go, trusting the students, changing your perception of your 'role' are hard to do until you have the confidence to take the risk, trust the students, let happen what will, watch and support as it seems appropriate.

In this case, Gaynor was ill and felt unable to stand in front of the class and talk to them. She sat at the back instead and watched. The students wanted to learn, wanted perhaps to please her. The tasks had been defined and each had a learning map to 'keep track' of progress. They could refer to her for feedback and reassurance that they had got it right.

We have noted already how important it is to define tasks. Learning skills, implementing the applications software of computers is experiential, you learn it by doing it, but it is much better if the focus is on the product, tasks, rather than on the mechanics of the application. You ride the bike to go somewhere.

Discussion

Generally, discussion is handled least well of all teaching methodology. It seems to come so naturally that there appears to be no need to intervene. But it is the one area where you, as the teacher, have to be at your most skilful and where you can most easily lose control of the learning.

Discussion has to be deliberately organised in teaching. Because it is one of the most common of human activities this is hard to do. The level of heat in the process depends on the personalities and the passions involved – the context. Outcomes depend on the level of interest in the topic that the students have, what it is for, its appropriateness for the experience of the group, and the quality of the initial input information. It has to seem purposeful to all those involved.

Discussion may be dominated by one or two people. Some, even the majority, may take no part or do very little. There are intervention techniques to be learned to try to ensure that all have the opportunity to contribute, that those who are shy or reluctant to speak are brought in and find a level of confidence to engage in exchanges, that those who have too much to say are made to listen as well as to speak.

Discussions can be very unproductive, can turn into arguments or shouting matches or even fights. Well-managed, they can help to solve problems, promote coordinated activity and generate enthusiasm and commitment. They can be used to clarify thinking and ideas, tackle misconceptions and bring to the surface deeply held convictions which may be the cause of misunderstanding.

'How do I know what I think until I hear what I say?'

Putting your thoughts into words is the only way to discover what you yourself think. That is what I am doing in writing this book. Listening to others with genuine interest to discover what they think is even harder. Watch televised sessions of Parliament. Is anyone actually listening? Or, if so, are they listening only to those they already agree with?

When we say that communication within a social unit has broken down, we usually mean that the parties (boss and trade union, husband and wife, parent and child) cannot discuss their differences, they remain isolated in their own positions.

Learning the skills of discussion must be something education should promote, but it rarely does. Why? Mainly because teachers tend to lack the skills themselves. Learning the skills of controlling discussions may be harder. A committee is usually only as good as its chairperson. Sometimes it is the quiet, rather reticent thinker, listening to others in the committee, who has the most penetrating ideas to contribute. How can you ensure s/he is heard?

Mentors and tutors rarely come to visit seminar work, preferring to see student teachers with formal classes or in practical sessions. Yet, if we are to negotiate learning programmes with groups of students, we have to genuinely listen to what they have to say. A pretence will not do. We must learn to manage group discussions to ensure they are effective. Sharing is two-way communication. Teachers have to learn to listen. And they must create the right conditions for such communication. See 'Barriers to Communication' in Chapter 21.

Discussions are easier in seminar groups; they are extremely hard to do with sizeable groups. They tend to be unsatisfactory with whole classes. The best way forward is to divide the class up into groups of no more than six with a time-scale, questions set out to discuss, and a requirement that each group reports its conclusions to the whole class. This needs careful planning and timing. Clearly, it is not possible without sufficient time for input (brief but very pointed), discussion, reporting and some drawing together of the outcomes at the end.

Agree the purpose

'*Gee, Mr Stravinsky,*' said one New York socialite, '*how do you know when to stop?*' The maestro replied, '*Before I begin, madam.*' If you have listened to Stravinsky's driving rhythms which seem to just speed on and on without signposts or punctuation, and then stop, you understand her question.

Generally, we can tell the beginning, middle and end of some activity. Not so with discussions which often appear to have none of these. Why is that? They lack shape because they lack a sense of purpose – they appear to be going nowhere.

However much pulsing energy and forward drive there may be in any discussion, students need to know where they are supposed to be going, why they are doing it – and when to stop – before they begin. Only then can teachers hope to control the interactions, monitor what happens, intervene to shape the discussion or stop unhelpful activity. Students and teacher alike must know the direction of travel, so that when the discussion starts to stray the teacher can bring it back on course. Student satisfaction or frustration depends critically on this because most adults are impatient of time-wasting, getting nowhere. They want to feel a real sense of progress. Those who know where they are going are more likely to arrive and to have some sense of having arrived.

Nor can teachers revisit rambling discussions that have little shape or pattern. How can they consolidate learning from them? The brain works with patterns; we must assist the process. There has to be some perceived structure. Structured questions help. They must also agree the rules which govern what happens.

Committee meetings have an agenda to make minute-writing possible. That is a useful model. You need to recognise that no one comes to discussion without an agenda of some kind. There may be as many agenda as there are persons involved, and this is a problem. Misunderstandings are avoided if the agenda is agreed, overt and purposeful, if the rules are understood and if someone takes the chair.

The best discussion has purposeful outcomes or action plans involving groups and individuals. People know what it is for: it is to clarify ideas and make decisions. Committees that meet simply to meet are wasting time; the main agenda item is fixing the date for the next meeting.

We all need to be clear: what happens next? As a result of discussing it here, what is supposed to happen? Discussion that has no purpose is best avoided, though there is value in the development of language skills in a foreign or second language, for example, in open-ended discussions. But even in this kind of class, discussion of questions in groups with a requirement to report findings to the whole class can be a very effective technique for overcoming reluctance to speak in that language. General social discussion as the glue for binding the group can happen in coffee breaks. Class time has to be seen by all to be used purposefully.

Structure: the teacher's role

Students expect you to take charge. It does not mean that it is always you who takes the chair. You can set up whole class discussions, but it is much better to set up groups, and usually without leaders, so long as the students have a clear agenda, structured questions to know where they are going within a time-scale and when they have arrived.

You will have to encourage openness, a willingness to explore issues, even bring out emotions and deeply held beliefs, as well as helping the students to restructure their ideas and their thinking by sharing with others.

The structure, therefore, is more to do with purpose and process than with content. This may be the opportunity to break out of a mind-set, to be ready to listen, look at things from a new angle, perhaps to reconstruct a value-system.

Discussion of closed questions, or where outcomes have been determined beforehand, are soon exposed. 'The chairman had the minutes in his pocket when he arrived.' It is too easy for teachers to arrive with the answers in their pocket – at the end of a supposedly open discussion to present the conclusions on a prepared handout or slide. The students quickly become demotivated, and may feel that the teacher is simply showing them how inadequate their efforts are. If you don't listen to them when you've asked them to speak up, why should they listen to you? It will probably create barriers to the 'message' you are trying to get across. The views of all students must be seen to be valued, taken into account in whatever decisions are made or conclusions are reached. Any summary should be of what they have discovered. Clearly, after that it is sensible to look at the conclusions and help them to see where they are inappropriate or inadequate or whatever.

All group activities involve group dynamics. These are not predictable even from one class to another. The clearer the structure and the goals, the easier it is to maintain control. Groups exhibit patterns of dominance and/or withdrawal. Try to involve all the students, and inhibit those who seek to dominate or use things for their own purposes in pursuit of a personal agenda.

You can make the structure loose or tight, and establish more or less teacher control the way you set it up. You can give the group(s) specific questions with guidance as to the kind of answers you will accept, or you can set out a series of structured (but still open) questions, intended to lead discussion down particular paths almost to a predetermined conclusion. You can make the questions less pointed but it may be very hard to come to any group or class consensus or to write up 'the minutes'.

The students should all have a copy of your lesson plan. It should state clearly when and how discussion is to occur, time constraints and intended outcomes, what they are supposed to achieve or where it fits with other learning activity. The clearer the guidance the better: preparation matters.

Chairing

You may appoint a chairperson for the discussion, or one for each group, to keep it going along the right path. You could make it rather like a committee meeting, perhaps, with a secretary to report back. If you want to be more in control, you can chair it yourself.

Who chairs the group discussion matters. Some let discussions ramble; others keep speakers to the point, inhibit interruption and defuse conflict, emphasise issues and avoid personal or emotive interactions. Teachers in the chair often seem to have the minutes already in their pockets. It is another lecture in disguise. The questioning may seem like 'guess the teacher's right answer'.

Reporting back

The discipline of reporting back is important. It concentrates the group's thinking if there is a need to report, to explain to others the conclusions and decisions about 'action' arrived at. The reporting method should be agreed. An excellent way is to supply each group with OHP acetates or flipchart size paper and pens and ask them to make a keyword structure for the reporter to talk to. This puts additional discipline into the discussion; the students have to agree words and structure and create it. It all takes time and this has to be planned. But it concentrates attention on the need for demonstrable outcomes.

A composite can easily be made, comparison with the conclusions of other groups is simple. It is not unusual to pin up around the room the keyword charts of all the groups. It overcomes also the tendency for the teacher to resume control by writing the conclusions of each group on the OHP or the board, or perhaps using a computer keyboard or tablet. If the technique is used in an inductive discussion with the whole class, one of your students could be asked to write up conclusions instead of the teacher. Students can take away the structured reports. If they have also specified 'action', they know what to do and who is to do it. This serves to consolidate the learning.

The minutes of effective committees have a strong structure, with minimum reporting of the discussion, but clearly stated outcomes and action points, with individual responsibilities that are also clearly defined.

Human factors

People unconsciously take messages from the arrangement of furniture, and are annoyed by messages that are contradictory or confusing. People sitting in rows talking to the backs of each other's heads miss subtleties of communication such as facial expressions, eye-contact, humour. How can they see this as a discussion? You have to move people and furniture to create the right environment.

Students know immediately what is to happen if they find chairs round a central table: this is to be a committee. But that is only one possibility. We can think about how to manipulate messages or how to create group space, group territories to get people working more closely together, identify each other and break down barriers. (See Chapter 21 and 22.)

We have to think about sound and vision. Groups competing at 'shouting levels' in the same room, for instance, create a great deal of 'noise' in all senses. How will they identify their space and their equipment such as a flipchart? If there are seminar rooms, use them.

Plan ahead. Define spaces and equip them for what you want the groups to do. For example, some teachers favour the use of flipcharts, some OHP, some may want to use laptops, perhaps, but to the same purpose: to present keyword structures to the other groups. Flipchart sheets can be put up around the walls for others to walk around to compare the great variety of ideas. Set up chairs, tables, screens, OHP, flipcharts or whatever. Give each group the tools for the job. Make it easy for them. Be businesslike. Do not try to invent on the hoof and create confusion.

What have they achieved?

Did the students achieve the goals and the intended outcomes? Are the ideas practicable? Does all or even any of it make good sense? What will they *now* do with the new structure they have created? Discussion is not usually about new information, although sometimes it is a way of focusing input by restructuring information they have already and making it group-orientated. In the end, it is mostly about attitudes and behaviour.

Seminars

Seminars are not lectures with small groups though they are often perceived that way. Their purpose is sharing, and most of the input should be by the students themselves. The normal approach is as a discussion, which is loosely structured but not formless. No progress is possible unless it is informed discussion with a shared and sound basis of information: to avoid rehearsing and arguing *ad nauseam* of unfounded, often passionately held opinions. Addition of new information may change suddenly the direction of an argument, and may then hasten agreement (or throw things into confusion).

The means of 'adding information' varies. Sometimes a lecture, a film or video can be the starting point, sometimes reading matter all the students will be expected to digest beforehand. If the input is complex, it is necessary to revisit it somehow. Often, it involves research by individuals or pairs, finding out from libraries or websites or local information centres or wherever.

A seminar's purpose may be to revisit and clarify earlier input to ensure that it is fully understood, usually by providing fresh input. Seminars should be used to provide and consolidate an information base the group can then work on. Many go much further and generate creative thinking. Often, someone is invited to lead the seminar, and to make a short introduction to supply a basis with questions for the group to address. A preliminary paper with information plus a working paper (with questions and keywords) will help to give shape to the seminar, maybe as 'challenge and defence' as in a debate.

There are advantages in someone producing a draft paper which the group then modifies and improves to present as a group paper. It hastens things along and helps to give shape and direction. This is, incidentally, the best way to arrive at clear action plans in committee work. It is a good way to make one individual responsible for at least one part (say each week) of a seminar programme.

If the purpose is to encourage all members of the seminar group to research a topic and then share what they discover (and if each is clear as to his or her specific contribution), this can rapidly increase the information base available. This technique is valuable when the contents of a syllabus seem extremely large and the teacher is faced with problems of covering *some* of it *somehow*. (See Case Study 22 on page 141.)

Structure

Most seminars are structured with clear time constraints and schedules. If someone is to produce a paper, it must be available to read beforehand. Input must be punchy and short, and discussion must be focused and to the point. It is its narrowness of focus that makes the session a seminar.

A seminar is strongly goal-orientated. Goals must be clear and agreed, and the group must be committed to them. Where action is required it must happen. Everyone carries equal responsibility for process and outcomes, that is, for success.

Competition

It is not unusual for seminar groups to become competitive. It may be deliberately arranged. 'Games' as tools for learning are based on such groups, which frequently become very tightly knit as a result, with both benefits and costs. The tasks the groups are given determine what happens. Watch carefully how groups interact and come together. If each is to produce an agreed view to present to others there will be less energy than if they are asked to come up with solutions to a problem, to discover the best solution, either for kudos or for a prize.

Many projects run like this, particularly in management training courses, where tremendously energetic seminar group work frequently happens.

CASE STUDY 26

An elaborate seminar game was devised at a weekend Department of Trade and Industry conference. Seminar groups were set the task of designing a science kit that would enable a learner in any country in the world (and without the difficulties of any language barriers) to learn and understand a principle in science. There were constraints: it had to work with minimum technology available anywhere (it must not need electricity), it had to pack flat but be possible for anyone to assemble using diagrams as instructions. Similarly, learning had to be experiential, by using the kit and diagrams. To achieve these goals, each group had to decide on a scientific principle, then decide how learners would understand what they had to do and what equipment they would need to learn it. Finally, the group had to decide how to do this within the constraints.

Each group had a seminar room with OHP, flipchart, whiteboard, pens, paper and so on: a group territory properly equipped for the job. There was a workshop with craft materials to make the kit once it was designed to ensure that it worked. Each group was required to demonstrate a working model to the other groups, and explain how it would be used.

Initially, each group had to formulate ideas and a design plan and explain it to the others: this was to share thinking and ideas and to get feedback. The final demonstration was required at the end.

One group set out to facilitate learning 'kinetic and potential energy'. They agreed that everyone would have water. Water has potential energy if it is stored at a height. If the water falls its energy is converted into kinetic energy, which can be used to drive a turbine. This in turn could be converted into electrical energy and used to light a bulb. The only remaining requirement was energy input to raise the water. If the learners had to put in their own energy they could learn about work. The important thing was that the system had to be 'closed': no extra energy had to be added other than the learners' own work.

A kit was designed, and then built out of simple craft materials, to raise the water and store it in a tank. A tube with a tap led the water to turn a turbine (slats in a spindle) and so a simple dynamo to light a bulb. The water was collected in a lower tank to be returned to an upper tank by the energy supplied by the learner, using a shadoof to raise the water. This energy was the only thing to be added to the system.

The whole apparatus could pack flat for assembly on site. Instructions for building the kit and for running it were in diagrams. The group wanted to use the nineteenth-century 'flick-book' technique here: by flicking the edges of a series of photographs the images can appear to move.

Discussion

1 Can you think of a way of involving your students in inventive activity?

2 What will you need to do to prepare for such activity?

3 Obviously, it would only be possible to do something as complicated as this with the right kind of equipment and in an appropriate environment? What facilities can you use?

4 Do you have the confidence to trust your students if they cannot do it under your eye?

5 What do they need as input and instructions/guidance to set about the task?

6 What sort of things would your students find exciting and interesting to do in your context?

7 Would it help to make it competitive, a game of some kind?

Comment

This inventiveness resulted from competition against others within tight parameters and constraints. The essential feature was that it presented a problem to solve. Motivation is important. The activity must seem purposive, possible to do if a little intimidating at first, and interesting. Solving problems is like that. In many good primary schools, a great deal of the most interesting work is group tasks to solve problems: *how could we keep pets in the school*? Or *how can we make everyone aware of the dangers of …?* Why do we not use this excitement more in FE/AE?

Promotional seminars

Seminars occur in commerce and industry, where ideas are shared round a table with a presentation of some kind by one of the members. But they may also be about selling an idea or a product, and so in actual fact small-scale lecture presentations, with the chance for questions and discussion afterwards. The difference is that in the former the outcomes are 'open', in the latter they are 'closed' and have the single purpose of persuading the audience to buy or not to buy.

I noted under AVA on pages 162–163 that today these are often computer-generated with Powerpoint using a light and portable projector linked to a laptop computer and a portable screen. The technique has led to the spread of the idea outside the boardroom. An advertisement in a WA newspaper read:

Free First Home Owners Seminar

This FREE seminar is an absolute must for all people considering purchasing their first home. This seminar will provide FIRST HOME BUYERS with an invaluable insight into a number of important issues, including:

- $7000 First Home Owners Grant. Are you eligible?
- Fees. Do you know what to budget for?
- Making an offer. Is this a legally binding document?
- Financing your dream. How much can I borrow?

You will have guessed that it was offered by someone selling mortgages. It is cleverly set out to tempt people with a free offer hook, baited with a government cash handout. The buyer is led on by questions you could reasonably guess s/he would want to know to the 'important' question: *How much can I borrow?* The first three questions are simply answered, a matter of facts to be found in any number of easily obtained documents. Obviously, the whole 'seminar' is about borrowing and this will certainly be 'as much as possible'. You could write the Powerpoint presentation for him, as long as you had access to the figures he will work on. Presumably, individuals would fix a time to work out their borrowing with him.

As a learning simulation, getting students to set up such a 'seminar' might prove enlightening for them. They could learn a great deal by discovering the relevant information, fees and mortgage lender rates and linking them to case study examples of young people buying for the first time. Then using Powerpoint to put it all together as a presentation and selling it to the class. In their case, yes it would be an excellent seminar activity!

Simulations

Teachers sometimes confuse the activities of simulations, games and role play, but they are really quite different. In a simulation a teacher must mimic a real situation. Many teachers may not be conscious of the fact that they already use simulations because it is the norm in training skilled tradesmen. The closer the simulation is to the 'reality', the better. It has to work in exactly the same way, but without the pressure of real time schedules. To set up a workshop simulation it is necessary to scale things down to what will fit into a booth rather than a house, if students are doing plumbing, say, or electrical wiring. Booths are normal practice in workshops. Stripping down and building an engine in a motor-vehicle shop is an example of a simulation. So is a catering kitchen and restaurant, or a hairdressing salon.

Students learn skills and confidence to deal with 'reality', but in a controlled environment in which constraints can be carefully chosen. The important thing is that real pressures, such as the dire consequences of failure, can be removed. But rules that apply to real encounters apply to simulations.

A simulated committee meeting has a real agenda and clearly identified roles. Students 'play' roles, but constraints of money, time, production targets, or whatever the committee is about, have to be real. The group is learning to run a committee effectively and purposively. Such simulations differ in many obvious ways from practising with tools in workshops. They involve time-scales. We need to be able to reflect on the experience, to look at the process and the outcomes. It is easier if the experience is relatively short. But there are many long simulations, like caterers in a training kitchen and restaurant, or apprentices working as a team to undertake a project in design and construction in a production simulation, where many different skills are being addressed beyond those of the craft itself. (See Case Study/Lesson Plan 2, caterers running a business, page 65.)

In all cases, what is to be assessed is not simply the quality of products or tangible outcomes, but changes in attitudes, insights and the intelligent application of skills. As most simulations of this kind are by groups, assessment of what each individual has contributed and achieved may be difficult.

The advantages of this kind of simulation are:

- removal of the consequences of failure, leading to a greater willingness to take risks
- opportunity to experience roles and responsibilities which are not one's own, but normally those of more senior people, and so provide insight into levels of decision-making
- elimination of arbitrary problems through the tutor's control of constraints
- feedback and reflection on the experience
- flexibility to change the constraints, goals, time-schedules and so forth
- simplification of outcomes and criteria for assessment, at least for group achievements/learning.

Real life experiential learning can be painful, slow and confusing. There are many risks that managers and learners deliberately avoid. Much of what is going on in the learning experience is missed because of limitations in sensory perception and the attention you can give it. Teachers in simulations can help their learners to see much that they would otherwise miss. And because learners never can acquire all the necessary skills together at once, learning of skills is easier if they are practised under controlled conditions.

But teachers can also make simulations 'closed' or 'open'. Catering training is closed, almost rehearsing a script, with very strongly defined role-models and procedures to follow; invention comes later. Other simulations are deliberately left to develop. Having catering students simulate setting up a business, for example, as in Lesson Plan 2. A design project like the one above demands creativity within constraints. Teachers have to trust the students and monitor what happens.

In the end the learning has to be tested in the fire, in a real context, because most simulations do not begin to match the pressures in the employment base. Other factors beside skills and insights come into play forcefully. Much carefully trained and desirable behaviour is often set aside; that may lead to mismatch and disillusionment for the learners.

This also happens all too often when teachers go away for training courses. It was one of the arguments for on-site training in commerce and industry and away from simulated environments like workshops and offices; and the political pressure discussed later for training on employers' premises.

CASE STUDY 27

On a CGLI 730 teacher training course, some tutors of an establishment to train firemen redesigned a course to deal with accidents on a motorway. They had available a sophisticated simulation. No expense was too great when it was about life and death decisions. Fire fighters of all ranks were seconded to this college from all over the UK and overseas for periods up to a month. An old airfield was converted into a training ground with concrete 'mock-ups' of motorways, railways, ships, tower blocks, and other structures. Fire could be set in any of them, and accidents staged, emergencies of all kinds simulated. Firemen had to enter and negotiate tunnels and towers with breathing apparatus, in the dark, or whatever might be devised as experiential learning under controlled conditions. There were lavishly equipped lecture theatres and dormitory accommodation.

Once these tutors had designed their course, making full use of all the above, they evaluated it against agreed criteria. One real problem was how to assess the learning. They looked for methods of assessing it *as a course*. It was, however, a simulation of teamwork with some input lecture style using video-playback and so on for discussions and feedback.

They agreed that the only sensible way to assess the learning was to watch these firemen in action. The acid test was whether the trainees under pressure of 'the real situation' performed more effectively or not. It was transferability of learning from the simulation to reality that mattered.

Discussion

1 Can simulations play any useful part in your own field of teaching?
2 Consider again Case Study 10 of Karen's Office Skills class. Would a change of that kind be appropriate with your students?
3 What are the benefits of this kind of activity?
4 What are the possible problems?

Comment

Clearly, simulations are much easier in some teaching fields than in others. Nor does it make sense to do something just because it might be interesting to do. It has to seem purposeful to the students. But this kind of activity can often enable students to find a new excitement in the learning process. The major problem is how to create an appropriate simulation of a 'real' environment or context.

Improving simulations

Ensure that the match with real world experience is close. Unless the learning is transferable, it will soon be lost. It is transferability of skills and insight (attitudinal change above all) to a real context which matters most. It is true not least in teaching, and it has been one of the main criticisms made of specialist college courses that tended, at least in the past, to value talking about it above doing it. But it applies in all fields. If students are trained in a workshop to work with lathes, say, to do it in a particular way, and then go back to work where the employer tells them to forget that because they do it differently, it is easy to imagine the effect on the learners. This happened regularly.

Matching reality for the learners has implications for the resourcing and organisation of the simulation, and for methods of assessment. You can only learn good working practice with the right equipment and in a supportive environment. In this sense, much vocational training may be seen as simulating real world working conditions.

Much of this kind of learning is caught rather than taught. It is in part the argument for the present proposal that all student teachers should have a mentor in their own specialist area. The Inspectorate reported that too little teacher training was in how to teach specialist subjects. What is not proposed is the training such mentors should receive. Nothing is new. Juvenal in *Satires*, published in the first century AD, asked: *Quis custodiet ipsos custodes?* (Who will guard the guards?)

CASE STUDY 28

A tutor of a teacher training course encouraged the student teachers to take risks and experiment in order to create varied learning experiences for their students. He encouraged them to have a flexible approach in their class planning and to respond as far as possible to student needs.

The student teachers were mainly in full-time employment seconded for half a day a week to attend the course. This pattern is now standard practice in colleges because of the requirement for all teachers to achieve a QTFE certificate. A great benefit is sharing of experience across disciplines by bringing teachers together from many departments, together with those from industry, part-timers in AE as well as FE, and from many other backgrounds such as Social Services and Nursing.

On going to observe a male student teacher in a vocational department, the tutor discovered that he had been given a roasting by the HOD because he had not used the set lesson plan that teachers of those courses were required to use. Naturally, the teacher had agreed to conform. Flexibility was out.

Discussion

1 What would you do if you were this tutor?

2 What would you do if you found yourself the teacher in this situation?

3 Do you agree that in some courses there is a right way to teach and it is a good idea that all do it the same way?

4 Why did the HOD insist that all the teachers conform to a set lesson plan in the department?

5 What are the arguments for and against that idea?

6 What do you think could happen at college level to avoid conflicts of this sort between training staff and the expectations of teachers in departments?

7 What are the pressures on institutions that might lead them to behave in this way?

Comment

This kind of mismatch begs the question as to what is the right way to do things. It is often the case in commerce and industry that employers are more interested in their profit than 'doing it according to the book'. The pressure on HODs and institutions is to make sure that students achieve the 'standards' and obtain the certification for courses they enrol on. Like administrators in American colleges, the need for control of what happens in their classes is strongly felt by administrators of UK colleges. In reality their jobs, the teachers' jobs, the finance of the institution all depend on demonstrable results, students achieving criteria specified outside the control of the institution. Failure or serious dropping out by students threatens the survival of a course. Imposing one lesson-plan, one methodology, on all the teachers of a course may appear to ensure control.

Can the HOD or the institution afford to take risks or allow their teachers to take risks? It is easy to believe that a particular formula works best and to insist that all conform.

Playing safe is at a premium. It is also possible to see this built into NVQ course guidance. Read more in Chapter 23 'Assessment' and the Appendix, where DfES in *An Agenda for Reform* addresses matching in-service training, the induction of new staff and staff development to overall college development plans on a college-wide programme with agreed aims.

What is needed is negotiation to agree what is good working practice. It is not unusual in any field for the trainers and employers of the trainees to have conflicting views, for the students to be confused by what they are asked to do. What students and employers want is demonstrable results. If you do it differently from the accepted norm, it had better improve performance.

It is absurd to deny that in many cases there is 'a right way' of doing something. Most kinds of machinery must be stripped down and assembled in the right way. Standard practices in trades are the result of years of experience. It is possible, must be right, to insist on specific instruction. But that does not necessarily mean that the same teaching/learning methods, or a standardised lesson plan, are right. Trainers of teachers have to recognise such constraints. Nevertheless, there are many fields and areas of training even within such trades as plumbing where narrowness in training is undesirable. Competence is not simply 'can do correctly', but 'can do intelligently' according to the context and circumstances. If one wants an automaton one should employ a machine. Read Bruner's concept of 'Competence' on page 327.

There are techniques for playing the piano, singing or any other form of artistic expression, but the variety of methods students might meet in going from teacher to teacher is amazing. It is not in fact possible to say precisely how any individual will learn right techniques.

To ensure meaningful competence in addition to motor skills teachers should promote

- development of cognitive skills
- affective learning such as commitment to the job
- positive attitudes
- intelligent decision-making
- problem solving skills
- insight.

The problem is that external assessment seems to value demonstrable skills as competences in many of the areas of FE training, because they are much easier to observe.

Games

In games the important thing is the pressure of competition; look at Case Study 26 on page 190. The skills required are not necessarily the same as those needed in real situations. Games have 'rules' that are arbitrary and meant to even out the odds, to eliminate certain aspects of reality, to concentrate on the insights the students are intended to learn. The rules can be changed, the situation manipulated. It is the arbitrary nature of games that makes them unlike simulations. Nor is it intended that what is learned, or the behaviour, should be practised or transferable to any real context.

The learning is about

- insights into human behaviour and how things happen
- the factors involved in decision-making
- psychology of 'gamesmanship'
- competing with others
- working as a team
- problem-solving
- winning and losing – both with equanimity
- binding groups together.

Games like Monopoly and Chess are played with boards and symbolic pieces. Others are physical as problem-solving in the round (the Army uses 'field' games to reveal officer potential). They can be intellectual power games, or playing the stock exchange, or being Wellington at Waterloo, or solving murders in a country house.

Ten thousand kinds! To use a game, you must first think through carefully *what it is for* and what is involved.

Games are dangerous if handled badly. They can take over, they gain their own momentum to become extremely 'noisy', so that it becomes very hard to know what is being learned. You can lose control of any game once it is set going. All the same students love such things and they can be great fun, which learning undoubtedly should be much of the time. But the students must know they are playing, it is not real, and the rules are arbitrary. It is too easy for a game to become 'real', to become too serious, emotional pressures and anxieties take over. Students in a losing team can become angry or demoralised.

The learning can only be revealed in the evaluation by asking: What happened? Why? What have we learned? Students and teacher should agree what the game was for, but they cannot begin to focus on that while the game is in progress. It has to happen by reflecting on the experience. There must be plenty of time to do that or there will be little learning, just a glow. Equally, the teacher must intervene if things are really not going in the intended direction or if emotional factors are likely to create negative outcomes.

Management training uses a combination of simulations and games where the boundaries may become blurred. There are good books with compilations of Management Games. In these, teams are often set the task of offering solutions to difficult situations, such as being adrift in a raft at sea when your yacht sinks and your team has to evaluate a list of items according to their usefulness to ensure survival till rescued, or your team has to rescue cavers trapped underground by rising flood water. The context is carefully modelled with strict constraints.

CASE STUDY 29

David had a group of students learning English in a Japanese University. In groups of six they tackled the Game of rescuing trapped cavers, taken from a compilation of games and other training activities in management training. It is a leaderless game where ideas are shared, but all must agree on what to do, a course of action. They were asked to offer their solutions to the whole class after 50 minutes to reach a consensus. Their decisions were written on the chalkboard in columns, so that groups could compare what each had decided. They had also to explain the rationale for their decisions.

Six cavers are trapped by a rock-fall and rising water in a cave system; they will all die unless they are rescued. The job of each team is to organise the rescue under severe constraints. They can bring out only one caver every hour because of a shortage of breathing apparatus and the cave will be full of water in four hours. The conclusion seems to be that two will die before they can be rescued. Each group has to decide the order of rescue for the people in the cave. There is no correct solution.

To help them the Game gives a brief biography of each of the cavers. These are designed to appeal to stereotype images and prejudices, so that the 'rescuers' will make decisions based on these rather than on rational consideration of the situation. A young, rich, beautiful Japanese girl; a middle-class woman cheating on her husband with the leader of the cavers – but she has four young children; a neurotic doctor who molests young women, but who is doing important research that might be lost; an African communist with 11 children, who is a church minister and political 'thorn in the flesh' to the British; an ex-soldier decorated for bravery as an under-cover agent in Northern Ireland, but now a drunk having an affair with the house-wife; an industrialist in his sixties 'from up north', a member of the Conservative party, whose death will lead to loss of an order that will cost 200 jobs.

David gave them a sheet inviting them to identify 'Priorities' and their 'Criteria' before the decisions were made. He told them to consider the situation, how terrifying it was to be trapped in a cave in the dark with water rising around them. Think of *what* and *how* as well as *who*.

The groups laughed a great deal as they talked about who they would leave to die!! and why. Their reports at the end confirmed this, especially how the 'lovers' would be happy to die together. There was no consistency of choice in the order of rescue, but the drunk having an affair was nearly always last. David had used the Game with groups in England and America with similar responses and decisions from the students.

Discussion

1 What is this game actually about? The rescue or the prejudices of the 'rescuers'?

2 What is the purpose of this game?

3 Why did the groups laugh so much when talking about leaving people to die?

4 How should games of this kind be conducted?

5 Is it best to leave it totally 'open' rather than to try to point it in a particular direction?

6 David tried to make the students think about the reality and what their priorities should be. Why did the students ignore all of that?

7 Is it a good thing that games are so separated in the mind from reality?

8 Were you surprised at all by the kind of decisions the students made?

Comment

All these biographies contained 'political triggers' of the mid-1980s in the UK, when the game was written. The fascinating thing for David was that he used this game in England, America and Japan, but there appeared to be no cultural barriers, the results were the same. 'A week is clearly a long time in politics.' Students everywhere thought about the 'value' as people or to society of the cavers and their emotional relationships and ignored the political triggers and the practical considerations of the rescue. They did what the designers of the Game meant them to do: they concentrated on biography as if this were a novel, not real people in danger. TV images of rescues in caves or wherever were the same worldwide and so removed cultural barriers. Such images also distance the viewers from reality.

The designers of the game manipulated information to control what the players did. The way information is skewed leads to the wrong kinds of questions; it is another example of 'bottom up'. All the information about the lives of the cavers is irrelevant to the kinds of decisions needed in the context of a cave rescue. Students were asked to measure the value of people's lives and then to act as judge and executioner. They found that great fun!

Clearly, no one can play God to judge people, which is what they all enjoyed doing. The first 'priority' must be that no one will die! If you start with that instead of deciding which of the six will be left to die, you will probably ask the right kind of questions about what to do and how to save all of them. The Game brilliantly made the students focus on unhelpful, confusing information and daft questions. It is actually about practical solutions. What is important is to have a clear model in the head of the job you are trying to do. You have to decide on your priorities and criteria for making choices. When dealing with problems most information is 'noise' and produces confusion. You must find the right questions to sift out useless information, to concentrate on what will be helpful in making the most sensible decisions. Armed with the right questions and not allowing your personal prejudices to influence what you do, rational and practical decisions will emerge. In the evaluation after the Game, David was able to draw that conclusion. The two factors of greatest importance here are *speed* and *panic v. calm organisation*. From those one can easily identify criteria for decision-making.

Games can and should be used in this kind of way, to face students with themselves and their own behaviour. They can learn how to tackle problems and how unhelpful information and prejudice can lead to wrong questions and irrational decisions. There should be transferability of the learning to real decision-making as a result of reflecting on the game: on what happened and why.

Teams

Evaluating and learning from games

Simulations and games bring us increasingly up against ourselves. What we learn is not simply how to do something, or even insight into the way things work, but most importantly what it feels like to be there, to be under pressure making decisions, taking responsibility, making things happen. '*Can I cope?*', '*Is this really me?*' We are faced with the challenge of performance. We adopt roles and take on responsibility, we cannot avoid it. We also learn what it means to work as part of a team, relying on others and they on us. With any luck, we find a good team and lots of support, but it doesn't always happen. Some people may be badly hurt, their self-esteem and self-image damaged not improved. That is what real life does to people.

In management training, such as that described by R.M. Belbin in *Management Teams: Why they Succeed and Fail,* teams were manipulated into different patterns by selecting personality types, those who will meld into efficient teams and others who will clash or fail to adhere. Belbin predicted that good teams need a leader (an Apollo) to generate ideas, but s/he is rarely good at getting things done, so you also need a good planner/implementer, another as a negotiator and so on. In particular, if two strong ideas-people try to impose their ideas, they will destroy the effectiveness of the team: he called it the *Apollo syndrome*. Out of the experience of being in competing teams, some that fail and others that succeed, trainees learn to become more skilful in their roles within teams, partly as a result of identifying what role they are best suited for. Belbin's conclusion was that someone had to consciously choose people with different strengths to put together successful teams.

Many games involve teams, but many pitch individuals one against another. There is in the main much less transferable learning benefit from such games, you just get better at winning that sort of game. Many examinations work like a sophisticated game of that kind, of course. To draw benefit from simulations and games, students have to focus on the positive learning that comes from the experience, for them personally and for the team. Tutor support is essential if they are to gain fully from these learning activities.

It is difficult to define learning goals as specific, demonstrable outcomes in activities where so much of what will occur is unpredictable, and deliberately so. It is possible, though, and in some cases, such as the catering simulation in Lesson Plan 2, it is desirable to make the outcomes 'closed' and quite specific as learning goals to be assessed.

To consolidate the learning, students need to agree what learning occurred as a result of the game, as a process of reflection on it. To assist that process, it is helpful to agree a statement of the intended learning, what the activity is for, before they undertake it. As an example only, apart from learning how to win, the list might include:

■ to understand the value of teamwork and planning
■ to gain insight into roles and responsibilities
■ to discover what 'my' strengths and weaknesses are
■ to discover how to work effectively in a team
■ to discover how to tackle problems systematically
■ to learn how to use information, to find the right questions
■ to discover skills such as [...]
■ to discover how to deal with frustration and stress
■ to gain confidence and coping skills.

Knowing what you are trying to learn before you set out will help you to identify questions that should be addressed to the experience when it is over. It is obviously difficult to specify learning goals in such activities because much of what occurs is unpredictable, unless it is 'closed'. But how do you 'close' a game? It is necessary, however, to agree at the end what has been learned in an evaluation by both teacher and students. Otherwise, consolidation becomes impossible.

Role play

Many simulations involve taking on 'roles'. Sometimes, as we have seen, there is a script (actual or implied) that controls what is allowed of the 'characters' involved.

Often, specific roles are needed to make a simulation more real: in a committee, say, people who are eager to get things done, those who want to block things, those who are pursuing a personal agenda, personalities that clash, and so on. Teachers can deliberately identify such personalities, and spell them out to the students concerned. In some cases, the teacher allows only the person in the role to see his/her description.

When exploring roles takes precedence over all other factors, the exercise becomes role play. As someone goes into role, they must adopt a level of belief about themselves as the person they are to become. There is liberation in role play: '*There are a hundred different 'mes' trying to get out*', said one American student.

Since it is not 'me', the usual constraints on 'my behaviour' may be relaxed. This is great, if that is what we want to happen. Many students can only get past their own inhibitions this way, and it can be most important in learning languages, or in learning to deal with people in social situations. Such methods can be used with excellent results.

In most contexts, role play should be used with care. It is a very powerful tool, and teachers can use it effectively or dangerously. It may turn into discovering feelings, releasing deep emotions, revealing images, stereotypes, unconscious values and so on that lie hidden in our subconscious. Both adults and youngsters can be quite startled by what they do, since they are not consciously in control. The most hilariously funny things I have seen have occurred during role play, but so have traumatic breakdowns. You are allowing people to discover things about themselves, about relationships with others, perhaps about deeply held values, and bringing them into the open.

Taking on a role may uncover one of the hundreds of 'mes' trying to get out, some of which may not be at all 'nice'; it can remove barriers, inhibitions, which make it difficult to talk rationally about things. Alcohol, of course, has a similar effect. The images youngsters have of their parents, for example. Relationships, like sex and space, are hard to talk about. Acted out, we may discover what we really feel and truly believe, even if we wish to deny those feelings and beliefs in a rational moment. It is best to avoid role play that explores suppressed strong emotions such as anger or fear or jealousy.

To use role play as a learning tool you must maintain control. You must remain in charge in an activity where it is impossible to predict what is going to happen. You must be ready to stop it or intervene if things take off in ways that are not helpful to the intended learning. Be prepared for participants to use stereotyping they hardly know they have even when roles are incidental to simulations: the stereotype union negotiator, the manager/boss, the wife/husband, the mother-in-law, the customer. Students are exploring their images of such persons. You will need to evaluate such images with the students and help them to talk through where they have come from and what effect such stereotyping has on their own behaviour.

Use role as a way of getting at aspects of learning students find difficult because of attitudinal problems or inhibitions. There are many examples: speaking a foreign language is a good one. Or you might get students to negotiate a price for a catering buffet, or for a product they want to sell, or for insight into relationships.

Guidance

There is no value in going into a role play without clear guidance to everyone concerned as to what role they are to play and what is to be discovered from the exercise. In Drama, there are advantages in improvising scenes, situations and experiences. Those who want to become actors have to be able to 'experience' the physical and emotional sensations of others – or themselves in strange contexts. It is an exercise in stimulating and freeing the imagination, to release the hundred 'mes'. But that is not the purpose of role play in most other teaching contexts.

It is not always easy to set out guidance because people will only see what they expect to see. People just look at the name on the label and not the contents of the bottle. It is the same with any information. Ensure that there is a preliminary session when things are carefully discussed, explored and explained. Get them each to tell you what their role is, so that you can share their perception of it before they begin. This will help the evaluation at the end, of course.

COURSE DESIGN

ACTIVITY 9

As part of your course design, consider the place of any of these methods in your lessons. A lesson is itself a mini-strategy. It is important to build in as much sensible variety as you can.

To learn you must tackle each method systematically, then afterwards look carefully at what happens to ask why it happened. You will discover where you are lacking in skill and understanding, so that the next time you will be better prepared and will tackle that method more effectively.

Suggested reading

BACIE. *Management Games*. BACIE, 1965.

Belbin, R.M. *Management Teams: Why They Succeed or Fail*, Heinemann (London), 1981.

Bligh, D.A. *What's the Use of Lectures?*, Jossey Bass Wiley, 2000.

Bligh, D., Jaques, D., Piper, D.W. *Seven Decisions When Teaching Students*, Intellect Books, 1981.

Coombes, B. *Basic Teaching Skills*, Heinemann, 1995.

Coombes, B. *Successful Teaching*, Heinemann, 1999 (simplified advice).

Cunningham, U. and Andersson, S. *Teachers, Pupils and the Internet*, Stanley Thornes, 1999.

Gardner, P. *Teaching and Learning in Multicultural Classrooms*, David Fulton, 2001.

Gardner, P. *Strategies and Resources for Teaching and Learning*, David Fulton, 2002.

Gelb, M. *Present Yourself*, Guild Publishing (London), 1988.

Jaques, D. *Learning in Groups*, Kogan Page (London), 2nd edn. 1991.

Joseph, R. *Stress-Free Teaching*, Kogan Page, 2000.

McCarthy, P. and Hatcher, C. *Presentation Skills*, Sage Publications, 2002.

Russell, T. *Teaching and Using ICT in Secondary Schools*, David Fulton, 2001.

Shannon, C. and Weaver, W. *The Mathematical Theory of Communication*, University of Illinois Press (Illinois), 1949.

Sutcliffe, J. *Adults with Learning Difficulties: Education for Choice and Empowerment*, NIACE/Open University Press, 1990.

Thomas, G. *Effective Classroom Teamwork*, Routledge, 1992.

von Mente, M. *The Effective Use of Roleplay*, Kogan Page, 1989/99.

Wheeler, M. and Bligh, D. *Counselling in Study Methods*, Intellect Books, 1985.

Woodcock, M. *Team Development Manual*, Gower Press (Farnborough), 1979.

<table>
<tr><td>**CHAPTER 17**</td><td>**Managing flexible learning**</td></tr>
</table>

DESIGNING TASKS

It is essential that *before they begin* students know clearly what they have to do individually and together, what each task is for, where it is going, how to get there and how it will be assessed. Analyse carefully what it is you are asking your students to do.

- What are the learning goals? Have the students agreed them?
- Is it appropriate in form and standard for the students in terms of their background and ability?
- Is it clear what the task is for? How does it contribute to the learning?
- Is it clear how the learning will be demonstrated and assessed?
- What is their role? What is your role?
- How much is required of individuals and how much full participation by the class?
- What level of difficulty and challenge do you perceive? How will they know it?
- Have you thought through what is required to achieve the task?
- What are the criteria for success? How will they know?
- What level of preparation and guidance is there?
- What resources will you provide and what must they devise or find for themselves?

Process

The students will do tasks in a sequence. You should ask:

- How will the sequence be known?
- Who will make the decisions?
- How will targets be set?
- What time constraints will there be?
- Will there be 'complete by' dates?
- How much of all this is negotiable – or renegotiable – with the tutor?

Students may need to be guided through early tasks:

- finding out where they can get help and resources
- how to use the library/multi-media/resource centre or any specialist areas
- how to manage equipment
- how to seek help and information in any other place
- how to explore major resources such as city archives.

You cannot assume that students can do any of these things, they must be shown how. Some tasks mean dealing with people rather than with books or things, especially if it is about social skills and the ability to work with others. Students need help in understanding how

- to deal with people
- to interview them, perhaps
- to conduct negotiations
- to do a survey.

None of this can be taken for granted: it is courting disaster simply to tell students to do such things and hope it will be all right. Teachers cannot know what is involved, how hard it is or the kind of difficulties that are likely to occur, unless they experience the task themselves. Every task needs validating by experience, preferably by the teachers doing it themselves.

Task design

This is the essential skill. Patterns help. Establish a format that is understood. Ask yourself what the students need in the way of information and guidance in order to do the task. Provide an overview of how this task fits into the whole. Before setting out to do it they need to know clearly:

- what they are setting out to learn
- what they have to do
- why they should do it
- what they will use in order to do the task
- where it is to be found
- how they will get hold of the necessary resources they will use
- criteria for successful completion
- some view of what an appropriate response is: e.g. the length of an essay
- preferably models to show the level or standard required
- where the task and its completion fit into overall grading of achievement
- any other things you have to think about.

If the task is to achieve a product – a tangible object, a demonstration of skill or an essay – they must know what form it should take, and the criteria for success. Obviously, in some fields such as art or poetry or creative writing it is not possible to be precise without limiting the imagination of students. But for judgements to be dependent simply on subjective responses of judges will not do. Students need to understand what the assessment process is, how it will be handled, and how achievement will be recorded and profiled. It must therefore be clear to them how successful achievement of each task contributes to achievement of major learning goals.

Each task needs to be appraised for the demands it makes on an individual student in terms of pace, readiness, ability to meet a challenge: all must be thought through. Is there sufficient flexibility in the guidance and criteria to allow for variations in ability to cope with the demands or to interpret the tasks to meet personal learning needs? And above all, clarity and simplicity in the guidance matter. The less the better, so long as it is complete and unambiguous.

Using resources

The teacher is an important resource for students, but not the only one they may use. Teachers put intolerable burdens on themselves to deliver if they feel all learning must be funnelled through them. Increasingly, teachers must become managers of learning that uses all manner of resources, not least those the students bring with them. Teachers need different skills to become such managers because they are handing over much of the responsibility for learning and control to the students. Teachers need confidence and trust in students and in their own ability to cope.

Much managed learning happens under controlled conditions. An engineering workshop, for example, is a major resource and an example of managed learning: students perhaps using lathes and worksheets are on individualised programmes. Or reading an English literature text quietly and then discussing it in groups, or writing an essay to show insight into a writer's style. Hardly revolutionary. What is intended is a total change in methodology, with different roles and responsibilities for teacher and students.

Teaching teams design whole learning packages: how students learn, resources in order to learn, the context/environment and the learning materials. They provide the guidance and monitoring: negotiating action plans with individuals, writing programmes of study and giving tutorial support. In this project, developing learning materials, designing and writing tasks or learning kits are the major functions; along with supervision, monitoring and assessment of the programmes. Tutorial functions include setting targets and schedules, devising and monitoring performance criteria, assessing achievement and handling feedback.

The responsibility for the learning is firmly with the students. The teacher has to manage the resources, the tasks and the programme rather than the students, ensuring that they can access what they need and controlling the learning process. If it is computer-based, it may be called VLE/MLE (Virtual Learning and Managed Learning Environments).

Costing of programmes becomes important. The cost of making materials is offset by the freedom teachers have to do other things, perhaps more effectively than regular classroom teaching. All this means a redefinition of teaching time and scheduling. Decisions must be made about input sessions and group activities, if there are any. Do they happen regularly week by week, or as needed to maintain progress? Since programmes are individualised, there has to be time for tutorials. How are they to be paid for? Preparation pays off, but setting up is expensive. Time and effort to design and create useful, valid resources will have to be paid for out of whole budget planning.

Managed learning programmes work well if:

- there are teams and resource-bases for developing materials
- learning structure and design are carefully thought through
- tasks and assignments are well designed and well presented
- the learning is interesting, stimulating and relevant
- there is clear understanding of learning activities
- there are agreed criteria for successful achievement through the completion of learning tasks
- there is effective monitoring
- there is sufficient finance and good technical support with appropriate facilities
- students are taught study skills and how to organise their own learning
- feedback is immediate at a point of need, and is supportive and positive – preferably in tutorials
- there is sufficient flexibility and adaptability to individual need
- record-keeping and tracking of achievement are maintained.

Distance learning/Flexistudy

Flexibility of provision by educational institutions is a response to difficulties that confront so many adult students on training or educational opportunities. Programmes of study and training have to be devised that allow learners (or employers or who ever requires the service) to negotiate how, where and when learning programmes, courses or whatever, happen. Time-scales, attendance patterns and assessments may need to become more like the American model of Community Colleges: students at any age can pick up any number of 'credits' over any length of time. This is the pattern chosen by the Australian university Sarah used in Case Study 20. A student makes his/her decisions in consultation with advisers about how and when, but not usually where. The present British system of accreditation does not allow for this kind of provision at every level, but it may have to come. Obviously it is difficult to allow for any possible pattern. Regular attendance on a course is still the preferred model, but negotiated provision related to the needs of the employers or the employees or individual learners is a stated aim of all departments. Students may or may not have to attend at a college or educational institution on particular days at specified times.

Institutions are no longer 'closed', they allow open access to expertise and facilities not limited in time or place. They are ready to meet the needs of individuals, employers and their employees and other groups wherever appropriate; and to do so on their premises as out-reach provision. It requires a responsive management; flexibility in the delivery of programmes; readiness to tailor provision to the individual's availability and time for study; a counselling system to guide students through their learning programme, which has been negotiated with/for them. There is a monitoring service that is intended to ensure that students are supported and achieve the goals identified in their programme.

Courses are now mostly based on tasks and assignments supported by input reading, computer software programs and other materials. They may involve sessions on premises other than a college ('out-reach' courses). They may be designed as a 'distance learning' programme on the same model of reading, assignments, assessment and feedback. In all cases, the teacher is tutor to individuals and must be readily available for consultation in a variety of ways. When there is no regular attendance, blocks of time for groups of students to get together may be set for weekends or on a Saturday only, or maybe even a residential week along Open University lines. This has clear implications for the flexibility of the teaching staff also.

Resource-based learning/CAL

Individualised learning is a strategy in which a teacher is just one of many resources a student is able to *access* (in the new jargon) in order to learn. Resources are the essential part of teaching/learning programmes; for no strategy can be successful that does not have the right resources. But resources of themselves are not a substitute for a strategy.

These programmes can be 'open' or 'closed', exploratory or structured. What is really new is the technology available and techniques for accessing it. Workshops always afforded individualised learning for trainees, what else can they do? For centuries, scholars researched information wherever they could find it, usually in libraries. For centuries, individuals have undertaken learning tasks under the super-vision of tutors. The present emphasis on individual learning programmes is a response to developing demand. Resource centres have replaced libraries, and yet books remain the most valuable comprehensive resource likely to be available for research. Students can 'read' a book on a computer screen, and 'search-engines' make it simpler to discover where information is located, but searches on the Internet can cost hours of frustration and students must have full instructions on how to do them. Writers of these 'searches' have to guess what questions people will ask. Computer programs exclude all but 'spot-on' questions, so that 'near misses' in questions won't work.

Computer Assisted Learning (CAL) has developed as a huge area of expertise. The student on a computer-based individualised learning programme must know what s/he is looking for and why, what s/he is trying to learn, how s/he will get feedback and how learning will be assessed, what s/he is going to do with the information s/he accesses to achieve 'ownership', to give it structure and meaning for their own pur-poses. These are strategic decisions made by someone other than the student. Searches may be instrumental within a linear programme monitored by the instructor. On the other hand, in an 'open' strategy, learning tasks can promote interactive exchanges using websites and e-mail. But students cannot be expected just to be able to cope. Many give up unless they have available 'Help', either from the program, on-line, or from a tutor, or staff in a resource centre, and many have to get it from other students.

Individualised learning does not have to use this technology. Distance learning packages have been available for half a century which are entirely paper-based, with exchanges facilitated by mail, but the same considerations apply. What is vitally important is the quality of the feedback and support. The great majority of stu-dents, however, feel very much more confident if they can actually talk to someone, or meet the tutors, or work as part of a group. The Open University has recognised for decades the need for weekends or weeks of seminars to supplement their TV/paper-based packages.

Developing technology is the way forward in many places. 1:1 or 1:10,000 are both possible. In Australia, where for people outside metropolitan areas there are huge distances to travel in order to get tuition at an advanced level, it is possible to use video-links via the Internet to be face-to-face with a tutor 1,000 km away. Conservatoires in Adelaide offer instrumental tutition to the Outback, in playing the trumpet, for example. In Japan, for most of the 90s, teachers using satellite in Tokyo have been teaching 10,000 students at a time across the Kanto plain. It is not the technology but the relative costs/benefits of delivery systems that will determine what happens.

Teaching teams who have experimented in setting up individualised programmes have found that it involves a huge amount of work and a long learning period before satisfactory material can be produced. They have also found it very difficult to provide the help and support on-line at the point of need for individual students. Paper-based programmes are simpler, but are time-consuming if there is to be more than minimal feedback. Grading is simple to do, but provides little guidance as to what a student still needs to learn. There is in practice no getting away from the fact that for tutors to be able to support students, it is 1:1 teaching, either on paper, on-line, or much better face-to-face. But tutorial functions of this sort need different skills from classroom teaching – skills which are acquired by trial and error learning, if at all.

Assessment

The process of assessment and the process of learning are linked. One feeds back into the other. It is possible to treat each task as separate for the purposes of assessment with its own criteria. But that is to lose the process and to concentrate on outcomes. The tasks become a series of coconuts in a shy.

Where courses are designed as separate Units, as in the Australian university course in Case Study 20, it is hard for students to make sense of the course as a whole. They will learn what is required for tests or to complete assignments as tests, and then most probably forget it. This will have an unfortunate effect on motivation. Tutoring must be concerned with overall learning goals and progress towards their achievement.

Tasks identify the process by which progress is made. To develop an action plan with each student, a tutor needs to monitor what is achieved by the completion of each of the tasks; and what has been identified as learning need in order to provide feedback. That is what assessment is fundamentally about.

Careful monitoring and regular review, preferably in tutorials, are necessary if students are to have ownership of their own assessments and focus on the extent of their own learning. Their tutor needs to keep careful records of what has been achieved – what is still to be done. S/he can draw up fresh action plans to meet individual learning needs as they emerge. These records are, of course, for the student, not just for the tutor or the team, and are shared with each student in tutorials (even if it is on-line or by post), so that each student can feel in charge of his/her learning. Just having a printout of your grades for completed Units is meaningless, as anyone who has tried to counsel students to transfer from one institution to another will know, when they turn up with their computer printout of grades. You can use a 'tutorial log' proforma to keep track of students' achievements. It is a simple form showing goals achieved and new goals set in the tutorial. These log sheets make up the basis of the student's Record of Achievement at the end of the course.

Evaluation

Programmes of this kind need constant review; all aspects of the process need revision in the light of experience. Each task must be evaluated for

- its level of difficulty, the way students coped with it
- its effectiveness in promoting the intended learning.

The same is true of resources, guidance, support and so on. **The aim is to make the learning programme as effective as possible**. **The learning path overall, or the tasks, or the assessment process, or all of them, may fail to achieve intended outcomes**.

In 'programmed learning', where students are taken step-by-step through a fully structured learning path, if students fail to achieve the goals the fault must be with the programme, not with the student. In the more 'open' programmes as intended in this book, we are not necessarily measuring or addressing an inability of students to achieve the goals in our evaluation, but the quality of the programmes we have designed. But evaluation should be team-based, with teams refining their techniques and action plans.

Real life/prior learning

Teachers cannot control what students learn from reading, from magazines, watching films or TV at home, or what they pick up in places where they work or visit, the people they meet, where they go on holiday, or the games they play, social groups they join and spend time with, life as a whole. This learning is unconscious, so it becomes their perception of reality and creates their values, much more so than learning in a structured environment. It is their understanding of 'normality', acquired when they are relaxed and enjoying life. Consider the way magazines deliberately shape tastes and desires, creating images and models which distinguish social groups, men from women, the young from their elders. If you really want to get to know your students, you could not do better than study magazines they buy, programmes they watch on TV. It is these that have the greatest effect on their image of themselves and where they belong in the world.

Because this learning constitutes nearly all that people learn it is far too important to ignore. It is shared with groups they are part of; and expressed in their use of vocabulary, their clothes, their homes and their body language. When people know they are learning in an educational context, they are likely to put up barriers to the learning that are not present when they are at ease.

Students need to focus their unconscious learning – to have a view of what they have learned, so that they can evaluate it and integrate it with conscious learning in a controlled environment such as a college. Learning gained at work or in family or leisure settings can be formally assessed and put forward to count towards certification; it is called *prior learning*. Systems exist to enable individuals to present such learning for assessment, to complement conventional learning on courses. If prior learning is accepted, it is 'accredited' as part of the overall achievement for certification. For more information on APL (Accreditation of Prior Learning) see page 281 under 'Assessment'.

The richness of this resource is immense, but it is usually left untapped. There are forms of prior learning which are easily identified and catalogued, such as experience in jobs, especially if it involved some responsibility, or demonstrable skills, or courses of training. One real difficulty today is that such expertise quickly goes out of date because of rapid technological innovation. If this prior learning is to be accredited it has to be adjudged 'current'. Another major problem in using 'life learning' is lack of structure. How does one select what is good, relevant and valuable? After all, no one said at the time that there would be a test. Many occasions arise when the learning can be tapped. If there is shared experience it may be used to enrich group work. Whenever they tackle tasks, students can be asked to match what they learn against their own experience. The more mature the students and the greater their breadth of experience, the richer this resource is likely to be. There is an increasing need for teachers to work closely with employers to integrate real life imperatives, those felt by employers and the community, with what teachers – or examining bodies – feel important.

An aspect of the real world that has been more fully integrated into courses is the workplace. 'Out-reach courses' are run where employers provide the resources, and colleges supply expertise. In the past, students were sent from workplaces to colleges to learn; now they can study work-based tasks, processes and procedures on the job itself. They are assessed in the workplace to meet the demands of real life interactions, at the normal pace of work and under the pressures of a real context and to a standard of work required by employers rather than in a college simulation with generalised criteria for performance. However, where students are wanting certification by an Awarding Body, what they achieve at work must be married to the examining board assessments.

Teachers have to develop skills, not only in working with students, but with those who share joint responsibility for tasks and assessments that students undertake. And they need to ensure coherence. It will be clear that the skills needed for negotiating contracts and programmes are becoming increasingly important for teachers as managers. FENTO describes this as 'collegiality'.

Roles

Teachers need to adopt many new roles, which require training and development of novel skills and techniques. A teacher may be 'manager of resources', 'liaison officer for outside agencies', 'adviser', 'external assessor', or 'counsellor'. Yet teachers need to approach their changing roles in all these capacities with a view of themselves primarily as teachers. The skills and insights developed by the programme in this book will remain as relevant as ever. Consider the schematic overview of role on pages 338–341.

Tutorials/monitoring progress

For a new teacher it may be enough to know that all the above possibilities exist, since it is unlikely they will find themselves doing any of them immediately. But one role teachers will find themselves undertaking is 'tutor' to individuals. As each takes responsibility for his/her own learning, it becomes necessary to monitor and control the learning programme. One obvious effect is that time must be found to spend with each individual in face-to-face tutorials.

Tutorials serve many purposes. They are needed to check on progress and to give support; or they can be like small-scale seminars to clarify ideas and create/monitor action plans. They are very expensive of time for teachers, the major cost to institutions; they are usually 1:1 or at most 1:3, so, tutorials must be cost-effective, contract-based and goal-orientated. Student and tutor are equally to be responsible for achieving the agreed goals. The major skill is in handling the relationship of tutor/adviser with individuals. The tutor has to try to understand each one of his tutees, but an easy-going tutor is of no benefit to anyone. There must be two-way exchange, a tutorial is certainly not a lecture! Tutors have to listen to each student, to act as a mirror. The agenda must be agreed, not imposed. Students must feel able to control their agenda to some extent to meet the needs they perceive if they are to trust the tutor, to be open in discussion. After all, it is their learning programme and their action plan.

Tutorials provide feedback in both directions. Students need to know their progress relative to agreed performance criteria. The teacher needs to know whether the tasks an individual has been set make sense to them, whether the individual can cope. S/he needs to decide how to make progress and whether to renegotiate the programme, or to put in additional learning activity, provide support in a new way, or find additional input or extra resources.

Tutorials are an important part of assessment to shape the learning process, define individual learning paths. Checking on progress is vital. Schedules matter. There are negotiated targets and they must be met. But there has to be flexibility because individuals learn at their own pace and bring their own barriers and problems. The major purpose of assessing is to advance the learning, and not to put a mark on it as a grade; although there is no avoiding it at some point.

The frequency of tutorials relates to the way the programme has been designed. But for time to be available, less time has to be used in full class teaching. The learning programme, therefore, has to be sustained by student learning activity in group and individual tasks.

Handling tutorials

Choose a suitable environment. You cannot conduct a tutorial in the refectory or a bar or in a room shared with other teachers. Set it up to give the right messages. Appear organised and serious. It is terrible if the student feels that the tutorial is just a formality or if it is treated as of little importance by the tutor. The tutorial demands your full attention. You have to listen. Eliminate 'noise' and make sure you won't be interrupted by the telephone or other people. Come prepared. Know about this student: what he or she is doing and what has happened already. At the very least know his/her name! Decide on your level of familiarity; if you are to use first names make sure that is acceptable to them as well as to you and that the level of respect and authority between you is maintained. You have to decide what students call you. Try to avoid any suggestion of 'talking down', especially to adults.

Think about personal space. Chairs should preferably be at least comfortable. Avoid barriers to separate you; like desks that create distance. Chairs may be close but not confrontational, better to set them at an angle so that eye-contact can be made and broken easily – it is embarrassing to look at another person continually, so looking away must not be a problem. Whatever you do, do not give wrong signals by dress or manner or by making physical contact. You have to establish a professional formal relationship, which must be perceived to be just that.

Timing matters. Start on time, finish on time. It is not a counselling session, where time can be flexible to accommodate emotional stress. Students need to learn how to handle time effectively, and to say things clearly but succinctly without 'beating about the bush'. More time does not mean better communication or under-standing. You need to practise economy of language and lucidity, too. Listen carefully, and wait for the student 'to say it'. Teachers tend to be impatient. One of the skills you need to develop (as in class interactions) is to be patient and wait. Jumping in quickly to fill a silence too soon stops important things from happening. When teachers do this as a matter of habit, students just let them get on with it. Interactions need space and time in order to happen, as in the theatre. Encourage the student to be open, and don't take over.

To listen is to show concern. How hard it is to find someone who actually wants to listen to you, who will find the time to do it! Try to see it from where they sit, so that you reflect back what they say and do, then match it against the agreed criteria, where you and they are going.

Students mainly need support and reassurance. They do not usually need bullying. If they are slipping in terms of targets, they have to perceive the need to achieve them. Tutorials are feedback, enabling them to see things more clearly themselves. You are their mirror. Target-setting, keeping to schedule, yes. Most students want to succeed. Matching the programme to individual needs is the tutor's responsibility. Keep records of tutorials with a copy for the student. Negotiation of the learning programme and action plans for individuals (and revisions) need documenting. Targets and progress towards them need monitoring and recording. Above all, be businesslike, but be human.

Suggested reading

Bell, J. *Doing Your Research Project*, Open University Press, 1993/1999.

Bourner, T. and Race, P. *How to Win as a Part Time Student*, Kogan Page (London), 1991.

Cottrell, S. *Teaching Study Skills and Supporting Learning*, Palgrave Macmillan, 2001.

Cottrell, S. *Skills for Success*, Palgrave, 2003.

Cottrell, S. *The Study Skills Handbook*, Palgrave Macmillan, 2004.

Marshall, L. and Rowland, F. *A Guide to Learning Independently*, OUP, 1998.

Talbot, C. *Studying at a Distance*, Open University Press, 2003.

Wisker, G. and Brown, S. (eds) *Enabling Student Learning: Systems and Strategies*, Kogan Page (London), 1996.

| CHAPTER 18 | **Student guidance and support** |

The current scene

The emphasis in post-school education, FE, AE and HE, is on individualised learning and supporting students while they are learning. The distinction between full-time and part-time students, the 16–22-year-old cohort or mature students, is blurred. Flexibility, now built into the provision of educational services, courses and learning opportunities by institutions, allows for patterns of attendance, length of courses, access to expertise, workshops, resource bases, workshops, laboratories, computing facilities, assessment procedures, all to be open-ended, no longer tied to a college timetable or to a calendar for examination preparation.

In America, there is provision for life-long learning, the opportunity to 'return to school' to obtain qualifications at all ages. There is a lack of pressure on youngsters to make a commitment to any one kind of employment in a society rich enough to allow all to put off decisions till their mid-twenties. If the consequences hardly matter, it is easy to drop-out of school, so long as there is the chance to return when you do know clearly what you want to do. Indeed, there is a lot to be said for it. There, too, students generally 'work their way through college'. Full-time attendance is 4 credits of 3×1 hour classes a week, 12 hours a week for 2 semesters of 16 weeks each year. Students work at part-time jobs round their pattern of attendance at college. Grades depend as much on attendance at classes as on work done in, before or after classes. The assumption of instructors is that all students have chosen to be there, but as in Case Study 22, page 141, they find that in courses which are 'required', motivation of students is often low. The only thing keeping them there is the need to get a Grade C. Instructors will be asked, '*What do I have to do to get a C?*', in effect minimum attendance. Courses are Units each worth one credit; they can be taken at any time to cumulate to enough credits for the award of a degree. There are required courses and options according to the 'major' study program.

Life-long learning is also the goal in the UK. It is essential in a technological society, where the only permanent thing is change. The impact of developing technology, globalisation, movement of industry and of employment to the most advantageous locations in terms of profitability, all this means competition by governments and regional bodies to attract investment, with opportunities for employment or the collapse of them. All of which has social consequences that are impossible to calculate. There is a constant need for companies as well as the workforce to update skills and knowledge, and levels of educational competence, with access to developing technology and confidence in using it, in order just 'to stay in the game' at all. But the pressures are very different; there is no system such as that available in the USA for the accumulation of credits and there is not the same level of wealth.

Education and training must be able to respond rapidly to changing demands. Dinosaurs were enormously successful, surviving for 200 million years slowly evolving in a non-changing world, until their world changed catastrophically and 'overnight'. Evolving slowly is no longer an option. For all institutions, accountability has become synonymous with survival, not only in financial terms, but in relation to the demands of the society the institution serves.

It is not unusual for well-qualified people from Africa to come to the UK for experience and further training. A man in his thirties from Zimbabwe was invited to teach a course in business management at a college near London. He had management experience and qualifications from his home country. There, anyone who had the chance of education at any age was totally committed and hard-working; they knew how privileged they were and what it meant to have good schooling, to be well educated, especially at a higher level. In the bush, not far from the main cities like Harare and Bulawayo, it is not unusual to visit village schools where a teacher has a chalkboard on an easel as his only AVA and the children sit on benches under a tree – even today. Learning is serious and important.

In his teaching in the UK, he found that most of his students were reasonably well motivated, but he had difficulty with some and with one in particular, whose attendance at class was irregular and who seemed unwilling to respond to even individual counselling. The young man round 20 years old had already received career counselling, but was apparently uncommitted to his studies. The teacher had tried several times talking to the lad's parents and they to their son, but it seemed to have little positive effect. None of them knew what to do, but clearly unless something was done the lad would fail the course. His behaviour was also disruptive of the work of others. The Zimbabwean could not understand such a lack of appreciation of this great educational opportunity.

Discussion

1 Why is there such a big difference between the value attached to education in an African country, in the developing world generally, and in the UK?

2 What can be done to help most youngsters attach more value to their educational opportunities?

3 What would you do to help a young person in your class who showed this pattern of behaviour?

4 What is the policy of your institution in regard to attendance and completing assignments?

5 How is a full-time student defined? What is required of them in terms of patterns of attendance?

6 What is the policy about tolerating absence, continued attendance, drop out and counselling?

Comment

The value attached to anything in general depends on supply and demand and what you can trade it for. It is not unusual in the UK for teachers to find in their classes full-time students of any age, from 14 to 20 or so, who have little motivation to be there or to learn. Why are they there? In many cases teachers find that the students have hardly 'chosen' to be there at all. The situation is complicated by their accountability to ensure that no one drops out of their courses and all achieve pass grades; it inevitably leads to a dilemma for the teachers and a challenge to their integrity. Should they award a pass grade to a student who has to be forced to learn, who has poor attendance and has done little or no work? Government insists that colleges only run courses where students do not drop out and do find employment after them, so that having students drop out of courses could lead to their closure. Pragmatism may lead to dishonesty at all levels.

In this case, even on a high level course of business management, problems of motivation are evident with some students. On lower level courses, the problem is more acute, employment is often difficult to find, even part-time jobs, so that students are counselled to undertake further training but with little genuine prospect of employment afterwards. One college has adopted a policy of a 4-day week for full-time students to raise attendance of full-time students, whose commitment is no more than 15 hours a week in any case. Perhaps, educational opportunity should be seen as a privilege not a right, and students should be discouraged from attendance until they are strongly motivated to want to learn. Maybe, this lad should be told to 'drop out' until he is mentally ready to study; a policy it is much easier to pursue in America than in the UK unfortunately.

Making choices/marketing

Since the problem of motivation is as much at institution level as in the classroom/ workshop, it is hardly surprising that a great effort must be put in to ensure that students do find 'right' courses and programmes of study, which can only be done at the level of need of individuals. The consequence is that teachers have a significant role as part the specialist counselling team in the college. There must be interchange of information in both directions. Not only must institutions facilitate what students perceive as their needs, but teachers also must recognise the importance of accommodating learning programmes to meet those needs effectively.

Perception of needs, however, is not a simple business, as we have noted earlier. Individuals can only discover their needs by matching their perceptions with those of others, or by undergoing a series of tests to reveal the level and currency of their skills and knowledge. It will also indicate their readiness to undertake further study or training, their potential, and so on. Schools offer computer-generated interactive programs through which youngsters can identify the direction most appropriate to their personality and aptitude. This involves yes/no gates and options to choose, which define the path by narrowing the possibilities. They may end up with a precise conclusion: '*Your aptitude is to run your own business, in hairdressing or in beauty therapy.*'

Assuming it really does make sense, a pupil can discover what s/he has to learn and achieve in order to reach this long-term goal.

Colleges and career advisers may use rather more sophisticated tools of the same kind. These services include information, advice, guidance, tutoring and counselling – a process that begins before students enrol, using highly sophisticated marketing strategies. Investment in marketing has become an established priority. Two areas of growth in all institutions have been guidance and marketing.

Before potential students have a personal interview, they can visit college websites to search for information and guidance. The websites are becoming increasingly professional, some more than others since it is a game with winners and losers that all must learn. But colleges also have teams who visit schools, and Advice and Guidance evenings, College Open Days and other techniques built into a marketing strategy.

Institutions have had to enter the marketplace as businesses, with as much a business ethic as educational. The 'bottom-line' approach to accountancy and to accountability has revolutionised all provision. Colleges must have a business plan, a marketing strategy, strong financial controls, short- and long-term goals and other approaches taken from successful business enterprises. To ask, exactly what business are we in? What do we need to make that business successful? How do we develop our product, do our market research, market our expertise, channel students into appropriate courses? How do we monitor success of the institution and of our students? How do we ensure quality control and financial controls? And so on.

In the past, heads of department and senior teachers interviewed students and 'selected' them for courses. Now every college has a professional guidance and monitoring team and college structure is as flexible as the provision it needs to make.

WEBSITES

ACTIVITY 10

Visit the website of any large college to discover the wide range of courses on offer. A useful exercise is to make a comparison between the websites of a number of colleges to discover what is similar and what is different about the way they approach

- marketing their provision
- professionalism in presentation, use of animation and so on
- providing an overview and a picture of the college
- patterns of attendance, being a student
- courses and qualifications available
- enabling potential students to explore the options
- guiding/assisting them in finding out more information
- guidance and counselling services
- making applications
- advising on support services available, including financial support
- possibilities of interactive exchanges
- location of the college sites and how to get there.

It is impossible in a book to anticipate what has been developed in response to demand in any particular area or institution. But it is important for teachers in each institution to know and be part of the provision for guidance and channelling into courses or programmes of learning, and in the monitoring of student learning and success.

Other factors

Government intervention has had a major impact on the kind of provision made in all institutions. There is a discussion under 'Assessment' of ongoing changes in certification and assessment processes. Apart from identifying individual learning goals, potential students now need far more guidance than formerly to discover their best learning route to certification. As an overview:

1 There is a wide range of qualifications available, some in modular or unit form, some with core and optional studies, some with placements or work experience; in addition students can claim credit for previously certificated but also uncertificated learning (APL).

2 Full-time students are now taught for fewer hours and encouraged to work independently in the college workshops and resource centres; they need help with the study skills to make this a viable learning route, with time management, self-motivation, use of catalogues, use of ICT and so on (see Chapters 12 and 19). Their needs and yours are almost the same in this regard.

3 New client groups are coming into further education: mature students on Access courses, refugees and asylum seekers, women returning to study, many who are seeking jobs and career change.

4 There is an increased need for guidance on financial, legal and welfare matters as well as language support for those for whom English is not their mother tongue. Even among native speakers, there is a significant number whose level of literacy and numeracy is a barrier to study or employment.

5 The government has set ambitious National Training and Education Targets (the percentage of the working population with qualifications by a certain date). The funding received by colleges has been made dependent on taking in more students each year; many of whom are unused to systematic study and require help with study skills as well as induction to the expectations and requirements of college life. These study skills may involve attendance at workshops in numeracy and/or literacy.

6 Many students are unemployed or receive benefits; they need advice on how to combine job-seeking with studying, on sources of financial assistance and on welfare services.

7 Too many students drop out because they have chosen the wrong course, have inadequate skills, or have too many personal difficulties to enable them to cope. It is tragic for them, disappointing for teachers and unfortunate for government figures; consequently funding has been tied to retention of students until they achieve their qualification goals.

8 Colleges are in competition with each other and with schools for the 16–19 cohort of students; a major marketing advantage is good student support services to match the school tradition of pastoral care.

9 As a result of trends and intervention advice and guidance, services have become centralised rather than peripheral, systematic rather than *ad hoc,* properly funded and operated by a team of qualified professional staff. They are now seen as vital to the business success of the centre.

The support team

There is no 'model', because centres respond to their own context and students, but in most centres you will find a team of people who work together to offer students advice, guidance and support on academic, study and personal matters; a core team who organise and manage these services, a wider team of specialists looking after medical, legal, financial, career, disability and child care matters, and also teachers with particular responsibilities, e.g. ESOL students or Basic Skills in literacy, numeracy and now in ICT. There are support staff in learning resource centre areas who advise on finding and using information.

In addition to this team, there may be teachers who act as academic advisers about particular subject areas and courses, and who may also help students with applications to higher education and further study.

Being a personal tutor

Teachers all have an important role to play. You may be asked to be part of a personal tutoring system of support and guidance, mainly for full-time students, managed by a senior member of staff who briefs, trains and supports the teachers who act as personal tutors.

How does this work? Groups of students are attached to a member of staff, who may or may not also teach them, for the period of their studies. You, as their tutor, are responsible for first line support. You help them settle in, keep an eye on their progress, discipline them if necessary, respond to their requests for help of various kinds and refer them to your team of specialists for further help if you think it is appropriate. You may be asked to help them to complete a Record of Achievement if they are in use in your place. It is an important document in which students and staff collect material as evidence to show how the student has progressed. It lists achievements, contains certificates and, importantly, has commentary as statements about progress by teachers and the students themselves. It is an important part of negotiation to identify and agree needs, learning paths, learning goals in knowledge, skills and attitude change, progress chasing, modification of the programme and achievement of goals.

In order to work with the students in this way, you set up tutorial sessions, either as 1:1 or as a group. Younger students tend to prefer a group setting. Some centres have a Tutorial Programme of activities for the year you can run in these sessions. Of these the most important is 'induction', part of which will be organised centrally; you follow this up in sessions with your own tutees.

Your knowledge and skills

You will need to be part of the counselling and guidance system within your institution, even if you are not officially part of the tutoring team, so that you will have to familiarise yourself with aspects of it, particularly in regard to the students in your classes:

- how they came to be there
- what part in their learning programme your course plays
- what support they can get elsewhere in the institution
- where to refer them in case of difficulties.

If you are part of the tutorial team you will need to know about the following aspects:

- the support services available in your centre, the names of the key advisers, the locations and times of access
- the courses/programmes on which the students are studying and the staff involved (with whom you will need to liaise)
- the duties and responsibilities expected of you, particularly boundaries around your area of work and reports you are expected to provide
- where to go for information and help on your own account.

The skills you need to develop

The most important element you bring to the tutor role is the normal friendly relationship you have with your students. You are not expected to be a social worker, priest and lawyer all in one. You are there to help with a range of fairly everyday difficulties; the team of experts is there to pick up the more specialist work. **Your chief skill is that of knowing your limitations and when to refer students.**

REMEMBER! … You are not a professional Counsellor. You must not attempt to take on roles which demand a high level of professional skill and training. It is easy to make tragic mistakes if you attempt to do it.

Important skills for you are:

- noticing if a student is acting out of character, and approaching sensitively to see if s/he wants help
- listening attentively to what the student tells you
- clarifying your understanding of what s/he has said
- exploring possible courses of action
- helping to decide what to do
- maintaining contact while s/he works on his/her decisions
- acknowledging progress and success
- most importantly, referring students with problems to the appropriate service.

Attitudes are all important

How you are is as important as what you do. Students identify the people they can trust, whether or not you are designated as a tutor. They look particularly for people who have time to listen to them, who accept that they have a problem but who do not designate them as a problem, those who have a generally positive attitude to the whole business of sorting things out. They require confidentiality in their dealings. You don't need to be a personal tutor to behave like this; it is an extension of normal teaching roles.

Sorting out the terminology

You may be unsure of the difference between the various terms. Most of us would see *advice giving* as something fairly directive, based on information which we make available on request. *Guidance* is seen as showing people the options available and suggesting some courses of action. You don't need to be involved with the enquirer to carry out these functions.

Tutoring and *counselling*, however, are dependent for effectiveness on the relationship which you build up with the other person. This lasts over a period of time during which you get to know the person so that you can understand how best to help him/her. But there are some crucial differences. *Tutoring* is closely related to study matters; the tutor takes the lead, organises activities, can be directive about a tutee's behaviour and discusses his/her behaviour and progress with other staff. The content of the exchanges is fairly routine. In *counselling*, the content is deeply personal and around serious issues. Strict confidentiality is essential. A formal contract between counsellor and student is set up with agreed boundaries, times and location. The counsellor works to help the student explore routes which might be taken to try to resolve difficulties. Solutions are likely to be long term and will involve much more than academic matters.

Counselling is a highly skilled professional service that should be offered only by those who are qualified to do it. You may find yourself using some basic counselling techniques in your tutoring or helping with relationships, like listening, for example. But the centre will have designated staff to carry out counselling and it is to them that you must refer your students if you think that they have this need. Your professionalism lies in being able to make that judgement. Don't be tempted to think that you should do counselling yourself. This is not in the student's best interests. Task 20 will help you to sum up this chapter.

SUPPORT AND GUIDANCE SERVICES

Imagine yourself to be *a student in the institution or context in which you are teaching.* **Construct** a 'coral diagram' (see Figure 18.1) to show what is available to support students. Most of the information you need is in the Appendix, but you need to look carefully at your own context.

Students could share this Task, with the teacher in a tutorial role. They may cooperate in completing the chart, perhaps in groups.

TASK 20

1 You, *the student,* are naturally at the centre. What support and guidance services might there be which you could approach or access to help you? You will need all kinds of advice and help because your life is complex; you are not simply a learner in this institution.

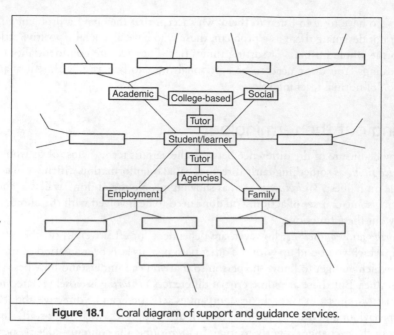

Figure 18.1 Coral diagram of support and guidance services.

2 Where is *the teacher, adviser or tutor,* within the framework? Will the students see the tutor as a first line of approach, an anchor while they are learning? It is the tutor who will bring it all together for them: they may wish to refer to him or her as well as to the specialist services.

3 The services vary from place to place and will change. It may require some research to discover: what is available, where it is located, who to approach.

4 You may continue adding to this chart as you (tutor or student) discover more; especially, where to find information or which services are provided. They may not be located in your own institution. Many government, local government and employer-based agencies are available. This is a constantly changing field.

5 You may wish to place some of these into the chart, or others you discover. The place and order of such things in the chart need discussion.

Careers guidance	*Study skills support*	*Academic guidance*
ESOL support	APL/APEL guidance	Tutorial guidance
Grants, sources of funding	Child care facilities	Mentorship system
Home Office Regulations	DHSS Regulations	Accommodation
Learning difficulties	Equal Opportunities	Chaplaincy
Employment guidance	Counselling	ICT support
Basic Skills: Numeracy	Basic Skills: Literacy	Medical Services

6 The chart is a starting point only. You may find the headings unhelpful, so *choose your own.* This is **your** chart, **your** framework to help **you** where **you** are.

Suggested reading

Bovair, K. and McLaughlin, C. *Counselling in Schools*, David Fulton, 1993.

Cottrell, S. *Teaching Study Skills and Supporting Learning*, Palgrave Macmillan, 2001.

Cottrell, S. *The Study Skills Handbook*, Palgrave Macmillan, 2004.

Corson, D. *Changing Education for Diversity*, Open University Press, 1998.

Cunningham, U. and Andersson, S. *Teachers, Pupils and the Internet*, Stanley Thornes, 1999.

Daines, J., Daines, C. and Graham, B. *Adult Learning: Adult Teaching*, Univ. of Nottingham, 1993.

FEU *Managing the Delivery of Guidance in Colleges*, FEU (London), 1994.

Lewis, G. *One to One: A Practical Guide to Learning at Home Age 0–11*, Nezert Books, 2001.

Marland, M. *The Tutor and the Tutor Group*, Longman (London), 1989.

Marland, P. *Towards More Effective Distance and Open Teaching*, Taylor & Francis, Routledge, 1997.

Mason, R. *Using Communication Media in Open and Flexible Learning*, Kogan Page, 1994.

Moseley, D. *Helping With Learning Difficulties*, Open University Press (Milton Keynes), 1976.

Nierenberg, G.I. *The Complete Negotiator*, Souvenir Press (London), 1987.

Sutcliffe, J. *Adults with Learning Difficulties: Education for Choice and Empowerment*, NIACE/Open University Press, 1990.

Wheeler, M. and Bligh, D. *Counselling in Study Methods*, Intellect Books, 1985.

<table>
<tr><td>CHAPTER 19</td><td>Developing study skills</td></tr>
</table>

It cannot be assumed that students can cope with learning on their own. Most people have poorly developed study skills; your own may need further development. In this chapter you will find some ideas and activities that should help **you and your students** to improve the ability to learn.

Students may need to be guided through early tasks:

- finding out where they can get help and resources
- how to use the library/multi-media/resource centre or any specialist areas
- how to manage equipment
- how to seek help and information in any other place
- how to explore major resources such as city archives.

You cannot assume that students can do any of these things, they must be shown how. Some tasks mean dealing with people rather than with books or things, especially if it is about social skills and the ability to work with others. Students need help in understanding how:

- to deal with people
- to interview them, perhaps
- to conduct negotiations
- to do a survey.

None of this can be taken for granted: it is courting disaster simply to tell students to do such things and hope it will be all right. Teachers cannot know what is involved, how hard it is or the kind of difficulties that are likely to occur, unless they experience the task themselves. Every task needs validating by experience, preferably by the teachers doing it themselves.

ACTIVITY 11

TARGETS AND SHORT-TERM GOALS

All skill learning depends on practice and repetition. Skills are developed as habit-forming practice by doing them over and over until they become 'unconscious' acts. But you will only achieve a high level of skill if you clearly understand what it is you are trying to do and you set yourself targets.

There is a problem with motivation. Long-term goals take so long to achieve and may seem to get no nearer and they may become disincentives. We need short-term goals and targets that are attainable within weeks (or even days), which can build towards long-term goals. The same is true for students.

Think of useful things as short-term goals. Set yourself attainable tasks such as these:

- I will master the search facilities in the resource centre.
- I will be familiar with the work and functions of the resources centre; work closely with the staff.
- I will find out how to get AVA and use technician support services.
- I will learn to use a computer.
- I will learn to write text using a computer.
- I will learn to use electronic mail.
- I will learn to use computer networks and how to do searches.
- I will make a list of books and other materials in my field and where to find them.
- I will increase my reading speed by searching for answers to my questions.
- I will look carefully at documents I produce to make sure they are clear and easy to understand.
- I will cut out unnecessary words in memos, and so on, I send.
- I will reorganise my resources file and review its contents.

All this sort of activity will encourage you to work closely with staff in resource centres and libraries and technicians who are there to support you. It is essential to develop these skills, so as to create and gather a bank of resource material your students may learn from, and to be a creative and supportive member of a team with your colleagues.

NOTE-TAKING/LEARNING FROM LECTURES

ACTIVITY 12

The worst kind of notes are verbatim scribble. Listening, watching and addressing questions to what the lecturer is presenting are more important than getting down everything that is said; it is hard to do both. To be followable a lecture must have a structure. Properly handled, lectures make a structure plain, with a plan using keywords. The listeners can add notes of their own.

If you listen carefully, a pattern will emerge, with alerting words about the links, or 'now I want …' statements, or rhetorical questions that are really the same thing. Keywords are usually not too hard to pick up if you listen out for them.

This skeleton pattern is what you need to take away so that you can look at it again. Come back to it as soon as possible afterwards and reorganise the outline so that it makes sense to you. This allows you to clarify it as you review it.

Look again at my advice in Part 1. This is the time to flesh out the notes – it is useful to add your own comments and questions, too.

Begin your learning before the lecture, approach it 'armed with questions', an alert mind.

Decide

1 What are you hoping to learn? Are you ready? Are you mentally awake?

2 Create your working space, with note-pad and writing material, or a small laptop, perhaps.

3 Listen to the preamble. If the lecture is one of a series, there should be a recap.

4 Note the links to previous learning.

5 There should be a 'map' of what is to come, even a plan to help you to know where you are (in case you or the lecturer wanders, as lecturers are prone to do).

6 Listen for keywords, structural statements and recap statements – to consolidate as it goes along.

7 Listen for feedback, voice inflections, gestures and so forth that show important points.

8 Watch: if there are OHP or other presentations, they should offer keywords or patterns to note.

9 Use keywords only for your notes. You have to listen, not write.

10 If you lose track, if the lecturer wanders, if you do not understand, ASK. The lecturer knows it already, but cannot know your difficulty unless you say so; you are the one trying to learn. The lecture is not intended to be a sermon in church.

11 There should be opportunities for anyone to ask questions. Don't hesitate to ask for clarification.

12 Go armed with questions; if they are not covered by the lecture, ASK THEM.

13 Listen to any summary and consolidation and check your notes.

14 Review soon. Within 24 hours you will have lost 70% of it.

Learning from written materials

You can employ similar techniques in written materials such as this book. Be proactive. Books have maps in the form of contents pages: use them. Take charge of your learning. It is important for you to identify clearly the structure the author uses, and how parts relate to the whole. Try to see what the questions were that this book is intending to answer.

Your needs are not the same as those of other readers, nor are you starting from where the author is. Approach the material with your own questions as well as those the author addresses. You should certainly make structure notes. In Part 1, I discussed 'forgetting' curves and your need for regular revision/revisiting of the learning. This problem is easier to tackle if you make notes and you review the notes in the sense of restructuring them whenever you come back to them.

You will change with growing experience to make comparisons of your own, your perception will change with fuller understanding of the author's intentions.

USING TELEVISION ADVERTISEMENTS

How can you practise observing a structure and making notes?

You need short, repetitive activity. Television advertisements can provide the shortest, most accessible and punchiest 'lectures'. They are highly efficient in the use of time in getting the message across. Within about 30 seconds, they grab your attention and hold it. They are very efficient in the use of words and compelling images. They convey a message (of some kind). They must make it memorable, not necessarily simple in meaning, but effective for the purpose of the advertisers. They may appeal to viewers in quite subtle ways, which it is interesting to analyse and explore.

One advertisement will usually be repeated several times, so that you can check what you do. Address questions to the experience. Once you have the skill, you can apply it to any experience, including this book.

Be proactive. Write down the questions. Revise them as new ideas occur to you. Try to see the script behind words and images. Visualise the script as camera shots that hardly ever last more than a few seconds. Then you can add the words. It is unusual for sound and picture to be recorded together. Nothing happens without detailed, meticulous design-work first. You are trying to get behind the presentation to the structure – to see how the thing has been put together and how it works. Find the questions the designers posed to themselves:

- How many camera shots? How long for each shot? Why choose those?
- What is the message? How is it built up, conveyed?
- What are the words? How do they work with the images?
- What is the advertisement appealing to? And to whom?
- Is it effective? What makes it so? If not, why not?

MAKING NOTES

Why make notes at all?

- to be attentive, proactive learners; humans are exploratory animals and need to be 'searching' in order to learn
- to get at the structure in order to see the whole and how it all fits together
- to produce a pattern you can absorb, match with your knowledge and experience
- to avoid the necessity of constantly re-reading everything
- to enable you to revisit and review and so consolidate: it is important that you learn it 'right', for unlearning is harder than learning
- to challenge and restructure your own understanding.

USE OF KEYWORDS IN NOTETAKING

(a) Linear style

COMMUNICATION		
Individuals	*Channels*	*Groups*
barriers	signals	sharing
self-image	messages	boundaries
attitude	interference	identifying
mind-set	noise	signals
emotions	redundancy	measures
prior learning	(radio/TV)	rules
experience		bonding
knowledge		common goals
skills		teams
convictions		support
messages		individuals
reading		personal needs
interpreting		common language
sending		concepts/group
concepts		experience
formal thinking		leadership
vocabulary		roles
		decisions
		action plans

(b) Linking pattern

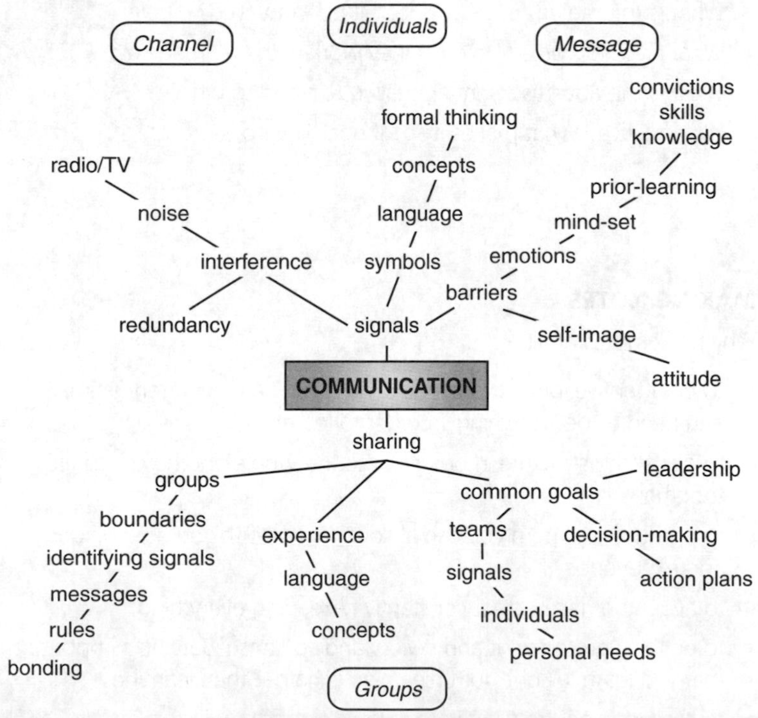

Figure 19.1 Patterns of ideas.

Patterning and sequencing

Notes are not verbatim reports. They are for you. To be useful they must provide:

- triggers to facilitate recall
- a means of showing links, patterns of ideas that make a whole.

You will develop your own pattern for notes. Some people prefer to make linear structures, to see a spine of argument developing. Others prefer to start with a central idea, and then to use links by keywords to related but not necessarily sequential ideas, forming what has been named a 'coral' structure (after the branching coral). I have heard it called 'spider notes', too. The preference may be related to certain dominance patterns in our behaviour overall. Figure 19.1 illustrates these two different types. Both rely on keywords as triggers.

Other clues to structure and relationships can be added by drawing circles and boxes to enclose related ideas/words, with arrows to show direction and connections. But you must develop your own methodology of making sense of the information.

Once you have something that works well for you, you can use it to get your message across effectively to others on handouts or transparencies or on the whiteboard or using a computer. Experiment with different structures. See which one is the most useful or meaningful for you.

REMEMBER! ... Your students will have their own way of 'visualising' and dealing with information you present. Some will respond to linear structures, others to patterning. Do not assume that what works for you works for everyone.

Brain behaviour

Brain behaviour works by pattern-making, by parallel processing of sense data and matching; which is unlike linear processing by a computer. Some psychologists differentiate pattern-making from rule-making, to be explained as differing ways the two halves of the brain work: left and right hemispheres appear to have different functions. Although it is speculative and far too simplistic, it is a useful distinction. In the 1970s Dr Roger Sperry's pioneering research led to a concept of *dominance*. Studying signals as electrical hot-spots generated in the brains of people doing different activities, indicating the parts of the brain that seemed to be responsible for each of these activities, his team observed that left and right hemispheres appeared to be differentiated in regard to such activities. The hemispheres seemed to specialise.

Many researchers have used the concept as a basis for explanations of experimental results in perception and behaviour. For other experiments read Chapter 28 pages 317ff. One recent Australian study developed the concept of 'switching' between hemispheres as a cause of manic-depression, which is an excessive concentration on a single activity. If someone looks at an image made up of a circle of bright dots, as on a TV screen, relaxes and just keeps looking at the figure, they will find that there is a definite 'switching': one moment they see all the dots, the next some have disappeared, then they pop back again. It suggests that the brain is switching, possibly between the hemispheres because the optic nerve from each eye goes to 'the opposite brain'. It is maintained that in studies of the speed at which this occurs with differ-

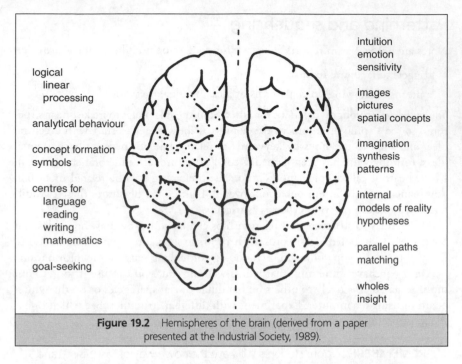

logical
  linear
  processing

analytical behaviour

concept formation
symbols

centres for
  language
  reading
  writing
  mathematics

goal-seeking

intuition
emotion
sensitivity

images
pictures
spatial concepts

imagination
synthesis
patterns

internal
models of reality
hypotheses

parallel paths
matching

wholes
insight

Figure 19.2   Hemispheres of the brain (derived from a paper presented at the Industrial Society, 1989).

ent groups of people, those who have an aptitude for activities in which decisions have to be fast, as in dancing and playing music, switching is fast, in those with an aptitude for maths it is slow, in manic-depressives it is very very slow. Again, a speculative interpretation but interesting. It hardly explains Beethoven, who was the world's greatest musical genius and known to have been a manic-depressive!

Logical thought, language and mathematical processes, reasoning and analysis are activities to be identified with electrical heat in parts of the left hemisphere. 'Left brain dominance' is said to be responsible for a preference for analytical behaviour, goal-seeking, logical or linear thinking, activity identified as rule-making and linear-structuring, all of which could be said to be highly focused action. Centres that appear to control language, reading and writing and concept formation are located there (Figure 19.2), which has been verified by examining the brain activity of those who have suffered strokes or physical injury when these functions are atrophied; or when the two hemispheres have been surgically divided, an operation that used to be performed to 'cure' certain kinds of psychosis.

The brain tends to work on many parallel paths, matching and hypothesising to produce new structures. Activity in centres in the right hemisphere is associated with rhythm, spatial visualisation, imagination, image-making and colour. 'Right brain dominance' is characterised by a preference for patterns and 'wholes', for symbolic representation, synthesis rather than analysis. It facilitates those mysterious insights and 'leaps in the dark' that all of us experience. It seems to allow us to respond intuitively, emotionally, sensitively, working with images, mental pictures, internal representation as models and patterns. Music and musical memory may be located here rather than in language centres, since atrophy of the language centres in the left brain does not affect the ability to sing the words to songs. One could argue that this confirms the idea of rapid switching of parallel processing to match patterns.

It is a simplification to say all this is to do simply with different hemispheres of the brain. It is a fact that we do exhibit these quite different ways of behaving in the way we think about and deal with the world and social life. Many also associate the one as more male behaviour, the other female.

They are clearly different kinds of activity. One promotes more creativity, essential in order to set about problem-solving and exploring alternatives, to cope with multifarious tasks at once. The other is essential for planning, getting things done, organising and communicating in a logical fashion.

It is an unfortunate feature of modern education that emphasis is put so heavily on left-brain behaviour. Both at school and work, left-brain behaviour is valued, considered clever. Creativity and imagination in students are not rewarded with high marks in examinations because they are harder to observe with precision, to measure or to quantify. Consequently, we tend to feel we should do things logically, to find reasons and arguments to justify what we do: a preference for linear structures.

An interesting observation is that those who enjoy writing programs for computers are pre-dominantly left-handed. What does that say about brain dominance? Interestingly, too, it includes very few females.

You will have seen that I have repeatedly stressed the need for structure, but I wish to modify that once again. Structure does not necessarily imply linear constructs. As we have seen above, there are perfectly valid structures that are circular constructs, spiral, inter-linking, and often idiosyncratic mental models. It is a fact that people see the world differently, have different models in the head, work with different mental constructs. Teachers have to recognise that people do 'think' differently. We cannot analyse our own thinking because we cannot watch ourselves think. But we can have a view of our preferred patterns and seek to exploit them, to work with our brains. We should ensure, however, that we improve, where we need to, those activities which we personally find less attractive. We must also recognise that others will do it, see it differently; which means we have to try to see it as they see it, too.

Studying

Studying requires us to be able to handle both pattern-making and rule-making. We have to be able to grasp the whole to make sense of the parts; and we need to see the structure. We need to follow the logic of an argument and to analyse the validity of the evidence; we also need to match these to our experience and insights gained elsewhere. We must construct our own picture of it all.

In setting about studying, be aware of how you perform best in order to maximise the benefit. Establish for yourself what you find the most effective procedures for you. It is experiential learning, so experiment, try various approaches to see what works best.

Once you have settled on a formula which seems to work well, you should make what you do habitual. Habits are patterns of behaviour we do not have to think about. Some are beneficial, others are certainly not. In learning, it is important to establish good habits and eliminate those that inhibit you, get in the way and slow you down. One of the worst culprits is the inability to concentrate on one thing at a time, to welcome distraction – many do! One advantage of using a computer is that it focuses attention. Remember Dr Johnson's famous dictum: '*The prospect of hanging concentrates the mind wonderfully!*' Deadlines are quite a good way of concentrating the mind.

Networks, electronic mail and interactive programs

New technology has revolutionised the way we think about information. Searching for information on networks and databases using computer modems and e-mail (electronic mail-boxes) appears to be far superior to searching for what we want to know in books. Accessing is much simpler, less time-consuming and less tedious than reading through long sections of a book to find what we want. There is all the new vocabulary to be familiar with, of course. The joy of reading has been replaced for most people by the fun and excitement of the increasingly magical possibilities conjured up on a computer.

I have advocated a 'top-down' strategy for finding information. Use it in a text-book as long as there is a reasonable table of contents and a comprehensive index. It is the strategy the Internet exploits: you cannot avoid searching by questions, you cannot flip through pages. Yet once directed to a website you can be in the same trouble as with a book. There is always much more information you don't want or don't need than useful stuff; your searching really begins once you get to the right website. Even finding that is time-consuming and very often frustrating. Search engines and websites are structured in ways, sometimes it seems idiosyncratic ways, that appealed to their creators. In this case, there is no escape. First, you really do have to 'find the right questions to ask'.

In this regard, books are still far superior. The computer is no substitute for having a book in your hand, and being able to look through pages, read a little, jump on, jump back, look at a diagram and compare it with text or another picture elsewhere in the book. You just can't do it in a computer program. A book is a 'whole', computers can only offer 'bits' that you will construct into a 'whole'.

You are limited to what has been put into databases, but the range, the depth, the quality, the sheer volume of material accessible on websites through the Internet is increasing 'exponentially' by the day. One of the best ways to get students going is to organise a 'treasure hunt' for 'pots of gold' buried somewhere in all these quicksands. Every day you can find new websites, new data-stores, new interchanges by groups with similar interests to share, new software, up-dates of older software. Any or all of this you can 'download' into your own computer 'hard disk'. Hard drives now can take up to 200 GB of memory, a whole library of books!

Not only can you find information, usually in edited or précised form (because it is difficult to read on the screen what is much better presented in a book), you can select and print out what you want, including illustrative materials, diagrams, maps, pictures and photographs, and all in colour. All can also be exchanged in moments by e-mail. For any scholar or student it is a wonderful time-saver. They just collate and edit the material to produce 'well-researched' written assignments. Tutors will be conscious of this danger, but the purpose of an assignment may be properly achieved this way if no more is required than showing you have read and understood the material (see Case Study 20).

Nevertheless, none of this is a substitute for a well-written book. Publishers have agreed to books of all kinds being published on CD-ROM/DVD-ROM with study notes and study programs, some of them sophisticated and interactive to allow the student to search for information. You may buy study packages to use on a desktop machine or a laptop. You may download these from a website. Many dictionaries, thesauri, and other standard reference books are available in a much more convenient form as a DVD-ROM, such as the Britannica and OED, with free 'download up-dates' and extensions to other databases. You no longer need two or three shelves to house large, heavy books with tiny print. 'Compression' on to DVD puts it all on one disk; and powerful 'search and compare' facilities make it easy to look up a word and to print out information as we need it.

One of the really useful technological advances is the scanner. What a time-saver! Linked to OCR, a program that converts a scanned image into the original text, which can then be inserted into a text-processing program, along with scanned diagrams, photographs, pictures – and all in colour – there is no limit to the number of articles and books one can produce with minimal effort. Software exists that enables you to produce professional-style articles, even full magazines. The danger naturally is that the presentation will become far superior to the content, but what's new in that? Almost all popular magazines are about selling the product, not about stimulating reading!

Textbooks are going out of date as they are published, but 'principles' do not change with the developments in technology. Such techniques are to be encouraged, to promote proactive learning we need to develop ourselves and to have our students enjoy. From a very early age, many have already become absolutely at home with computers, which have become very much cheaper and increasingly sophisticated; the operating systems and software are much more 'user-friendly'.

Computer games fascinate all ages, encouraging interaction with machine-generated images. 'Virtual reality' is for many superior to reality and a wonderful stimulus to imaginative and creative activity. Educational institutions and teachers should make positive use of the new enthusiasm for learning that this creates; they will need to become deeply involved in this new technology.

Interaction with a computer is not the same as passively, mindlessly watching TV. The brain is alert and active, even in video games that seem to be highly repetitive because of the need for very quick reactions and the strong desire to learn how to beat the machine. Interactive video software in computer programs and on DVD enables students to interrogate video material and a great deal of other information in other forms. The volume of such information is staggeringly large.

This possibility of interaction has opened up an exciting world of learning activity: what the computer does and where programs go are controlled by action/reaction of the person(s) using the program; it is a two-way exchange not just a one-way channel for information passing. A problem with material recorded on film or video-tape is that its sheer volume, its richness, makes it verbose and hard to comprehend, certainly to structure into your own knowledge and use. It is the main argument against the kind of university course experienced by Sarah (Case Study 20). Individual Units are overloaded with information that cannot be other than 'out there'. This is compounded by the sheer number of Units, which are self-contained, non-referential to other Units, and designed as 'closed' packages. The other side of the argument naturally is that traditional courses at UK universities are very narrowly specialised, and can hardly be expected to provide a broad education. Some balance is clearly desirable here.

With a film or video this richness can be exploited. Teachers can help by explaining how the video is structured, creating a list of questions to address to the material or by selection. Computer programs linked to video material allow us to search for answers to questions and to select the parts of the video material that are relevant to each question. This selection is usually programmed in as it is hard to design the program to enable random access. It would be better if we could ask our own questions rather than those stored in programs. Nevertheless, the system does allow students to plan their own learning paths through the material.

Fully structured linear and branching programs with or without video clips use feedback loops to ensure a thorough grasp of the material by repetitive testing and questioning; with gates to allow progress at the pace of the individual learner and to enable leaps as well as crawling on all fours. Program writers for more open courses can easily produce material to test learning; and are particularly useful for self-testing to give learners instant feedback or to guide them back to revisit sources of information and instruction. There are many forms of computer and linear programmed tests readily available.

Information may be made available in different formats: on screen, in print or on disks. One enormous advantage is that the information can be kept up-to-date, which is much more expensive to do if it appears in book or even pamphlet form. This makes it particularly valuable in areas such as careers advice or economic forecasting when you need accurate, up-to-the-minute data. Of course, someone has to up-date the material constantly, too.

Teachers and students accumulate visual and textual computer-based materials via networks and databases or develop their own, and they can be shared with others through a network. You can link to desktops or networks using the Internet or e-mail from home or office.

Electronic mail and networks are for sharing, but not only information. Many groups worldwide, since there are no longer language or continental barriers to the Internet, share the excitement of creative activity, problem-solving, debates, attacks and counter-attacks in scholarship or politics or games or gamesmanship. Individuals or groups on separate continents can work together with ease on projects. I have a great deal of fun with distant friends this way. It hardly matters where you are any more. I travel between three continents regularly, but it has no effect on my communicating via the Internet across the world. How the world has changed!

You can print out what you need to a high standard of presentation, incorporating pictures, diagrams, photos, text within pictorial images, all in colour to the standard of glossy magazines. The hoped-for 'paperless office' has proved to be a fantasy; computer-based data seems to demand 'hard copy' for one purpose or another. Whole forests are disappearing to feed the demand. This does not mean that books and all kinds of professionally printed material are no longer of value. People must continue to read for enjoyment as much as for information, to stimulate their creative faculties and to share and generate ideas. Not least to develop competence in and a 'feeling for' language and words. Libraries have become resource centres with multimedia facilities; teachers must be at least as comfortable with 'multimedia' as students; and exploit its possibilities to the full.

Training

Training in the use of new technology is straightforward for teachers and students and there is an ongoing training function required, usually provided by computer-based training packages, in regard to new software and updates for older software. There is an unending need for updating knowledge and skills, too.

Text-processing is now standard practice for recording and creating one's own and linking to database and professionally produced materials. The range is vastly extended by the use of graphics software and scanning functions. The level of skill and insight you develop and the relative speed at which you can work depend on how many hours you are prepared to give to producing and collating materials, as does the range and quality of the materials. On the other hand, you can do your preparation in any convenient place, even on a train using a laptop, and access information and send text by mobile phone. Linked to a palmsize computer, you can download from the Internet as you travel. None of this just happens. You have to work at it, but the fact is that it is a tremendously absorbing activity to which people become quite addicted. Hence, the learning progresses enormously fast even for those who seemed to achieve nothing in formal education.

Like any map, this brief description of new technology and its effect on the way teachers and learners interact will not come fully alive until you actually use it yourself. Try to work closely with the staff in your resource centre and those who are using multimedia to do their jobs. You really will need to become almost as adept as they are, even if it consumes more of your time than you feel able to afford. You might well become swept up in the excitement of it all, as millions are already.

But this excitement and fascination mean that time spent in front of a computer is likely to increase, may even take over one's life. There is a danger that interchanges with machines will soon replace interchanges with people. The danger was evident as many as 25 years ago when teachers in infant schools and anyone dealing with small children began to notice that infants did not respond to the human voice as they used to. It was very hard to get their attention, while play patterns changed. These children were reared by sitting in front of a TV for many hours, their attention was 'fixed' on screen images, and the mothers did not interact with them or they with their mothers as in 'normal' child-rearing.

This inability to concentrate without the focus of a machine has proved a worrying trend. It has had an impact naturally enough on social skills, creating more self-orientated adult behaviour and people who show an inability to 'put yourself in the other person's shoes'. It reinforces the tendency to go into situations without thought of consequences for others, noted when discussing strategies for teaching and learning above. Playing team games can have exactly the opposite effect.

Suggested reading

Buzan, T. *Use Your Head*, BBC Books (London), 4th edn, 1995.
Buzan, T. *Make the Most of your Mind*, Pan Books, 1977/1988.
Cottrell, S. *Teaching Study Skills and Supporting Learning*, Palgrave Macmillan, 2001.
Cottrell, S. *Skills for Success*, Palgrave, 2003.
Cottrell, S. *The Study Skills Handbook*, Palgrave Macmillan, 2004.
Fry, R. *Improve Your Reading* (*How to Study*), Kogan Page, 1996.
Fry, R. *Use Your Computer* (*How to Study*), Kogan Page, 1997.
Marland, P. *Towards More Effective Distance and Open Teaching*, Routledge, 1997.
Turner, J. *How to Study*, Sage Publications, 2002.
Wheeler, M. and Bligh, D. *Counselling in Study Methods*, Intellect Books, 1985.

<table>
<tr><td>CHAPTER 20</td><td>Aids to learning</td></tr>
</table>

The Wow! factor

One important way in which teachers and students become adept in the use of computers is to use them for presentations. Children in schools in Australia from the age of 10 use their resource centre to research and prepare presentations with computers in many subject areas. They do this either as individuals or in groups. Microsoft Powerpoint is the dominant software program used for this. It is relatively simple to put together different styles of text and images, which can be downloaded from a website or scanned into the computer. In a number of senior schools, every student has access to a personal laptop linked by a radio hub, so that s/he can work almost anywhere, carry the computer to where other resources such as books are. Or literally sit in a comfortable chair with it on her lap!

The fascination of producing presentations which look so clever and professional is a great motivator to find the materials for the content. It encourages children to search for information, to go at it with questions: discovery learning with a structure and clear purpose. They find pictures and photographs, other visual materials as well as text, in a wide variety of sources available in the centre or other resource areas. The quality of the product is raised by comparison with others, as in all cases of competition. The presentation, however, is usually recorded on disk and presented on a computer screen to the subject teacher. Where appropriate there will also be 'hard copy' for a file of work.

Teachers are therefore expected to use the same kind of presentations in their teaching, and classes are equipped for computer projection. But there is a problem. As a motivator for learning it is a resource without parallel. Children and the teachers who use it become computer literate, skilful in the use of the keyboard for writing text and knowledgeable in research techniques. As a teaching tool, it is demanding of time for preparation; after all, the quality should be a model for the children. More importantly there is the usual curve with anything new; now the novelty of computer-generated presentations is past its peak. Australian researchers report that the reaction to a lecturer using it is most likely to be, 'Oh no! Not another Powerpoint presentation!' The Wow! factor will no longer work.

The old-fashioned methods of presentation are much simpler to prepare, more versatile and lend themselves much better to two-way interactions. Content, as we have seen, needs to be acquired in small digestible amounts; it is better built up as a structure rather than displayed as a grand edifice. If a computer presentation is used in the same way as the earlier techniques on an OHP, building up links with keywords as structural elements, but supported by the exciting possibilities of the imagery the computer can access, there is a great deal to be gained.

Obviously, the teacher needs to be competent and have confidence in managing this resource. Equally, s/he needs to understand the principles of audio-visual presentation in classrooms. The use of new technology does not invalidate what has been researched extensively; and the chalkboard or whiteboard is still a teacher's most valuable audio-visual aid, but it is often very badly used. A board may be replaced by an OHP or flipchart of large sheets of white paper; these days, where the finance is available by an interactive whiteboard.

Read again the section on Audio Visual Aids in Chapter 16, on pages 159–169.

Audibility and visibility

Consider the acoustics of the room and the lighting conditions. Do not assume that people can hear or see. The screen may be masked for some students by others or by the OHP or the projector. It is often a problem when the lighting, artificial light or sunlight from windows, creates reflections and/or shadows, especially on a chalkboard. The greatest visual aid is useless if the image can't be seen. Always ask the people furthest away or at the widest angle if they are having difficulty. But if possible test it out yourself, walk around to see. In particular, check any material you have put up on the board for legibility and structure, preferably from the furthest point; this has the added advantage that you can make personal contact with students and experience it from their point of view. It is too easy to remain fixed at the front when using any AVA, including the chalkboard.

In many teaching rooms the position of the board determines how students will sit relative to the teacher. Some are wide rather than long and set up so that if there are rows of desks, the students sitting at the front are at a very wide angle to the board or screen and can only see part of it. Other rooms are long and narrow so that students in the back rows are a long way from the teacher/board or hidden by other students. If at all possible, get students to move to where you and they can see and be seen, and can hear properly.

Many students deliberately choose to sit in places where communication is far from easy. A teacher with a class of any size, when they are sitting in rows (and it is not inappropriate if you are doing a lecture-style presentation), may find s/he can only talk to this side or that of the room, or to the front or the back. A teacher really should be mobile, try to establish contact with all the students some of the time. Don't just talk to one group of students as in Gillian's class (Case Study 14) because they respond to you. This is much easier if they are grouped to make it simple to do.

Particularly when the acoustics of the room are difficult, students and teacher must get close. What do you do about difficult acoustics? For instance, the hum of the OHP is a distraction; turn it off whenever you do not need it. Rooms near busy roads, or construction sites, or workshops can be very noisy if the windows are open, but also very hot, stuffy and airless if they are closed in summer or if the heating is set high in winter. How will you resolve such a difficulty? Sometimes you can't do anything about it. Ask for another room!!

Think about the personalities involved. Are there any in the group with poor eyesight? They may be too embarrassed to put on their spectacles; this quite frequently happens! Is anyone colour-blind: 6% of males? Maybe colour differentiation is important. Some cannot distinguish lines that are too fine or present narrow angles. Ask people to move if it might help. Think of brightness of the image or contrast with general brightness in the room. Draw the curtains or switch off lights. There may be angles at which reflections make it hard to see. Experiment; move the screen (or the class). Take control. Many classes are designed with windows down one side, which on a sunny day may make for problems of seeing images. If the sun is on the desks, they can't see to write and then look up to see the board. Perhaps you should lower the blinds or draw the curtains. Take control.

Deafness tends to be more embarrassing and more difficult, and people are often less aware of the onset of deafness than they are of failing vision. Both affect people gradually, usually as they get older. A physical decline seems inevitable, though people compensate with greater effort too. You need to be alert to problems, to your clarity of diction and your pace of delivery, too. It is up to you to ensure that everyone can hear and everyone can see.

Listening skills

Listening skills require a great effort to develop. We are surrounded by a cacophony of sounds. Most students have been conditioned to be unhappy with silence. Some may wake up listening anxiously to silence in the middle of the night. So, we routinely block out most of what we hear. Listen to a tape-recording of an hour of your life in normal circumstances. What sounds are there you did not 'hear' when they were actually happening? About 90%?

Yet teachers expect students to listen more than to do anything else, without recognising the problems involved. Students may be 'talked at' for an hour or more. They are also often expected to take down notes at the same time. Apart from the difficulty of trying to do two things at once, there are many problems of inaccuracy, mishearing, misunderstanding and so on. Many teachers take the cynical view: 'As long as they've been given the information, what the hell! If they can't make use of it, it's nothing to do with me.'

All social behaviour depends on listening to others; and most people are very bad at it. Teachers are also notoriously bad at listening to students. Parliament is a public display of egotists talking and no one listening. Eventually, people have to scream and shout, even become social vandals, to make others listen. Watch the huge noisy rallies that seem to be reported regularly on TV newscasts. In tutorial roles, your listening skills are vitally important. Very often tutors fail to hear let alone understand what a student is trying to say. Of course, the student may need help to say or to articulate what is important to him/her.

Alerting signals

If you want students to listen it is essential that you give them cues, alerting signals, and questions to think about. They need to be able to follow your structure easily. Give them the pattern. It can be built up using keywords. There should also be opportunities for feedback as two-way communication, loops or links to consolidate learning at least every 15 minutes or so.

Take stock of your delivery, pitch and tone of voice. How fast do you talk, how monotonous is your voice? Inexperienced teachers tend to let their voices rise, become rather strangled or shrill. Relax, slow down. A slower pace gives you and them thinking time. Try to pitch your voice lower, and to vary its pitch; it will be nicer to listen to and will probably carry better. Try to improve your diction, too. Always imagine you are talking, not shouting, to the person at the back of the room, the one furthest away from you. Ask him/her if s/he can hear you.

Do you miss consonants off the ends of words? Most English speakers are very lazy about articulation of words. Remember that in English the ends of words are more important than the beginning, yet the great majority of English speakers are careless about their diction, especially the ends of words. It is hard to hear word patterns. Listen to anyone in normal conversation: do they finish their words clearly? It is partly a matter of speed and partly of concentration: on ensuring the other person understands. Many people don't actually care if the other person hears them or not! Listen to yourself on a tape-recorder after a class. Better than video, it can be quite revealing.

OHP: projector and screen/laptop and projector

The OHP is a most versatile tool, which, as suggested above, can now be duplicated by use of a laptop computer. It has the advantage that you can prepare material beforehand, but also add to it or adapt it in the class. You can use it as a substitute for board work – and maintain eye-contact with students to encourage their participation. You have to turn away to write on a chalkboard and risk losing the contact. You should develop techniques that will not divide you from your class. Some teachers treat the projected image as if it were a chalkboard and do all the explanation at the screen, so losing the advantage of projection. You can do all the pointing and explanation on the OHP/computer screen and it will be projected behind you. You can sit to be part of the group when appropriate, or invite them to work with you, especially if you are adopting an inductive approach.

You can point out relevant detail on the transparency on the OHP, perhaps using a pen to lie as a semi-permanent pointer, moving it as needed to focus attention. You can reveal and mask parts of the structure or diagram as you want to concentrate on particular things. You can use all the visual clues, exploiting the four basic factors set out on page 160 above. The computer is even more versatile in regard to adding, revealing, dragging text and images and so on; the cursor is a pointing device and highlighting is simple.

All that I emphasised earlier about structure and sequence applies to projected images. Have a clear structure, take the students through it. Too much all at once is difficult to grasp, but they need to see the structure 'as a whole' by the end. Build it up gradually, revealing a bit at a time, elaborate the keywords or diagrams with your explanation. It helps to eliminate all the image except the bit you want to concentrate on (easily done with paper on an OHP), then gradually reveal the building blocks. Remember that the OHP/computer is an aid for your explanation, not a substitute for it. Think, too, about the density of information and verbosity. It is easy to make transparencies of A4 printed pages or scan text to make presentations: teachers frequently do. The result can be illegibility and incomprehension. Much better the other way round, to construct text in a computer, or on the transparency and then print it. A projected image must be read at a distance, a paper is held in the hand. Keep that difference in mind.

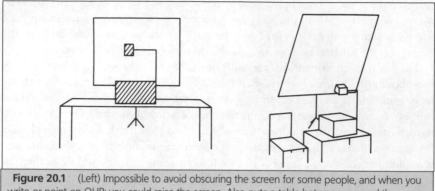

Figure 20.1 (Left) Impossible to avoid obscuring the screen for some people, and when you write or point on OHP: you could raise the screen. Also puts a table between you and the group: creates distance, formality. (Right) OHP not on sight-line or dominating. Screen needs angling forward. Easier to see in most illuminations, feels comfortably closer. Barriers removed.

Setting up the projector and screen

Where are you going to place yourself in relation to the projector? In many classrooms designed to use computer projection, the projector is in the ceiling. Nevertheless, the teacher has to be aware of the problems of getting between the projector and the screen. The OHP/laptop allows you to face your audience or to stand or sit among them; you are close, you can maintain eye-contact. You do not have to stand, presentation-style. You can use it with a group in a much more relaxed way. You can sit beside the machine, which signals that you are part of the group. This allows you to interact more easily with the group rather than with the screen. This kind of teaching is about sharing, not telling.

If you are using a portable set-up like an OHP, make sure the machine itself is not preventing students from seeing the screen. Try putting it on a low table (even a chair) rather than obstructing sight-lines for people sitting down (Figure 20.1). It helps if the screen can be tilted forward at the top.

The laptop is even more versatile. If you are using a desktop computer with a remote control mouse, you can easily move around, but it is not so possible to do inputs of text to build up materials inductively with a class. (See Case Study 24 on page 180.)

Look carefully also at Figure 16.2 'Faces of ICT'. The interactive whiteboard is the same in three images: in the first a teacher's shadow is thrown on to the board by the projector and s/he is remote from the students; in the next s/he uses a remote control with a laptop, it allows the teacher to work among the students; in the last the teacher is projecting on to the board from an OHP and using a flipchart. ICT of itself neither helps not hinders good teaching. It is still much easier to use the old technology. The two seated images show a teacher standing at the board when the technology intended to allow her to sit with the students; which is what is to be seen in the last image – the teacher among the students – or the students working as a seminar group. Consider the lessons about presentation techniques with projected images.

Building up resources

Materials produced by using computer software, OHP transparencies, teaching/learning aids are all a developing resource bank, which requires organising to allow for order and retrieval. Computer files are relatively easy, but can become confused and so need regular reorganisation. Transparencies need to be framed and covered. The photocopier can be used in conjunction with OHP to produce good-quality transparencies quickly. A structured lesson plan, for instance, should be in handout form, but also on OHP acetate to provide an overview of learning goals and activities. The computer is linked to a printer and scanner, quite often as one machine. Colour copier/printer/scanners are so relatively cheap that you can have your own. With so much versatility, the only constraint is your creative imagination. You can produce materials in many different forms for different uses; the contents can be mixed and matched, cut and pasted, supplemented and rejigged. I have already suggested colour-coding for your handout materials.

Storage of all computer-generated materials on the computer hard disk needs back-up on CD or DVD disks and as 'hard copy'. The latter needs filing, possibly in a box file with all other teaching aids you use. There is little more annoying than having to search for things when you want them or to have to produce them again because they are lost.

Nevertheless, you will find that you cannot just use the same thing over and again. You have to evaluate it with the benefit of hindsight, experience and growing understanding and 'redo' it so as to improve it. Where the original work is in the computer, that is much easier to do. Handouts need to be filed in date order and by topic/sequence; the use of colour-coding is helpful. The same is true of hard copy of any kind. Be organised. Be work-person-like!

Boardwork

Structure matters in boardwork too. It is easy to use the board as a jotting pad; this is quite helpful to concentrate attention and move the focus, but it doesn't produce a pattern that is easy to remember. Plan your boardwork, whenever you can, or at least determine some structure, within which you can make notes on the board. Look at it at the end and see if the pattern makes sense for your students to take away. You need a 'model in the head'. You can put up an outline before they come. Whiteboards have the advantage that you can use colours for differentiation and boundary.

Write legibly. This requires practice, it's quite different from any other writing you do. Can the people at the back read it? If it is too small or the letters are poorly formed, no! Try to look at it from the back to see it as they see it. You could use columns, circles, or section off the board, or use lists with headings, or arrows to show relationships between ideas. The coral diagrams on pages 222 and 228 work well on a board. If you add information, words and so on, on the board as you go along, you must differentiate different information, ideas and topics by boundaries (lines) around each part and possibly indicate the links. Go through it with your students to consolidate at the end if you can. Ask them if they can understand what it is you want them to take away, before you wipe it off! But you must do that, too.

Handouts

The most valuable, least understood resource is the photocopier. It is often used to reproduce masses of 'stuff to give the students', generally without thinking through what they are going to do with it, or whether it will contribute effectively to learning. As with every other aid, a handout needs careful planning. There are many questions that will occur to you as you prepare it:

- What is it for?
- How should it look?
- When do they need it?
- What is to be the sequence?
- What will it contain?
- What colour should it be?
- What size is it?

Here are some examples of useful handouts.

1 A teacher has to assume knowledge, breadth of experience, to be able to concentrate on what can be done in class. There has to be a lot of learning elsewhere. A handout ensures that all will have the same accurate and up-to-date information. (Of course, they have to read it!) It must be readable, too.

It is most important that students read widely. It is much better if they do this before a session, so that what they have read is a basis for their work. It is easy to use material as if it were a textbook – to let it run the class. It is better to see it as a committee paper circulated as a basis for discussion, to take as read and somewhere to start from.

Students must be encouraged to find their own reading. They need access to photocopying in the library/resource centre to make up a 'reading portfolio'. They should be encouraged to adopt the approach I set out in my advice on the development of study skills in Chapter 2.

2 Reduce a handout to be used in a lecture to a skeleton of keywords, which students can 'flesh out' with their own notes. Use it to help students to grasp the structure and pattern of the whole, the flow and sequence. Wordy handouts are confusing 'noise'.

Structure and linking, alerting and outline notes, are much better than the (usually) selective and inaccurate notes that students scribble while their attention should be on listening and watching. The brain cannot be alerted with questions while the ears are trying to catch the answers. A 'gapped handout' will assist note-taking and consolidation by enabling students to recall accurately what was covered in class. It can also be used to test recall, words, whole sentences, labels or whatever that needs to be tested. It can be filed for revision.

3 A handout can be designed as an instruction sheet, an action plan or a working document. Guidance, outline drawings to complete, questions to find answers to, maps, treasure hunts, so many creative ways of using handouts. They all need design to ensure that they are effective to their purpose. This is much better than inventing material on the hoof, and then getting the group to copy it down from the board. Distortion and misunderstanding become inevitable. Once you have designed a handout, have it validated by a mentor or someone else for clarity, ambiguity, what it is like for someone coming to it fresh and possibly not already knowledgeable.

4 Use handouts to 'share'. As with OHPs for groupwork, handouts can ensure that all have the same ideas – and can focus them through revisiting – and have the same richness of resources to work with.

242

REMEMBER! … Check your handout, especially if it contains visual material, to see that it does not use stereotypes or other material which could offend some students or distract them from their learning. Be particularly careful with humour. Material, visual or in words, that seems innocent or amusing to you may be offensive to someone else of another gender, age or culture.

Resource bank

A most important feature of handouts is that they accumulate along with other teaching and learning aids as a personal resource file. They need organising: given headings and dates, and perhaps colour-coded. Using different colours for the different kinds of handouts can be extremely helpful. Sensible use of handouts ensures a structured, clear, non-verbose, accurate information-base for students, too, with a linking pattern.

REMEMBER! …It is unhelpful for students to try to revise from material that is as wrong, incomplete, ambiguous, illusory or fictional as student notes so frequently turn out to be.

Simple learning materials are often as effective as complex ones. All AVA is expensive in time and effort. Time spent making AVA or handouts will only make sense if the products solve a real problem in learning; it is also far better if they can be used for more than one session or class. An advantage of working in a team, or with colleagues, is that you share ideas and the effort of creating resources. There should be a team resource bank to use.

Problem-solving

One good exercise is to identify real learning problems in your field of teaching. With colleagues, think of creative ways to tackle the problems. You could use models as well as presentations or slides. You could think of games or activities that require setting out as instructions.

I have seen extraordinarily inventive ideas in a wide range of disciplines from such an exercise. I gave an example in Case Study 7 on page 33, in which a doll's house was used to help students who had difficulty in visualising things, and to 'see it happening' for real somehow.

A group (or an individual) may pose themselves a learning or visualising problem: for example, to show how far away the nearest star is by taking the Sun to be the size of a pea, where the planets are on the same scale. Or how you might explain planetary motion. Or convey the idea of a standing wave in physics, or the menstrual cycle, or the circulation of the blood. Or how to deal in stocks and shares, or decision-making in a business enterprise. Or to analyse the action of the four-stroke engine.

These have all been designed as models, charts (some with parts that move), board or card games; and some were highly competitive. If a visual stimulus can be helped with action, all the better. Think of the 'sculpting' in Case Study 6 on page 31.

What matters is not the cleverness of the technology but the inventiveness of the designers.

Team-based resources

Teams share expertise and creativity building up a team resource bank of teaching/learning materials. Awarding bodies and examining boards increasingly promote team approaches which help to integrate areas of the curriculum. Students are to learn through projects that cross subject disciplines, while teachers work as teams to produce the learning materials.

A resource base is needed where materials can be located and are accessible to the team. It has to be equipped not only for the storage and retrieval of materials but for creative work too. This is a base where the team can generate ideas and activity-work for a whole curriculum programme. Clearly, since it consists mostly of handouts and consumables, there must be a system to track usage and ensure replacement, as happens in supermarkets. All team members carry responsibility. The production of AVA, models, computer graphics, computer-generated presentations and so on requires work-benches, computers, printers, copiers, scanners, video machines, materials such as acetates, and so forth. The control of expenditure and decision-making is important, so that record-keeping must be well organised.

Under 'Study skills' above I suggest ways in which teachers can develop their skills to contribute more effectively to such work. Institutions have multimedia and resource rooms with technicians and other support staff. If you are lucky enough to have such support for teachers, you should make sure that you work closely with them. They are often linked to the multimedia centre to exploit technological advances in the use of computers and networks. It makes economic sense to put major resources of this kind together with trained staff to ensure that they are used effectively.

Desktop publishing

It is a major priority to learn to use text and graphics software; no one in FE can reasonably expect to teach without these skills. They make the production of good-quality learning materials possible. You can manipulate text in a word processor to ensure that it is presented in the most effective way without the tedium of having to rewrite or retype. Learn to compose, to 'invent', at the keyboard.

Most computers have a range of fonts and allow the use of graphics which will enable you to produce excellent presentation materials. You can link many software applications together. Learn to use a copier, a printer and a scanner, too.

All computers can now support desktop publishing programs that allow teachers to produce materials that look as attractive and as well produced as the printed page, but at a fraction of the cost. Once the basic text and diagrams have been set up, they can be manipulated all the ways magazines use to make them visually exciting. But you can also make them work the way learners learn using all the visual techniques mentioned above: simplifying, structuring, sequencing, headlining, boundaries as lines and boxes, integrating diagrams and other images with the text. Poor visual presentation of learning materials fails to stimulate students, so they 'switch off'. Look at almost any commercially produced material and see how it depends on visual impact for its effect. Even quite awful content can be made compelling reading. Teachers need to exploit every possible technique to the full.

Films and television

There are good and bad ways of using films and television programmes. All are by nature 'verbose': they contain far too much information and visual imagery for students to make sense of, certainly if they see a progamme or film only once. Their main purpose is to entertain, or to stimulate interest. Where they set out to inform, they assume some general audience. Students will find it hard to select what they need. Even instructional films may not be particularly easy to digest so that information is selected out by the students' lack of attention. The dimly lit and comfortable environment is not conducive to attention. Only the strongest of images will be remembered. Almost everyone goes to sleep, at least mentally, under hot, dark, non-stimulating, often rather airless conditions.

Using films and television well

You must see the material first (simple advice, but often ignored). Analyse the film into structure to see how it is put together; after all, someone planned it. Provide students with this structure (as keywords) to help them to grasp the parts in relation to the whole. Alert students to what they can learn, what to look out for. Pinpoint the questions the film addresses; otherwise they will not know what to look or listen for, and will certainly miss most of it. And it is no good asking them afterwards, 'did you notice ...?'

Even better, select those, possibly short, parts of the film or programme which contain what you want students to learn. Show only those. This has the added advantage that you can show these parts more than once. Using this technique:

1 Prepare the students with questions and structure.
2 Show them relevant and important extracts from the whole.
3 Revisit these with the questions to elicit answers – or maybe more searching questions.
4 Reshow the extracts to consolidate the learning and link it to other learning experiences.
5 Encourage them to ask questions.
6 Possibly in groups, ask them to talk about what they have seen and what they remember.
7 Have the groups report back to the class what they thought important.
8 Evaluate the learning with them.

If this technique is used with video-recordings, the students can have material available as part of a databank (for example, in a resource centre) to consult when they need to revise.

<table>
<tr><td>**CHAPTER 21**</td><td>**Barriers to communication I**</td></tr>
</table>

Language barriers

In order to make progress in engaging students in the learning process, we must ensure that we and they recognise the barriers they bring with them and those we create for them. Teachers should be able to recognise the learning problems that students create for themselves or behavioural characteristics that hinder learning. It is not easy for us to see our own.

Mind-set and emotion

Emotional or attitudinal barriers result from cultural conditioning or in response to past experience. We all have a mind-set about things that relate to us, our self-image that inhibits our willingness to believe we can do certain things. They can turn into attitudes and beliefs that we will defend against overwhelming evidence.

Perhaps you know someone who is a banker. What image does that word conjure up for him or her – or for you? *'There are certain things bankers do, wear, enjoy, don't do, don't wear, don't feel comfortable doing, aren't there? I couldn't possibly ...'* It will inhibit certain kinds of behaviour. Girls (or their parents) still reject the idea of engineering as a possible career. *'Do women actually enjoy science or engineering or maths? Isn't that what men do? It's not for women.'* Many men see nursing or primary school teaching as an inappropriate career. Where do such attitudes come from? They clearly relate to our perception of ourselves, a powerful self-image we have developed as a result of our experience. Many, such as that of the banker, we derive from models around us. It is not unusual to meet students who genuinely see themselves as 'thick', not 'clever like these others'. It may be a result of painful experiences in education in the past or as a defensive posture to protect them from possible failure.

We have our needs for personal space and territory. Our value-system, our likes and dislikes, our images are often firmly embedded; they are inextricable from 'me – who I am' and exhibited both in our words and in our body language. We can all read such body signals easily. They are the one and only international language; for that reason the most useful means of teaching any other language. It is clear that most of this language is built-in genetically into all human beings. Someone who has a mind-set that says *'I can't do maths'* is never going to succeed in maths, however hard the teacher tries, unless that mould can somehow be broken. This learner has had past experience of failure in maths, perhaps reinforced by a role-model, that has established a conviction that 'it's not worth my trying'. The same happens in most areas of learning. Ball games will defeat some people utterly; some are all thumbs in craftwork; some are word-blind; some can't draw even so much as a straight line. You will have heard people say these things. All are self-fulfilling prophecies.

It is far from easy to tackle such attitudinal barriers. Yet if someone discovers a way through the barrier, the effect on their self-image and their lives can be quite dramatic. The discussion above on motivation (page 126) may suggest ways forward.

Jargon, symbols and specialised vocabulary

All subject areas employ jargon: words and symbols with precise meanings in that context – to share understanding, to avoid ambiguity. Jargon is a response to the need to be specific within a particular context. In some cases the use of jargon can lead to incompleteness. It fails if the student does not know the words or the symbols we are using.

Even in the use of non-jargon, ordinary language, it is easy to misunderstand someone if the words they use, though they appear to be the same as words we use, carry implications or references to values or expectations different from our own. *We are not coming from the same place.* Clearly, this is the major problem in helping students to grasp *uses* rather than *meanings* of words in a second language. Most translation dictionaries, especially the electronic wallet-style, offer a choice of one-to-one equivalents, with little help as to when to use one rather than another. In English the shortest words like 'a' or 'the' and prepositions are the hardest to use correctly. Long words are much easier because they usually have more restricted and more specific meaning.

Even when teaching native speakers of a language in their own tongue, teachers frequently do not share the same cultural value-system as their students. The problem may be greater for the older Japanese or Chinese or even European teacher of young students within their own culture than for a foreigner because cultural values are changing so fast in all these countries. Cultural divides are clearly widening across generations in all countries. In many cases it involves whole new vocabularies.

Even if we speak what is apparently the same language, we are not all interpreting the words the same way: Mark Twain's wisecrack of 150 years ago: *the English and Americans are two peoples divided by a common language.* In order for you to follow me in this book we must share a common interpretation of words in a common value-system.

Do you in fact share the same cultural value-system as your students? These values are built into words. Even when you speak the same language, are they interpreting your words as you intend? How much more likely is it that you will miss each other when you use words or symbols which are unfamiliar to them?

The cartoons in Figure 21.1 are taken from a refreshingly different way of helping English-speaking adults come to terms with Chinese characters. The writer is a Chinese laughing at changes in value-systems he sees embedded in these characters.

Teacher's questions

How can teachers handle questions? What should teachers do? These two sentences are really pseudo-questions, rhetorical questions, alerting statements: all teachers use them. They are not looking for any creative response, but merely aiming to alert the students' brains – here the readers' brains. They prepare them for 'my' answers, without stimulating them to find their own. Having a student actually discover answers different from 'mine' can seem to be bad news for many teachers. They want

Figure 21.1 Fun with Chinese characters (T.H. Peng, *Straits Times Collection*, Federal Publications, Singapore, 1980).

students to remember the 'right' answer, in other words 'theirs'. Great weight is given to this procedure through the examination and testing system. The level of restructuring by the student depends not so much on curiosity as on extrinsic motivating factors such as the teacher's pleasure or anger, or passing the exam, or just 'getting it right'. It depends critically too on how easy it is for the student to link the information or concepts into what is *known* already. If the pace of arrival of new information (new words or new definitions) is too fast, or if the volume of information is overwhelming, learners cannot deal with it. But in any case, just being exposed to it once will not work. It has to be revisited and rethought.

It has to 'arrive': be put into familiar language or symbols. Teachers need to pitch it at the level a student can receive and understand it; and recognise the barriers to learning all of us bring to any learning experience.

Effectiveness depends on the students' readiness to learn and on the control exercised by the teacher, who must manage the form in which the new information is presented, and decide how much at one time or how often. It must match the students' readiness to deal with it. Too much overwhelms them and simply produces 'noise'. There has to be time for mental processing. Pace matters.

It is easier for learners if the structure is clear, if it leads them through identifying questions which build one from another, even if they are presented as statements of keywords. It will ensure that the brain is alert to deal with the information and will assist their mental processing.

A hierarchy of questions

In a hierarchy, higher levels will depend on successful achievement at lower levels of skill, knowledge and understanding, which are a prerequisite of further advance. Higher levels include all lower levels.

Level 1: Focusing on what is happening now

Think, for example, of an experiment in science: the students need to observe and record accurately what happens. Learning activities in all subject areas, from practical skills like dress-making to the study of a text in a literature class, require the same level of concentration and accuracy. Students should be alert, questioning what is happening for them or around them. To observe accurately they have to develop the right skills. This is only the first level of questioning, and many fail even to achieve that satisfactorily.

Level 2: Describing experience

It is essential that students achieve at least Level 2. To do this, they need questions to address to the observations they have made. Questions like: *What have I observed? What has actually happened?* These will give shape and meaning to the new information. Level 2 facilitates construction of a frame of reference and language and symbols to describe the observations. One valuable effect of this learning will be an enlarged vocabulary. In this sense, it is a truism that 'all teachers are teachers of language'.

Level 3: Comparing and interpreting experiences

This is concept formation, the ability to think in abstractions, to make mental models. It is the way we link experiences into the 'wholes' which we call 'knowing'. Reflection on the learning will be necessary for achievement at Level 3. Students must match a new experience with previous experiences and with 'knowing' already acquired. They must be given activities to ensure processing of the new information so as to link it with previous 'knowing' into a newly structured 'whole'.

This process we call 'understanding'; it may lead to leaps to new mental models: 'insight'.

Questions that promote activity of this kind are much more searching. *'Compare the results of this experiment with those you got in Experiment C. What do you think is happening here?' 'If we change x, what do you think will happen? Why? Consider principles we discussed yesterday.'*

Questions may not be in obvious question format as we can see here.

Level 4: Generalising, thinking creatively

Problem-solving involves first having a clear mental picture of the problem to be solved. We should not assume that most people can 'visualise' problems, make mental models, even 'see' the context within which the problems exist. Modelling in the head is a sophisticated skill that many find impossible. It is the major problem that faced teachers of science when students had to demonstrate/explain how something worked rather than remember right answers for examinations.

Tackling problems, however, can accelerate learning dramatically, so long as the problems to tackle are set at a level appropriate to the readiness of the students. Problems that are too complex, or assume knowledge or experience the learners do not have, will simply defeat them.

Questions at this level are related to problems to solve. They do not have to be particularly clever questions. Problems set to children in a primary school are effective in getting them to think creatively, 'to turn the problem over in their heads' and suggest possible ways of tackling it; and then argue for one solution against another one. One class was asked to come up with ideas about keeping pets in school.

Teachers can help their students to frame the problem in a tractable way through structuring their questions. If they fail to tackle the problem successfully, it may simply be that the questions they are addressing are unhelpful or are not setting enquiry off in the right direction. Consider again Case Study 29 of the cave rescue.

Closed and open questions

'Closed' questions assume the right answer exists. They can often be answered *yes* or *no*. Many tests are of this kind: true/false, objective tests, computations and so on. So much of education seems to be about closed questions, especially in Japan and the USA. Teachers have a preference for them in many of their classroom interactions. Examiners love them because they are independent of bias or subjective judgements. As an alerting exercise a closed question can be successful. But to be effective as a technique the teacher must name students who are to answer. General questions addressed to the whole group are ineffective in alerting all students; most will leave it to clever-clogs to answer.

The teacher is not looking for competing answers, nor even for students to reframe the new information in their own words. This last is vitally important; questioning can be used effectively to promote Level 2 activity. The questions may still be closed. But if students are to achieve Level 3 or Level 4, they need 'open' questions that stimulate them to think and to find their own words. 'Open' questions receive unpredictable answers: 'messing about here for a bit to see what we can discover'. Their principal purpose is not to elicit answers but to generate increasingly searching questions. Open questions are about an attitude of mind, stimulating natural curiosity to explore and to find out. They involve openly valuing each student's answer however improbable it might be. It is easy to demotivate students so that they will not try to find answers or generate original ideas.

A class of silent students who will not respond to questions is a depressing experience for any teacher. People experience damage to their self-esteem if they find themselves competing with others in discovery learning when they can't answer or are made to feel rather stupid. The most successful approach is usually to set students up in groups to explore problems and ideas. Individuals feel less exposed and can give each other mutual support.

A great deal of wasted effort is also caused by asking questions of the wrong kind, looking for unhelpful answers. We must first find the 'right' questions and validate them to make sure they alert the students to 'useful' activity and that they will look for answers in the right sort of places. Think again of Case Study 29.

Structured questions that define a linking path are better than a series of unconnected general questions, at least until students have sufficient experience to structure their own paths. But students may still arrive at the 'wrong' answers or go off in the wrong direction.

A teacher using inductive methods has to decide when to intervene, and certainly if discovery learning is intended. For unlearning is much harder than learning, so students need to get it right first time. There is frustration in letting them get into a mess, nor should they be trying to reinvent the wheel. The appropriateness or otherwise of discovery needs appraising. Again, it is a matter of clearly formulating what has to be done and controlling the learning activity through structure. The main purpose might be to promote group bonding rather than what the students in fact discover for themselves.

Inductive methodology is the use of open questions. But it has to be genuinely 'open'.

CASE STUDY 31

A television programme on teaching methods showed a teacher using 'Inductive Methodology' in a Police training context. A sergeant in uniform in a very crowded classroom was teaching cadets also all in uniform indicating rank. He asked a series of questions in order to elicit a structure of ideas to be used to formulate a problem.

He would ask a question. After each question, he walked halfway down the class and took the answer from one particular male cadet. He returned to the whiteboard and wrote up the answer. No other answers were sought or taken, although many of the cadets offered their replies. In particular, he ignored the only three girls in the predominantly male class, who had sat at the front eager to participate. They put up their hands, but he walked past the girls every time, deliberately it seemed so that he could not see them.

At the end, he projected an OHP transparency with precisely the same answers presented in the same structure. It was rather like a committee meeting in which the chairman arrives with the minutes already typed out in his pocket.

Discussion

1 Was this questioning inductive? If not, why not?

2 What do you think was the effect of having teacher and students in uniform?

3 Would these students be willing to challenge the teacher or to offer their own ideas?

4 Is that possibility appropriate in contexts like this one? Why, or why not?

5 The cadets were eager to reply. Why was that, do you think?

6 The girls sat together and at the front of the class. How would you interpret that behaviour?

7 The sergeant walked past the girls sitting close to him. Why do you think he did that?

8 What were the messages in this class?

Comment

I do not see this approach as inductive methodology. Inductive implies that the questions are open: we're going to see what we can discover. The sergeant knew the right cadet to ask to give him the right answers. It seemed the last thing he wanted was competing answers, and certainly not from girls. It was a good example of closed questions.

Messages

Teachers must watch all the time. Video-recordings of classes can be very revealing so long as they are about the whole experience and not just what the teacher does. My questions in this Case Study are about what I observed happening. Clearly, this brief description is highly selective, it ignores the content of the lesson, for example. It says nothing of language registers, vocabulary, tone of voice and you must take my word for what occurred. Maybe, I got it wrong! Everything in this class was transmitting messages: the people, the uniforms, how the room was set out, the technology used, the body language. All of this is read instantly by those within the class and those watching the video-recording. The same is true of all classes – yours and mine. After more than 40 years, students still surprise me. Every class is a fascinating study in behaviour.

What messages were the people in this class transmitting? Students were eager to participate. Does it mean that it was a good lesson? What were the learning goals? What did they actually learn? Was the lesson effective for its purpose? The answer to the last question is probably yes, but what was the purpose?

The class was in rows of three students either side of an aisle. The teacher walked away from the rostrum at the front to get close to students towards the back of the room. He was conscious of the problems of distance. He returned to the rostrum to write up student responses. However, he did not appear to try to involve all the students, especially not the girls sitting at the front. Clearly, the students were watching him carefully and reading his messages. What were they? What was his message to the girls? They were eager to learn and had sat right at the front, but they were separate from the boys. They knew they had to try harder than the boys, and it seemed that it was fairly new to have girls in this class at all, at least from the behaviour of the sergeant to them.

In this case, the teacher felt the need to control the questioning so that the answers he wanted the class to learn were 'correct'. The students took away a structured handout of keywords that they could use to revise the learning. The alerting was effectively done. Since all the students appeared to know the answers already, the lesson was itself consolidation of earlier instruction. Why did the BBC call the class Inductive Methodology? It was clearly part of Instruction to ensure that the students learned the right procedures according to police regulations. Its purpose did not seem to be to develop a creative approach to tackling problems.

Language in use

Words more accurately have *uses* rather than *meanings*. A strong cultural element is built into words so that it is almost impossible to really understand speakers of any language, including one's own, if you have little insight into the values and assumptions conveyed by words and symbols that are used. Language works by accumulated meanings or nuances according to the context. We must know who is using the word and for what purpose.

A lecturer was talking with a group about children and how important 'security' was for them. She discovered after half an hour or so of discussion that some members of the class thought she was talking about Social Security Benefits. What an enormous difference this made to their understanding of what the teacher was actually talking about!

I was recently talking to a Japanese girl who wrote in English for a sophisticated magazine in Japan called *Roots*. I jokingly suggested she might translate this as *daikon*, '*big root*' in Japanese, a favourite vegetable. The joke was much funnier for her as *daikon* suggests 'unsophisticated country-bumpkin' against 'city-slicker' for a Japanese, which she explained when she stopped laughing.

In many subject areas, there is a large specialist vocabulary to be learned. The use of symbols is vitally important in others. Interestingly, symbols work similarly to *kanji*, the Japanese version of Chinese characters, where the meaning of the visual symbol is independent of the word that is used to 'read' it. They are very much like Arabic numbers, which may be expressed in many different words even in English, let alone in other languages, but convey the same meaning visually. Using the Arabic numerals how will you write: two, twice, twenty, double, squared?

Jargon (like symbols) is intended to facilitate sharing between those who work in a particular field. But initially, jargon, specialist vocabulary, use of symbols, and so on are more likely to confuse than to enlighten, as anyone coming new to ICT will know.

Maybe, we could help students to learn our symbols in an amusing way, as these cartoons do with the *kanji*. But we should make sure they do understand them, and that we have a shared context of meaning. Students quite often feel isolated in class because they may feel they are visiting 'foreign parts'.

Look again at Case Study 3 on page 26. Sandra wanted her 'students' to go through a difficult experience: to feel what it was like to face something they just couldn't make head or tail of because they couldn't read. Anyone who visits a foreign country where the writing system uses symbols that are quite different from those you have learned becomes 'as a little child'. There is something awful about suddenly finding yourself 'illiterate'. Go to Japan or China or Arabic-speaking countries!

Language register

Language register is also most important. We choose a style of speaking which is appropriate for the context we are in. We use a range of styles, words, phrases, sentence structures, formal and informal expressions and tones of voice. These are our 'language registers'.

Consider the difference between making a speech at a wedding and chatting in the lounge with your friends. Would you address your boss in the same way you would your husband or wife, or one of your children? Or your dog? What about your 'tone of voice'? In many cultures, choosing the right level of politeness in speech is more important than what is said. In others, anything goes apparently (though probably not!).

The words we use, our whole language register, show how we value the other person relative to others and ourselves. 'Talking down' to adults is to show that you do not value them as equals. On the other hand, if your choice of vocabulary is wrong, your sentence structures are too complex or idiosyncratic, or the speed at which you talk is too fast, you will fail to communicate with them. It is a fundamental problem facing writers of books like this one. What language register should I use?

YOUR WORDS

We need to look carefully at the words and symbols we use in our teaching and at our language registers. There are many questions you could ask yourself.

- How much of what I say is 'jargon' – part of my specialism?

- What level of vocabulary have these students achieved?

- How can I ensure that my students understand and are comfortable in using these words?

- Can they use them accurately? How much is still a totally 'foreign language' to them?

- How fast do I speak? Most lecturers/teachers eventually discover that slower is better.

- How complex do I make my sentences? Can students follow me easily?

- How far am I conscious of my use of language at all? When I talk, do I consciously choose words?

- What 'language register' do I need to ensure that my students share a common level of understanding?

- Are they, in any case, a homogeneous group? Do they share a common language?

- In my handout material and teaching aids, do I look at words and symbols as carefully as I should?

- Do I ensure that they are within the comprehension of the students?

- Are they clear, unambiguous, easy to follow and so on?

- Are they culturally 'neutral' or at least inoffensive? Is there covert bias such as sexism or racism?

Again, it is sensible to have a second person vet your materials for such problems, and especially the last, because they can cause strong barriers to communication and learning. Students also need to recognise what barriers of this kind they bring to interchanges with teachers and materials. Any evaluation must be a preliminary to action to make things better.

Curiosity

Many classes seem to operate like the showing of holiday slides. There is no communication, because there is little sharing. Students are excluded. They have to approach the experience alert – with their brains switched on and eager to find out. Teaching activity can switch them on or switch them off. Humans are exploratory animals; exploring is behaviour we share with the animal kingdom in general. Curiosity must be an important part of the human psyche. If the brain operates by pattern-making it must be searching to discover patterns. To make progress we must be challenged by things we find puzzling or hard, we must tackle and solve problems.

Much of inherited behaviour relates to coping with the world we live in, built-in to our brains. It is the same with all nature: how else would you explain what beavers do? What distinguishes human behaviour is the ability to distance ourselves from reality and experience, to construct concepts and to make mental models, for which we invent words. Many words explain and control our experience. If we cannot find a word for something, we are baffled, we feel at a loss.

It is this level of curiosity, this exploratory, discovering activity, that questioning relates to. We need language to deal with our discoveries. Children are full of the word '*why?*' A baby is asking a question when s/he puts a rattle in her mouth to explore hardness. As the child grows and wants to control experience, the questions s/he asks require language, words, concepts. But would a child ever develop concepts without this physical exploration?

Questions have to do with alerting the brain to a new experience that is coming and might be a challenge to present 'knowing'. The same is true of ideas and word-patterns. Knowledge, according to Jerome Bruner in *The Process of Education* (1977), is the *process* of the constant restructuring of concepts; learning and knowing may be the same thing. It is not lumps of stuff to transmit somehow from here to there. Nor can I hammer knowledge into my students' brains: they must be made ready to absorb it, process it, restructure it, in order to deal with what is new. Information can only become personal knowledge when it is processed in some way. Consider the cartoon on page 70.

The radio must be switched on, as it were. Nor is it a small transistor radio designed only to receive messages. It is a two-way radio that responds and seeks further clarification of the news. It is useful to imagine antennae on the heads of your students: which direction are the antennae pointing? Without preparation the brain cannot deal with new information. It will ignore it, just as it ignores most of the sensory data around us most of the time. We just do not notice it. We perceive consciously only things we alert our brain to; the rest passes unnoticed and apparently unrecorded. That we have in fact recorded it can be shown by hypnosis, but concept formation does depend on conscious alerting.

What do you remember of the last 24 hours? Why those things and not all the rest?

Hence the importance of questions. Rote-learning, although powerful, actually has no effect on how people think. The learning has not become part of their own structure of concepts, the way words work for them. They have no ownership, it belongs to someone else.

Levels of questions

We can alert the brain to explore present experience or revisit past experience. Questions work at various levels:

- Level 1: Direct experience – focusing on what is happening now.
- Level 2: Describing experience, to ourselves and to others; this is a second level of abstraction.
- Level 3: Comparing and interpreting experiences (a third level of abstraction) – this involves mental models/patterns; we restructure our conceptual understanding when patterns do not match.
- Level 4: Thinking creatively, generalising, transferring learning to new contexts, using it to solve problems.

Much brain activity is to do with processing information. We may use questioning to make the brain receptive so as to take the information we want it to have and to provide us with perceptions of the world, to create mental models. We do this all the time, learning is unstoppable, or we would never be able to deal with our world competently.

What does this button do on my new camera? What happens if I press this? Would that new dress, hair-style, tie suit me? We try to imagine it on us: it is our mental modelling. It is Level 1 questioning. But we can set the brain actively forming new concepts and abstractions from experience by patterning information into new insights. There is a social function of language, which allows us to share and bond. It happens when we try to tell others about this information and experience – what we now *know*. We can compare it with the new structures they have created, and which they in turn express in their words, what they *know*.

Working with other people in this way helps us to refine our ideas, create hypotheses about the world that allow us to attempt to predict what will happen or what people will do. To explain and predict is necessary in order to try to control what happens. It is how technology works – how most human and social activity works. It is also how words acquire and constantly change and refine their usages and meanings.

Programmed questioning

Many institutions have developed programmed questionnaires to enable students to explore options – to make decisions about career paths, negotiate their own learning pattern and for progress-chasing. There are thousands of examples out there. One we are all familiar with is an Inland Revenue Tax Return. Many are now accessible on websites; which assumes that the respondents do not need any interchange with another person. Usually, completion of the form in institutions is a preliminary to face-to-face interview with counselling staff. Websites offer e-mail assistance, but what happens is often a prepared general response. It is hard to get a one-to-one interaction with an adviser. The designers of the questions start with factual information, then lead a respondent towards various pathways which branch or narrow according to the answers chosen. The process is simplified in many cases by 'yes/no' choices or 'a, b, c ...' options at decision-points as in programmed learning. There is a range of options, from which there are leaps and loops to other structured questions: each path leading to more specific decisions. With a computerised program, there may be a printout summary with pointers to the outcomes of the decisions that have been made.

In regard to this kind of questioning, there has been a great deal of research into the effects of the way in which questions are framed or worded. It is not necessary for the ordinary teacher to learn this level of sophistication, however. That is for specialist counsellors, who are also trained to lead the interviewee by a series of questions. Clearly, they can also reply to open questions from the interviewee, which might be more revealing. It is hard to predict in practice what students really want to know, what is really worrying them. Questionnaires may miss the essential problems. It is almost impossible to find a questionnaire of this sort with open questions, because there are prepared answers to each question, which may be further questions. Questionnaires are meant to be a form of instruction as well as to facilitate decision-making. They might have a number of purposes, of which the most important is to help the respondent find the 'right' questions, for various reasons.

- We need to be told what the questioner wants to be told and the information we must supply.

- We often don't know what questions to ask, what the range of options is or what is possible.

- We have to explore possibilities and it is most helpful if we have a guide to show us the pathways.

- Wrong questions or the wrong kind of questions produce unhelpful answers.

- Open questions deny the possibility of structuring in advance.

- Unstructured questions lead to unstructured interviews so that advice and decisions are vague.

- The negotiator/tutor needs to address the needs of individuals, but can only do so within constraints.

What the designers cannot account for are the personal circumstances, home pressures, work pressures, the barriers to learning, the self-image and other problems of individuals. Those are what counsellors and negotiators are really exploring with students. Questionnaires can only be a starting point.

YOUR USE OF QUESTIONS

Examine carefully the way you use questions

What level in the hierarchy of questioning above do you generally expect your students to deal with? Could you help them to achieve a higher level of skill? A deeper level of understanding?

ACTIVITY 16

Are your questions generally closed or open?

At Level 1 they will be rather closed, because we are concerned with accuracy of observation. It may depend, however, on the kind of answers you will accept or are looking for. Even at this level it is perfectly possible to encourage students to explore their observations, as 'discovery learning', so long as what they observe is described properly at Level 2.

On the other hand, even problems tackled at Level 4 may be rather closed if the students are informed that there are 'right' solutions to them. Emphasis may be put on the methodology used by the students or their understanding of the nature of the problem to be solved.

Now look carefully at your use of closed and open questions

1 How do you handle class interactions using questions?

2 Have you thought carefully about what you do and why you do that?

3 When you use closed questions, what techniques do you use to ensure that all your students are alert?

4 How far would the use of open questions be effective with your students in your context?

5 What would you need to do to ensure that your students found open questions helpful rather than disruptive of what you are wanting them to learn?

| CHAPTER 22 | Barriers to communication II |

Human factors

Human factors, also called ergonomics, can be defined as 'managing work': a study of the interaction of human beings with things they use and the environments where they work. Research measures the amount of effort it costs to do something, to discover what needs to be done to make it more human and more efficient because of the way it affects the people involved. All things, whole environments intended for human use should be designed to take account of the human users.

In industrial and commercial enterprises, there have been scandalous cases of mismanagement of this interaction, leading not just to inefficiency but quite serious industrial injuries. Forty years ago in an industrial town in northern England, I taught groups of platers, apprentices employed in marine engineering concerns making enormous boilers for ships. The lads spent whole days inside the boilers using riveting guns. At college they were deaf and unable to concentrate on anything.

How often do teachers have to do battle with badly designed rooms or workshops? How many are expected to teach in environments set out and equipped on assumptions of what is to happen as teaching/learning activity which are no longer valid? How hard is it for them to get things they need, or do adequate preparation? How hard is it for the students too? How can you maintain motivation if it is just too hard? How can they be expected to be efficient if the environment works against them?

Industrialisation in all countries traps workers in desperately uncomfortable, noisy, machine-dominated, production orientated, so dehumanised and exhausting environments. Think of the early cotton-mills. Imagine what it was like to drive and stoke great steam engines on the railway, where a man had to shovel six tons of coal between Leeds and London as the engine bounced around at speed. It was and is still in many countries grossly inefficient.

Ergonomic studies have made great improvements, as the cost of the human has to be measured in with the cost of the machines and buildings. As teachers, we must try to ensure that factors under our control support what we ask the students to do rather than get in their way. Read again Chapter 11, 'The learning environment'.

Risk-taking

Studies of road accidents show that the compulsory wearing of seat-belts did not bring about dramatic reductions in deaths on the road in the UK. Why? Psychological research shows that human beings need 'arousal' to keep 'perception of risk' and 'sense of danger' in balance. Such research papers are laden with 'new speak' words: 'risk-compensation' is necessary to keep our 'arousal' at an acceptable level. What this means in practice is that straightening roads merely makes people go faster. A sense of security, or lessening of a sense of risk when people fasten their seat-belt, makes them drive faster and brake later. In Australia, a recent study found more people buying large four-wheel drive vehicles to use in the cities because they felt safer and protected. The result was a significant increase in the number of fatalities caused to other road users in accidents with such vehicles. There was a campaign to persuade people not to use them in towns.

We need to maintain a balance between our pleasure and excitement in doing something and what we perceive as the risks involved in doing it. Theme parks are full of rides which provide danger thrills under controlled conditions. We need these thrills and it is better to find them in such places than, say, in 'hot-rodding' around the streets of a town. Where there is too little excitement young men in particular will find ways, quite often antisocial ways, of getting it. But those who 'play safe' learn very little. To be alive is to be in danger of dying. All human activity, even lying in bed, involves some risk. We all need to take risks in order to learn. I wonder if children know this somehow. The development of adventure playgrounds near bomb-sites in London after WWII was a response to what children did in uncontrolled play. The designers set out to create an environment that was as adventurous, as exciting as the ruined houses, but where adults supervised and controlled the risks.

Teachers must take risks, too. It is risk-taking in every human activity that leads to progress. It is obviously risky to share decision-making with students, to experiment with unfamiliar methods of teaching/learning, to let go control in some measure over what occurs: maybe to send out a group to do a survey of traffic, to ask questions of people, to do a piece of field research, or to use resource centres, rather than to 'keep them where I can see them'. Look again at Case Study 22. Growth as a teacher must involve a willingness to experiment, a growing confidence to let go control, to involve students and so give them ownership of their learning. But it has to be controlled risk-taking. The building of adventure playgrounds was not to minimise the risks but to supervise and control them. Just sending students to a resource centre will not be successful unless there has been a consultation with the staff there, and some planning of the activities and support they will receive. Your responsibility for the safety of students is a legal requirement. If there are hazards that are avoidable, you must take action. I once banned students from using a theatre in Florida because of the many dangers I discovered there. The college was very quick to act to remedy those problems. You are a role model, students will watch what you do, so think carefully about what they see: 'do as I do'. Students must accept their responsibilities too; to do that they will need proper guidance and organisation. You have to define what they can and cannot do. It is best if that is clearly spelled out; rather than picked up, as it will be, from their experience of what they can do under your supervision. We want the right kind of risks taken to bring about the most profitable kind of arousal.

REMEMBER! … Your principal responsibility is always to ensure the health and safety of your students.

Personal space

Personal space is an invisible area surrounding someone in which there are perceived 'boundaries' for their interactions with other persons. It is defined by zones of social contact. The types of possible interaction vary with distance, which is shaped by the context and environment. A study by E.T. Hall simplified this into concentric circles. He identified four zones, which he called: intimate, personal, social and public as distances from the centre (see Figure 22.1). The behaviour of a person whose space is violated may change considerably when the 'wrong' person enters a closer zone or if 'wrong' interactions are attempted there.

Closeness increases the effect of one person on another, partly because of increased sensory stimulation when smell and sound are added to sight. The kinds of physical contact allowed between individuals varies in different cultures. For example, it seems greater among the French and Italians than the English, who like to keep others at arm's length (a distance confirmed by research). Middle-class people in England seem to be more likely to hug and kiss each other than do the working class, and women more so than men – except on the football field, perhaps.

People who work together tend to use closer social distance, while business is conducted more distantly. It probably has to do with seeing the whole person, with the enlargement and importance of the head as people approach, and with maintaining eye-contact. This distance is important also in screening out other people. Public distance is well outside the circle of social involvement, and at this distance other communication problems occur. Teaching is at a 'business' distance, but it is

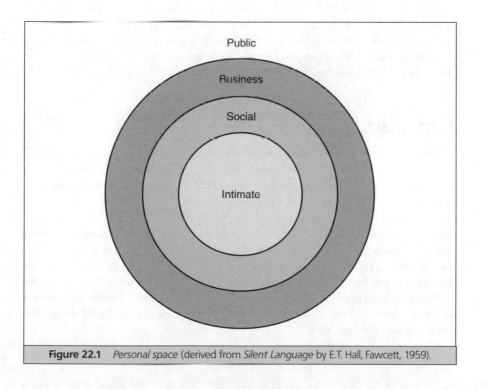

Figure 22.1 *Personal space* (derived from *Silent Language* by E.T. Hall, Fawcett, 1959).

possible to enter a student's 'social' distance for some activities, as long as it does not cause anxiety, a sense of discomfort, or even threat. It is difficult to predict individual reactions. Teachers need to be very conscious of distance-related problems.

Establishing right relationships involves identifying appropriate zones for social contacts. To be intimate in behaviour, one has to be close and both must feel comfortable there. Men and women behave differently in this zone. Invasion may seem threatening: there may be tension, discomfort or even flight. Working together in a physical way requires contact; indeed, team behaviour requires a redefining of everyone's personal space zones, perhaps creating group space instead. Drama-training uses techniques to overcome barriers felt to physical contact by getting people into a scrum, the way they are broken down in sports like rugby. In almost all normal interactions, actual physical contact must be avoided. This has become a matter of legal prohibition today.

Typical reaction to invasion of personal space is to face away, avoid eye-contact, stiffen, pull in the shoulders – leave! Defensive behaviour is typified by lack of verbal response, or by abusiveness. Hall says, '*We treat space as we do sex. It is there, but we don't talk about it.*'

Studies of crowding and empty space on trains identified a stress chemical in the urine of the passengers who had travelled in crowded carriages. Invasion of personal space creates responses that are complex, intended to distance the intruder from the victim: turning, leaning away, withdrawing into oneself, moving apart, changing seats. In crowded trains, people shrink their private space and control discomfort by staring at the floor or into space. Their body language projects 'non-relating to non-persons'.

In classrooms, workshops or wherever, you should observe the behaviour of individuals to ask yourself how each is relating to others in the class. How does each deal with distance in interactions? If you observe patterns of behaviour which are getting in the way of what you want to happen there, it is always possible to do something about it, move people perhaps. Students will move of their own volition if they feel strongly uncomfortable. Consider again Case Studies 13 and 27.

Territoriality

Concepts such as personal space and territoriality are borrowed from analyses of animal behaviour to explain how such factors may affect human performance. You will have watched a dog mark out his territory. Most male animals have some way of doing it, why not humans? But it is not just males.

Like personal space, territoriality exhibits unwritten but clear social rules of space behaviour that are learned in a culture. Infringement of the rules will cause discomfort and quite often hostility. Territoriality differs from personal space: a territory is a fixed location that does not move with the person who defines it. Boundaries are sensory, marked by stimuli such as scent for animals and visible cues such as coats and bags for humans. You will see your students, male or female, mark out personal territories this way. Why do people feel more comfortable if they always occupy the same seat and the same table?

We all know the rules that govern territory. We can distinguish that which is 'mine', such as a house or a flat which can be controlled even when 'I' am not there, from that which is for anyone like a park, and from a park bench, say, which becomes semi-private, can be claimed by someone on a temporary basis, just as someone 'claims' a seat on a train or in a restaurant or in a classroom. It is not unusual for people to become very possessive if someone 'steals their' chair. In some cultures, it can seem amazingly selfish behaviour. I have seen towels left on recliners around a pool in hotels in France from early morning to mid-afternoon when the 'owners' come to use them. Other guests will lie on the grass and not dare to remove them. The English tend to just take the towels off. Behaviour in semi-private territory is of importance to teachers. Students will reserve seats, mark ownership of a chair and boundaries with their equipment. Studies in trains found there was no verbal exchange, passengers just placed 'territory markers' like bags and coats on the adjacent seat. Students use bags or books. An invader is forced to ask for them to be removed, '*Is this seat taken?*' Removing them oneself breaks the social code, causes embarrassment, even annoyance.

Well-designed teaching spaces need to take into account not only the more obvious things (though often ignored) such as acoustics, lighting, noise levels, temperature control and ventilation, but the spaces that are occupied for particular purposes. Teaching spaces may be rendered ineffective if seating arrangements mean that students are unable to mark territories (they can't spread out), or if they feel impelled to withdraw into themselves to preserve their need for personal space. Density and crowding threaten personal space and territoriality. Having too many students in a class makes social grouping difficult.

Teachers need to control spaces that students occupy. They should try to define group territories where they want group activities to happen. Students sitting in rows merely defines teacher's space. Consider also Case Study 14 on page 91.

Gillian had set up her classroom in an open square with students on three sides, to encourage communication not only with her but with other students. Unfortunately, the students had decided to occupy the three sides as separate group territories: girls to the left, boys to the right, mature women in the centre. Gillian lost control of the interactions between herself and two-thirds of the class. She maintained eye-contact and interacted only with the mature women who sat directly in front of her. The younger students took no part in her lesson, partly as a reaction to her unconscious messages. You need to be constantly watching: what are the messages you are giving and what are your students' reactions to them? If students define group territories, you should make sure they are used to good and effective purpose. You should be party to decisions about such groupings. Consider what the students in your own class have chosen to do. In some cultures, the girls always sit together and separately from the boys. Should you insist that they mingle?

Activity has to be planned in relation to physical distance, eye-contact, territories identified for working groups with 'their' resources. Ensure that space is right for each particular learning task. Groupings may need to be restructured frequently to prevent small cliques becoming fixed. You want your class to be one community, not several with separate boundaries.

ENVIRONMENT, SPACE AND TERRITORIES

A *Make a detailed study of the environment where you teach.*

1 What factors influenced the design? What was assumed to happen as learning/teaching activity?

2 Is that appropriate to your chosen methodology?

3 Did you choose it because of the way the room was set up and equipped?

4 What would you consider to be the right conditions, taking into account all the factors involved in achieving your learning goals?

5 What action is necessary and by whom to create these conditions?

B *Look carefully at the use of space and territory in your class*

1 Do you mark out your territory? How? Some teachers have a desk with their papers in between themselves and their students, perhaps as a protection. What signals do you use?

2 How close do you get to students, or let them get to you? Where would you place the socially acceptable zones around yourself? How do you indicate those to the students? (Remember that they will take you as a role-model.)

3 How do individuals in your class define their personal space or territory? If it creates difficulties, what can you do?

4 Has the class broken up into more than one group? Do they define group territory, group space and behaviour in a way that is appropriate for what you want to see happening?

5 How can you ensure that there is positive use of space?

It is up to you, as teacher, to take control, to establish rules for group behaviour, to define territories if need be by moving people around, and to set up different groupings for varied activity. Whatever you do, try to avoid groups settling into one fixed pattern.

MANAGING GROUPS AND STUDENTS

Managing groups

Watch your class carefully as it becomes a social group, and in particular when people join the group late. What happens? Why?

1 What action should you take if they form not one cohesive group, but several cliques?

2 How will you ensure that they come together and agree purpose, goals, rules, patterns of sharing and working as a team together?

3 How will you help them to define their boundaries?

Managing your students

Consider the performance criteria below.

Performance criteria

22.1 Students establish with the teacher a supportive and positive group identity. They have agreed and shared purposes and learning goals.

22.2 Social and personal interactions are carefully observed. Groups as they form are noted, as well as the behaviour of students in the groups.

22.3 Dominance patterns, effects of personalities and personal factors are noted. So too are students' reactions to teacher language and behaviour. The teacher takes appropriate action.

22.4 Individuals and groups are managed well.

22.5 The teacher responds to feedback. Teaching method, language and behaviour are modified.

22.6 Teacher language and stimulus material are appropriate.

22.7 The teacher is sensitive to learning problems and students' difficulty in comprehending materials used to present information and instructions.

22.8 There is variety of pace, presentation, activity and skilful use of open and closed questions.

22.9 The teacher is respected by students, and has established an acceptable role relationship with them and with colleagues.

Community

Human beings are social animals. Most people prefer to work in social groups, such as a class, rather than be alone with a machine, although young people today seem to be more and more conditioned to such isolated experiences. Generally, people look for support and understanding, to share learning and other social activities. We have noted already how important it is from the growth of clubs and support groups for slimmers, cyclists, those who want to quit smoking and so on. When people are 'on-line', they are more comfortable if they feel they are communicating with someone, even if it is in a 'virtual environment'.

Communication is sharing within a community, which is a group with defined boundaries with common purposes, language and values, roles and responsibilities and common territory. Findings of studies of group behaviour apply to all communities, of which a well-integrated class is an example.

SOCIAL GROUPS

1 Think about the groups to which you belong. How are they defined and what are their boundaries, shared purposes and understanding? What did you have to learn and do to be accepted as a member?

ACTIVITY 17

2   Consider the social group that is your class. Try to clarify:

- what you consider to be the purposes that you all share
- how those purposes are to be identified and agreed to
- what the rules are that should regulate group behaviour
- what roles you expect your students to adopt
- what role(s) you see for yourself
- how you ensure that students 'join the club'
- how you should deal with outsiders coming in.

EXPLORING AS SOCIAL BEHAVIOUR

Learning is an activity on the part of learners in which formal teaching may play a minor role.

We describe a picture, or a building or a statue as communicating with us. What do we mean? Clearly, pictures just hang there. The energy for anything to happen has to come from the viewer, whatever skill the artist had. Albert Einstein invented the 'thought experiment' to try to understand behaviour of objects when approaching the speed of light. Here is a thought experiment for you to do, preferably with colleagues.

What can we learn about 'communicating in a context' from these below?

- visiting an art gallery alone
- listening to a classical music concert or a rock concert
- going to a foreign country for the first time
- becoming a member of a club
- practising with a sports team
- watching a television programme
- telling friends about a holiday, using slides or a video-recording.

The important thing is to think: what actually happens there? With colleagues you could divide into groups of three and report what you have discovered to the whole group, to see if any principles about communicating emerge that apply to all the contexts.

Joining groups

Most of this book is about communicating. After all, that is what teaching is, isn't it? But we need to be clear what we are trying to do. Many are content to understand communicating as the efficient transmission of information one-way and look to the Shannon–Weaver formulae for guidance. If we start, however, from the concept of building a community, different questions arise. We need to bear in mind the idea of groups with boundaries.

Competition between groups will define boundaries more sharply. Members of each group will invent all sorts of glue and banners to proclaim 'us' against 'them'. In extremes, it might turn into secret societies with handshakes and coded signalling, but frequently it is a matter of dress or uniform or other open signals. You will notice how quickly students conform in matters of dress – downwards it may seem if you like to see people reasonably well-dressed.

In most societies we recognise groups that adopt pseudo-military uniform with indications of rank: police service, fire service, ambulance service, nurses or security guards. Putting on a particular uniform means also adopting a behaviour pattern, even a mind-set along with it. One covert purpose is to ensure 'the whole is greater than the sum of the parts'. Groups that gel, work well together, can achieve much more than the same individuals would on their own. Where does this added value come from?

We can see analogies in the animal world. Some are mysterious. Ant-hills created by termites are remarkable structures with a complex ventilation system, including chimneys, that extract stale air by heating up and generating air currents through the tunnels. But where is the 'model in the head' that enables termites to build it? There is no possibility of the parts existing alone, how do individual termites know in their tiny blind world what each has to do to construct the whole? Communication within the hill is by chemical pheromones excreted by the Queen. Can it be within the genetic code? In human groups too there is a mystery as to how purposes and direction arise, and how they are communicated to all involved.

Joining a sports team engenders a spirit of competition. Team spirit is exhibited in dress and observation of specific codes of behaviour and often of written rules. It is derived partly from agreed purposes (goals!), partly from perceived antagonists (other teams). Team members rely on the rest to display a commitment to the team that supersedes other social commitments. The same is true of a drama group or an orchestra, even without obvious opponents. There is implicit competition: to do at least as well as others have done and to win praise for their performance. Teachers can exploit this competitive glue when setting up learning 'games' in classes, too.

Group behaviour imposes a need for individuals to discover a role in the group. This is no less true for you, as teacher, than for any other members of the class, unless you choose to remain as an 'outsider'. But to be the disruptive outsider cannot be right. To be effective, you will have to establish that you are working with the students as part of a group together, to be one of 'us'. The unhappiest experience you can have as a teacher is to find a group ganging up against you while you try to establish common ground. You may help to create that distance by your actions, unconsciously signalling lack of sympathy with them. Of course, this does not mean that you have to join in outside class activities, drink in the pub with them, although going with an adult group to some outside activity always helps. Think rather of how welcome you are within their 'social' boundaries. Nevertheless, they must not lose respect for you as the teacher.

REMEMBER! … Your first job as the teacher is to establish the class as a group with agreed goals, roles, rules of behaving and personal responsibilities.

If you think of an evening class as a club, complicated things may be going on. Rules govern all the operations of the club. What are they for? How are they arrived at?

Anyone joining has to learn and observe them, to adopt the code of behaviour of members; and has to take the trouble to see what it means. People who have dealt with adult groups know that breaking into established groups is not at all easy, as strangers may disrupt the group in unpredictable ways. It is easier if the rules are stated explicitly, but the important ones are usually exhibited only in the behaviour of the club members: what is acceptable and what is not. Peer-group pressure and a desire to become, or remain, one of the group ensure that members learn rules quickly. New members arrive feeling 'foreign', but wanting to be accepted as one of 'us'. They look constantly for clues as to how to behave and are extremely sensitive to modelling and feedback: they will conform in dress and language use, even if it feels odd or wrong. They will absorb club values and ways of thinking too.

Sharing

Sharing is the most important element of communication. Searching, wanting to share and to belong is another. Being part of a group, or a valued and effective member of a team, working with others to achieve a goal, is all part of being human, our sense of community. Shared danger creates the greatest bonding, as is evident in wars – the greater the danger, the greater the bond. Communities are strongest in defence against perceived enemies, as all politicians know, who exploit all kinds of threats, real or exaggerated, to gather support for their cause. You can watch it nightly on TV news broadcasts.

Being an outsider is painful. Being isolated by a language barrier or cultural difference is highly disturbing, particularly if it involves loss of self-respect because you can no longer do things yourself, such as use a telephone or order a meal or go shopping alone. It can happen when joining new groups or classes as well as travelling abroad. We have noted how bad it feels to be suddenly illiterate when you can't read in a foreign script.

In many aspects of communication, the energy has to come principally from the 'receiver', wanting to know, wanting to share. We are more acutely aware of this in activities we do alone than in those we do with others. In looking at pictures or walking through a city, we respond in individual ways to stimuli. We may quickly get bored or may experience a high level of excitement, depending on our receptivity. In other situations, even where we are totally passive, when listening to a concert in a concert hall, or watching a play, or an opera maybe, or a play in a theatre we are infected by the shared emotional responses of the audience; and this affects the performers enormously, too. In rock concerts shared responses are dominant, taking over individual behaviour as part of a crowd.

Television has become the major source of entertainment worldwide and has had a profound, mainly destructive, effect on traditional cultures. It tends to be a private experience, except sharing the excitement of a crowd watching a football match perhaps. We share the TV experience, not just with those who make the programme but with all the many people we know are sharing it with us. It is obvious that television has become the most powerful educational tool, far more effective than the majority of college courses, because we learn more readily if our attention is strongly focused, and we are not putting up barriers to the learning: if we do not know that we are learning, just 'having fun'.

From observing behaviour we can understand a great deal about how people learn and what is needed to stimulate them to learn. It comes back again and again to watching what people do, and for a teacher what students do in his/her class. How can we ensure that learning is fun? How can we make our students so enthusiastic about their experiences in learning that they want more and more and are distressed when it is over? Have you ever heard of students crying because their class was finished?

In the present climate for educational institutions in the UK, so much seems to be driven by fear, not by the excitement of learning. If assessment is seen as about someone else's needs and not about the process of learning for each individual, it can turn into a threat. How can teachers make it a stimulus to greater commitment to the learning?

Suggested reading

Berne, E. *Games People Play: Psychology of Human Relationships*, Grove Press (New York), 1964; Penguin (Harmondsworth), 1970.

Chapman, A.H. *Put Offs and Come Ons*, Putnam Berkley (New York), 1968.

Coombes, B. *Successful Teaching*, Heinemann, 1999 (simplified advice).

Cottrell, S. *Skills for Success*, Palgrave, 2003.

Gardner, P. *Teaching and Learning in Multicultural Classrooms*, David Fulton, 2001.

Gardner, P. *Strategies and Resources for Teaching and Learning*, David Fulton, 2002.

Gelb, M. *Present Yourself*, Guild Publishing (London), 1988.

Harkin, J., Turner J. and Dawn, T. *Teaching Young Adults*, Routledge–Farmer, 2001.

Hills, P. *Teaching and Learning as a Communication Process*, Croom Helm (London), 1979.

Hollander, E.P. *Leadership Dynamics*, The Free Press (New York), 1978.

Jacques, D. *Learning in Groups*, Kogan Page (London), 2nd edn, 1991.

Joseph, R. *Stress-free Teaching*, Kogan Page, 2000.

Mason, R. *Using Communication Media in Open and Flexible Learning*, Kogan Page, 1994.

McCarthy, P. and Hatcher, C. *Presentation Skills*, Sage Publications, 2002.

Nash, R. *Classrooms Observed*, Routledge & Kegan Paul (London), 1972.

Peng, T.H. *Fun With Chinese Characters*, Straits Times Collection, Federal Publications (Singapore), 1980.

Rackham, N., Honey, P. and Colbert, M.J. *Developing Interactive Skills*, Wellens Publishing (Northampton), 1971.

Sotto, E. *When Teaching Becomes Learning: A Theory and Practice of Teaching*, Continuum International, 2001.

| CHAPTER 23 | Assessment and testing |

USING ASSESSMENT

Design assessment tools and procedures and use them effectively within a teaching programme. The assessment procedures should integrate clearly with the learning process. In order to match the intended learning outcomes, what is assessed must be what students set out to learn. They should be valid and reliable measures of change and achievement. They should be of a kind which are 'do-able' and which candidates have the required insights and skills to produce as evidence of their learning.

The methods should be varied as necessary

(a) to provide feedback to achieve short-term and long-term learning goals

(b) to test and validate achievement of stated criteria

(c) to match examining board assessment criteria and procedures for certification where necessary

(d) to provide, identify and categorise evidence for this achievement

(e) to help all students to achieve their learning goals.

Performance criteria

23.1 A variety of methods of assessment is planned and used appropriate to the intended learning outcomes.

23.2 Chosen methods are used skilfully and effectively.

23.3 There is clear and sufficient evidence provided by work that students do and by the assessment tools.

23.4 This evidence is used to support statements about achievement of learning goals for individuals.

23.5 Assessment is used for feedback to individuals to inform decisions about learning and adapting the learning programme.

23.6 There is sensitivity to the problems of individual students and they receive appropriate support.

23.7 Evaluation of both the scheme of assessment and individual tests and tasks is carried out.

Introduction

In Part 1, you were introduced to basic principles and practice in feedback and assessment within the learning process. You are now going to take those ideas further. Assessment is an important part of the teaching/learning process, one taken more seriously by learners and teachers than almost anything else. The government monitors standards in certification of achievement of school-children and adults and regularly intervenes in the way they are assessed. It devises and publishes policies and sets up bodies to regulate certification according to current concepts of learning and achievement; and these change over time.

Examining boards have been restructured in the last 20 years. Government-backed bodies were set up to develop a national system of assessment for vocational qualifications based on demonstrating 'competence'. Part of the rationale for developing NVQs was to reduce an array of qualifications from a host of awarding bodies. It was difficult to see how the various qualifications related to each other, in which people with 'equivalent' qualification might perform very differently in practice. There was the need for equivalence in qualifications not just in the UK but across the European Union. If you need to know how the National Vocational Qualifications (NVQs), Scottish Vocational Qualifications (SVQs), General National Vocational Qualifications (GNVQs) work in practice, find a colleague to show you. You will be introduced to some of the theory in this chapter.

First, however, you are going to look at assessment in general, picking up on the ideas explored in Part 1 of the book. First find the questions. Below is a list intended to indicate the range of possible questions that this chapter addresses.

Assessment as learning

Every activity in teaching is about learning; assessment is no exception. There are many questions to think about before designing an assessment scheme; they are again: *who, what, why, how* and *where.*

REMEMBER! … Thinking it through, proper preparation pays off.

- What is it for? Who is it for? What are you hoping to learn? What are they hoping to learn?
- What do they: the students, employers, examining bodies or whoever want to find out? What do you want to find out? Why do they and you want to know? What will they do with the information? What will you do with it?
- Is it a means of selection? part of an accreditation scheme? or a personal profile?
- Is it intended: to help to define a career path? to enable students to make choices? to assist in guidance? to accredit learning towards certification? to justify an award/certification? to verify competence?
- When will you assess? How often will you assess? What effect will assessing, especially testing, have on the learning process?
- Is the assessment *formative* or *summative* or both? Is it part of coursework as *continuous assessment or a final exam?*

- What evidence will be produced to justify the judgements made about achievements? How will you determine the quality of that evidence?

- Is the assessment *before* placement on a learning programme? Is it to find out what an individual knows and can do at the beginning of a course? or *part of* a course process?

- What part does assessment at this point play in this process? Where is it going? Is it intended to feed back into the learning? Is it to be used to award a grade?

- Is this a *final* assessment? Is it internally set and devised? Is it externally set as a test/exam?

- If externally set and marked, do you/the learners have to surmise the contents of the test/exam: what is to be tested? questions? the standard expected?

- Are you preparing 'a mock' as a preparation for an external assessment? How will you know what kind of test to make? What level to set the test and to mark it?

- What is the assessment about? knowledge? understanding? insight? cognitive skills? practical skills? specific abilities? learning behaviour? attitudinal change? problem-solving skills?

- What level of learning, performance/certification is assessment to verify: beginner? intermediate? advanced? How is the level perceived? How is it standardised? How is it certificated?

- What is a hierarchy of learning and assessment? How do these assessments, these students, fit into the hierarchy? How is 'level' identified? Is it formally as, for example, NQF Level 4/HE Level 1?

- What criteria are used to judge the quality of the evidence in relation to achievement at this level? How will you know when a group or individual is ready to tackle this level of assessment?

- How will you ensure that it is fair? unbiased, not skewed? fair to all? comprehensive? How will you ensure that it is *valid* (it assesses what it is supposed to assess and not something else) and *reliable* (will all those who need the information be able to rely on the results and the evidence for making decisions)?

- Is the achievement *criterion referenced, normative, self-referenced*? Does it identify competence? potential for further study? training? employment? responsibility? promotion? certification?

- Is it once for all? or integral to a learning process? Is it to be repeated to improve performance?

- How do the students perceive the assessment: as a signpost? a gate? a barrier? a coconut in a shy? a hurdle to jump? a river to cross? a chance to shine? a display of skills and knowledge? a challenge? a boost to self-confidence? a terrifying ordeal? exciting? fun? boring? repetitive? a waste of time?

- What form will it take? on paper? oral/aural? practical activity? an assignment/task? multiple-choice test? short answer test? essay? project? case study? video-recording with commentary? computer-generated presentation?, etc. There are as many options as there are learning strategies.

- Is this the most efficient, economical, effective way of assessing what you/they want to find out?

- How will you validate the assessment if it is (a) subjective, as in, say, judgement of 'competency' or in marking essays? or (b) objective, as in correct/incorrect responses in an objective test?

- Where will you conduct the assessment? Under what conditions? Under what constraints? Over what time-scale? Is it intended to simulate a real situation? Is it intended to be a formal occasion?

Appraisal and evaluation

The questions are comprehensive and legion; they need to be asked *in all the stages of the assessment process*: i.e. before you devise assessments, when they have been devised, after students take them. This is a process of appraisal and evaluation.

In appraisal *before* we do anything, we have to ask the kind of questions above. To design assessments to do the job we want to do, we have to know first what that job is. Particularly we must decide what we are about before we set off. It is no good getting half-way and finding that we are on the wrong train, or that we are building our house on quicksands, or where it is exposed to a likelihood of flooding or forest fire. We have to anticipate difficulties, constraints, outcomes.

In evaluation *afterwards*, when we have observed what occurred. Did it do what it was intended to do and was it effective for its purpose? Could we have done a better job? Did we arrive where we wanted to go? Could we have got there by a simpler, less complicated route? Could we/they have enjoyed the journey more? Could we have built a better, more solid, more live-in-able house? If we did it again, would we do that way? What have we learned from what occurred? After all, the main purpose of doing an evaluation is as part of the next appraisal: what do we need to do *now*?

Assessment is to provide an informative profile of learning or achievement with good evidence, on the basis of which reliable decisions can be made. Numerical/letter grades alone do not provide useful information for evaluation or appraisal. Confusion arises if we are not clear about the uses of words. Too often, self-assessment, self-appraisal and self-evaluation are used interchangeably. It should be clear that they are different parts of the process. We start with appraisal – but appraisal again and again throughout the process – each stage or element must be evaluated and the next stage appraised. But we need the evidence. Assessment procedures are tools for obtaining information with which to do these things.

The teacher's main job is to make him/herself redundant, not needed. We are about fostering independence, not teacher-dependence. The strategies for teaching, learning, assessing that enable a learner to take responsibility for his/her own learning, assessing learning, making strategic decisions, are preferable to those where all the decision-making, appraisal, evaluation, assessment, remain the prerogative of the teacher or examiner or institution; where learners are informed of their results and their needs are identified for them; where others make strategic decisions about learning, careers or whatever else. Individualised learning means that total responsibility for all decisions lies with that individual.

Standardised achievement testing (SATs) that school-children have to take every two years or so in the USA, Australia and the UK, is to facilitate control over schools by governments. SATs are overtly testing schools not children: schools, not children are identified as 'failing' if too many children fail to perform well in tests of literacy and numeracy in particular; the intention is to ensure that schools do put sufficient effort into making sure that children pass those tests. This is a blunt instrument, of course. The causes of underachievement in any area are likely to be complex.

In the UK, where there is a plethora of externally set and marked examinations in addition to SATs, the more publicised examination results are also used to rate schools on a scale which assumes a level playing field when everyone knows that some schools are knee-deep in mud or are fighting a force 8 gale. The use of results to make judgements in terms of 'accountability' has also moved the goal-posts for teachers and institutions in FE and HE.

Evaluating

The Open University has published many models of evaluation. The range is wide: from comparing starting conditions with outcomes to see what has changed (and ignoring everything in between – the process) to 'goal-free' evaluation which tends to look at the process and what happens (and ignoring intentions and goals).

It helps to see the activity properly linked to the appraisal. If we know where we are going and how we intend to get there, we can match our expectations against what actually happened. We can then learn how to do it better next time. We also learn what we have achieved and what is still to do. First, we must be sure of the facts, be able to demonstrate to someone else the evidence. But evidence is not only about things we can measure. The most important changes in learning are not easy to measure.

REMEMBER! … State the facts with the evidence so that the emphasis is on the nature of the evidence.

To ignore goals and intentions is to pretend that the activity is purposeless. The matching of one to the other is of importance in terms of motivation and satisfaction. But we cannot ignore the process because how we learn is also how we improve learning.

When evaluation happens matters. If we are too close to something, we cannot see it except with peripheral vision. Or we distort or we see bits and not the whole. We need distance – and that is the same as time. But we must evaluate what has happened in order to know what to do next – before we set off again.

What is assessment?

Assessment is the devising and use of tools to find out the nature and quality of the learning. In most cases it provides the most important evidence of learning. Learning is change in many things; we can assess *change* and *achievement* which usually involves some kind of *measurement*. Feedback is meant to accelerate progress towards achieving goals in skills and knowledge, together with behavioural and attitudinal changes. And to identify goals that still have to be addressed and achieved, so that learners and teachers can decide what to do *now*, what still has to be learned, and what still has to change. The process of assessment is part of the learning process: to formulate models in the head of good practice in learning. It is also about learning how to achieve good grades in assessment, and some teaching programmes concentrate fully on the latter.

There is an assumption that assessment and testing are synonymous, where tests or exams are seen as measurements of achievement. It may be a matter of the way we perceive what we are about. I can assess whether a person can bake a cake by evaluating a product. I may examine it and compare it with a 'model' it should approximate to, I may cut it, taste it, even eat it. Clearly, the more often a student bakes a cake, the more competent s/he is likely to become, as long as s/he receives the right kind of helpful feedback. S/he has to learn to do it right. Now, is baking the cake a test? Here, the task is the way to achieve competency and a way to demonstrate that learning. From the point of view of an assessor it is a means of testing learning. There may be identified 'competences' to be demonstrated in the performance of the baker, as well as qualities of the cake; procedures which are transferable to 'competency' in any practical sphere. In other cases, testing is a procedure which is separate from the learning process. It is possible to set up baking a cake as 'a test' where there are identified constraints of time and procedures. But it should still be feeding back into that learning process if it is to have other than grading value.

There are a very large number of testing procedures. You can only learn them by doing them and doing them right. When you assess, you measure achievement against standards previously laid down either by an external examining body or as internal criteria as devised in this book. You will be expected to compare what this learner knows and can do with what a learner should know and be able to do at a given level and in the kind of assessment you are using, against 'models' as stated standards written and published, or as 'norms'. In many programmes, this will be a test of some kind. Many aspects of learning do not lend themselves to tests of the formal kind, but they have to be observed and judged.

Criterion-referenced assessment

You measure achievement against a standard, a set of criteria that represent *mastery* or *competence* at a determined level. Criteria at more advanced levels include those at lower levels in a hierarchy. National Vocational Qualifications use this approach. In NVQ, a learner must meet *all the criteria* to qualify for a pass; a pass is 100% of possible achievement. Nor can a learner progress to a more advanced level without demonstrating, or being accredited with, the full range of competences at the standard of the lower level. For students who fail to complete all the competency programme of an NVQ, there is no mechanism for accrediting achievement of the parts that are completed; as is possible in an American system of 'credits'. What then?

Norm-referenced assessment

A learner's achievement is measured by testing against the standard normally achieved by a candidate at that level in that kind of test. The standards, or 'norms', are arrived at by *piloting* tests on very large numbers of people, called '*standardising the test*'. In this kind of test, examiners can set the pass mark at different levels; 40% is common; it could be as high as 80%. The learners' achievement is graded by deciding bands of scores: as pass, credit, distinction. For example, numerical grades may be 85% = distinction, 70% = credit; or use of letters A to G. Large-scale national examinations like GCE A Levels use letters. In this case 'pass' equals 'good enough', acceptable, rather than mastery or competence; a candidate is not expected to demonstrate achievement of the whole learning package defined by the contents of a syllabus.

Unlike criterion referenced assessment, which provides a profile of what a person has achieved in all the areas assessed, norm referenced testing does not necessarily show strengths and weaknesses in a learner's achievement. Of course, some examiners do like to make very 'fine' distinctions in the absence of numbers: I have seen B+?+. There is no avoiding subjective judgements.

In America, each instructor grades student achievement on their courses without reference to any others, since there is no mechanism for standardising the *grade models* of individual instructors. It is common practice in an American college for instructors with a reputation as an easy grader to have huge classes and those who insist on a high standard to have small classes. In the UK, internal and external verification of *grade models* is vigorously pursued.

Criterion-referenced programmes rely on subjective judgements of levels of skill that are to be demonstrated in performance, as in the baking of a cake. As Madame said to me in Villefranche when I asked for the recipe for a dish of garlic mushrooms, '*Monsieur, it is not what, it is who.*'

Grade models are shaped by experience of similar tasks or activities in the past. If I want to write a 'good' essay, I must have a model of what a good essay is. As with baking a cake, it is part of the learning process for a teacher to provide sufficient practice in the writing of essays for students to acquire the right *grade model* for themselves. The same is true of grades for assessing teaching.

The DfES publication, *An Agenda for Reform of the Initial Teacher Education System for the Learning and Skills Sector* has on page 22, '*Comparison of teaching practice assessments*':

> A college has developed its standardisation of teaching practice assessments in order to give it a level of attention comparable with that of the moderation of written assignments. On a programme with over 100 part-time trainees, two tutors/mentors jointly carry out about 10% of the 6 teaching practice assignments of trainees. Each independently completes the assessment of a teaching practice session delivered by a trainee and variations in judgements are discussed as part of the college's normal moderation procedures.

Clearly, in order to do this the tutors must be looking for the same things and using the same criteria. The purpose of the exercise is to ensure fairness and consistency in making judgements.

Self-referenced assessment

The learner's performance is compared with performance in previous tests, activity or tasks s/he undertook of the same kind and at a given level. Feedback in the learning process is self-referenced assessment. Students need to map and monitor their own learning, as you are doing in the Reflective Diary you are keeping. Without such a map, you can hardly tell where you are on your journey. This form of assessment is most appropriate for measuring attitudinal change, e.g. confidence or responsibility. It is used where external assessment of any kind has little place, as for learners with learning difficulties and disabilities who may only be able to achieve a small amount of progress at a time, or in leisure classes, or in personal attainment programmes such as slimming.

The purposes of assessment

Your reasons for assessing will determine the kind of approach you adopt. Within a learning process the principal purpose is to provide evidence for feedback to learner and teacher – and/or progressive accreditation for overall achievement. Assessment provides information and demonstrable evidence for the judgements that are made. Information about learners' achievements is important to people such as employers or admissions tutors for further courses, who want unambiguous information they can rely on. Employers and advisers need to know how capable the applicant or worker is and his/her potential for taking responsible positions or for further study and development. Naturally, they are also very concerned to know the personal attributes of candidates.

Your role in tests

You may be involved in operating tests which have been devised by others or in creating your own. Most tests used in further and adult education are externally devised and marked (GCE A Levels, for example). Your role may be to prepare your students for tests by carrying out *mock assessments*. In these the students practise on questions which you have devised to be as similar as possible to the ones you expect them to encounter, and which you mark at what you consider to be the same level. You need to know how you will identify the questions and the standard, how you will verify that. One way commonly used is to study past papers and the reports of examiners, which are intended to be helpful feedback to teachers and schools. You must in all cases study published *criteria for grading*.

If you are working on an NVQ programme, all the criteria and other assessment requirements will be laid down for you by the awarding body. Your role will be to check your interpretation of the criteria with your team (or with your '*internal verifier*' if you do not have a team); to prepare your candidates for assessment; to observe their performance, question them, scrutinise written material if any, or items they may have produced; then make your judgement and give the learners feedback.

The role of the internal verifier in NVQ is important to ensure that judgements made by one teacher do not deviate from those made by other teachers in the same or other institutions. All other certification by Awarding Bodies in general will involve internal and external verification of *grading models* used within institutions where the grades are internally awarded. Clearly, the more precise the statements made of performance, the more 'objective' they are. In the past, 'behavioural object-ives' were set down in '*be able to ...*' lists that were often remarkable for their preci-sion as to '*what, how, under what conditions, to what standard*' and so on. But such a procedure was in danger of becoming tedious and tightly controlling the process of learning. Competence is not identified in such detail. You may assist in devising

GNVQ assignments with a team according to national criteria laid down by an Awarding Body. You may be given sample assignments as models; there will be guidelines to grading achievement available, so that you can judge how to grade the work. GNVQ assessments are checked by an internal verifier and periodically by external verifiers, whose role is to ensure that there is a consistency in standards of grading between institutions. In this regard, the evidence is all important. The use of new technology makes the production of evidence much easier, as discussed later. You may, however, be able to design your own tests and assessment activities for your own students, which you mark and on which you give them feedback.

At whatever level you are working, you will need to follow certain principles if you are to be able to conduct assessment in a professional manner.

Subjective/objective

Some things are relatively easy to measure and record as a score; accuracy in recalling information or simple skills or solving puzzles where right answers are not in dispute. The more unambiguous learned behaviour is, *objective in the sense of being independent of personal judgement by anyone*, the easier it is to measure against criteria. The reverse is also true. Accuracy of recall is more easily tested than imagination and creativity, responses to which are by their nature subjective and hard to identify by agreed criteria. That does not mean we should not attempt to agree criteria for them.

Already, sophisticated measuring devices are available to measure more tenuous things: levels of introversion/extroversion, anxiety states, aptitudes. If something is observable, it should in theory be measurable against 'norms'. Orthodoxy assumes that attitudes and values, though clearly exhibited in behaviour, are not measurable: i.e. you can test *can do*, but not easily measure *will do* or *will do always* or *will do intelligently*. We need to think carefully about that.

Is it *sufficient* in testing competence to *assume* underpinning knowledge? Behaviourists used to state that if someone does it, you do not have to insist s/he knows why: for they had *conditioned* the learner to behave that way. Equally, can we assume that if a student demonstrates a competence or a range of competences that we can safely ignore attitudes: commitment, confidence, motivation, or important personality characteristics, or the ability to work in a team? It is normal now to test the underpinning knowledge, the '*why*', the '*why not*', the '*so what*' to ensure intelligent application of competences. This is not the same as requiring demonstration of decision-making and thinking or insight into principles. Many people can use an applications software program or drive a car very well with no understanding of the principles involved. But real behavioural change requires insight. The deeper one goes from ability to do something in observing behaviour the more subjective the judgements become, so they tend to be ignored in criteria for assessment. It is relatively straightforward to measure cognitive and behavioural change. But if accident statistics remain at a constant level when all sorts of preventative safety measures are introduced, such as compulsory wearing of seat-belts front and rear in a car, widening roads, a higher police presence and cameras, steep fines, it may be because we are changing our perception of danger. There is compensating behaviour, we need arousal and risk-taking, excitement, challenge, fun, fulfilment – like children in adventure playgrounds. Bad news with operators of lethal machines like cars, though.

Aiming for good-quality evidence of learning

Assessment should be at all points in the learning process: to decide before, during, and after, what is needed if you are to meet the needs of individuals. It is very helpful to know where individuals will be starting if you are to monitor their change or progress. The whole process should be designed to help to find out about a learner's capabilities. What learners do in tests or tasks, whether practical, written or spoken activity, is evidence of learning. Properly constructed tests give a great deal of information. They indicate what a student still needs to learn and master. But learning tasks also test capability. It is equally true of writing an essay, solving a crossword puzzle, or crossing Antarctica alone on foot. The evidence needs to meet certain criteria if it is to show a learner's achievements reliably, that is, without distortion. Some of the criteria are that evidence must be

- current – a picture of his/her capability now, not something s/he did some years ago
- authentic – the learner's own work
- sufficient – there should be enough of it of the right kind and at the right standard.

Currency is common sense if we think how rapidly skills in most fields change, most notably in any area where developments in technology have an impact. *Authenticity* is hard to judge in a distance-learning programme or any programme where there is a requirement for coursework that contributes significantly to the grading of achievement. The reason institutions require candidates to sit examinations periodically is to check for inconsistencies between their results on such tests and their coursework for Units or overall. *Sufficiency* is a matter of personal judgement; more does not mean better. *Quality* is of greater importance than *quantity*, so is underpinning knowledge and insight in skilled performance. You have to judge whether you have sufficient evidence of the right kind and at the right level, which is why it is so important to have a policy agreed by internal and external verification.

Validity and reliability

Are the tests you are using valid and are they reliable? These are the two fundamental criteria by which to judge evidence. Look back at Part 1 where these ideas were introduced (pages 111ff) A test is valid if it does the job it is supposed to do – it tests the targeted knowledge and skills and not something else. Does it do so at the identified level? Does it discriminate between those who understand and those who don't?

You need to be clear what it is you want back from the test before setting or constructing the questions. Drawing up model answers for a written test is quite a good guide, and *validating*, that is, discussing the questions with colleagues to see how they interpret them. If possible, pilot the test: try it out on a group of learners to see if you get back the kind and range of responses you expected. Check that successful or correct responses are indeed based on knowledge and understanding, not just the ability to speak and write fluently. The ability to write an essay shows that a candidate can write an essay, but that may not be what you want to know. Often, the opposite occurs, where a candidate has the necessary knowledge and understanding but lacks the linguistic skills to express it adequately. The test is reliable if it produces results that other people can rely on. It would produce a similar spread of results if it were given to a similar group of students. You can continue to use it with confidence.

Objective tests

The most reliable tests are those whose questions have only one right answer. In a multiple-choice in a simple form, a candidate chooses one answer from a choice of four possibilities. The three wrong answers, the '*distractors*', are designed to be as plausible as possible, so that it takes real knowledge and discrimination to pick out the correct option. It is not uncommon for such tests to become multiple-guess, a lottery, however. Much of the difficulty may lie not so much with the recall that is being tested as with the linguistic level assumed in the wording, or other extrinsic factors such as cultural assumptions or experience; so there is a need to check such barriers to interpretation. Is the language used in the test at the right level for those taking the test? Are there invalid cultural assumptions and implications?

Multiple-choice tests are more effective in testing *recall* than the *application* of knowledge to an 'open' context. One answer must be correct, which implies that the context must be 'closed'. It takes ingenuity to design a test to apply the knowledge to an unfamiliar context without making the distractors obviously wrong. For testing this kind of application, *short answer tests* or '*yes/no*', '*true/false*' *tests* structured to test levels of understanding are often better. In multiple-choice, every question should be answerable correctly without knowledge required to answer any other question; it doesn't matter if a candidate gets all the others wrong. Every question must be at the same level of difficulty. All objective tests used by examining bodies undergo rigorous validation to eliminate those distractors that are not definitely wrong, by piloting all test questions and statistically processing the results: if any distractor is selected by too high a proportion of candidates, it is too 'possibly right'. Such tests almost inevitably become easier. Objective tests of this kind can be marked by computer, which cuts out any risk of subjective judgement by the assessor, while short answer tests require an examiner.

Using a range of tests, reliability may be increased if internal tests (set and marked internally) are combined with tests set and marked externally as with GNVQs. Can a single test be made sufficient? If it is testing recall, is there a wide enough range in questions to 'cover', or to properly sample the knowledge required? You will probably need a very thorough test or series of tests to feel you have sufficient information to determine the learner's achievements. A single demonstration of practical competence is unlikely to be enough, for example. Your judgement will be more reliable if you have sampled a learner's skills and knowledge using several different kinds of test, as written assignments, oral assessment and a practical performance test.

Essay questions are less reliable, because they can also be much more 'open'. To be fair, the criteria for marking them should be known to the candidates. If a majority of marks is for accuracy of recall, the essay is easier for the examiner to mark (it is 'closed') than if more marks are given for application of knowledge to an 'open' context. The greater the range of possible interpretations or levels of response, the more carefully criteria for acceptable answers has to be specified in relation to grading at the different levels. Awarding Bodies organise checking systems: examiners standardise the marking of sample questions to avoid any significant divergence in judgement. Nevertheless, such a system cannot be made error-free.

The criteria used to be carefully guarded and known only to the examiners. The government in the UK insisted that examining boards publish detailed criteria for all examinations to be fair to candidates, with the inevitable result that teachers teach to the criteria and candidates now achieve higher grades than those of comparable ability did previously. The response by government and in the media has been to complain that standards have been lowered.

If a learner is a student on a course, you will be able to assess progress and offer feedback on a *continuous assessment* schedule and at the end provide evidence of *current capabilities*. However, some candidates for an award may judge that they already have knowledge and skill to enable them to proceed directly to assessment and have no need to undertake a course of study first (as some people do with the driving test). The test will then either show that they were right in their judgement, i.e. competent, or show up areas of work for further practice, after which they must be tested again. A case such as learning to drive shows how many patterns of interaction between teacher, learner and examiner are possible. It is this flexibility the institutions are asked to match.

APL (Accreditation of Prior Learning)

Usually, you will be testing students in the present. If you are involved in APL as well as their level of experience and expertise, you need to check that the applicant's knowledge and skills are current and up to date. Where a candidate for an award is asking for competence based on previous learning and experience to be judged in an APL system, it is essential to be sure that the claimed knowledge and level of skill is *current*, whatever previous experience s/he may claim to have.

It is probably most obvious in relation to vocational qualifications where the commercial or industrial context may have changed radically in as little as two or three years. This is why the role of advisers to APL candidates is crucial; they can help applicants to review their learning in relation to the criteria for assessment, so that they have a clear picture of what is required before they opt for assessment.

The authenticity of a student's work is carefully monitored on a continually assessed course, and there are elaborate safeguards built in to public examinations to prevent cheating. However, you need to check carefully on the ownership of material presented for APL. Practical performance tests or oral tests can usefully be combined with written submissions to check authenticity.

Being fair

The criteria for good-quality evidence described above all contribute to a system that aims to be fair to all candidates. Tests which have high validity and reliability are based on relevant material at the right level and are sufficiently rigorous in gathering suitable and sufficient proof – so that candidates cannot succeed by coincidence or luck. A great deal of work has been done by individual teachers and examining bodies to eliminate bias in test questions, just as they have established test procedures to give everyone the same chances to succeed. It involves looking very carefully at the way questions are phrased so that there are no ambiguities which could mislead candidates. You must also validate questions for anything a candidate may find offensive in terms of gender or racial bias in particular.

You need to be sure that questions you devise do not rely on understanding a cultural context, or access to an experience which some candidates might not have, e.g. going to the opera or using ultra-modern equipment. We have seen in some earlier Case Studies how difficult it is to ensure that students are not disadvantaged by lack of experience or cultural bias. In the USA, intelligence tests used with children were the same across the States, until it became clear that those in the South were disadvantaged because of assumptions about their experience, for example of open fires for heating. With the movement of personnel by international organisations such as the United Nations and the immigration of large numbers of people from very different climates, multicultural classes are often the norm. If a child is asked how many seasons there are in a year, the 'correct' answer may well be two: wet and dry. An Australian woman complained that it was intolerable in Melbourne when the north wind blew, it was so hot!

What are you going to assess?

You need to think about what exactly it is that you want to assess – what *knowledge*? which *skills*? which *attitudes*? You cannot make decisions about the kinds of tests, or the kinds of tasks to devise, until you have decided their purpose and what they are about. Once you have a clear idea of what you are aiming to achieve and the areas of capability which you want to pinpoint in assessment, you may find it more straightforward to choose or devise an appropriate set of tests or tasks.

REMEMBER! … Students are entitled to expect to be assessed on what they have been taught or led to believe will be in the assessment schedule, not something else.

On a course of training in the workplace, basically you test mastery of the objectives or outcomes in the subject/skill area which have formed the basis of the teaching. One of the advantages of NVQs is that the whole area to be tested is set out for the candidate from the start. In public examinations, although the syllabus has been outlined, questions can sample a candidate's understanding of any part of it. Some candidates may be lucky in the exam in getting questions on topics they have prepared or where they are particularly proficient, others may work enormously hard and maybe no questions are asked on topics they have studied. So, a huge effort goes into question-spotting to beat the examiner. The teacher needs to be canny in choosing a syllabus which has a narrow focus, not one which roams far and wide, especially in subjects like History. It is not unusual, however, for examiners to want to win in this game, and to occasionally 'bowl a googly', to everyone's annoyance.

If you are designing your own questions, remember that you should have the same pattern of emphasis in the test you had in your teaching. If you stressed one area as particularly important, this should be reflected in the test. This is a concept called *weighting* discussed later.

When are you going to assess?

Formative assessment

The primary function of assessment is to tell the learners how well they are performing, how they have done so far and what they still need to learn. It is an essential part of the learning process. None of us can learn without feedback. Students come to formal learning partly to receive this feedback and so come closer to achieving their goals. This is as true of those who attend leisure classes as of those who embark on national qualifications.

This process of receiving formative feedback is very valuable to the learner and calls for considerable skill in the teacher. It also helps the teacher, in that it shows up areas of strength and weakness in the teaching in time for corrective action. If all the students do poorly in one area while achieving reasonably well in other areas – as, for example, if you use tests which usually show a spread of marks, but in one area all perform poorly – it is reasonable to assume that the fault lies with some aspect of the teaching, or the learning programme or the assessment procedure, not with the students.

Continuous assessment

Accumulated grades for completed tasks or tests during a course may be the principal evidence for accreditation, as in Coursework for GCSE and GCE A level or competency programmes.

Summative assessment

Assessment at the end of a period of learning, such as a course, may have a variety of intentions. There is an unfortunate tendency to use achievement at one particular time and in one set of circumstances to remain an indicator of ability and 'value' (or lack of it) for years to come in education and employment. The reason for abandoning the 11+ exam 40 years ago was that it channelled individuals into one or another category – and into different kinds of schooling – far too early in life. When an individual is labelled, examining may be seen as a barrier rather than as an aid to learning.

'One-off exams' are notoriously unreliable in the case of individuals, even when they produce reliable results on average. Many people do uncharacteristically badly or well in tests conducted on a single occasion; some perform badly in any kind of exam because of emotional barriers. Students and teachers may come to see external exams as a lottery. It is the rationale for continuous assessment, or a number of assessments over a period of time of which the scores are added, or a combination of scores on continuous assessment with a final summative test. GCSE examinations have this format, and some GCE A levels.

These results are used to allow or prevent a student's entry into other spheres of activity or to more advanced courses. In SATs, and many other externally set and marked tests, it is the overt purpose to control what happens in the teaching. Since exam results become of such importance to a person's life chances, to the jobs of teachers, even to the survival of an institution, one effect of once for all testing is that teachers teach to the exam, and this skews the learning programme.

Assessment and grading are not synonymous. Final grades may be replaced by a sophisticated profile of overall achievement. The purpose of grades is usually to compare achievement of one with another in a group of learners, one group with other groups or a whole national cohort. It is intended to predict how an individual will go on to perform at a higher level of study or in employment, but it is obvious that a profile is a better instrument for this purpose. A report of the grades a student has achieved and in what range in GCSE and/or GCE A level is regarded by employers and institutions as a profile.

Where are you going to assess?

There are obvious disadvantages to the candidate for assessment if a formal test is set up in a place, an environment, that is unsuitable for what is to be tested. Practical tests, in testing competency for NVQ, say, can only be undertaken in workshops, swimming pools, kitchens or wherever the technical proficiency can be demonstrated. But they are unlikely to be suitable places for written tests, or even oral/aural tests. You cannot test competence in using a software program without a computer; or ride a horse without a horse. If you are teaching a course on an employer's premises, do you test learners there? or in a neutral context? Some tests require projection facilities: if the room is to be darkened, what safeguards are there?

Fairness implies fair to all; some candidates should not have advantages over the rest, nor be disadvantaged. It is as much a matter of assessors ensuring fairness by control of the conditions as in preventing candidates from skewing results by wiles and cheating. People are good at devising ways of beating any system; teachers have to become equally canny in spotting what they are doing. Some examining takes place very formally in rooms set out to prevent cheating and with monitoring by a number of 'proctors' together.

As with environments for learning you need to be aware of the effects of environment when assessing learning; the same considerations apply but there are more rigorous constraints. You want to ensure that candidates do justice to themselves, and that the testing is fair to all. You will also need to decide what they can use during a test/exam. Can they bring dictionaries or lecture notes, calculators or textbooks? Must they provide their own materials, e.g. for cookery? Must they wear appropriate clothing and safety equipment? Must they provide a supply of pens? In most examinations there are also strict rules related to entry and exit, where to sit, behaviour … If you are new to the procedures, make sure you know them well beforehand. It cannot be experiential trial and error learning.

Assessing cognitive skills

'Cognitive skills' means those (for example, memory/recall, applying knowledge, problem-solving) required in the process of learning. Cognitive skills are important also in acquiring understanding, demonstrating knowledge and in social interactions. They include linguistic and symbol-using skills: recognising patterns, using symbolic presentations and language, spoken and written. They also include visual modelling and using abstractions such as numbers. The range of cognitive skills is the same as that of human achievement. A brief survey of the assessment of cognitive learning cannot offer more than a glimpse through the curtain of this complexity.

You will need to decide what to include and what to leave out (if there is a choice), where to put the emphasis and what level of cognitive processing you wish to target. Selecting the level of questions or tasks and phrasing them correctly to imply this level is a challenging task, although it is equally difficult to identify levels of achievement when marking tests and assignments. It will be made easier if criteria are carefully structured and defined and if the nature of the evidence is agreed by all.

Objective tests may seem to be a simple recall exercise, but generally what is needed is to test principles behind the facts, e.g. recalling mathematical formulae before going on to use them to solve problems. You are more likely to be interested in getting students to demonstrate their understanding beyond simple recall, to manipulate formulae, perhaps, or to explain the significance of certain facts and principles, selecting some to support, others to destroy an argument; and describing relationships between them. You want your students to explore the '*why?*', the '*why not?*' and the '*so what?*'. Objective tests cannot reasonably be expected to do that. You want students to use knowledge to show understanding in new applications usually in an 'open' context, that depend on their grasp of principles they have learned.

These three levels, recall, understanding and applying, make up at least 50% of testing in college and adult centre courses. Read again Levels of Questions on pages 247–250. The hierarchy of Testing is clearly related to the hierarchy of Questions.

You may wish candidates to demonstrate insight or problem-solving skills, which depend on capabilities other than those targeted in your teaching. It requires intelligent thinking-it-through as well as application of principles. Older students are more likely to have relevant experience to relate to a context in which a problem is perceived. With appropriate students, you could look for analysis and synthesis in a context, to pick out important factors and how they interact; for instance, factors that contribute to an economic recession. You could ask them to synthesise existing factors into a solution; as an example, to propose ways in which juvenile crime might be reduced in urban areas or a failing business returned to profit. At a higher level, you could ask them to evaluate a situation, weigh up its strengths and weaknesses, to recommend ways forward; or to carry out a feasibility study, say, on setting up an irrigation system in a desert area, or introducing road safety awareness to junior school curricula.

The higher the level of questioning, the higher the level of cognitive skills the learner must demonstrate, but it is best to build up skills over a series of tasks designed to facilitate use of the skills within the hierarchy.

In a *case study*, you will see that to deal with it successfully students have to

- recall the facts
- understand their significance
- apply them to a problem situation
- analyse the causes of the problem
- propose various solutions
- weigh up the feasibility of their proposals
- argue the case for one of them.

Each of the later cognitive skills has within it all the earlier ones. It is what makes the case study such an effective assessment instrument. The higher the level of questioning and of cognitive skills, the harder it is to define criteria for assessing them. After all, it is not the solutions students may come up with so much as *how* they generate the ideas and process them that are of importance. It is made more complex if the problem is set as a group task. In mathematics at GCE A level, more marks are awarded for method and working through than for a 'correct' solution. In Art as well as in Maths, students are required to show their 'working': how they arrived at their result. A girl I knew once was a brilliant mathematician, but she failed to gain admission to an Oxford University college, let alone the scholarship she deserved, because she just 'knew the answer' to a mathematical problem but she could not explain how she knew it.

The key point is that you need to choose assessment tools at the right level(s) for the course and award concerned. If the levels are too low or too high your test will lack validity and may well be unfair to the candidates, especially if this test is at a higher level than they have been led to expect. It is equally important that you identify clearly for yourself and for them the criteria for success. A tool of assessment that might be effective under certain constraints will be a disaster if introduced at the wrong stage, in for example an assignment-based continuously assessed programme.

CASE STUDY 32

A group of students on an Access to Social Science course were faced with the following as their first assignment; they were mainly mature students who were returning to learning after a career and study break, several without formal qualifications. You might consider what level of linguistic achievement is needed simply to understand the assignment.

Investigate the recent changes in employment law as promulgated by the European Parliament. Prepare a short paper which covers the implications for employers and employees and estimate the likely consequences for small employers in the UK. You will have 10 minutes to present your key ideas to the rest of your group and to answer questions on them.

Discussion

1 What assumptions did the teacher make about these students?
2 What are the assumed learning goals of this course? How would anyone know them?
3 Did the teacher attempt to discover where the students were starting from? the base-line?
4 Did the teacher see the task as a learning exercise or a testing exercise? or both?
5 How many distinct tasks are contained in this one assignment?
6 What skills and knowledge would these students need in order to understand what they had to do?
7 What skills and knowledge would these students need in order to do any or all of these tasks?
8 What would be the criteria for success in completing any or all of these tasks?
9 How would the students know these criteria? How would the teacher know them?

Comment

Clearly, this is far from effective as a tool either for learning or for assessment. It reads more like a statement of what the teacher might be intending as a lecture series. The sheer complexity of it as a task is intimidating. Assumptions are made about the students, their knowledge or experience, their level of cognitive skills and linguistic ability, their experience of conducting research; and all are way off beam. It is not even clear that they could hope to deal with such complexity at the end of the course.

Where possible tasks chosen should suit the learning group. The above is an assignment which, in the right context, could be a source of interest and learning. But what is it testing? At the outset it begs all sorts of questions about familiarity with library and/or resource accession systems, academic papers, techniques of oral presentation; then it demands a challenging 'public' performance before the group has had time to establish any sense of belonging or rapport. Clearly, students would need preparation in much more than the subject matter before it would be fair to test them in this way. At the very least they would need an induction to study skills and opportunity to practise techniques of information retrieval, plus pair work in the group and individual tasks to build up their confidence.

You might like to consider whether this test would have met criteria for validity or reliability which you looked at earlier. The main key to validity is the learning goals. For this test to be valid the learning goals for the programme would have had to include these areas among others:

- knowledge of how to retrieve information/data from paper and electronic storage systems
- knowledge of employment practices and their legal base, both in the UK and in Europe
- cognitive skills: (a) to apply knowledge in the analysis and evaluation of specific cases; (b) to précis knowledge for report purposes; (c) to plan a presentation to a target audience; (d) to take into account language register and time constraints
- interpersonal skills: to communicate orally with a group in a formal setting to make a formal presentation to a class.

If the teacher had set out to help students to do such things, developing cognitive and interpersonal skills like these, it would be fair to assess them. The test would be relevant to the objectives, set at the right level, would discriminate those who had knowledge and skills from those who did not. The test would be invalid if the cognitive skills and interpersonal skills were not in the learning goals of the course in the first place. In any case, it would make no sense before they had had the chance to practise and to learn them.

Would the test be reliable? Would it yield the same results if it were used with a similar group of students on another occasion? Could you trust the results? The test would be reliable, provided a set of assessment criteria had been worked out for it which matched the objectives. These would have to be unambiguous so that all assessors interpreted them in the same way, and each assessor kept 'strictly' to the criteria when marking the test. Only the factual basis might lend itself to unequivocal criteria.

You might consider whether as an 'activity' designed to promote learning this approach has an appropriate place in your learning programme; at what point could students undertake it? If you try to identify carefully the criteria for success in presenting such an analytical assignment, you will begin to understand the complexity of in-course assessment in a field such as this.

Progression and new technology

The reorganisation of FE/HE with the blurring of boundaries has led to confusion over levels in courses and certification. Unfortunately, it is difficult to define criteria to specify Levels within Levels, unless a course is identified as Units at the same Level, which may be to deny the possibility of progression as levels of maturity in understanding, skills or performance. There is, therefore, a dilemma for designing courses. Stages may be replaced by Units presented purely in terms of content rather than related to a learning process. (See the Appendix.)

It is clear that in no higher level course are students graded in the foundation years at the level to be expected in subsequent years. The difficulty may be addressed by criteria in terms of the maturity of approach, and thinking, as in GCE A Level Maths and Art above, rather than as achievement. Performance in teaching is expected to show greater skill and insight with time and experience, but maturity in the approach, in thinking through, may be at a high level of behaviour which can be observed at the outset. After all, it is how someone sets about the job that matters.

There is, however, a tendency to demand demonstration of linguistic skills and other cognitive skills which are not dissimilar from the case study above. Many assignments take a written form which may be looking for skills the candidates have not yet acquired. This problem can be overcome by the level of flexibility allowed in the nature of the evidence which is considered acceptable.

There seems to be no reason why a teaching session in a hairdressing salon, say, should not be video-taped and presented with a voice-over by the teacher to explain why s/he did what s/he did, what happened, what s/he observed in the group and/or individual behaviour, what action s/he took. It will be a valuable tool for evaluation as well as valid evidence of performance. It can be more easily related to performance criteria than, say, writing a report about the lesson, and it can be shared with a mentor or tutor to compare perceptions. It is 'praxis evidence' as a permanent record. Teachers in skills areas such as these are frequently not confident of their level of linguistic skill to cope well with any writing, let alone assignments for grading purposes.

There is a reluctance to use new technology in designing assessment tools, despite the relative cheapness and miniaturisation of such things as video-recorders, voice-recorders, hand-held computers. Software that enables users to speak into the computer and have their words converted to text on the screen should overcome some of the difficulties those with poorly developed writing skills experience. It is possible to record experiences as they occur, to note observations as text or voice, to record and edit any number of things that happen with a voice-recorder, of which data is fed into a text-processor in a computer via USB cable. The advent of computing was heralded as foreshadowing the paperless office. Almost all examining, recording, evidence is still paper-based. It is hard to know why.

DfES, *An Agenda for Reform of the Initial Teacher Education System for the Learning and Skills Sector*, discussed in the Appendix, gives examples of *good practice*. *Moderation by video*, page 22, states:

> A consortium of colleges in the south of England has evolved a way of addressing the issue of standardising their assessment of teaching practice. All those involved in the summative assessment of teaching practice meet to review video clips of actual teaching sessions. They independently assess the teaching and learning sessions and complete relevant documentation. This allows comparison of judgements to occur and grade boundaries to be confirmed or amended. These sessions also identify any requirement for further training of assessors across the partnership to ensure consistency of assessments.

The sensible way to deal with such information is to treat it as a case study: i.e. to find questions to elicit what can be learned from it. *Video-clips* are selected and edited versions of something. How are they edited? What criteria are used for deciding what to include? What does the camera 'look at'? Are the 'teachers' invited to comment by voice-over on what occurs in the classes? Have they received feedback using the same video-clips? How does summative assessment relate to formative feedback? And so on …

Developments in distance learning using video and computer links are accelerating. It is only a matter of time before they become standard. TV correspondents send video-link live reports by facing a camera via the Internet and satellites, so that we can all be 'present' at events anywhere in the world. In Australia, a person hundreds of kilometres away in the outback can have trumpet lessons face to face with a teacher in Adelaide by video-link and receive instant feedback from a top professional.

Clearly, uses of new technology will revolutionise all teaching/learning/assessing, including what is acceptable as evidence, how it is presented, how skills are demonstrated. What you can do in learning to play a trumpet you can do with anything. Since the mid-90s, teachers in Japan have been 'teaching' 10,000 students at one time by satellite link to classrooms nation-wide. Obviously, 1:1 tutorial using a satellite is very much more expensive, but between the extremes everything is possible.

Assessing motor skills

The same general points about level apply in judging performance in motor skills; you will be looking for levels of accuracy, coordination, speed and economy and technical proficiency; in some cases, however, imagination and style are what really count. You can add to the level of demand of a task by combining skills, changing a context or increasing the pace of performance. You have to validate tasks you set to ensure that they are appropriate for the level of candidate and award concerned. Are they at foundation level, or intermediate, or advanced?

You will find validating tasks easier if you compare your perceptions with those of colleagues. I suggested earlier you might validate tasks by doing them yourself; and that this will help to identify the criteria by which to judge performance and achievement. Remember to check that the tasks reveal sufficient of the candidates' skills for you to make a valid judgement of their capabilities. Motor skills, even more than cognitive skills, are more dependent on native talent than on teaching. No amount of teaching of its own will make a footballer a Manchester United star or an opera singer a prima donna.

Motor skills are the means to an end, not an end in themselves. This complicates the criteria. If we are assessing a step in ballet, for example, it is almost impossible to isolate it from the context in which it is performed. The same is true of driving a car, a swing in golf or turning metal on a lathe. Obviously again, the higher the level of skill the more subjective the judgements are likely to be, so that it is essential to share your criteria with others, with a mentor or an internal verifier or whoever. The judgements are bound to depend on the level of skill, experience and insight of the assessor.

Assessing attitudes

It is inappropriate to set levels for attitudes, but it is possible to describe the behaviours you want to see demonstrated. You may have to add a time dimension: the candidate must demonstrate attitudinal change over a period of time and apply it on all occasions, i.e. habitually. The lathe operator must *habitually* use the safety guard, the chiropodist must *habitually* treat the whole person. What then is the evidence to be? You may also need *proof* from more than one witness or assessor, by comparing your perceptions and interpretations with those of others. This is likely to be fairer to the candidate because judgement of attitudes is much more subjective than judgement of skills. And what a person does in an employment situation may not reflect what has been required at college. Attitudes are not always transferred from one situation to another.

When assessing attitudes you will either be working to a given set of criteria, or you will have devised your own. Naturally, you will have explained these to the learners so that they know what is expected of them. When we say that someone exhibits a particular attitude, we are usually referring to lots of small pieces of behaviour which add up to the approach required. It is these which you need to list so that you can check that they are really demonstrated, and that you are not being misled by a general impression or bias based on other factors. Here is an example from customer care for a leisure centre, set out as performance criteria. The receptionist:

- is punctual on arrival for her duties
- is correctly dressed
- has a good standard of personal hygiene
- gives priority of attention to the customer over routine duties, e.g. answering the phone
- looks alert and interested (sitting and standing)
- greets the customers with a smile
- gives the customers full attention while dealing with them

- listens carefully to any requests
- gives full explanations to queries
- makes generally friendly but not personal comments if appropriate
- acknowledges the end of the encounter; e.g. with thanks.

If you still find the idea of a checklist difficult, try compiling a list describing appropriate teacher behaviour towards students in class.

Compiling tests

You are now armed with much of the information you need to put tests together, if this is your role. You know the syllabus and its objectives, the level of the award, areas of knowledge, skill and attitude you want to assess. You know the characteristics which your tests must meet to produce good-quality evidence. You may or may not know the actual students who will sit the tests, but you do know what they have been expected to learn, the learning goals.

You can now decide how you will assess them: what kind of assessment instruments you will use as tests. This book is full of examples of inventive assessment as well as teaching/learning in all the discussions and case studies. The way a student learns is an appropriate way of testing learning. It is right to sample motor skills, for example, by practical tests, while oral questioning is one way of complementing judgements of technical proficiency by assessing underpinning knowledge.

In this case, you may find it helpful to think of tests in four groups:

- things you ask candidates to do
- things you ask candidates to write
- things you ask candidates to say or explain
- things you ask candidates to provide as other evidence.

These groups are not necessarily separate; you will be increasing the validity and reliability of your tests if you combine them. You might want candidates for a catering award to cook vegetables in several different ways; you might ask them questions about the processes they have used, you might ask them to write about the nutritional value of the food, you might ask them to present the cooked vegetables in a particular form. Together they give you a reliable body of evidence of their skills and understanding, which each alone cannot provide.

But you can choose from a wide range. If you wish to test recall or application of knowledge or cognitive skills, you might choose to use an objective test; they are often, but need not be, multi-choice tests. You can test aural skills in a language by using a cloze test where a candidate must enter correctly from dictation gaps in a printed document. Short answer tests allow of a level of inventive response to test understanding as well as recall. Many tests are of the true/false form, a binary test more adaptable to testing application of principles. A student listens to a dramatised conversation in a targeted foreign language, say, and then has to answer true/false questions about what was said. At a higher level, questions may probe implied meaning, implication, attitudes or a candidate's thinking in predicting what happened then.

So-called intelligence tests may require a candidate to spot the differences in two pictures, or to memorise in a specified time a list of objects, or what is occurring in a picture, say, of a robbery: what was the burglar wearing, who was standing in front of him …? or to match shapes, or to rotate shapes in the head to identify which of a number of examples is correct. The number of such tests is legion and many books are available to provide examples. We have noted above the possible danger of cultural bias in such tests. Pictures can contain things which are much more familiar to some than to others. Tests often make assumptions of what the child/adult brings to the test from his/her own life-experience. Would you do well in a test which assumed you knew from experience about life in an African village or attendance at a Shinto shrine in Japan? What if the picture was of an object you had never seen before in your life?

Written assignments and essays, performance tasks, interpretation in music and drama, case studies, media presentations, all can be designed for learning and assessing at many different levels, or even the same task repeated over and again as you will have discovered by what is involved in the tasks in this book related to developing good practice. When you look back through your Reflective Diary you will discover how your thinking, your behaviour and your attitudes have changed. You are implicitly learning how to appraise, assess and evaluate your learning.

Suited to its purpose

Whenever you choose or devise a test, you need to be sure it is appropriate for its purpose. You do not use a written test to assess someone's competence in life-saving, for instance, although it is not inappropriate to ask him/her to write a report on what happened and why decisions were made after the event. As suggested above, it might be more effective to have the candidate make a commentary on a video-recording of what happened. Merely being able to do something, even if you do it with considerable technical proficiency, does not imply that you can do it intelligently, whatever it is. If you want to test competence in motor skills, you do need a practical performance test. You might couple this with an oral test to ensure that candidates knew why they were carrying out those actions in certain ways – or what to avoid doing: they understood the consequences of their actions. For example, if you only wanted to know if the candidate was familiar with the names and uses of certain drugs, if there are no shades of meaning or interpretation, you could use a multi-choice objective test. If you wanted the candidate to demonstrate analytical skills, producing a reasoned argument setting out advantages/disadvantages of using a process, say the use of a new drug regime in an intensive care unit, there are a number of appropriate ways to do it; a structured short-answer test may be the right format, or better an essay.

You must make sure that the chosen test is appropriate for the kind and the level of abilities which you want to assess. This is part of your check on the validity of the test. For example, a technically brilliant performance in playing the piano may not be good musically in terms of phrasing, interpretation, decisions about speed and dynamics. Examiners in music are asked to grade performances; to do so, they have *grade models* to define levels as Grade 1–8, usually in the technical difficulty of the pieces. Within these grades, they give numerical scores against a range of criteria to determine pass, credit and distinction, but mainly in interpretation and understanding of the period and style of the music, and musicality in the performance. The grading relies heavily on the experience of the examiners in the judgements they make. There are other tests besides playing prepared pieces, including aural tests. It would not be inappropriate to ask the candidate to write the decisions that led to the interpretation of the piece s/he played, but it is never required. Essays may be used to test other learning, such as the history of music. Some examiners will discuss pieces with candidates, however.

Clearly to be completely fair, a recording, preferably by video, would be helpful, at least for feedback, to replay elements, single phrases maybe, to discuss with the student, to provide criteria and to make judgements based on criteria; this is what happens in 'a master class'. Top professionals are asked to judge at music festivals when their 'grading' comments are tested against other people's perceptions, especially those of the teachers. One famous singer told of awarding a prize to a girl who performed a piano piece beautifully, but she did so with lots of body movement. Another girl's teacher afterwards told him that in future *she would teach her pupils to wiggle their bottoms when playing!*.

Checklist of characteristics of an effective test

To see if you have chosen the right kind of test for your purposes you could subject it to the sort of checklist which follows.

- It is valid, it tests what it set out to test and not something else.
- It is reliable, it will provide the same range of scores, say, whenever used and whoever marks it.
- It discriminates between those who know the (correct or appropriate) answers and those who don't.
- It is relevant to the learning goals.
- It is not biased against any candidate by reason of language, background or culture.
- It is at the right level of difficulty for the candidates and the award (if there is one).
- It is interesting in itself and will promote learning.
- It is clearly expressed in appropriate language at the right level for the candidates.
- Its instructions (rubric) are clear and straightforward.
- It covers a reasonable amount of skills and knowledge to ensure sufficiency.
- It is not likely to take too long to administer or to mark.

The best way to find out if you have made the right choice of test is to *pilot* it on a group of people and analyse the results. If you can't do this, meet with a colleague to go over your test questions and procedures rigorously, looking for potential hazards, cultural bias, misunderstandings, ambiguities and so on.

Frequency of testing

You need to decide how often you will use tests with your students, to make sure the testing process does not dominate the learning process. You can use tests effectively as progress markers, to give students feedback on their strengths and weaknesses in a way which remotivates them and prepares them for later summative assessment. Be careful of overloading the learning time with tests which check on but do not enhance the learning, or which seem to be an end in themselves.

You will need to draw up a scheme of assessment if you are working with a group of learners over a period of time. Remember that you need to leave time to teach the material, to give students practice in the thinking or skill acquisition required, to prepare them properly for the testing, carry out the assessment, mark the tests and then give the students feedback. Feedback weeks after the test is of little use in accelerating learning. I need to know if I am holding a tennis racquet correctly now, not next week. I need to know what was wrong with my first essay before I can begin to know how to write a better one.

If you are operating a scheme of continuous assessment, you will have to do all this formally and compile the appropriate records. You can afford to be more flexible if you are using this kind of test framework to prepare students for an external examination, but none of the stages above should be skimped.

Getting the balance between learning and testing right takes thought and practice; and if the assessment tasks will promote higher order skills and imaginative thinking, this is a clear advantage.

Making judgements and recording test results (marking)

The secret of making judgements on work submitted for assessment, whether that work is practical or written or in some other form, is to have a very clear picture of what you want to see as evidence of understanding and competence. Where it is to be an agreed list of criteria this must be written down, not left to your memory.

When you design the assessment and draw up the assessment checklist you should allocate marks to each group of criteria, unless this is already done for you. These marks represent the value which you are giving to aspects of the performance from a total number available. At its simplest, you might have 10 marks available and 10 key points which you value equally, so that each point gets 1 mark. You may decide that all 10 marks must be gained to achieve a pass, or you may decide that 4 out of 10 is acceptable. If you express this as a percentage, 40% is your pass mark. If you want to identify grades with marks, you can decide that 5–7 inclusive represents a credit grade; i.e. 50–70%, and that 8–10 inclusive equates to a distinction; i.e. 80–100%. It is your marking scheme. In the example above, all the points counted equally. This is a very simple scheme; you can make it progressively more complex. You can give more *weight* to some points than to others. You could make some points half a mark and others 2 marks to achieve this. You could say that a pass is only achieved if certain points are achieved as part of the necessary 40%, rather than any 4. In a written paper, it may mean that certain questions are compulsory while others are optional. But you need to be sure that whatever you decide matches the emphases that were placed on topics or skills when they were taught or outlined in the scheme documents. This rubric must also inform the candidates of your weighting in the questions.

It is also vital to record your decisions correctly; assessment information is among the most sensitive information you will be dealing with. It should be passed on only to those with a proper right to know about it. One of these people if you are working on an NVQ or GNVQ, will be the internal verifier for your team, whose function is partly quality control: to check that what was supposed to happen did happen. Did you follow all the procedures correctly? Were all the candidates treated fairly? S/he does this by sampling your assessments, accompanying you while you assess a practical performance, and looking at the way you handled submitted work. This process is designed to ensure that all candidates get a fair deal and that the level of the award is maintained. External verifiers who work directly for the Awarding Body check their work in turn.

Weighting

You can *weight* the marks so that you acknowledge the greater importance of higher levels of skill than lower levels. For instance, it is obvious that students need knowledge of facts and/or formulae before they go on to use them in argument or calculation. If the point of the assessment is to test application of the facts and formulae rather than their recall, you need to give more marks for the more difficult operation. You can make this distinction within one test question or in a whole test. Certain maths tests commonly give 20% of the marks for recalling formulae but 80% for using the formulae to solve problems.

Let's take the question '*Show how the effects of global warming might influence agricultural practices differently in different parts of Europe in the next 30 years*'. Here, the student could obtain 20% of the marks for knowing about current agricultural practices in relation to geographical area, 20% of the marks for knowing what the effects of global warming are, but 60% of the marks for a discussion of changes implied by global warming in a sufficient number of geographical areas to show an understanding of the principles involved.

Dealing with failure

Tests are inevitably linked with the fear of failure. The consequences of failure as a motivator, as a threat, generally has negative effects. It is always better to be positive with students, to boost their confidence and motivate them to do better by praise and emphasis on what they *can* do. Since one of your roles is to prepare students for assessment, this should include being as positive as possible about what happens if they do not do as well as expected. It is a positive process in NVQ, where the candidate is first of all advised to delay assessment till s/he feels that s/he is competent, reducing the likelihood of failure (it can also save everyone's time). If an individual does not meet all the criteria, s/he is given feedback about areas of weakness but also of strength, and a new action plan is drawn up for a date by which s/he can prepare so as to retake the test.

Within your teaching you should manage testing processes so that they are routes to learning and not events to fear. You can be very influential in setting the appropriate tone, and in demonstrating its reality through constructive feedback to individuals after in-class tests. You can help them to feel that if they fail a national examination, there are always further opportunities, failure at this time or on this occasion does not mean that *they are a failure*.

If you act as personal tutor to a group of students, you may be able to give positive guidance during the run-up to examination periods.

Your scheme of assessment

You have looked at approaches to assessment, its organisation, and what you need to consider for a single test. Now analyse what you want out of an overall scheme of assessment; i.e. one which spans a period of time and includes several types of test. Here are the kind of questions to ask; they are a summary of the material in this chapter.

Will my scheme of assessment:

- use only valid and reliable tests?
- cover all or a sufficient sample of the knowledge, skills and attitudes which I need to assess?
- match the learning goals and outcomes of the course?
- suit the characteristics of the group as learners?
- be at a level of linguistic and cognitive skills appropriate to the students?
- provide sufficient evidence overall of the candidates' capabilities?
- fit into the pattern of learning and not skew or unbalance it?
- communicate requirements clearly?
- give candidates interesting things to do?
- have fair deadlines, reasonably spaced out?
- use straightforward, open and clear administrative procedures?

Suggested reading

Boud, D. *Enhancing Learning Through Self Assessment*, Kogan Page (London), 1995.

Boud, D., Keogh, R. and Walker, D. *Reflection, Turning Experience into Learning*, Kogan Page (London), 1985.

Castling, A. *Competence-based Teaching and Training*, Macmillan (London), 1996.

Cocker, D. *Successful Exam Technique*, Northcote House, 1987.

Ebel, R.L. *Essentials of Educational Measurement*, Prentice-Hall (New Jersey), 1972.

Hoffman, B. *The Tyranny of Testing*, Crowell-Collier Press (New York), 1962.

Hudson, B. (ed.) *Assessment Techniques*, Methuen (London), 1973.

Jessup, G. *Outcomes: NVQs and the Emerging Model of Education and Training*, The Falmer Press (London), 1991.

Redman, P. *Good Essay Writing*, Sage Publications, 2001.

Rowntree, D. *Assessing Students: How Shall we Know Them?* Harper & Row (London), 1977; Kogan Page (London), 2nd edn, 1987.

Satterly, D. *Assessment in Schools*, Blackwell (Oxford), 1981.

Willmott, A.S. and Fowles, D.E. *The Objective Interpretation of Test Performance*, NFER Publishing (Windsor), 1974.

You are now aware of the basic requirements for assessing, but it is an area which can be taken much further. The following books (available from City & Guilds, Sales Department, 1 Giltspur Street, London EC1A 9DD) will be helpful:

Assessment Handbooks (priced):
Setting Multiple-choice Tests (compiled and edited by Norman Gealy).
Coursework Assessment
Setting and Moderating Constructed-Answer Question Papers (by Chahid Fourali).
Profiling Systems Assessment
Assessing NVQs

Glossary of Terms – used in standards development, curriculum design, assessment and accreditation (by Chahid Fourali).

Introduction: discoveries in psychology

When I complained to my Head of Division in a Florida college that the sheer size and volume of the Humanities 2 syllabus made it unteachable, he replied, '*It's only a survey, Dave*'. I think he meant it amounted to a 'naming of parts'. They were to be 'covered' briefly, so as to ensure that the students had heard about them. What for? I wondered. Why learn these things unless they are to be significant to you in some way?

What I hope to show in this part of the book is that psychological discovery as applied to learning and teaching is exciting and fascinating. It is not 'out there somewhere', but fundamentally important to what teachers do. Even if I had the space of a large book, indeed many books, devoted exclusively to it, I could not cover it. I can only provide a glimpse through chinks in the curtains at some major theories of learning. It is my hope you will want to read more, and use what you find out to try to understand what is happening for your students.

A great deal of what happens, even in good teaching, is intuitive. Teachers learn by trial and error and role-modelling, sometimes by *diktat*. They do not always know why something works, but are glad that it does. They are just too busy to be curious, and do not have the time to stand back and think or to read the educational literature. Nor, in any case, will the reading have value unless they think about it in relation to what they decide to do with their students in their context. This book started the other way about: to try to develop good practice in real teaching before exploring theories in any depth or to test theories against practice. The test of a theory is whether it works: does it predict usefully what will happen *here* under certain conditions? It is not enough that it should offer an explanation of what *might* be going on. There could be many other explanations that are equally valid. The history of education is littered with failed theories, even those that were the result of years and years of research.

The model of teaching/learning set out in Parts 1 and 2 is not invention arising simply from my own experience. There is well-documented research in psychology and practical teaching. I have also worked closely with many teachers of adults in many contexts, and I have benefited from their knowledge and experience. It is usual in academic texts to direct the reader through use of footnotes and references to sources for statements and assertions made. I have resisted doing that, as I do not find such texts helpful. I have added some suggestions for reading intended as a guide, but not as a comprehensive list.

The literature on learning and teaching is vast. I have tried below to direct your attention to those beliefs and thinkers I believe have had an important influence on what has happened: to try to show the sources of the ideas and practice exhibited in the model which informs the book. Moreover, academic books usually present a dispassionate and non-advocative description of learning theorists. This survey is intended to go beyond that: there is a thread of argument. Selection and distortion are inevitable. I urge you, where you can, to read original texts for comparison.

CHAPTER 24

Behaviourism

In the 1900s, psychology was dominated by the School of Behaviourism, under the leadership of John B. Watson. They were inspired by brilliant results in animal psychology achieved by Morgan and Thorndike. Human beings, Watson declared, should be studied like any other animals. Behaviour, human behaviour, should be observed like the phenomena in all other natural sciences. No Behaviourist, Watson declared, has *observed* anything that can be called consciousness, sensation, perception, imagery or will. All such terms are unusable in descriptions of human activity, because they cannot be observed or demonstrated objectively. This assertion was held to be true and self-evident. Experiments were to be confined to *objective observations* of the results of *stimulus and response*.

Decision-making was effectively ignored, as was 'thinking it through'. These are mentalistic terms, which a few examiners still think you cannot test and therefore, for the sake of objectivity, must ignore. For the same reasons, 'goal-seeking', 'the will' and other attitudinal terms cannot be part of the examination/criterion-referencing system, although they were to be accepted by some Behaviourists, such as Tolman, as important. Why such puritanism, particularly since they seem to exclude intelligence in the behaviour we are trying to assess (and improve?)?

Mental 'representation' or 'conjectural modelling' of the world is an idea the early twentieth-century psychologists tried to eliminate in the effort to give their discipline the appearance of an objective science. '*Any reference to consciousness was carefully excluded for fear it would introduce the scientifically unmanageable idea of a causal principle that was not immediately accessible to public observation*' (quoted by George Miller in *States of Mind: Conversations with Psychological Investigators*).

The conditioned reflex

Behaviourists developed a programme of research based on the assumption that behaviour of all kinds could be explained in terms of the measurable stimuli impinging on the sense organs and the nerves which controlled the muscles. The *stimulus–response bonds* most often quoted are reflexes such as the knee-jerk, and the reaction of the iris of the eye to light. There is a stimulus, light, and an immediate unlearned response of the iris muscles. The important thing is that it does not have to be learned. It is obvious that most behaviour in all plants and animals essential for dealing with the world is of this kind. A baby is born with peristalsis in its digestive tract. Without conscious control, it pumps blood around its body and constantly produces the thousands of proteins necessary to its functioning as an organism. What then is learning? What is it necessary to learn? How is it learned?

How does it become embedded so that we do not have to employ consciousness? The Behaviourists thought they had discovered the mechanism by which this happened: the *conditioned reflex*, a reflex that was transferred from a direct stimulus to a surrogate stimulus. They believed that by analysis, it should be possible to show the *chaining* by which each of the conditioned stimulus–response bonds came to be the particular behaviour they were studying, however complex that behaviour might appear to be.

The idea of the conditioned reflex that was built into the doctrine of the Behaviourists began with observations of dogs by I.P. Pavlov early last century. In studying the digestive system, he had noticed that his dogs would salivate without the presence of food, just the sight of the man who gave them the food would do the trick. Pavlov showed that any stimulus a dog can perceive could be made to evoke salivation after it has been paired with food often enough. Pavlov offered, it seemed, an objective way to explain how ideas become associated: as Pavlov's dogs associated food with seeing the caretaker.

The salivary reflex is not under conscious control. You cannot say: I will now secrete saliva, and thereby cause my mouth to start watering. You could think about dinner, and that might make you salivate. This is a conditioned reflex. Psychologists came to believe that they could build any arbitrary system or hierarchy of behaviour by simply conditioning people in the same way. Bechterev, a rival of Pavlov's, experimented with voluntary movements, like lifting the paw, rather than involuntary reflexes. Pavlov's ideas, with Bechterev's methodology, were then picked up by John B. Watson and others. In the 1920s, Behaviourists redefined psychology as the Science of Behaviour, not the science of mental activity. They wanted to exclude the mind from psychology.

As different people introspect differently, they thought a researcher could not rely on what people said about mental activity. '*There's no way I can verify you really had the experience you told me you had.*' Behaviourists knew they were conscious, but they were convinced they could not study conscious experience scientifically. They had to be hard-headed scientists: nothing was allowed that a physiologist would or could not do.

They thought that any complex pattern of behaviour, such as human speech, could with sufficient analysis be reduced to reflexes, and to chains of reflexes. When a *stimulus* elicits a *response*, and that response in turn becomes the stimulus to elicit the next response, and so on, the result is a *reflex chain*. 'How simple,' they thought. People are not complicated after all. Psychologists had discovered the unit of analysis. Given a response they should be able to figure out what the stimulus was that led to it, and so on back up a chain of reflexes. *This would allow control of the process.*

What was being studied was transfer of response to stimuli of one kind to stimuli of another kind. Learning was defined as *relatively permanent change in behaviour* that could be observed and measured. The programme was to analyse and simplify the complexity of behaviour so as to describe it as chains of stimulus–response bonds. A trained person could teach by controlling and reinforcing each of the links in such defined chains, or so it came to be believed.

Teaching programmes

The facts are hardly in dispute. Dogs do salivate if they hear the sound of the biscuit barrel. I can be made to feel fear in the cinema by visual or auditory stimulus made possible by conditioning; it makes it easy for the advertising and propaganda industries to work on people's emotions. Techniques that are applied to advertising and politics have made *emotional engineering* a high art, even a science. Conditioning happens, it is very powerful. What is in dispute is the mechanism, how it works, and how it can be used in teaching. Later psychologists of the Behaviourist School sought to extend and modify the early doctrine, to make it viable as a means of instruction. B.F. Skinner (born 1904 and formerly Professor of Psychology at Harvard University) set out to identify the 'how'.

Operant conditioning

Skinner claims that one can describe behaviour in terms of external stimuli and their positive or negative reinforcement. He argues that learning is accelerated by reinforcement: a stimulus that increases the probability of a response. In operant conditioning, the most important stimulus is that which immediately follows the response, not that which triggers it. In order to predict how a person will behave in the future, we must look at what happened as a consequence of similar behaviour in the past, not at his expectation of the consequences that will follow his behaviour. This may seem rather mentalistic after all. What Skinner is trying to avoid is the idea that future expectation – goal-seeking – affects present behaviour. It must relate to what has happened in the past in terms of reinforcement. This shapes our behaviour by using our desires and our fears.

Strength of a response can be determined by the intensity of the stimulus. Prolongation or repetition will also increase the intensity of a stimulus. For instance, if an animal like a rat is starved, the stimulus of food and the reward of food will be greatly increased. Skinner used this to show how rats can be conditioned to find a path through a maze with food as the stimulus. A rat, which is an exploratory animal, searches a box until by trial and error it discovers how to get food. It can then be conditioned to follow more and more complex paths through a maze to reach the food. Thus, the experimenter can control the behaviour of the animal and establish patterns in that behaviour. From this, Skinner believed that you could predict behaviour: you could control the process of learning and shape the behaviour as you wished.

The systematic application of reinforcement has been Skinner's principal study. He believes a technology of learning/teaching can be devised. It could be all predictable (in the scientific sense) and so *programmed*. So, teachers should not be learning by experience in the classroom. '*Teachers need the kind of help offered by a scientific analysis of behaviour.*' This kind of programme has been tried and with some success.

Comment

Does conditioning work? Yes, certainly. Animals and children, no doubt adults, can be conditioned. It happens in normal nurturing. We observe strong conditioning into sex roles and status expectations. I find it very difficult to prevent myself making responses that have been conditioned into me, even though I am conscious it is happening. Positive and negative reinforcement work. Skinner did it most effectively, at least with rats, by systematic use of his techniques. Parents and teachers use conditioning much more simply, through rewards and punishments, to try to shape the behaviour they want. Peer-groups quickly establish conforming behaviour in dress, language and the rest by reinforcement. Most human behaviour in social situations, societies, groups, tribes, can be seen to be the result of conditioning. People condition themselves to 'need' salt, nicotine, alcohol – an inexhaustible number of electronic gadgets – almost anything. With considerable effort, they can decondition themselves.

But powerful as it is, conditioning is not the only type of learning. It cannot be ignored and teachers should take careful note of what has been discovered about reinforcing learned behaviour. As a systematic approach to education or even training, it fails to take into account many other aspects of human behaviour, most notably motivation and attitudinal change. For this reason it tends to fail to achieve the intended programme. Humans develop resistance to conditioning. It is hostile to the development of cognitive and intellectual skills. Surely, teachers must promote intelligent thinking. The most highly skilled practitioners, if their skills are largely robotic, soon find their skills are out-of-date, non-current, almost useless; but they have no means of learning new ones.

CHAPTER 25	Neo-behaviourism: structural analysis

The most influential of the Neo-behaviourist psychologists from the mid-1960s was R. Gagné (born 1916, and Professor of Psychology at the Universities of Princeton and Florida). His concern is the structural analysis of learning processes and design of teaching models to match the kinds of learning they are intended to facilitate. He devised a systematised approach to instruction that influences the design of many teaching programmes.

Learning is seen as '*a change in human disposition or capability, which can be retained, and which is not simply ascribable to the process of growth*'. He compares organic processes in the body such as digestion to describe a process taking place in the learner's brain. The analogy is a computer program, but it is *a total process*, not fragmented but systematically described. It starts with *apprehending* what is in the environment, the stimuli; followed by *acquisition*; then *storage*; and finally *retrieval*. Learning is analysed into descriptions of *changed behaviour in terms of an observable type of human performance*.

There are for him *five* major categories of human capability that are outcomes of learning; each requires a different learning strategy and teaching that recognises the type of learning and the strategy. Instruction is to be designed with different characteristics that depend on which particular class of performance change is the focus of interest:

1 verbal information
2 intellectual skills
3 cognitive strategies
4 attitudes
5 motor skills.

Clearly, this goes a long way beyond Skinner in identifying a range of types of learning and needing to match the appropriate process of instruction to the intended type of learning. It is certainly not simple stimulus–response bonding. It is Behaviourist in placing emphasis on *structure* imposed from outside. While acknowledging the importance of *process* in the learning, *outcomes* are seen as the main criterion of successful instruction. And yet the range in the types of learning that are to be *systematised* is limited.

Gagné sets out *eight* conditions or types of learning:

1 *signal learning*: stimulus–response at the level of signals
2 *stimulus–response learning*: involves discrimination between stimuli

3 *chaining*: stimulus–response bonds are chained in sequence at a motor level – what others might call 'memory in the muscles'

4 *verbal discrimination association*: verbal chains are formed – involves making of individual links, discrimination and chaining to 'associate' (in Pavlov's sense)

5 *multiple discrimination*: more sophisticated discrimination between apparently similar stimuli – with correct responses

6 *concept learning*: responses to 'classes' of stimuli – recognition of relationships or 'classes'

7 *rule-learning*: chaining concepts: a rule is 'an inferred capability that enables the individual to respond to a class of stimulus situations with a class of performances'

8 *problem-solving*: a natural extension of rule-learning where the most important part of the process takes place within the learner 'who discovers relationships'.

This is a hierarchy of learning. The word is taken from the organisation of priests, and implies a pyramidal structure from many at the base to one at the top. By extension, however, as in this case, it implies that each capability has within it and necessary to it all the previous lower capabilities. For example, I cannot chain stimulus–response bonds unless I am capable of making the individual bonds first.

Gagné proposes *use of instructional sequences related to the hierarchy*:

- *informing* the learner as to what form of performance is expected after completion of the learning
- *questioning* the learner to elicit recall of previously learned concepts
- *using cues* to elicit the formation of chains of concepts or 'rules'
- *questioning* the learner so as to obtain demonstration of rules
- *requiring* the learner to make a verbal statement of the rule.

As a teaching programme this is clearly desperately limited, and entirely teacher-centred. Gagné identifies *eight* phases in an act of learning which implies *voluntary learning activity* only, what the learner does:

1 *motivation*: goal-seeking – induced by creating expectations

2 *apprehending*: differentiation of stimuli by focusing attention

3 *acquisition*: storing the learning by encoding it

4 *retention*: extended memory storage

5 *recall*: the process of retrieval

6 *generalisation*: transfer of learning to new contexts

7 *performance*: demonstration of what has been learned

8 *feedback*: the process of reinforcement.

Comment on behaviourism

Gagné's programming of learning derives from how he sees the teaching–learning interface operating. Certainly, the statement of learning goals is of major importance, but who identifies the goals? The instructor alone it seems. Gagné has *instructors* as designers and managers of a process of instruction, providers of immediate feedback to the learner to reinforce learning (Skinner-style), and assessors of learning outcomes. Assessment is the instructor's prerogative. This language has become standard as a description of teaching in American schools and universities. It is an attempt to *systematise* instruction. A great deal of effort, in training in particular, has gone into such systems, it has dominated much of the provision. There is little room for dynamic or organic change in such a programme. It has within it implied conditioning of learning by shaping and reinforcement, called feedback.

Nor does it acknowledge that all humans are exploratory animals. Decision-making is for the instructor. How can this produce independent learners, let alone independent thinkers? The emphasis in the end is on demonstrable, observable performance. Those aspects of learning Gagné identifies as important, such as developing cognitive strategies and attitudes, because they are not demonstrable in performance are ignored in instructional/assessment/feedback programming.

The eight phases of instruction appear to relate systematically to outside rather than inside need, to the American style of instruction as *tell and test orthodox right answers*. But where then are 'discoveries of relationships' or 'leaps ahead beyond the evidence'? It would be impossible to imagine 'leaps' that miss out whole parts of the chain.

Yet we know the human mind does make such leaps. We leap to conclusions, often enough with very inadequate evidence, then fill in the gaps in the chain afterwards. But this is desperately untidy for such a system as Gagné proposes. Where is 'trust in the students'?

The whole Behaviourist programme was based on a misconception of how science worked. It was thought to be the accumulation of experimental facts, analyses, theorising, the demonstration of proofs, and replication: a misconception that was prevalent until the last war. Behaviourists thought they could build up a supremely thorough-going system which would inevitably be effective, because it was designed on the basis of scientific research. It could be systematised: each building block was to be made up of conditioned behavioural patterns, using reinforcement techniques (teacher-centred).

Gagné appears, like Darwin and Freud, to wish to impose a rigid finality that cannot allow of challenge from the learner. Dynamic, unpredictable change must imply unpredictable outcomes. You cannot make the outcomes totally shape the learning process, unless your purpose is conditioning to preconceived patterns of behaviour; i.e. indoctrination. How much of *what* people actually learn, let alone *how* they learn it, is really in the control of teachers/instructors? Do teachers need to perceive a much more modest role for themselves?

Unfortunately for the Behaviourists, science just does not work as they thought. It generates hypotheses, sometimes no more than 'hunches', and looks for evidence to support but more to invalidate them. It starts from questions and/or guesses rather than from evidence: i.e. top-down, not bottom-up.

Sir Karl Popper in 1958, in *The Logic of Scientific Discovery*, proposed a new philosophy of science. Scientific method since Bacon had been thought of as demonstration of proofs, and research was concerned with proving the theory correct. Scandals occurred when contradictory evidence was suppressed. For Popper, a theory must be falsifiable, not verifiable. The proper business of science is 'rejection of hypotheses'.

It starts with a conjectural hunch that often goes way beyond the available information; then the programme is set up to check the hypothesis against the world: does it explain the facts? Will it predict what will happen if … ? A good theory will predict outcomes in the given circumstances. The test is whether or not the prediction is false in *every* single case; one miss and it is necessary to modify the theory.

Einstein's theory of gravity made very different predictions from Newton's. For example, he said light rays from distant stars would be bent if they passed close to the sun, a prediction that could be first tested during an eclipse of the sun in 1919. Measurement was very difficult, but it seemed to confirm Einstein against Newton. He was also correct in predicting that clocks would run slow in a spacecraft. But Newton's equations are easier to use and more practical than Einstein's, so Newton is preferred in our everyday world.

Scientific theories, since Einstein and Heisenberg's *uncertainty principle* in relation to the structure of the atom, are no longer expected to demonstrate objective truth: it is enough that they work. So long as they will predict what will happen they are useful, and that is what is required. The great optimism about being able to explain everything has largely died.

Positive conclusions: Gagné's insistence on matching teaching to intended learning and analysis of 'how that is intended to happen' is extremely important. We must surely do the analysis. We must understand how to design a strategy of learning and a strategy of teaching to match it. We must agree learning goals with students. But they must be signposts rather than goalposts, because we cannot predict what will happen or how the goals will need to be redefined as the process evolves. In any case, a point of arrival is also the next point of departure. Nothing is once for all.

We also need to use feedback in a formative way, but not to shape the learning to conform to predetermined, teacher-centred and fixed outcomes. For thousands of years people have taught bears to dance by conditioning. We will no longer pay to see bears dance; we consider it cruelty to animals, although we still go to a circus to see other animals 'perform'. Who is the learning for anyway? We are intended to admire and applaud the trainer, not the performer.

Feedback is not to reinforce learning in the Behaviourist meaning and technique, seeking to shape learning to teachers' predetermined models. It is better seen to be in the nature of a mirror, to allow the students to match what they are doing against models and criteria that we have agreed with them and which they perceive for themselves. This will enable *them* to measure their progress and so to improve whatever they are setting out to learn, to set about learning consciously and intelligently, to take responsibility for their own learning.

Suggested reading

Annett, J. *Feedback and Human Behaviour*, Penguin (Harmondsworth), 1969.

Berelson, B. and Steiner, G. *Human Behaviour: Inventory of Scientific Findings*, Harcour Brace Jovanovich (New York), 1964.

Block, J.H. *Mastery Learning: Theory and Practice*, Holt, Rinehart & Winston (New York), 1971.

Coating, B.F. *Science and Human Behaviour*, Macmillan (London), 1953.

Gagné, R.M. *The Conditions of Learning*, Holt, Rinehart & Winston (New York), 4th edn 1985.

Hilgard, E. and Bower, G. *Theories of Learning*, Appleton-Century-Crofts (New York), 1966.

McConnell, J.V. *Understanding Human Behaviour*, Holt, Rinehart & Winston (New York), 1983.

Skinner, B.F. *The Technology of Teaching*, Appleton-Century-Crofts (New York), 1968.

Reynolds, V. *The Biology of Human Action*, Freeman (Oxford), 1980.

Watson, J.B. *Behaviourism*. B. Lippincott (Philadelphia), 1924.

CHAPTER 26	Insight learning: Gestalt

Intellectual progress, psychology is no exception, occurs by challenge and defence. The school that arose in vehement opposition to the Behaviourists was the Gestalt school. All great eras have been characterised by competition for excellence.

Where Skinner spent many years studying rats, experimenters who wished to challenge the Behaviourist School of Watson studied chimpanzees, our nearest cousins. I once had an 'intelligent' cat, who discovered how to get me out of bed in the middle of the night by rapping the knocker on the front door of my house: he climbed up slats on the door and lifted it with his paw. I certainly did not condition him to do it. How did he learn it?

Kohler (1887–1967) was interested in the chimpanzees' *ability to solve problems*. Since they could not tell experimenters their introspections, he observed their behaviour and created hypotheses to explain it. You may well have seen these experiments, since they were filmed. One was to give a chimpanzee the problem of getting bananas that were suspended out of the ape's reach. To solve this the animal placed boxes one on top of another.

How would you explain what the ape did? Surely not by stimulus–response chaining. Had the ape had experience before that had been developed through reinforcement to produce a capacity to make such inventive use of the environment? Or was it creative thinking of some kind? Was there a reorganisation in the brain of structures in the world? Did the ape perceive a different relationship of objects to make an 'artificial tree' that it could climb? Did s/he 'visualise' the problem mentally first? Another experiment used the ape's frustration at not being able to reach a bunch of fruit that was outside the cage. The ape apparently 'experimented'. Some jointed sticks had been provided, and after several attempts s/he succeeded in putting them together to reach the fruit. Studies of behaviour of similar kinds have been filmed in the wild with various animals. What hypothesis could one invent to explain this? How would you explain *problem-solving* of this kind?

You can watch birds in a cage solve problems, using their beaks as we would use our hands to climb about or *play* with moving parts, just like my cat's *experimenting* with my front door knocker. Kohler saw this behaviour as '*not connected with previous trial and error*', not linked step-by-step as a chain, nor as reinforced patterning which, in order for it to be stimulus–response bonding, such links must be. Could it have been recall of past learning? And of what kind of learning? Most young animals do seem to enjoy *playing* and *learning through play*. It is why this is the preferred approach in infant schools. It is a necessary stimulus to exploration, finding out by doing it, experiential learning. Kohler called it *insight learning*. It was, he thought, a restructuring in the mind to see how the whole thing might work: *Eureka! I've got it.*

We have the experience ourselves quite frequently. It was said to happen as a Gestalt: the *structural essence of the total situation* posed by the problem is *perceived* by the learner. You will have experiences like this with your own pets, and similar personal experiences to reflect on. We quite often use the phrase: '*Oh! I see it now!*' This implies some kind of *visualising* of the problem in a new way. We see how the bits make sense together. For Gestaltists, 'the whole is greater than the sum of the parts'. 'Seeing the whole' makes sense of the parts.

What distinguishes *insight learning* for these theorists is that:

- the solution is a sudden leap, as if pieces were fitting together
- once it has been accomplished, it is easier to solve similar problems
- it leads to permanence in learning – it appears to become part of our way of dealing with the world
- we can transfer that learning to unfamiliar situations in different contexts.

In other words, it appears to be about how we *subsequently* do things. It improves our intellectual and problem-solving skills and processes. Transferability is essential: cognitive skill must be applicable to new, unfamiliar contexts.

This suggests that if we want to improve people's skills we need to look at how people deal with things '*in the whole*', and not try to improve skill performance by analysing it into constituent bits. It doesn't work that way. Gestaltists argued that a phenomenon like learning has to be studied as an organised, complex structure which changes as a whole by sudden leaps from one state of being to another. The pattern of brain activity that made this leap happen they called *insight*.

Certainly, most things, from the simplest to the most complex such as human behaviour, are much more easily grasped and understood when we have a view of them as a whole. We cannot even begin to see what each bit does on its own for we can understand it only in relationship to the whole. There are multitudes of things of which the whole is not analysable into constituent parts. A painting or a photograph is perceived only as a whole, the parts may be taken separately but are then seen as another 'whole'. So is a piece of music, or a tree. Analysis of constituents and processes helps you to appreciate it more, but to take it apart is to destroy it. William Wordsworth, in an early poem, wrote, '*We murder to dissect.*'

Comment on Gestalt

The Gestaltists' explanation of how learning happens is important – that it is best seen as a dynamic process, it is not linking nor even associating with previous experience, but creative restructuring that arises from thinking problems through to a sudden restructuring in the mind. Challenge to the mind by new experiences is essential to learning.

Acquisition and retention of *insight* are the core of the learning process for them. Since this comes about through problem-solving, it will be most effective when learners are challenged by being given problems to find solutions to; they must ask questions rather than wait for answers. The best practice in primary schools is exhibited in problem-solving group projects. It demands a very different kind of learning programme from that proposed by Gagné with his structural analysis. It must be dynamic and 'open' in terms of the intended learning. It must be productive thinking in a dynamic, creative process. It is in fact impossible to predict how any mind of whatever kind will restructure its experience, even a cat or a bird; it is what we mean by intelligent behaviour, and the size of the brain does not seem to prevent it happening. 'Bird-brained' is an error as anyone who has watched what crows do will know. Birds can be terrifyingly clever.

All decision-making must therefore be seen as a creative response to situations. It is creative because it involves making a new structure of the problem in order to discover a solution. And the process of learning is cumulative; it improves what we can do thereafter. This is to be contrasted with rote-learning in which creativity is suppressed. It can be seen to happen when we are faced with a familiar object in an unfamiliar guise. We might have to rotate it in our mind's eye, picture it some new way to recognise it. A favourite game of local newspapers is to present picture puzzles to their readers: where/what is this?

A capability for creative thinking will be present in most learners. This capability is already in the student and it has to be brought out. It is not in the teacher to be transferred to the learner by some technique of knowledge transfer. *How should the teacher attempt to bring it out, rather than to teach it or to put it in?* Asking a question of this kind changes the perspective of teaching entirely. Productive/creative thinking involves learners grasping the essential relationships within a problem, grouping them into wholes and restructuring the whole problem to find solutions. But we quite often might need to break down a problem into related stages in order to tackle it successfully. We may not be able to grasp the whole of something – if it is too big.

Teaching/learning strategies

Much of what makes a 'person' is a result of conditioning, whether it is consciously done by parents, teachers, employers, peer groups, churches, advertising companies, or just pressures to conform, such as sex-role conditioning. I could not possibly go out wearing a skirt and make-up. Many women feel naked if they are not wearing make-up. Unlearning such reinforced behaviour is extremely difficult if not impossible, particularly if it is accompanied by a mind-set of beliefs and attitudes, and within the context which has conditioned the behaviour in the first place. Given an entirely new social context, deconditioning is made easier. If I moved to a country where all men wore skirts or make-up I might find it possible to change, but not without some discomfort. We are at present trying to create the 'right climate' in which smoking is seen to be antisocial and make pressures to quit irresistible. This is happening even in Japan. It is helpful to understand the mechanisms involved.

Clearly, there is a place for rote-learning in teaching programmes. Memory rote-learning has an important place in the laying of foundations, let's say in number work, but used as a major means of instruction it stifles the very learning we are trying to assist. Indoctrinating clearly is intended to suppress creativity, but we don't want children to challenge the validity of multiplication tables, say. Unless they use the new information it will remain 'in a memory box'; you have to use the 'tables' to make them yours. There may be problems in overwhelming students with too much information at one time. But it is easy to test.

Creativity is not testable. It relies on personal judgement, and is only indirectly observable as outcomes. But it is obvious also that without a sound basis of information to build your speculations on, you will offer solutions that make no sense, no matter how creative. As in science, the criterion of feasibility in a theory is: does it explain the facts? It must make predictions that stand up to the facts. It does not require insight learning to memorise, but that seems a poor reason to require *only* memorising of facts – or opinions masquerading as facts.

Problem-solving is a powerful tool of learning. It is creative, related to success as an organism in the world, to social behaviour as a social animal, to intellectual growth and development of skills and capabilities; and through all this to self-esteem and independence. It has the additional advantage that we can use it to foster sharing and team effort, essential skills in a technological environment.

So, in designing learning programmes, we must vary our approaches to learning and fit them together to create successful learning strategies.

Right answers

The major problem with the Gestalt approach, as it turns out, is that there is too little information most of the time for learners to have a view of the 'whole'. They must make a leap with insufficient evidence (insufficiency of evidence hardly ever stops one, of course). Or the whole may be just too big a leap to make. We have to take smaller whole lumps, and hope to build them up into a greater whole later. I wonder if such a strategy would be acceptable as Gestalt? If we only saw parts of some painting a bit at a time, say, or single phrases of a piece of music, our picture would have to be built up by constant revisions, not by sudden leaps. There would be a final 'whole', of course, which would show us that our previous mental pictures were actually all wrong or misconceived. It is what happens in nearly all learning.

One consequence is that we often end up with the wrong 'whole', a delusion, a misconception of what it is we are about, which may lead us off in a totally unprofitable direction. Insight is great as long as we leap to the 'right' answer. What do we do in such a description of the learning process if, as is often the case, the answer is wrong in whole or in part? Ensuring that students have the correct response is the intention of reinforcement. Transmission of non-false information is important if we are to avoid very serious problems in later learning. It must be correct, if only because it is so hard to unlearn once it is established.

One of the great difficulties with discovery learning and problem-solving is this: at what point should a teacher intervene if it becomes obvious that students are on the wrong track? How vital is it that they do find the correct solution at the end of their effort? Obviously, wheels without an axle or bearings or gearing may well be ineffective for the purpose intended. The students need to have that pointed out.

The other great problem is that it can be very slow as well as very fast. Teachers and students easily become impatient. I remember well a student saying to me 40 years ago, '*Sir, why don't you just tell us the answer? It'll be so much quicker*'.

The method is intended to accelerate the learning by a sudden leap, in which the whole of the thing falls into place. This is how we often learn: we make a sudden leap beyond the evidence, and fill in the gap in retrospect between where we were and where we have arrived, with our knowledge of the 'whole' to guide us.

In support of the approach it is easy to show that a leap to a conclusion, cutting out a great deal of rather tedious unit-building, is efficient as a methodology *as long as students fill in the gaps afterwards.* Frequently, this last condition is unfulfilled, and gaps remain which later prove to be very inhibiting of future progress. Even graduates of famous universities, in History say, leave to be teachers, whose 'knowledge' of their subject is narrowly focused on two discrete centuries of history of the British Isles and no 'knowledge' of the centuries between or since or of anywhere else in the world, except in as far as it was needed to understand their specialism. Scientists usually have narrow specialist knowledge, too. It is often hopeless to employ a chemist to teach physics, or even maths. It may be very slow because students may not be very good at formulating or visualising the problem, discovering questions or a method of looking for answers. They may go down blind alleys or run up against gaps in their knowledge or understanding that inhibit progress. If they are working in a group they may have conflicting Gestalts or paths of enquiry to follow.

Teachers will want to provide 'teacher's Gestalt' to hasten the process. A major problem is then that the gap between where the learner is now and where the teacher is may be so wide that the 'teacher's Gestalt' is incomprehensible to the students. Teachers usually start from what *they* know, *their* picture of the world, and provide it as an insight for students. Or more often they may offer an author's 'picture of it all', a textbook solution.

This is the standard practice in complex subjects such as history, English literature, sociology and engineering science. The amount of detail is so huge that it is far too time-consuming a process to build up the students' 'picture of it all' by taking a tedious slow march through the details. In any case, from the practical point of learning, it is much easier to understand the detail and to know what you are looking for in the detail if you have a picture in your head of the whole thing. '*You can't see the wood for the trees.*' It is a fact that too much information is confusing. But we have to ensure that we do understand *where the student is starting from*: how he or she may *make the leap to the Gestalt*, and what has to happen then in terms of *filling in the gaps.* And this is not easy to do if we have no view of what the gap consists of, or even that gaps exist. This is part of what is wrong with providing the teacher's or the textbook's 'right' answers. They may make perfect sense to the teacher and the author because they are restructuring information that is already possessed to make a new 'whole'. On the face of it, it looks like an efficient approach, because it accelerates the students to a conclusion they might otherwise take a long time to reach, or which they might never reach at all because of lack of skill or information or motivation to discover.

But the whole without the evidential information makes little sense, especially if students do not know what the questions are to which these are the 'right' answers. Textbooks rarely state the questions: too often, answers are to be learned as facts when they are truly a person's reconstruction of the world to make sense of the facts. Teachers may be pleased with the efficiency of what they appear to have done, but in Gestalt terms it is an illusion of knowledge, since the students have not actually made any leap at all. They can only do that if they restructure their own 'picture of it all'. They have to process information themselves; they have to restructure their conceptual framework for it to become usable knowledge. To memorise and then to repeat accurately what they have memorised is not insight, but it is the way many examining systems work. Some students can answer any question you like on the content of a textbook, and have no idea what it is actually about. Enabling students to achieve insight learning provides a formidable challenge to teachers and that explains why it so infrequently occurs.

Suggested reading

Kohler, W. *The Mentality of Apes*, Harcourt Brace Jovanovich (New York), 1925.

CHAPTER 27

Cognitive development: concrete and formal thinking

Jean Piaget (1896–1980), for 50 years Professor at the University of Geneva and Director of the Rousseau Institute, studied hundreds of children, trying to understand how they learned. He believed, like Gestaltists, that children are born with certain *innate mental structures* that determine and shape their cognitive development. These innate structures provide their motivation to interact with their environment and guide the growth of their knowledge about the world. Children construct grammar in their minds as they learn to talk because their genes allow them to. He took a middle road in the prevailing 'nature–nurture' controversy. Piaget also thought the shape of the mind was affected by the environment in which the child grew up.

Piaget concentrated his attention on the mind. He paid little attention to behaviour itself. It was *mental functioning controlling behaviour* that interested him. '*The child is not shaped by the parents,*' he said; '*the child is the teacher.*' Your social environment merely provides 'inputs', your mind interprets and reshapes these inputs to create the knowledge you presently have. He was much more impressed by similarities that linked all children than by individual differences. In every child, according to him, intellectual development must proceed through four clearly defined stages, which occur in giant steps. They are not the slow and steady accumulation of knowledge and information. Piaget's *four developmental stages of cognitive development* are as follows:

1 *the sensory-motor period*: birth to 24 months
2 *the pre-operational stage*: 2 to 7 years of age
3 *the stage of concrete operations*: 8 to 12 years of age
4 *the stage of formal operations*: 12 years onwards.

Piaget maintained that the *average age* at which children attain each maturational level was about *the same in all cultures*. All infants explore and respond to their environment directly and rather automatically. Children explore the physical and maternal world up to around the age of 18 months, when they truly begin to 'think': when they build an internal representation of the external world, and learn to manipulate objects in their minds.

Between the ages of 2 and 7 children acquire sophisticated language. It gives them the ability to deal with many aspects of the world as symbols, by talking and thinking about objects rather than having to manipulate them directly. They can remember past events and anticipate their happening again. But they exhibit only egocentric reasoning: they cannot differentiate between 'self' and the environment. By the time children reach 6 or 7 they begin to acquire 'concepts' and see the objects as 'out there' not as part of me, but only gradually perceive them in relationships. Two halves of a ball they believe to be two new objects and expect them to weigh more than the original whole ball. They *perceive* weight and number in a non-adult way. Counting is not the same as the concept of number. For this reason, in infant and primary schools a great effort goes into teaching number using concrete examples, by handling objects.

At about the age of 12 Piaget believed for *all* children a cognitive leap occurs. They begin to use abstractions to manipulate thinking about the world. They can then tackle problems in the mind by isolating the important variables so as to manipulate them mentally or perceptually. Now at last individuals can draw meaningful conclusions from purely abstract or hypothetical data. They can now deal effectively with questions about how, what and why. Piaget identified this change as being able to *reason formally using abstractions*, instead of seeing the world and themselves in 'concrete', 'real out there' terms.

Is it true?

The main problem is that Piaget did not conduct experimental research under 'controlled conditions' such as present psychological research uses, and this kind of research does not confirm his assertions. Many of his basic assumptions are suspect: in particular, that there are general structures of the mind. There are also an embarrassing number of exceptions to his general rules. His are challenging ideas. I have found that many adults cannot deal with conceptualising abstract objects; they see things in concrete terms, or even 'me and the world' terms. They can deal well with counting objects, but not with number concepts. Perhaps, as many as 8 out of 12 adults have failed to make this cognitive leap, which Piaget asserted happened at 12 years of age. Assumptions we make about students' ability to cope with learning goals and programmes we teachers set up for them have to take account of such readiness or lack of it. We must recognise the need for cognitive growth.

The change to the National Curriculum in Science in the United Kingdom led to the need for a crash training programme for science teachers: biologists had to relearn physics to integrate it into their science teaching. To do so, they had to explore new student-centred methods and projects. But thinking scientifically is impossible if you cannot deal with abstractions, mental representations of the world and objects in it, visualise and manipulate them, perceive variables to differentiate between them. To do a science experiment you must isolate one variable you wish to study and try to keep everything else unaltered, so as to measure change in that variable alone. This implies quite complex thought processes. The problem comes sharply back. Many students have not made the leap from concrete to formal thinking by the time they come to do GCSE at age 16, and they cannot deal with abstract ideas.

The old input/output approach to memory training allowed teachers to get students through exams in science without any real understanding. GCSE will not allow that. Pupils must conceptualise and design methods for investigating phenomena. *You cannot do it if you are not capable of formal as against concrete thinking. Teachers therefore must tackle this cognitive change first.* The cognitive development problem exists, but not as Piaget envisaged; nor is the problem confined to science.

All creative thinking involves the ability to conceptualise and use abstractions. It relates in fundamental ways to vocabulary – the ability to use words and symbols as representations of the world.

Suggested reading

Piaget, J. *Language and Thought in the Child*, Routledge & Kegan Paul (London), 1926.
Piaget, J. *Behaviour and Evolution*, Routledge & Kegan Paul (London), 1979.

CHAPTER 28 | Perception

Common sense and my experience tell me that if I run headlong into a wall, I will do myself harm. But one nursing training officer once told me of patients she had known who had walked straight into walls without apparent harm to themselves. Perhaps, they did not perceive the wall to be an obstacle to them because of their 'insanity' at the time. How is it that people can walk on hot coals without apparent harm, or put skewers through their faces without bleeding? You can watch it from time to time on TV.

How far is what actually happens related to what we expect to happen? Does the *knowledge* come from experience, how we investigate the world? Or are there innate mental structures, inborn ways of visualising our world? Do we inherit cultural beliefs? And why do some people have such a different view of the world from ours?

Creatures receive information about the world from sense organs, of which for humans the eyes are the most powerful. It was probably because they used sight in preference to the other senses that our ancestors took to walking upright: to get a better look at things. Dogs, by contrast, evolved the ability to differentiate smells to which they are a thousand times more sensitive than humans are. Sight is not so important to them. We may wonder what their 'picture' of the world would be like. It would be fascinating if dogs could describe their 'view' of things. Would we recognise any of it? Could we even have a common language when their concepts would relate to smells we cannot smell, and our concepts to colours they cannot see? But all humans seem to be able to use the same conceptual ideas; encouraging because it suggests they have a similar experience of the world from which to derive them. Their perceptions are at least similar enough.

On the other hand, human common experience relates to physical capacity for sensing the world which excludes the greater part of the available information. We are familiar with the very different pictures of the world presented by television, our most powerful educational tool. There are images of galaxies and stars from radio telescopes, X-rays of the human skeleton, brain scanning that uses ultra-sound waves, and heat-imaging using infra-red light that appears to be used by snakes and other creatures; where ultra- and infra- mean beyond and below what we can perceive. These are all converted to visual images we can deal with, using visible light. We cannot have direct sensory access to those images of the world. Similarly, we 'hear' sound-echoing used by bats and dolphins to picture their world or for navigation, but only by changing the frequencies to what our ears can actually hear. We seem, in fact, to be genetically programmed for a particular *perception* and *knowledge* of the world we live in. We cling to our familiar picture of the world, brought to us only by visible light (the light we can see), as a *true* picture: the *only* picture. From a purely practical angle, what else can we do? But what has it to say about what the physical world is really like? Enormous parts – perhaps the most import-ant parts, who knows? – of information about even the most everyday aspects of our environment are not accessible to us through our senses. Or, if they are, we ignore them.

Clearly our brains also select from the experiences we do have; someone who loses the ability to see may become much more aware of what the other senses dis-cover, may hear things and smell things of which the sighted person is unaware. You can demonstrate it very easily to yourself. Make a tape-recording of an ordinary hour in a room while you are busy doing things there. Then listen to it afterwards; you will hear many things you did not notice at the time: clocks ticking, birds singing in the garden, the noise of footsteps or chairs moving, the sound of your own voice. Similar things can be learned by closing your eyes and exploring by touch only.

You normally filter nearly all of this out, presumably because there has to be a limit to how much information about your environment your brain and nervous system can process. Most of what is there you do not 'see' or 'hear' or 'feel' or 'smell'. What you select is what you need at the time. What do you do with the information such as it is when you get it? How do you *see* the world, for instance? Do you have *direct access by vision to an external reality*? Vision was once thought of as the experience of a spectator, seated behind a screen, watching a perfectly formed image. What is wrong with this idea? We are forced to ask: how does the spectator see what is on the screen? Is it to be the same way, as a spectator looking at another screen in his eye? Then another spectator another screen and so on *ad infinitum*: an infinite regression? It cannot operate like that.

Jonathan Miller in *States of Mind* gives the example of someone driving along a wet road. He *sees* a three-dimensional scene of slippery tarmac. What he actually *sees,* the image in the eye, is of course neither slippery nor three-dimensional. It can only mean that the person is *subjectively* and actively creating this image by conjur-ing up a model in the head of what is there. I gave, in Part 1, an example of driv-ing, of lights coming towards you at night. The amount of sensory information is very small indeed. Yet you usually have no problem with it. You build an image of *a vehicle* to which the lights belong, and decide what you have to do according to what you think a person driving that vehicle is going to do.

Without 'an image of it all in your head' you could not deal with it. A 'slippery road' is the same; you see it as 'wet' or 'slippery' because of your previous experience of such things. You might be wrong. It could be a mirage caused by heat on the road, I expect you have seen that too. But given alternative explanations, you nor-mally go for the most common first. Of course, you will know if it is raining or bright sunshine!

These are *alternative perceptual fictions*. They are fictions because you have invented them as explanations of what you actually see. What your eye receives is light: directly received from the headlights, received by reflection from the wet road. The eye makes an image on the retina. The important question is: What in fact happens then?

An analogy may help. Think how a telephone works using the principle of encoding/decoding signals. Sound waves, encoded as electrical impulses, are sent down a *wire* and decoded back into sound at the other end. Similarly, the optic nerves must take information from retinal cells and encode it as chemical messages, which operate like an electric current. Nerves that run from the retina are part of the brain, not separate from it. They are the means by which the central nervous system receives this coded information. What kind of code? By a complicated chemistry, the light seems to trigger pulses like electrical energy that are transmitted along the nerves and have to be decoded in the brain. The brain does not decode them back into light! What does it do with them?

All sorts of interesting things, obviously. For one thing the retinal image must be upside down since the lens works much like a camera lens. Look through a camera lens and you will see that. Why don't you see the world that way up? Again, the image must be constantly changing, you cannot hold your eyes still, they flicker. What happens when you move your gaze around the world? Try starting at one end of a wall and letting your gaze travel along to the other end. Does the wall seem to move? The image on the retina of your eyes is streaming past in reverse and upside down. How is it that you see a stationary wall.

How, in addition, do you see it as a solid wall if all the retina has to go on is the light reflected from the surfaces? What a complicated business it is! We also *see* a three-dimensional world. Having two eyes makes it possible to see objects in perspective, but how does it work? You can experiment if you want to. Put a patch over one eye. You still see the world as three-dimensional even if you find it hard to judge distances. You can stand on your head. Is the world upside down or are you? Cows and birds have eyes either side of the head, so they must work independently, but they still deal easily with a three-dimensional world. Birds manage to fly in straight lines and land with precision on tiny branches.

Your brain must in some way set up a constructed image of the world you are perceiving. It has to *know* somehow that the world is solid and motionless, it is your eyes that are moving across it. You are moving in relation to it, not it in relation to you. This is like Piaget's 'the world and me'. You will have experienced the confusion of not knowing whether it is you moving or the world when you were sitting in a train at a station and another train next to you appeared to move. Everyone, till Copernicus made his mental leap, thought the earth was motionless and the sun went around it. That was their hypothesis, his was different.

Your mind/brain interprets sense data to make it match the image it has constructed. If it fails to match, you become confused, you look for other information to help you. You look out of the other window of the train, you try out various other models to see which will match. It seems to be what your brain does without your thinking about it: it tests out alternative hypotheses, generating explanations or assumptions about what is out there.

What you actually do is to explore the world, set up hypotheses or models of what appears to be there, and then test to see how well it all matches. For much of the time, too, the hypotheses are constructed from very inadequate information. Even when there is very little sense data – as with the lights coming towards us in the car at night – we still make, must make, guesses, hypotheses, possible explanations in order to deal with it. It is like constant problem-solving. And we have to do it with whole objects and whole experiences. The biggest problems are caused by inadequacy of information.

Look at the drawings made by young children. There is a pattern to the way all children make drawings of their world and particularly the people around them – anywhere in the world. Fascinating studies have been made. Why are the people in the drawings almost the same? Where do children get their images from? Are they representing some in-built, innate models? This is how Gestalt theorists explained it.

Either all children see people and houses differently from the way adults see them or they all deal with what they see differently. African children will not draw the same houses as Europeans. But are their 'models in the head' different from those of adults? If they are the same for all children in a particular context, where do they come from? Or maybe it is physiological, something to do with the ability to coordinate hand muscles or hand and eye.

As we grow we accumulate experience: we appear to create more sophisticated models of our 'reality' to enable us to deal with the world and make sense of it. We certainly must have a larger and larger range of models to choose from unless our experience is very restricted even in adult life. T.E. Lawrence in *The Seven Pillars of Wisdom* tells how tribesmen of the Arabian desert, in a society with no representational images of people (it is taboo in Islam to make images of people) could not make any sense of a drawing he did of their Sheikh. The best guess one made was that it was a foot. It was apparent they could not *see* it. Lawrence said that their ability to visualise people had atrophied. The ability to see at all is acquired, the potential innate in the brain has to be switched on by the experience of using the optical apparatus. A baby who is prevented from doing it by defects or circumstance will lose the possibility of ever seeing: the neurons in the brain cannot make their connections once the critical period for doing so is past. How many other 'potential' capabilities are lost this way must be a matter of speculation. The capability for telepathic communication possibly?

Professor Richard Gregory of Bristol University has worked with visual puzzles. He writes in *States of Mind*,

> It turns out that the generation of fictions is very important for seeing the richness of reality from the very limited amount of data, or information, which the senses can handle or have available to them. So generation of fiction is intimately bound up with generation of fact.

He identifies *four kinds of illusion*. Here are just two: *ambiguity and fiction*. Try your own 'perceptual brain language' on the illustrations in Figure 28.1. The three boxes look like three-dimensional objects, but they are just lines on a flat piece of paper. How does that happen? Gregory wrote,

> Sometimes you find one face looks like the front and then suddenly it'll flip and become the back. You can make it happen when you blink, or when you move your eye about; it will also flip entirely spontaneously.

Try!

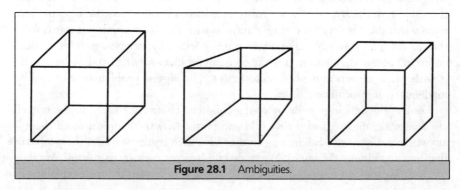

Figure 28.1   Ambiguities.

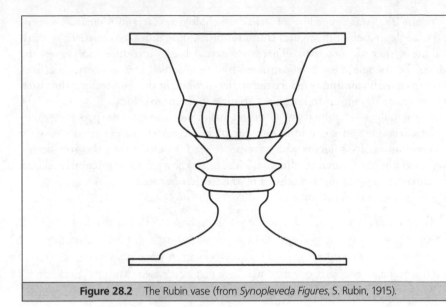

Figure 28.2   The Rubin vase (from *Synopleveda Figures*, S. Rubin, 1915).

It is the *ambiguity* that we have problems with. We set up and test one of possible alternative hypotheses of how this cube *is*, in a fictitious three-dimensional world we also create for it. We test out another equally probable hypothesis. We cannot come to a definite conclusion with the available evidence, so we try again … and again.

We do all this *quite unconsciously* too. It just keeps flipping from one to another. It is very difficult for us to control it. Try! It suggests that the part of the brain that is testing the hypotheses is not the same part we use to take conscious control, or even to think about what is happening and why. Is there a duality in the mind?

The 'Rubin vase' in Figure 28.2 shows two different kinds of object, the vase and a pair of faces, in profile. These are actually two different objects, and to get this to work, says Gregory, the objects must have roughly equal probabilities. The brain switches and tries out the two hypotheses.

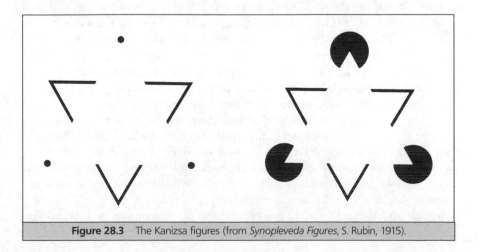

Figure 28.3   The Kanizsa figures (from *Synopleveda Figures*, S. Rubin, 1915).

Figure 28.3 was devised by an Italian psychologist, Gaetano Kanizsa. The central triangle in each of the figures is an illusion. Although we see the edges as sharp and clear, they are not there. There's no actual brightness difference across the edges: the triangle must be constructed by the observer, says Gregory. The lines seem to curve if you simply reduce the angles of white in the dark sectors: the visual system seems to join up an imaginary triangle with curved sides.

You actually *see* a white triangle, although all that there is on the paper is gaps in a black triangle and some little bits out of black circles. I have tried this with Japanese university students who have never seen it before: they also see the triangles, so it is not cultural conditioning. It seems to be a genetically determined trait in humans to make these hypotheses of 'the world out there'.

Gregory says in *States of Mind*,

> If it's a figure that's got surprising gaps which are unlikely to occur by chance, it's more likely there's something getting in the way, producing gaps, than that something is missing. This is the way the brain deals with experience. It is normally very useful to go on seeing parts of objects, or at least to believe that they're there, when they're hidden by something nearer.

Otherwise, we have to believe in bits of objects existing, like the Cheshire Cat's grin – impossible! You can experiment again. Ask someone what they see when you have a pen or something you are holding with only half of it or the tip of it showing above a desk, the rest behind the desk. Will they believe that half a pen exists? There are lots of child-play gags like nails that go through hands or noses.

Hypothesising

Professor Gregory has described many more visual experiments of this kind. The main conclusion he comes to is that *perceptions are predictive hypotheses*. The test of a scientific theory is whether it can successfully predict what will happen. We seem to behave in this fashion in the perception of our world. We make hypotheses and then test them out. As Gregory points out, in the Kanizsa figures it is *absence* of signals that makes us *see* the overlying triangles. We hypothesise the existence of these triangles to explain the gaps. And it is not something over which we can take conscious control. Even if we know something is wrong, we cannot *will* ourselves to *not* see it. You cannot stop yourself from seeing the white triangles that are not there. It is as if our *knowledge* of the world or of its objects is built into the brain somehow together with rules for making guesses and for matching, and which we cannot have access to by our conscious, thinking, problem-solving mind. We cannot observe inside our brains; *we cannot watch ourselves think*.

Gregory comments in *States of Mind* that the process of evolution created brain structures, as it shaped our noses so that we do not drown when it rains. Our noses are like roofs to keep out falling rain, so why not brain structures that '*incorporate a more and more accurate model of the universe in which it lives*'? The brain seems to have '*rule-observing processes which in brain language are more and more accurate pictures of the world*'. It exhibits pattern-making processes also. Are they the same? I suggested in Chapter 19 that the two hemispheres of the brain seem to have different functions or preferences related to pattern-making (images) and rule-making. Does this help to explain some of the enigmas of perception?

Teaching/learning

It is essential that teachers know how people perceive the world if they are to help students to learn. A carpenter works with the grain of the wood in order to shape it successfully. We must work with the normal processes of learning if we are not to create problems for students rather than help them to learn. This research however, shows, that the constructs that individuals make out of any experiences to make sense of them for themselves, are far from predictable, and are very likely to be idiosyncratic and personal. We don't all see the world the same way by any means. What matters is that we share our perceptions and come to some consensus about them.

Since our normal behaviour in learning is to explore, set up and then test hypotheses, we should recognise this in the strategies we devise in teaching/learning. Think, again, about the baby as it explores its world *using all its senses*; think too about the adults in Tony's class (Case Study 4).

People learn by testing hypotheses, but *they must want to*. What drives them to put a great deal of effort into it is equally complex. No doubt a part is played by dissatisfaction: we modify hypotheses or models when they do not fit. If people are very happy with the conditions as they are (and with what the world is for them), they are not likely to change. It may or it may not be a good thing for them to continue with their present models of the world and how it affects their behaviour. It may be that the models they have are appropriate for their need. Needs change, however, and then there is a need for more appropriate models.

Teachers must remember that change is painful. There are high costs in terms of self-image, insecurity, adjustment, and so on. Students need our support to deal with change. But since change is permanent, at least so long as we continue to evolve new technology, teachers will always be needed.

Suggested reading

Gregory, R.L. *Eye and Brain*, Weidenfeld & Nicolson (London), 1977.
Gregory, R.L. *The Intelligent Eye*, Weidenfeld & Nicolson (London), 1970.
Miller, J. *States of Mind, Conversations with Psychological Investigators*, BBC Books, 1983.

<table>
<tr><td>**CHAPTER 29**</td><td># The cognitive revolution</td></tr>
</table>

John Searle in *Minds, Brains and Science* comments,

> Most of the recently fashionable materialist conceptions of the mind, like behaviourism, functionalism or physicalism, end up denying, implicitly or explicitly, that there are such things as minds … they deny that we do really intrinsically have subjective, conscious mental states. … If a scientific account of the world attempts to describe how things are, then one of the features of the account will be the subjectivity of mental states. My present state of consciousness is a feature of my brain.

We make progress in thinking about new ideas according to the kinds of analogies we have available to us: we compare our new ideas with things that are familiar. Searle takes issue with those who believe the brain functions like a computer; that 'the mind' is an illusion created by the brain; and that we may be able to build a machine with 'artificial intelligence'. But we use analogies all the time. In the seventeenth century, clocks offered an analogy for the workings of natural phenomena. Plato (429–347 BC), the father of Western philosophy, showed the way. In order to make them accessible to people generally, his approach to problems in philosophy was to argue by analogies. His most famous comes from *The Republic*, where he invites us to imagine prisoners inside a cavernous chamber underground, chained in such a way that they must face a wall, onto which a fire throws the shadows of all manner of objects, including figures of men and animals passing by; and they hear only echoes of voices rebounding from the wall. Since they have no other experience to compare them with, they must take these shadows for 'reality'. But what if someone were to go out of the cave into the light, to be dazzled by its brilliance and the colours of the 'real' world? What if he came back and told them what he had seen? Clearly, they would reject him as deluded.

For Plato our world was merely shadows: 'ideas' existed in a 'real', that is a permanent and unchanging, world accessible only to a disciplined intellect. He distinguished *noumena* perceived only by the mind from *phenomena* perceived by the bodily senses; these senses in fact prevent our seeing the reality, a philosophical stance which has had a profound effect on all Western philosophy and religion. The concept of a permanent, real 'other world' accessible to the mind or soul is the basis of many great religions. Our world lacks permanence, everything is in constant flux so that it can easily be argued that it is unreal. This has provided a fertile ground for the mind–body controversy.

But the revolution which occurred in psychology was the result of the invention of machines which appeared to behave intelligently. That made it possible to use taboo words like 'purpose' and 'goal-seeking', which had been excluded from use in discussion of psychological behaviour since they were seen as mentalistic concepts: not demonstrable, objective, scientifically acceptable evidence. Ever since Newton's time, it was thought that if you couldn't point to an object, phenomena (Plato's appearances), observe an example which was accessible to all in the physical world, you had better ignore it. You could not study it scientifically. Behaviourists said: introspection is all very well, but show me 'a goal' out there.

Once you have radar that locks on to a target, an automatic pilot that is designed to keep on a predetermined course, you can argue that purpose and goal-seeking are eminently respectable 'out there' ideas to explain what happens. The new machines made it perfectly sensible to say: Look! it went for that target. The word 'target' is about the future. So is the future somehow controlling the present? In what sense do we talk of cause and effect if a cause is in the future? Machine-talk has crept into thinking about our mental behaviour. The language of 'encoding and decoding information' comes from information theory, intended to improve radio-signalling, and applied to processing by computers. Some experimenters in teaching techniques, such as Edward de Bono, see the brain as largely a pattern-making instrument that works by encoding information into patterns, which it can then store and retrieve in order to match with sense data as it arrives and is processed in the brain.

Cohen and Stewart in *The Collapse of Chaos* write,

> The late twentieth century has witnessed an explosion in ability to store knowledge in our culture rather than in our brains. We have invented a new phrase for such techniques: information technology. Information is treated as a commodity, something that can be bought and sold, measured in bits (binary digits, yes-or-no decisions). But information theory is a quantitative theory, whereas most things that are important to humans are qualitative … those aspects of a message that matter to human beings, such as meaning and understanding, do not fit readily into a crude information-theory mould.

The analogy above is with a digital computer that uses electronic processors to *encode* input as data and facilitate 'memory storage' of that coded information in 'data-base files' with a 'retrieval system'. Everything is 'systematised' in 'machine code' that only the machine can read. Since some of the functions of the brain appear to be describable in language of this kind, is the brain then a computer? Searle, *Minds, Brains and Science*:

> Because we do not understand the brain very well we are constantly tempted to use the latest technology as a model for trying to understand it. In my childhood we were always assured that the brain was a telephone switchboard ('What else could it be?')… or a telegraph system. Freud often compared the brain to hydraulic and electro-magnetic systems. Leibnitz compared it to a mill, and I am told that some of the ancient Greeks thought the brain functions like a catapult. At present the metaphor is the digital computer.

Searle argues that those who believe they may build machines with 'artificial intelligence' are wrong.

> Minds have mental contents; specifically they have semantic contents. … Computers do not 'think', they just follow programs: they manipulate symbols by computation, but they do not assign 'meanings' to the symbols; and they do not create 'internal, mental, models of reality'.

What is the process of encoding like? De Bono thinks of the brain as responsive to patterns that become etched into the fabric of the brain in some way. His simile is of water that makes deeper and deeper channels in a substance. Where the channels go depends as much on the qualities of the substance (its resistance to shaping) as on the incidence and persistence of the water. Material that is soft will be channelled more easily. The brain by analogy may be more receptive to establishing some patterns than to others.

In *Lateral Thinking*, he argues that the brain encodes into recognisable patterns. When new sense data is received, there is a matching process with encoded patterns. Clearly, the least resistance will occur where the deepest channels have formed from previous experience. Thus, we tend to have preferred ways of seeing the world. They are not innate but are the result of experience, whereas the Gestalt theorists would have argued for innate brain structures which programme us to perceive the world in a particular way.

De Bono sees the activity of the brain as setting up hypotheses related to pattern-matching behaviour. His view of creative thinking is totally different from that of the Gestalt school. It is not about the 'whole' at all, but about patterns that may build into wholes. The major problem he sees is that we will hypothesise the 'wrong' pattern; that this will inhibit our making sense of things when new information arrives.

One effective way of avoiding this happening, since we are now aware of it, is to try to avoid setting up any hypothesis that an experience is of a specific pattern, what he calls *vertical thinking*. Once you have set yourself on a particular path by such a hypothesis you will probably block out all other possible patterns and so are very likely to miss another more useful pattern which makes better sense of the whole. You should aim to 'keep your options open', and to allow your mind to generate numbers of different patterns out of experience. It can then match against a range of possible coded patterns as additional sense data provide additional information. This he calls *lateral thinking* which proceeds on a broad as against a narrow front.

Would he quarrel with Professor Jerome Bruner who argues that the most practical thing you can do is to have an hypothesis you can reject on the basis of further experience? This clearly echoes Popper's view of science.

Bruner (born in 1915 and Professor of Psychology at Harvard and Cambridge) argues that we *perceive the world by active selection from sensory information*. It depends on setting up hypotheses and testing them out as described by Richard Gregory. Previous experience is the key to what actually is perceived. It is also strongly determined by the society in which the individual lives – by its culture. **Knowledge is seen as a continuing process in the brain, not a product**. It cannot be packaged in 'lumps' to be put into some new brain in some way. It must involve active processing on the part of the learner. The brain of any individual will be selective according to such intangibles as needs, values and attitudes. Many are made part of an individual by cultural factors in the society s/he grows up in.

Learning will depend on how far attitudinal aspects of behaviour affect what the individual does with the new information or new sensory data. There will be rejection of those parts which are found threatening or culturally difficult to deal with.

New studies on attention and alerting have shown how the brain deals with the 'information-knowledge' process. *'Arousal of the nervous system with active scanning was seen to occur when the model of the world stored in the brain was violated in some way, i.e. when it was inconsistent with the incoming information,'* wrote Gregory.

How does the process work?

- There must be seeking of some kind.
- There is a selective mechanism.
- There is a means of reorganising concepts already established to accommodate new information to produce modified concepts – and from these 'internal models' of the external world.
- The process involves hypothesising to explain incoming information, and some testing of the new models/concepts to see how far they are meaningful when used to explain the world of experience.

Not patterns, but internal models of reality against which to match new data and experiences, Bruner argues

> physicists came to realise that the data of physics were related to the models in the physicist's head – the models he had constructed in order to build his theory of the physical world. ...
>
> Post-war psychologists were into mentalistic matters such as the selective filtering of experience, the construction of selective representations of the world in memory, strategies for co-ordinating information. Its sum total amounted to 'the Cognitive Revolution'.

Bruner dates it from 1932, the year in which Heisenberg was awarded the Nobel prize for physics for his statement of the *uncertainty principle*: a revolution in how scientists viewed their ability to observe the world. One outcome of which was to question whether the observer was in fact creating the phenomena he was attempting to study by the method he used for observing them; the phenomena he observed were not in existence until he made them appear. How often we seem to do that in social affairs! And in controversies in sociology, economics and history.

As the science of computing began to grow, it was possible to see *stimuli* as forms of *input*, and their significance depended on how you *encoded the input*, where you put it for *storage*, then how you *retrieved* it, and how you *matched it with other coded inputs*. You could store not only *information* in the memory of the computer, but *instructions* as well. *Instructions were like thought processes*. But the explanations of how the brain actually works now have moved from *linear* or *single*-channel computing to *parallel processing*, as it were, with many computers working in parallel. There is a similar scientific view of *genetic information encoded* in DNA: *replication and storage of information, genetic instructions and control genes* for switching on and off.

Competence

Bruner has the opposite view from that used in the UK/NVQ documentation about what students should be learning. Central to attainment of *competence*, rather than particular performances in skill or ability is *the acquisition of correct modes of thinking* or *cognitive change*, in which *perception* has the central role. It is *intelligence* which makes a person *competent*, not '*can do...*'

We live in an amazingly complex world. The brain can only deal at any one time with a limited amount of information, there is 'limited channel capacity'. An internal model of the world will make it possible to 'chunk' information into manageable packets, and to use this model to guide the search for, and processing of, information which is constantly arriving. If it is in fact what is happening in physics, *'objective, out there'* becomes a matter of *'interaction between the observer and the environment'*. If perception involves actively exploring the world with our senses, there must be a mechanism in the brain which enables us to tell the difference between sensations that result from what *we* do – our own movement – and sensations that result from the world's movement. If we explore the world with our eyes, the world does not seem to move. We are constantly moving and so are our eyes but we never get the impression of the world moving. Bruner states,

> Neurological mechanisms which anticipate the state of affairs which will result from a forthcoming action are called 'feed-forward' mechanisms to distinguish them from 'feed-back' mechanisms which provide information about the result of such movements. In fact, the comparison between feed-forward and feed-back represents one of the most important processes in the nervous system. The difference between what was intended and what actually occurred is what we process to correct the movement.

Learning behaviour relates to the learner's ability to create strategies, defining goals and ways of achieving them. This will involve feed-forward and feed-back. We can see Kohler's chimpanzees in this light. It also is necessary for learners to have a conceptual model to work towards. They must analyse available information and think about what is to happen. They must be prepared to take risks, to test out their hypotheses and so on – to come back from failure and try again – to explore and experiment. This is essentially *a creative process*. Since what we are striving for are *transferable models* to enable us to deal with changing conditions and new situations, learners have to be taught to see single instances in terms of principles and generalisations. They must develop the cognitive skills that enable them to grasp principles and to apply them to concrete instances in changing contexts: adaptability. Learning is mainly cognitive: acquiring information, transforming it by the assimilation of it with previous knowledge, and checking how the knowledge structure now constituted works in relation to explaining new situations.

It is not very helpful to separate learning about something from the process of learning to do it. It is better to learn physics by doing what physicists do. And it is the same with teaching. You learn to generalise about teaching by having experience of teaching. Realism and discovery come from actively doing what you are setting out to understand. So long as you do reflect cognitively on the experience, matching what you expected to happen with what actually happened.

Telling students about it in an expository way is useful in terms of alerting and attention (what I hope is happening now for you reading this book), but it will only become a part of your internal model of it through experience. Only then can it become transferable and usable.

Bruner proposed a 'spiral curriculum'. He meant that learning had to be constantly revisited. If knowledge is a process, so is the acquisition of skills, attitude formation, and so on. They are all part of growth. The most commonly occurring mathematical figure in nature, particularly in living organisms, is a spiral, because organisms grow by multiplying cells geometrically. Which creates, mathematically, a spiral.

Thus, in all our learning in life we repeat multiples of times the same experiences and activities, and we learn more about them and how to cope with them, do them well, feel comfortable with them the more often we do them. Our under-standing and insight grows with the experience and can be visualised as the spiral Bruner suggests. Teaching is no different.

No learning is once for all. We have to revisit it constantly to reshape our skills and knowledge. Rudiments early, and Bruner insists that learners must proceed by mas-tering each learning task or skill. The concept of mastery is a dynamic one: it is related to growth and maturity. Although learning does not occur as a continuum, but by spurts and periods of consolidation, mastery at each point is essential. Gaps in learn-ing can and must be overcome by revisiting. Development and redevelopment mat-ter. The model I have developed for this book attempts to interpret discoveries such as these about the human capacity to learn as a model of learning to be a teacher.

Suggested reading

Ardrey, R. *The Social Contract*, Fontana (London), 1971.

Ausubel, D. *Educational Psychology: A Cognitive View*, Holt, Rinehart & Winston (New York) 1968.

Bruner, J.S. *The Process of Education*, John Wiley (New York), 1977.

Bruner, J.S. *Actual Minds, Possible Worlds*, John Wiley (New York), 1986.

Cohen, J. and Stewart, I. *The Collapse of Chaos*, Fontana, 1997.

de Bono, E. *Lateral Thinking: A Textbook of Creativity*, Penguin (Harmondsworth), 1990.

Goldner, B. *The Strategy of Creative Thinking*, Prentice-Hall (New Jersey), 1963.

Miller, G.A. *Psychology: The Science of Mental Life*, Harper & Row (New York), 1962; Penguin (Harmondsworth), 1966.

Morris, D. *Manwatching*, Panther Books (London), 1978.

Searle, J. *Minds, Brains and Science*, BBC Roth Lectures.

Shostrom, E. *Man – the Manipulator*, Bantam (London), 1967.

Wertheimer, M. *Productive Thinking*, Harper (New York), 1959.

Whitehead, A.N. *The Aims of Education and Other Essays*, Williams & Norgate (London), 1950.

PART 4

Growing responsibilities

CHAPTER 30 | More to learn

Sir Karl Popper (1902–95) changed the way theoretical scientists were perceived as going about their business of generating and particularly validating their theories. *Conjectures and Refutations* reads,

> The acceptance by science of a law or of a theory is tentative only; which is to say that all laws and theories are conjectures, or tentative hypotheses, and that we may reject a law or theory on the basis of new evidence, without necessarily discarding the old evidence which originally led us to accept it.

An American theoretical physicist, Richard Feynman, said much more simply, *'We can never be sure we are right, we can only be certain when we are wrong.'*

What matters is the evidence: if the theory is in conflict with the facts or if it fails to predict what occurs, the chances are the theory either requires modification or is wrong. After publication of the *uncertainty principle* in quantum mechanics in the 1920s and *chaos theory* in mathematics in the 1970s, scientists no longer believe that one day they will be able to explain everything or predict the outcomes of events with other than statistical probability. Both show that it is impossible to observe phenomena, whether in the microcosm of particle physics or in the macrocosm of our normal world of experience, above a level of accuracy where predictions can be made as percentage probabilities of the kind used in weather forecasting: there is an 80% chance of rain. A favourite journalistic image from a paper given by Edward Lorenz in 1972 entitled 'Does the Flap of a Butterfly's wing in Brazil Set off a Tornado in Texas?' is a striking example of *chaos* in the modern scientific sense: minutest changes in initial conditions multiply exponentially to the most enormous effects. Science is content that theories which work will do very well until they don't work; and that this will then lead to better theories.

Popper argued in *Objective Knowledge: An Evolutionary Account* that evolution as a process is best understood as *trial solutions* to problems met by creatures in their environment. Each state is a tentative adaptation to the world the creatures live in; animals and plants incorporate the tentative solutions into their anatomy and behaviour, so forming the bases for later solutions equally tentative. He was not offering a simplistic Larmakian view of evolution as creatures evolving to take advantage of what they experienced in a purposive goal-seeking way: giraffes grew longer and longer necks to reach higher branches. When the environment changes as climates change, great droughts or floods or prolonged ice-ages, species that cannot adapt die out. But new species are part of environmental change, too, from viruses and bacteria, to the evolution of grasses that dinosaurs could not digest, to large animals in competition for scarce resources. But it also offers opportunities. Life will evolve to fill empty niches and in response to stimuli in the environment as eyes have evolved in five different ways in response to light. There has to be feedback into the genes from experiences of the world by complete species. It cannot just be Richard Dawkins' *Blind Watchmaker*, in which genes randomly throw up evolutionary change and those survive and prosper which *by chance* produce advantageous changes. The theory is much much more complex than the simple concept, survival of the fittest.

Popper did propose that theories and ideas develop in a purposive goal-seeking way, because they are the result of thinking and decision-making. A theory is tentative, and will serve till proved inadequate or just plain wrong. Each starts from what a previous theory proposed and challenges it against evidence and new ways of perceiving what is actually going on. For Popper, achievement in all human affairs happens thus: in politics, economics and art more so than in science or technology, because the objective 'out there' phenomena are much more tenuous to observe as 'the facts' against which to measure success of a theory in matching the reality of the world. Generally, theorists select 'the facts' that suit their theory and ignore the others.

Progress in all fields depends on changes that occur under the impetus of critical evaluation of predictions made by theories against what actually occurs. Recent history shows how much more successful dynamic, open societies are than those where their leaders defend unsuccessful, ineffective or unworkable ideologies. The twentieth century saw huge-scale social experiments with disastrous effects because the theories were wrong, but people persisted, still persist, in them against all the evidence. Popper showed that any task must start from a problem: we have to ask why it is a problem, and define it clearly. The degree of success we have in tackling, or solving, the problem is determined by how clearly we perceive and set it out. That depends again on the questions we ask, their validity and that of the evidence we are prepared to accept. To understand writers on any scientific enquiry, or social topic like education, we must know what the problem(s) was to which they tried to find a solution; what the questions were they asked; how they arrived at the answers they proposed; and the evidence they looked for. We need then to evaluate the answers and the evidence with more probing questions.

But in social research, questions are often not 'open', but skewed by a predetermined view of what the researchers are looking for; this affects the evidence they find. This is unfortunately the norm in education, which is closely allied to theories of social organisation and politics. What do we want the outcomes of education to be ? How does learning happen? Can it be shaped or channelled in ways to ensure those outcomes? Do we want independent thinkers or a population ready to conform? Are we about short-term goals or long-term effects? Many changes in educational theory and practice are part of a sociopolitical agenda, where the theory and the evidence are selected to justify change. Addressing questions of this kind at Level 4 of Questions (Activity 16 on page 257) will ensure that problems are not only defined, but repeatedly *redefined by critical evaluation* that compares an initial hypothesis, our educated guess, with what actually occurs. In all human activity, especially in teaching, this is the way we learn and progress. Of course, the questions you ask will be determined at least partly by the context in which you ask them and the kind of answers you are hoping to find. It is almost impossible to set about anything 'with an open mind', but we should try as far as we can to distance ourselves from our context and see it as others might see it who are apart from it.

It will be clear that the Tasks set out in this book are best seen as problem-solving exercises. I have encouraged you throughout to set up tentative solutions to learning problems that students face in the context where you are teaching; then to use evaluation as feedback to redefine the problems and look for better, more effective solutions.

Your perception of what is going on in your environment, and for your students, has changed through the process. So has the way you approach your students and your preparation. I advocate an integrated learning process, where learning is seen as cyclical and where we progress by using feedback and evaluation as the major assessment procedure. Where no solution is seen to be final, it is always tentative, and we can always do better on a future occasion. Thirty years ago, I knew a teacher in HND Engineering who had used the same lecture notes for 15 years, and another, famously, who had them written on 22 blackboards, which he selected and displayed for each lesson! The world has changed.

Keeping up to date

The major headache for doctors is constant change in the context where they work, trying to keep up to date with the evolution of drugs and treatments. A great deal of a doctor's time is spent in making sure s/he is up to date. New discoveries are made all the time. Drug companies spend billions of dollars to develop new drugs. New techniques using developing technology in medicine, hospitals and ancillary industries have revolutionised the treatment of diseases. But the diseases fight back and new diseases are constantly arising, because of the use of the same developing technology, the effects of chemicals which only emerge with time, and the environmental changes we often unwittingly make. One effect, naturally, is that doctors become specialists in certain narrow fields and must refer patients to other doctors for diagnosis and treatment outside their field.

What is true for doctors is true for most people in employment. In a rapidly changing world, new technology and economic forces not only change the rules of the game, constantly it seems, but they create new ball-parks and new kinds of games. There was a time when 'training' could prepare a person for a lifetime of employment. Now, many skills become obsolete and knowledge out of date. Education is part of that evolving scene.

One of the biggest obstacles is *attitude change*. Education and training should concentrate on preparing students so that they can cope with change, and know how to learn and relearn to adapt rapidly, as their world suffers revolution rather than slow evolution.

One purpose of the programme in this book has been to help you to learn how to learn: to appraise the tasks that you and your students need to undertake, to evaluate what is achieved, to find the evidence by asking appropriate questions, and to adapt the learning programmes to be more effective in achieving agreed goals. Another is to ensure that your learning is transferable to any new context. You must keep up to date. Education, institutions and methods of teaching and learning have been forced to change in order to keep pace with the world they serve. Many of those changes have perhaps been arbitrary, the result of ideological processes rather than pressures from employment in a technological society. Yet there is no sign that changes will become less painful in the future.

KEEPING UP TO DATE

Your own field of expertise will be experiencing development and change along with everything else. It is essential that you keep up with what is happening. Documents are produced by examining boards and awarding bodies providing guidance to teachers, tutors or senior staff who undertake training roles as new initiatives in education and training are introduced.

- How familiar are you with these?
- Where can you find them?
- Can you use them to make practical, workable schemes of teaching and learning programmes?
- What would it help you to find out?
- What other information is there?
- How can you discover that and use it to help you to make sense of what you are setting out to do?

  1 Make a list or a collection of relevant documents – at least know where they are kept and how to get hold of them.

  2 Try to identify what it is you need to find out; where to look for the information you need. This will change with time, so you need to review your needs.

  3 At an appropriate time you must decide on, undertake some research in depth into initiatives in your field as they affect what you as teacher or trainer need to do.

<table>
<tr><td>**CHAPTER 31**</td><td># Effectiveness and the curriculum</td></tr>
</table>

Welcome to the end of this part of your journey. What you have been exploring in this book is your role as teacher in a particular context. I hope you have found plenty to stimulate and interest you on your road. What you have learned will depend on what you have done: how busy and active you have been in using the programme of Activities and Tasks in the book, and reviewing and evaluating your experience in teaching.

You have probably discovered a great deal about yourself. Whenever I have asked teachers to evaluate their learning on a programme like this one, they have always said they have learned most about themselves. They have discovered strengths and talents and many things that surprised them. They have learned how to cope with demands made by circumstances and other people. They have also learned how to observe what is actually going on and take control of what they and others were doing.

I hope you have gained insight and skills. You should have developed a new way of looking at things, to be more observant, able to distance yourself to take a critical view, and so learned the skills of evaluation.

Where to now?

Learning is for tomorrow or next year. After all, we cannot change the past. Every arrival is a point of departure. We evaluate in order to decide what to do *now*, for we can always be better at what we do. There is no point in learning something as complex as how to teach effectively or how to engage students actively in their own learning, unless we make it a matter of habit.

Revisiting and consolidation are essential. So far, you have been thinking about your own class or group of students: what they need to do in order to learn with your help. Students in nearly all formal teaching/learning contexts do not, of course, learn just with one teacher. They have a programme of studies of which your class is part.

- Do you know the relationship between what they learn with you and what they learn with others?
- How far are you aware of what other teachers teach? What they expect their students to do? What kind of learning behaviour they are looking for?
- How does what students learn in one part of their programme affect learning in other parts?

It may be confusing for them to have contradictory messages from different teachers. In the past, it was left to students to try to make links between different parts of their programme; often enough it seemed that there were no links; learning, or rather teaching, was divided into discrete 'boxes'. Today in many school programmes, such as GCSE, subject boundaries are still clearly marked. Curriculum design is concerned to present an overview of the whole of a learning programme. The emphasis today is on *teams working together* and these include outside agencies, employers and others. Decisions by individual teachers must be modified to take account of what others are doing, and all should have a clear view of the intended outcomes of the learning overall. FENTO labelled this behaviour *collegiality and collaboration*, working well with colleagues wherever they may be.

CURRICULUM DESIGN

TASK 25

You have developed the necessary knowledge and skills to set about designing a learning programme with colleagues. So, working with a group in your own context, design a programme of study as a curriculum to integrate the learning activity for students in that context.

Unless you share a perception of overall learning the programme is setting out to achieve, and have an agreed sense of the curriculum design, you cannot contribute effectively to the achievements of your students overall. The design must integrate all the disparate elements of curriculum content to provide effective learning experiences which are coherent and make sense as a whole. The curriculum needs to motivate students and be designed to help them to learn efficiently by using appropriate strategies of learning. How far will the curriculum you design with your colleagues help students to become competent and effective in the roles they occupy?

Effectiveness is the keyword

In all advisory papers and reports, the single word *effective* appears again and again as the measure of excellence in every aspect of a teacher's role. The main use of the word is that it does well what it is supposed to do, whatever 'it' is. It is assumed that readers will recognise the *criteria for being effective* in the context, you will know it as you know the colour red. Unfortunately, some people are colour-blind and, in any case, red is a spectrum of colours.

Although many strategies could be used in the design of a curriculum, some are more effective than others and none is totally or predictably effective. Let me repeat: a strategy is a model in the head, an overview. It enables us to know what we are trying to do and how we perceive it happening. In considering any curriculum for students at any level, we must have a view of the whole as well as the parts. What is to change here? Surely, behaviour as a whole.

I have used the word *competence* repeatedly: it is another word found again and again in the same official papers. You may still be a little vague as to what the word means. Competence is a still developing concept, the use and the meaning change with time, with who is using it for what purpose. Nearly all words work like that. My use of the word derives from the view I take of what is involved in demonstrating competence both in a role and as a whole. I designed an overview diagram (Figure 31.1).

Competence can be viewed in a narrow sense: '*can do*' statements related to specific, defined tasks, or in a broad sweep: '*able to take responsibility for …*'. I choose to use the latter, mainly for the reason that training in specific tasks is highly contextual and does not allow for transferability to new contexts. Nor does it address the problem of '*can do … intelligently*'.

Whereas if we consider *roles* people occupy, we can design training that is generic and will be transferable from one context and level of responsibility to another. The *role of teacher* embraces many other roles and skills a teacher must be prepared to learn, as in the later chapters of this book.

Some training programmes identify up to 12 roles, and seek to develop them *in parallel* or *independently*. They may identify the role of *tutor*, at some levels that of *counsellor*, the role of *assessor* naturally. As you progress in your career, you will find yourself undertaking roles that may surprise you, but unless you choose to specialise in one field, you must avoid isolating any other role from your major role of *teacher*. *It is the level of responsibility that determines 'roles'.*

In designing the learning in this book, I assumed that you first have responsibility at the level of a class. The second part assumed greater responsibility, for a programme of learning activity with a group of students over, say, an academic year. Implied in that was a change in the way your role as teacher was defined, by deeper understanding and increased levels of skill. You were asked to consider *tutoring*, for example. This final part is about the growing responsibility you will undertake as you become integrated into the cooperative activity of teaching teams, and possibly take on the role of *mentor* for new teachers.

Analysis is fairly easy to do. We can break down behaviour into constituent parts. Identifying criteria does just that. We can, if we wish, train parts and test them. What is more difficult to do is to put the parts back together, to synthesise them into '*the behaviour as a whole*' we are really trying to achieve.

The language used in discussion of competence shifts. There is much more emphasis now on *effectiveness in the role*. This is to recognise that tasks do not make sense in a vacuum, they relate to a role in a context, where it is *the role that integrates the parts*.

There is much more to effectiveness in a role than technical skill in achieving specified tasks. To identify what is required a person needs a *conceptual framework*

- to grasp what the role is about
- to understand what purposes it serves
- what the essential qualities and attitudes are in order to fulfil the role successfully
- insight into the way this role fits with roles of other people
- understanding of theory as well as practice
- underpinning knowledge that enables the person
  - to use skills and expertise intelligently

- to get properly organised
- to think through problems
- to set targets, design action plans.

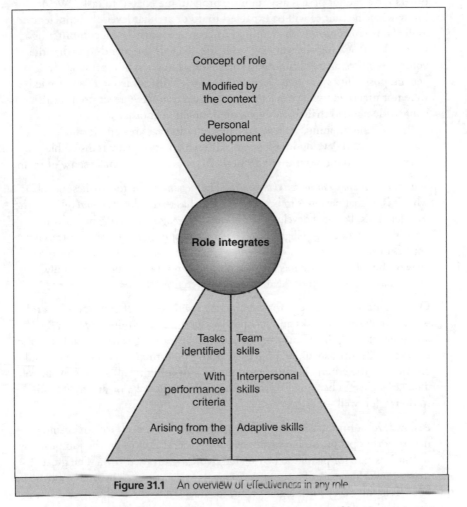

Figure 31.1   An overview of effectiveness in any role

Clearly, the 'higher' the level of responsibility, the more essential become acquisition and practice of higher level cognitive skills. Let's look at an example.

Personal assistant

1 If I say the words you will immediately have a view of what a person is likely to be doing because it is a concept you understand. Anyone undertaking the role has to work with this concept. But there are many other concepts, understanding, insights s/he is expected to grasp if s/he is to become effective in the role; whole books of guidance have been written for personal assistants. This is *a conceptual framework* that training must set out to develop.

2 The *concept* of the role is *modified to take account* of *the context* the person is actually working in. There is no such thing as *personal assistant*, an abstract concept; there are only *people who are engaged in specific contexts*.

The role of personal assistant depends critically on the role of others, especially the person they assist. Of course, you might say. Without full understanding of the context, and demands made in the context – and by others – we cannot design any training programme related to tasks. We do not know what the trainee will be expected to do or at what level of competence. Will *this personal assistant* be required to keep accounts? Use a computer or a fax machine? What skills will need to be developed? It depends on what the context requires. Much training in the past had to guess and provide for general possibilities. It often happened that the skills someone really needed were not practised, while others were practised that were never used, or the context demanded that the things were done quite another way.

In designing training, we have to develop tasks that are generic and transferable; and develop insights and skills which are equally transferable. Learners have to interpret the skills in their own context to make sense of them.

3 We *appoint people, not personal assistants*. The person in the role makes the job what it is. If that person is to be effective, s/he has to develop *personal qualities* the role demands. Personal development is *growth through experience*, but only by using that experience intelligently. '*It is not what, it is who, monsieur.*' A training course must concentrate on *self-assessment*, taking responsibility for developing a view of the role through one's own learning. It cannot be set up so that only external assessors test; and only test task competence.

4 Once we have a framework for a design that will deliver effectiveness in a role, we can analyse what tasks and technical skills the role requires. We can set about developing them, ensuring if we can that learning is transferable to other contexts. We can also apply quite demanding performance criteria. We should ensure that the criteria identify good practice in fulfilling all aspects of the role. The tasks have to become habitual because the skills are a means to an end – to do the job well.

5 At low levels of responsibility, it may be enough; there is clearly an absolute necessity that people do have sufficient insight and skill to do the job properly.

But it is rare for people to be isolated, working on their own. The great majority work as part of a team. A personal assistant can only be as good as the boss. Together, they form a good team (or not). In terms of effectiveness, it is essential that they do.

At all levels beyond that of no responsibility, there is a pressing demand for the development of *team skills* and *interpersonal skills*. Training programmes must provide learning activities that will develop these skills. How they work depends again on the context.

6 But no amount of good practice and developed skill are of much use if, when new challenges arise or circumstances change, they become outdated and they are an obstacle rather than a help. *Dinosaurs die: adaptable mammals thrive.* Dinosaurs were the most successful creatures ever to evolve. Why did they become extinct? It seems that they could not adapt to catastrophic changes that occurred in their environment. This has happened frequently in the past decades in our rapidly changing world as a result of developing technology. Training in

tasks can make for highly proficient skilled workers, but only so long as things stay as they are. Conditioning to produce robotic behaviour fails in the end.

Adaptability requires *problem-solving skills*, and the ability to design and take control of what you do. Training programmes have to make sure that learners are able to adapt, to learn how to learn, and to do it quickly and efficiently.

Competent teachers have to be effective in the roles they undertake. I hope it is clear that the design of the programme in this book for teachers exhibits the logic of the above argument.

Suggested reading

Bell, J. *Doing Your Research Project*, Open University Press, 1993/1999.

Boud, D., Keogh, R. and Walker, D. *Reflection, Turning Experience into Learning*, Kogan Page (London), 1985.

Brady, M. *What's Worth Teaching?*, SUNY Press (New York), 1989.

Bristow, J., Cowley, P. and Daines, B. *Memory and Learning A Practical Guide for Teachers*, David Fulton, 1999.

Corson, D. *Changing Education for Diversity*, Open University Press, 1998.

Cottrell, S. *Teaching Study Skills and Supporting Learning*, Palgrave Macmillan, 2001.

Cottrell, S. *Skills for Success*, Palgrave, 2003.

Cottrell, S. *The Study Skills Handbook*, Palgrave Macmillan, 2004.

Daines, J. W. *Adult Learning, Adult Teaching*, Welsh Academic Press, 2002.

Davies, I.K. *The Management of Learning*, McGraw-Hill (New York), 1971.

Fry, R. *Improve Your Reading (How to Study)*, Kogan Page, 1996.

Fry, R. *Use Your Computer (How to Study)*, Kogan Page, 1997.

Harkin, J., Turner, J. and Dawn, T. *Teaching Young Adults*, Routledge–Farmer, 2001.

Handy, C. *The Gods of Management*, Pan Books (London), 1979.

Hopkins, D. *A Teacher's Guide to Classroom Research*, Open University Press, 1993/1996.

Hoyle, F. *The Intelligent Universe*, Joseph (London), 1983.

Jarvis, P. *Adult and Continuing Education Theory and Practice*, Routledge (London), 2nd edn, 1995.

Joseph, R. *Stress Free Teaching*, Kogan Page, 2000.

Kounin, J.S. 'An analysis of teachers' managerial techniques', in Morrison, A. and McIntyre, D. (eds) *The Social Psychology of Teaching*, Penguin (London), 1992.

Magee, B., *Popper*, Fontana (London), 2nd edn, 1985.

Marshall, L. and Rowland, F. *A Guide to Learning Independently*, OUP, 1998.

Nierenberg, G.I. *The Complete Negotiator*, Souvenir Press (London), 1987.

Opie, C. (ed) *Doing Educational Research*, Sage Publications, 2004.

Popper, K. *The Logic of Scientific Discovery*, Hutchinson (London), 1972.

Popper, K. *Objective Knowledge: An Evolutionary Approach*, Oxford Univ. Press (Oxford), 1981.

Reeves, F. *The Modernity of Further Education*, Bilston College Publications, 1995.

Reeves, F. *Education NOJP.* Bilston College Publications, 1995.

Shostrom, E. *Man – the Manipulator*, Bantam (London), 1967.

Talbot, C. *Studying at a Distance*, Open University Press, 2003.

Appendix: Written assignments

Anything we do is an exploration that enables us to discover more about ourselves, nothing more so than writing down what we feel we need to communicate to others. Whatever we do, however well we do it, it is essential to come back to it from a distance and to try to see it as others coming new to it might see it.

Writing like everything else in life is a process not a product. You learn to write by writing, and you have to write something over and again, and again, to discover what it is you want to say – and to say it as you want to say it. Writing it once will not do that! All the sentences in my book have been rewritten by me many times, including these pages!

The use of a computer and writing software takes quite a lot of the pain out of what is reasonably tedious in revising written work. The spelling and grammatical errors are usually spotted for you also by the program.

Remember! make a priority of learning to use your computer's software and the keyboard skills to work quickly and accurately in writing into computer files.

For the purposes of developing cognitive skills and for their assessment, there is an inescapable need to be able to communicate effectively in written presentations, Usually, it is assumed that what is required is something in 'essay' form. What that 'form' is depends on the context and the purpose, but also the tutor's perceptions: there is no general formula for a 'good essay'.

But in the end you learn to write by writing and you have to begin at the beginning. The DfES Agenda noted that about one-third of all trainees surveyed in the inspection lacked level 2 qualification in literacy at the start of their courses, and one-third also lacked level 2 qualifications in numeracy. They noted that Procedures for the moderation of assessment of written assignments are generally thorough.

Emphasis by DfES is placed on how well a student communicates in writing. **But remember!** the purpose of writing is primarily to clarify for yourself what you have learned. You do this by trying to tell others and to receive feedback. It is not to prove that you have achieved a high level of skill in writing. In all communication be simple, straightforward and honest. Do not obscure what you want to say by 'cleverness'.

Remember! what matters most is clarity and the structure of the presentation so that it is simple, clear, easy to follow and says what you want to say.

I have made 'practical suggestions' throughout the book concerning the approach to writing in essay form, and of alternative methods to the formally structured essay, especially in regard to forms of presentation for assessment. This book has not set out to teach you how to write effectively. Nevertheless, there is an on-going discussion of essays in relation to the other skills teaching demands. Please look again at Assessment (pp. 111ff), Case Study 20 (p. 139), Task Design (p. 205), Assessment and testing (pp. 270ff) (Grade models and Aiming for good quality evidence of learning, Validity and reliability, Suited to its purpose, Weighting).

'How do I know what I think until I hear what I say?' is the purpose of a Reflective Diary. But if what we say or write is intended to be shared, so that we can get some feedback and make progress through the interchange of information and ideas, we need the skills that will enable that to happen. They are essentially linguistic and cognitive skills. It is one of the prime purposes of teacher training to develop those skills. This book is about the process by which a teacher can achieve all such skills to a level to be effective in a teaching context.

You also learn to learn by exploring and organising the evidence to support what you now know and wish to communicate. This should arise as far as possible from the experience of preparation, implementation and reflection on teaching.

Clearly, however, you need to read and explore the experience and wisdom of others. Where you quote from a source of any kind, or present supportive evidence for what you say, you should indicate with a note what that source is: whether in a book, from an Internet web page or wherever.

Remember! lifting sections of books or Internet pages and presenting them as your own is dishonest to yourself as well as to your tutor – you only learn by putting what you think into your own words. Usually, simply quoting without your own interpretation fails to achieve learning. It hardly ever becomes part of your own knowledge process and is extremely difficult to recall.

Glossary of terms

DfES *Agenda* has the following glossary of acronyms, terms and abbreviations.

Accreditation Approval by a regulatory body, e.g. QCA accredits; Awarding Body qualifications

ACL Adult and Community Learning

ACM Association of College Managers

ALI The Adult Learning Inspectorate inspects the post-16 provision of learning and skills sector providers. Shares a common inspection framework with Ofsted

AoC Association of Colleges

APL Accreditation of Prior Learning

Awarding Body An organisation that develops qualifications for the national qualification framework

Basic Skills Literacy, numeracy, ESOL and ICT; pre-entry Level to Level 2

Cert. Ed. Certification of Education: initial teaching qualification offered by HEIs

CPD Continuing Professional Development: learning, training and development activities a teacher undertakes after completion of initial teacher education

DfES Department for Education and Skills

Employment NTO Employment National Training Organisation

ESOL English for Speakers of Other Languages

FE Further Education: colleges serving learners from age of 14 upwards

FENTO Further Education National Training Organisation, has the key role of developing occupational standards and endorsing teacher education courses

Foundation Degree A new vocational higher education qualification

GTCE General Teaching Council for England: the schools organisation responsible for the registration of teachers, and teachers' continuing professional development

HE Higher Education

HEFCE The Higher Education Funding Council for England: the organisation that funds HEIs

HEI Higher Education Institution: a university, university college or Institute of Higher Education

ICT Information and Communications Technology

IfL Institute for Learning: a learning and skills sector body which sets standards for CPD. Membership is to teachers/trainers holding FE teaching qualifications or NVQs in Learning and Development

Individual Learning Plan (ILP) A learning and assessment plan devised between an individual learner and their assessor/course tutor and/or mentor, which allows the learner to progress at their own rate

Initial Assessment The process of identifying where the learner is before they start a course or qualification, to ensure they are on the right course and can achieve the aims and outcomes of that course

Initial Training Used in this document to refer to a course leading to an FE teaching qualification

IsNTO Information Services National Training Organisation

ITE Initial Teacher Education

ITT Initial Teacher Training

LEA Local Education Authority

LEAFEA Local Education Authorities' Forum for the Education of Adults

Learning and Skills Sector The post-16 (and increasingly post-14) sector as defined by the Learning and Skills Act 2000. Excludes schools and HEIs, but includes FE colleges, sixth form colleges, adult and community education, work-based learning and Ufl/learndirect

LLLSSC Lifelong Learning Sector Skills Council: not yet operational

LLSC Local Learning and Skills Council

LSC The national Learning and Skills Council: an organisation with 47 local offices responsible for funding and planning the learning and skills sector

LSDA Learning and Skills Development Agency

LTSN Learning and Teaching Subject Network: HE networks with 24 subject centres and on-line resources

MA Modern Apprenticeship

Masters Degree An HE qualification at HE Level 4: usually taken after a first degree

Mentor One who supports a newly-qualified or trainee teacher and may act as an assessor

NATFHE The University and College lecturers' union

NIACE National Institute of Adult Continuing Education

NQF National Qualifications Framework: a framework of Awarding Body qualifications monitored by QCA

NRDC National Research Development Agency

NVQ National Vocational Qualification: qualifications based on National Occupational Standards, available at Levels 1, 2, 3, 4 and 5

Ofsted The Office for Standards in Education

PGCE Post-Graduate Certificate in Education: initial training qualification offered by HEIs, normally taken by students who have graduated from a first degree

Post-compulsory Usually used to describe post-16 education and training as 16 is the legal school leaving age

Professional formation Used in this document to describe the trainee's entitlement, which includes initial training and workplace development

Providers Learning and skills sector term for organisations providing education and training to the post-16 (and increasingly post-14) sector learner

QAA The Quality Assurance Agency for Higher Education: organisation responsible for safeguarding the public's interests in the quality of HEI qualifications, and improvements in the management of quality of HEIs

QCA Qualifications and Curriculum Authority: the national body responsible for accrediting qualifications and national occupational standards, maintaining the national qualifications framework and developing curricula

QTFE Qualified Teacher for Further Education (proposed in this document)

QTLS Qualified Teacher for the Learning and Skills Sector (proposed in this document)

QTS Qualified Teacher Status: a school teacher who is awarded QTS has passed an initial teacher qualification and other requirements deemed necessary by the DfES

RDA Regional Development Agency

SFC Sixth Form College

SLC Student Loans Company

SSC Sector Skills Council: employer-led organisations that are taking over responsibility for the work carried out by NTOs

SSDA Sector Skills Development Agency

Standards Unit Unit set up within the DfES to raise standards and achievement in the learning and skills sector

Success for All A reform strategy for further education and training launched in November 2002 by Charles Clarke

TTA Teacher Training Agency: the schools organisation responsible for improving the quality of teacher training and attracting able and committed people into teaching

UCET The Universities Council for the Education of Teachers

UNISON The union for people delivering public services

Validation The HEI process of approving HEI qualifications

WBL Work-based learning

Suggestions for further reading: compilation

Annett, J. *Feedback and Human Behaviour*, Penguin (Harmondsworth), 1969.

Ardrey, R. *The Social Contract*, Fontana (London), 1971.

Ausubel, D. *Educational Psychology: A Cognitive View*, Holt, Rinehart & Winston (New York), 1968.

BACIE. *Management Games*. BACIE, 1965.

Belbin, R.M. *Management Teams: Why they Succeed or Fail*, Heinemann (London), 1981.

Bell, J. *Doing Your Research Project*, Open University Press, 1993/1999.

Berelson, B. and Steiner, G. *Human Behaviour: Inventory of Scientific Findings*, Harcourt Brace Jovanovich (New York), 1964.

Berne, E. *Games People Play: Psychology of Human Relationships*, Grove Press (New York), 1964; Penguin (Harmondsworth), 1970.

Bligh, D.A. *What's the Use of Lectures?*, Jossey Bass Wiley, 2000.

Bligh, D., Jaques, D. and Piper, D.W. *Seven Decisions When Teaching Students*, Intellect Books, 1981.

Block, J.H. *Mastery Learning: Theory and Practice*, Holt, Rinehart & Winston (New York), 1971.

Bloom, B.S. (ed.) *Taxonomy of Educational Objectives, The Classification of Educational Goals*. McKay (New York), 1956.

Boud, D. *Enhancing Learning Through Self Assessment*, Kogan Page (London), 1995.

Boud, D., Keogh, R. and Walker, D. *Reflection, Turning Experience into Learning*, Kogan Page (London), 1985.

Bourner, T. and Race, P. *How to Win as a Part Time Student*, Kogan Page (London), 1991.

Bovair, K. and McLaughlin, C. *Counselling in Schools*, David Fulton, 1993.

Brady, M. *What's Worth Teaching?* SUNY Press (New York), 1989.

Bristow, J., Cowley, P. and Daines, B. *Memory and Learning: A Practical Guide for Teachers*, David Fulton, 1999.

Bruner, J.S. *The Process of Education*, John Wiley (New York), 1977.

Bruner, J.S. *Actual Minds, Possible Worlds*, John Wiley (New York), 1986.

Buzan, T. *Use Your Head*. BBC Books (London), 4th edn, 1995.

Buzan, T. *Make the Most of your Mind*, Pan Books, 1977/88.

Castling, A. *Competence-based Teaching and Training*, Macmillan (London), 1996.

Chapman, A.H. *Put Offs and Come Ons*. Putnam Berkley (New York), 1968.

Coating, B.F. *Science and Human Behaviour*. Macmillan (London), 1953.

Cocker, D. *Successful Exam Technique*, Northcote House, 1987.

Cohen, L. Manion, L. and Morrison, K. *A Guide to Teaching Practice*, Routledge, 1996.

Coombes, B. *Successful Teaching*, Heinemann, 1999 (simplified advice).

Corson, D. *Changing Education for Diversity*, Open University Press, 1998.

Cottrell, S. *Teaching Study Skills and Supporting Learning*, Palgrave Macmillan, 2001.

Cottrell, S. *Skills for Success*, Palgrave, 2003.

Cottrell, S. *The Study Skills Handbook*, Palgrave Macmillan, 2004.

Cunningham, U. and Andersson, S. *Teachers, Pupils and the Internet*, Stanley Thornes, 1999.

Daines, J.W. *Adult Learning, Adult Teaching*, Welsh Academic Press, 2002.

Daines, J., Daines, C. and Graham, B. *Adult Learning: Adult Teaching*, University of Nottingham, 3rd edn, 1993.

Davies, I.K. *The Management of Learning*, McGraw-Hill (New York), 1971.

de Bono, E. *Lateral Thinking: A Textbook of Creativity*, Penguin (Harmondsworth), 1990.

Ebel, R.L. *Essentials of Educational Measurement*, Prentice-Hall (New Jersey), 1972.

Edney, P. *A Systems Analysis of Training*, Pitman (London), 1972.

Egan, G. *The Skilled Helper*, Brooks/Cole (London), 2nd edn, 1995.

FEU *Managing the Delivery of Guidance in Colleges*, FEU (London), 1994.

Fry, R. *Improve Your Reading (How to Study)*, Kogan Page, 1996.

Fry, R. *Use Your Computer (How to Study)*, Kogan Page, 1997.

Gagné, R.M. *The Conditions of Learning*, Holt, Rinehart & Winston (New York), 4th edn, 1985.

Gardner, P. *Teaching and Learning in Multicultural Classrooms.* David Fulton, 2001.

Gardner, P. *Strategies and Resources for Teaching and Learning in Inclusive Classrooms*, David Fulton, 2002.

Gelb, M. *Present Yourself*, Guild Publishing (London), 1988.

Goldner, B. *The Strategy of Creative Thinking*, Prentice-Hall (New Jersey), 1963.

Gregory, R.L. *Eye and Brain*, Weidenfeld & Nicolson (London), 1977.

Gregory, R.L. *The Intelligent Eye*, Weidenfeld & Nicolson (London), 1970.

Hall, E.T. *Silent Language*, Fawcett, Premier Books (New York), 1959.

Handy, C. *The Gods of Management*, Pan Books (London), 1979.

Harkin, J. Turner, J. and Dawn, T. *Teaching Young Adults*, Routledge–Farmer, 2001.

Heinecke, W. and Blasi, L. *Methods of Evaluating Educational Technology*, Information Age, 2001.

Herzberg, F. *Work and the Nature of Man*, World (New York), 1966.

Hilgard, E. and Bower, G. *Theories of Learning*, Appleton-Century-Crofts (New York), 1966.

Hills, P. *Teaching and Learning as a Communication Process*, Croom Helm (London), 1979.

Hoffman, B. *The Tyranny of Testing*, Crowell-Collier Press (New York), 1962.

Hollander, E.P. *Leadership Dynamics*, The Free Press (New York), 1978.

Hopkins, D. *A Teacher's Guide to Classroom Research*, Open University Press, 1993/1996.

Hoyle, F. *The Intelligent Universe*, Joseph (London), 1983.

Hudson, B. (ed.) *Assessment Techniques*, Methuen (London), 1973.

Jacques, D. *Learning in Groups*, Kogan Page (London), 2nd edn, 1991.

Jarvis, P. *Adult and Continuing Education Theory and Practice*, Routledge (London), 2nd edn, 1995.

Jessup, G. *Outcomes: NVQs and the Emerging Model of Education and Training*, The Falmer Press (London), 1991.

Joseph, R. *Stress Free Teaching: A Practical Guide to Tackling Stress in Teaching, Lecturing and Tutoring*, Routledge, 2000.

Kohler, W. *The Mentality of Apes*, Harcourt Brace Jovanovich (New York), 1925.

Kounin, J.S. An analysis of teachers' managerial techniques, in Morrison, A. and McIntyre, D. (eds), *The Social Psychology of Teaching*, Penguin (London), 1992.

Larkin, J.M. and Sleeter, C.E. *Developing Multicultural Teacher Education Curricula*, State University of New York Press, 1995.

Lashley, C. *Improving Study Skills: A Competence Approach*, Cassell, 1995.

Lewis, G. *One to One: A Practical Guide to Learning at Home Age 0–11*, Nezert Books, 2001.

Magee, B. *Popper*, Fontana (London), 2nd edn, 1985.

Marland, M. *The Tutor and the Tutor Group*, Longman (London), 1989.

Marland, P. *Towards More Effective Distance and Open Teaching*, Routledge, 1997.

Marshall, L. and Rowland, F. *A Guide to Learning Independently*, OUP, 1998.

Maslow, A. *Motivation and Personality*, Harper & Row (New York), 1954; Addison Wesley Longman (New York and London), 1987.

Mason, R. *Using Communication Media in Open and Flexible Learning*, Kogan Page, 1994.

McCarthy, P. and Hatcher, C. *Presentation Skills*. Sage Publications, 2002.

McConnell, J.V. *Understanding Human Behaviour*, Holt, Rinehart & Winston (New York), 1983.

Miller, G.A. *Psychology: The Science of Mental Life*, Harper & Row (New York), 1962; Penguin (Harmondsworth), 1966.

Miller, J. *States of Mind, Conversations with Psychological Investigators*, BBC Books, 1983.

Morris, D. *Manwatching*, Panther Books (London), 1978.

Moseley, D. *Helping With Learning Difficulties*, Open University Press (Milton Keynes), 1976.

Nash, R. *Classrooms Observed*, Routledge & Kegan Paul (London), 1972.

Nierenberg, G.I. *The Complete Negotiator*, Souvenir Press (London), 1987.

Oborne, D.J. *Ergonomics of Work*, John Wiley (New York), 1982.

Opie, C. (ed.) *Doing Educational Research*, Sage Publications, 2004.

Peng, T.H. *Fun With Chinese Characters*. Straits Times Collection, Federal Publications (Singapore), 1980.

Piaget, J. *Language and Thought in the Child*, Routledge & Kegan Paul (London), 1926.

Piaget, J. *Behaviour and Evolution*, Routledge & Kegan Paul (London), 1979.

Popper, K. *The Logic of Scientific Discovery*, Hutchinson (London), 1972.

Popper, K. *Objective Knowledge: An Evolutionary Approach*, Oxford University Press (Oxford), 1981.

Rackham, N., Honey, P. and Colbert, M.J. *Developing Interactive Skills*, Wellens Publishing (Northampton), 1971.

Redman, P. *Good Essay Writing*. Sage Publications, 2001.

Reeves, F. *The Modernity of Further Education*, Bilston College Publications and Education NOJP (Bilston), 1995.

Reynolds, V. *The Biology of Human Action*, Freeman (Oxford), 1980.

Rowntree, D. *Assessing Students: How Shall We Know Them?* Harper & Row (London), 1977; Kogan Page (London), 2nd edn, 1987.

Russell, T. *Teaching and Using ICT in Secondary Schools*, David Fulton, 2001.

Satterly, D. *Assessment in Schools*, Blackwell (Oxford), 1981.

Shannon, C. and Weaver, W. *The Mathematical Theory of Communication*, University of Illinois Press (Illinois), 1949.

Shostrom, E. *Man – The Manipulator*, Bantam (London), 1967.

Skinner, B.F. *The Technology of Teaching*, Appleton-Century-Crofts (New York), 1968.

Sotto, E. *When Teaching Becomes Learning: A Theory and Practice of Teaching*, Cassell (London), 1994 and paperback edition Continuum International Publishing, 2001.

Sperry, L. *Learning Performance and Individual Differences: Essays and Readings*, Scot Foresman (Glenview, Ill.), 1972.

Sutcliffe, J. *Adults with Learning Difficulties; Education for Choice and Empowerment*, NIACE/Open University Press, 1990

Talbot, C. *Studying at a Distance*, Open University Press, 2003.

Thomas, G. *Effective Classroom Teamwork*, Routledge, 1992.

Turner, J. *How to Study*, Sage Publications, 2002.

von Mente, M. *The Effective Use of Roleplay*, Kogan Page, 1989/99.

Watson, J.B. *Behaviourism*, B. Lippincott (Philadelphia), 1924.

Wertheimer, M. *Productive Thinking*, Harper (New York), 1959.

Wheeler, M. and Bligh, D. *Counselling in Study Methods*, Intellect Books, 1985.

Whitehead, A.N. *The Aims of Education and Other Essays*, Williams & Norgate (London), 1950.

Willmott, A.S. and Fowles, D.E. *The Objective Interpretation of Test Performance*, NFER Publishing (Windsor), 1974.

Wisker, G. and Brown, S. (eds) *Enabling Student Learning: Systems and Strategies*, Kogan Page (London), 1996.

Woodcock, M. *Team Development Manual*, Gower Press (Farnborough), 1979.

Wragg E.C. *An Introduction to Classroom Observation*, Routledge, 1994/99.

Index